Cliffo

of

Clifton

(1823 – 1893)

England's Youngest Catholic Bishop

Friend of Newman

Loyal Critic of the Pope

J. A. HARDING

First published in 2011

Alexander House
160 Pennywell Road
Bristol
BS5 0TX

© John Anthony Harding

The right of John Anthony Harding to be identified as the author of this work has been asserted in accordance the the Copyright, Designs and Patents Act, 1988.

British Library Cataloguing-in-Publication Data
A catlogue record for this book is available from the British Library

ISBN 978-0-9560617-9-9

Cover picture:
Dr Clifford's Episcopal Coat of Arms

Dexter (to the spectator's left) the arms of the See of Clifton.
Sinister (to the spectator's right) the crest of the Lord Clifford of Chudleigh. William was the second son of the 7th Baron.
Tassels: A row of three indicates a bishop. A row of four indicates an archbishop or an Assistant at the Pontifical Throne. The latter distinction was conferred on Dr Clifford just 16 days after his episcopal consecration.
Motto: 'Always prepared'.

Designed and typeset in Century 725 in Great Britain by Colour Graphics Printing Services Ltd, Bath. Printed and bound by CPI Group (UK) Ltd, Croydon, CR0 4YY.

DR WILLIAM CLIFFORD, BISHOP OF CLIFTON (1857 – 1893)

Dedicated to the memory

of my dear parents and sister

William and Mary Harding

and Mary Brain

R.I.P.

Foreword by The Bishop of Clifton

As the ninth Bishop of Clifton, I am delighted to recommend this study of Dr William Clifford, the third Bishop of Clifton (1857 – 1893). In many ways, Bishop Clifford echoes themes that the Church still considers important today.

The Second Vatican Council taught about the importance of Bishops as successors to the Apostles and their collegial ministry in shepherding the Church. Bishop Clifford was very aware of this and it influenced his thoughts during the First Vatican Council as well as the way in which he exercised his Episcopal ministry within the diocese and the country. It also had a bearing upon the way in which he understood papal infallibility. Though he had reservations about the way in which Pius IX acted, Bishop Clifford was always a faithful supporter of the Papacy and thought of schism as unthinkable.

Like John Henry Newman, Dr Clifford regarded the laity as having an important and active role in the mission of the Church and saw the necessity of an adult education and formation. He regarded the exclusion of Catholics from universities as a mistake which would result in the absence of Catholics within the professions. No less important did he regard the ordinary person as being influential in the way in which others understood the Church.

Within the diocese Bishop Clifford ensured a firm financial foundation by putting at the disposal of the diocese his own personal means. He re-purchased the Prior Park Estate to re-open the school and the seminary. He undertook a refurbishment of the Pro-Cathedral under the guidance of Charles Hansom. In 1882 to mark his silver jubilee as Bishop, he completed the church at Prior Park which had remained unfinished due to a lack of finances.

Having succeeded Bishop Hendren and Bishop Burgess, who both had a very short time as Bishops of Clifton, Bishop Clifford gave good and steady guidance to a newly formed diocese and pointed it towards a hopeful future.

Rt Rev Declan Lang
Bishop of Clifton   May 2011

AUTHOR'S NOTE

This study of Bishop William Clifford was submitted as a dissertation for the degree of Doctor of Philosophy at King's College, London, in July 1992. The title was *Dr William Clifford, Third Bishop of Clifton: His influence at the First Vatican Council and on the English Catholic Church*. The degree was awarded by the University of London, of which King's is a constituent College.

Nineteen years later, this same work is being published under a fresh title: *Clifford of Clifton (1823 – 1893) England's Youngest Catholic Bishop: Friend of Newman and Loyal Critic of the Pope*. Clearly it has proved necessary to make some corrections and other adjustments to what has been written, but, essentially, the text has remained the same. Parts of the first chapter on the Western District (1688 – 1850) – covering Wales (until 1840) and the present-day Dioceses of Clifton & Plymouth – were used to 'set the scene' in the volume entitled *The Diocese of Clifton 1850 – 2000*, published in 1999 to mark the 150 years of the Diocese.

All primary documents quoted in this book, unless otherwise stated, were seen and read by me in the archive named in the appropriate footnote. During the past two decades there may well have been migration of some papers and / or archives. A degree of caution is therefore advisable on the part of students wishing to examine these primary sources for themselves.

Finally, I have taken great care to be as accurate and sensitive as possible in rendering the meaning of Bishop Clifford's addresses at the Vatican Council and in translating various other occasional documents. In this regard I judge John Henry Newman's hitherto unknown letter (p. 272, Latin original p. 271) urging Propaganda Fide to maintain its prohibition on Catholic students going to Oxford – *Illud Periculosissimum Erroris Tabernaculum* – to be of particular significance.

I take responsibility for any inaccuracies in sense, tone or emphasis that may have inadvertently crept into any of the texts printed here in translation.

May 2011   J.A.H.

TABLE OF CONTENTS

Page

C: Final Years and Death

Appendices

Sources & bibliography

Index

ACKNOWLEDGEMENTS

Many people have in a variety of ways assisted me in gathering material for this book. In particular I should like to thank Lord Clifford of Chudleigh and his late father (1️⃣th Lord Clifford) who so readily made ther family archives at Ugbrooke Park available to me. I am slso grateful to the late Bishop of Clifton, Dr Mervyn Alexander, for the interest he showed, and to Abbot Aidan Bellenger and the community of Downside for their hospitality and the use of the monastary library.

Likewise Bishop Declan Lang has been most supportive and the Foreword he has written serves to remind us of our sense of continuitiy as a diocese.

The hospitality I have received from Mgr. John Kenedy and the staff of the Venerable English College, Rome, and from Mgr. Ronald Hishon and the staff of the English College, Valladolid, has been greatly appreciated.

I wish to place on record the help I received from my fellow archivists, some now deceased: Mgr. George Bradley (Leeds), Mgr. Charles Burns (Vatican), Rev. Michael Clifton (Southwark), Rev. Peter Dennison (Birmingham), Canon Anthony Dolan (Nottingham), Rev. Francis Edwards, S.J. (Generalate, Rome), Rev. J. G. Holt, S.J. (Farm Street), Rev. Dr David Lannon (Salford), Rev. Justin McLoughlin, O. F. M. (Forest Gate), Mrs Margaret Osborne (Northampton), Miss Elizabeth Poyser (Westminster) and Canon Christopher Smith (Plymouth). I am indepted to the late Dr. John Cashman, and to Professor V. Alan McClelland and to Dr. Judith Champ.

The Library Staff at the British Library, Bristol University, Brunel University and at the Public Record Office have been of great assistance; likewise the staff at the Public Libraries at Bristol and Frome.

Nicholas Lee readily accepted the challenge of compliing an index and gave me inavaluable advice in preparing the thesis for publication. Gill Hogarth and Emily Hogarth have helped me by re-typing parts of the t ext, and by identifying and enhancing contemporary photographs from the archives.

To all who have helped me I am most grateful.

September 29th 2011

J.A.H.

———————◆———————

'The thesis constitutes a significant contribution to challenging existing interpretations of the ecclesiastical politics of the nineteenth century' –

University Examiners.

———————◆———————

Andrew Patch and the staff of Colour Graphics Printing Services, Bath have at all times placed their professional expertise and guidance at my disposal and I now acknowlege the help they have given.

INTRODUCTION

William Clifford, third Bishop of Clifton, was a leading Catholic churchman of the nineteenth century and yet, despite numerous references to him in various histories of the period, no full-length study of him has so far appeared. This book – which does not pretend to be a biography – is a study of the man and his thought, particularly as seen in the context of the turbulent times in which he lived.

There are two crucial issues which are treated here in particular detail. First, the part played by Clifford in the succession to Westminster in 1865 which resulted in the appointment of Henry Edward Manning. The second is the question of Papal Infallibility as debated, and eventually defined, at the First Vatican Council. The perspectives of this study are both historical and theological and they are to be seen in the light of what happened at the Second Vatican Council which met some seventy years after the death of Clifford. Like his friend, John Henry Newman, Bishop Clifford may be seen as at least pointing the direction of some later developments in the Church.

Crucial to my study have been the family archives of Lord Clifford at Ugbrooke. I believe that most, if not all, the letters I have quoted from those archives are seeing the light of day for the first time. Particular attention should be paid to those relating to the Association for Promoting the Unity of Christendom, to the Errington affair, to Clifford's articles in the *Dublin Review*, and to informed reaction to his pastoral letters on the *Syllabus of Errors* and on *Catholic Allegiance* (his Reply to Gladstone).

The criterion used for the division of letters as between the family and the diocese of Clifton must remain something of a mystery. In general it may be said that there is nothing at Ugbrooke which concerns Clifford's duties as a diocesan bishop. On the other hand there are at Clifton two files of papers which belong to that corpus of material which pertains to the bishop both as a national and a literary figure, and of which the greater part is still with the family at Ugbrooke.

The following exchange of letters does throw some light on the subject. The first is from George Ambrose Burton (Bishop of Clifton 1902 – 1931) to the Hon. Charles Clifford and is dated February 21st, 1923:

> . . . Your Uncle, the late Lord Clifford, being the sole legatee
> of Bishop Clifford, took away with him to Ugbrooke nearly
> all the Bishop's letters. We have but one or two of his own,
> and of those addressed to him I may say none. Hence the
> great lacuna in our Diocesan Archives, beginning in 1857,
> the date of Bishop Clifford's consecration.
>
> I am frequently asked for information as to certain events in
> his long episcopate; and invariably can give but one reply,
> viz; that though a Bishop's letters on Diocesan and Church
> business are commonly allowed to be the property of his See
> after his death, "the late Lord took them all away." – I do not
> ask, of course, for any letters written to him by members of
> his own family: – but those received from ecclesiastics on
> ecclesiastical business or topics. – They would all be bound
> and added to the many volumes of our Diocesan
> correspondence.[1]

The reply, three days later, was as follows:

> . . . I believe that Bishop Clifford intended that my Uncle
> should deal with his correspondence – I have reason to
> believe that my Uncle used his discretion in deciding what
> letters should be kept. I imagine that my Uncle destroyed
> many of the letters addressed to Bishop Clifford by
> Archbishop Errington.
>
> My Aunt, the late Lady Denbigh, sorted out a considerable
> number of Archbishop Errington's letters to Bishop Clifford
> which my Uncle lent to Shane Leslie.
>
> I will look through these letters and let your Lordship know
> later whether it is possible for me to part with them. [2]

---

1   Clifton Diocesan Archives, *Letters to Honble. & Revd. William Clifford*
     (2 folders), Part I (loose inside cover). Letter from Bp. Burton to the Hon.
     Charles Clifford, dated 21.2.1923.

2   Clifton Diocesan Archives, *Letters 1923 - 24*, No. 37, Letter from the
     Hon. Charles Clifford to Bp. Burton, dated 24.2.1923.

Nothing further appears to have been said. [3]

I do not know whether all the documents referred to in this study as being at Ugbrooke are still there. During my visits in 1986 and 1987 they were tied together in bundles marked by years and that is how I have referred to them in the footnotes. At Clifton, apart from the two folders already referred to, there are papers relating to the routine running of the diocese and, perhaps more importantly, Clifford's *Diaries* for the years 1854, 1855 and 1880 – 1893 (inclusive). Sadly I have been unable to trace the whereabouts of the missing volumes.

The archives of Propaganda Fide in Rome are of particular value to one who is studying the history of the diocese of Clifton. Clearly the early years involving the trauma of Prior Park are of special significance but they are particularly so in the present context because it was precisely the parlous state of the finances of the diocese that in 1854 prompted Pius IX not to appoint an immediate successor to Bishop Burgess. Instead he decided that an Apostolic Administrator be appointed and in so doing he accepted the offer of Archbishop Errington. After taking such a personal interest in the diocese it was only natural that Pio Nono should show particular concern as to who should eventually be charged with providing the diocese with a fresh start. William Clifford was his personal choice.

Although Clifford's father (the 7th Lord Clifford) was known personally to the Pope whom he not infrequently came to visit from his residence in Tivoli, it would in my view be wholly wrong to see the appointment of his son as a thinly-veiled case of nepotism. Equally the appointment should not be viewed exclusively in terms of the Catholic aristocracy being at last given a place on the bench of bishops. Certainly those lay people of patrician background welcomed his appointment and in time communicated to him their views, but Clifford was of sufficient mettle to be his own man as his stand at Vatican I shows beyond all doubt. In a word, William Clifford was appointed bishop on his own merits and on the reputation he already acquired. To this the letters of congratulation clearly testify and they rule out any suggestion to the contrary.

---

3   Since Bp. Burton speaks of there being at Clifton no letters addressed to Bp. Clifford, it is fair to assume that the two folders of *Letters* that are now there, bearing Burton's hand-writing on the covers, are the result of this exchange. Even so, as has been noted, the division does seem somewhat arbitrary.

One book in which Clifford figures prominently is Cuthbert Butler's eminently readable *The Vatican Council 1869 - 1870*.[4] It was first published in 1930 and re-issued in paperback in 1962 in time for the opening of the Second Vatican Council later that same year. On one point, however, it needs to be read with caution, viz. where Butler is at pains to show that there was no lack of freedom on the part of the bishops assembled at the Council, either in the debates on Papal Infallibility or in the subsequent votes. True, he does narrate the unfortunate incident of Cardinal Guidi of Bologna who had spoken in council of his reservations about the proposed dogma and who that same evening was called to account by the Pope in a private audience. [5] This notwithstanding, Butler concludes his story of the Council with the following assessment:

> When all has been weighed up, the fact stands out that there was no real interference with freedom of speech, or thoroughness of discussion, or independence of voting; and so the ecumenicity of the Vatican Council cannot properly be called in question on the score of defect of liberty.[6]

The same opinion is implied in a personal letter which Butler wrote to Bishop Burton who apparently had lent him his copy of *Letters from Rome on the Council* by Quirinus[7] – A scurrilous book the professed aim of which was to bring into the open the story of 'the imposition of dogmas (which was) effected by all kinds of crooked arts and appliances of force'.[8] Butler wrote:

---

4   Cuthbert Butler, *The Vatican Council 1869 - 1870*, (Publ. London, 1930; republished Fontana paperback, 1962). All references are to the paperback edition.

5   *Ibid.*, p. 355.

6   *Ibid.*, p. 454.

7   Quirinus, *Letters from Rome on the Council*, (Publ. London, 1870). The author is generally understood to have been Döllinger writing in German for *Allgemeine Zeitung*.

8   *Ibid.*, Preface, p. vii.

I return with best thanks the "Quirinus" you lent me. It has
been useful to me to have it by me. But it is *pestilential* and
I hope my Vat. Council will definitely and finally put it out of
court for ever. [9]

All this is in stark contrast with the letters of Clifford to his Vicar
General, Bonomi, which are printed in the Appendix. In these Clifford a
man invariably temperate in language and moderate in judgement –
bares his soul –

. . . I can neither banish from my mind nor ignore the immense pressure
put on so many Bishops who were wholly dependant (*sic*) on the Pope . . .
The fear expressed by so many bishops both to me and to others of what
would be the consequences to them of giving a vote not pleasing to the
Pope were not without foundation. Even since the Council one Bishop at
least has lost his place by his vote . . . [10]

Now Cuthbert Butler certainly knew of these letters[11] when he wrote his
First Vatican Council, as did Bishop Burton.[12] One can only conclude
that they were suppressed because it was thought that sixty years after
the Council (when Butler was writing) was too near to the event to make
public these most sensitive documents. Be that as it may, it would have
been much more honest if Butler had let the matter go by default by not
mentioning the issue of freedom at all, than by giving a verdict on events
without even mentioning letters which he knew put a wholly different
complexion on those events.

---

9   Clifton Diocesan Archives, Letter (loose) inside the cover of *Quirinus*.
     Letter from Cuthbert Butler to Bp. Burton, dated 10.2.1930.

10   Clifton Diocesan Archives, File containing letters between Mgr. John
     Bonomi, V.G. and Bp. Clifford. Bonomi to Clifford, dated 13.11.1870.
     Clifford to Bonomi, dated 17.11.1870.

11   Cuthbert Butler wrote to Bp. Burton: 'Clifford's letter to Bonomi is
     interesting, but as I'm not writing about Clifford I would not want to cite
     it'. Clifton Diocesan Archives, *Letters 1923 - 24*, No. 306. Letter dated
     14.4.1924.

12   Bp. Keily of Plymouth (who had recently spent a few days at Clifton) wrote
     to Bp. Burton: 'I wonder if it wd. be too much to give me the vital part of
     Bp. Clifford's letter to Bonomi as it opened up a very wide field for thought,
     and also for prudent action when things are said in public'. Clifton
     Diocesan Archives, *Letters 1923 - 24*, No. 252. Letter dated 13.2.1924.

When Abbot (later Bishop) B.C. Butler came to edit the paperback edition in 1962, he wrote

> . . . no attempt has been made to revise the well considered judgements which make the book not only a history but a critique of the Council. To the best of the editor's knowledge, no progress in scholarship since 1930 has made such a revision necessary. [13]

He, however, was in a different position from his namesake. Scrupulous scholar that he was, it is inconceivable that he would not at least have mentioned the letters had he known of their existence. In any case it would have been right for him to assume that the archives at Clifton had already been thoroughly examined. In a word, Cuthbert Butler knew whereas B.C. Butler did not. [14]

The addresses which I have quoted from the First Vatican Council are all taken from Mansi's *Collectio Conciliorum*, tomes 49 – 53, which were published between 1923 and 1927.[15] Speaking of this vast literary undertaking, Cuthbert Butler says:

> Here is printed in full everything official or semi-official relating to the Council: public Acts, documents, reports, petitions, minutes of congregations and committees, and the stenographers' reports in full of all the speeches at the debates – everything. [16]

---

13   Cuthbert Butler, *op. cit.*, (ed. B.C. Butler), p. 5.

14   The probable explanation for his being unaware is that since the death of Bp. Burton in 1931, the Clifton Diocesan Archives had been in a virtual state of dormition with the result that first-hand knowledge of the letters had died with Burton and Cuthbert Butler.

      Bp. Clifford's letter to Bonomi was eventually published by F. J. Cwiekowski in *The English Bishops and the First Vatican Council* (Publ. Louvain, 1971), pp. 298 sqq.

15   Mansi, *Collectio Conciliorum*, Tomes 49 – 53, (Publ. Rome 1923 – 1927).

16   Cuthbert Butler, *op. cit.*, p. 489.

He might have added: even the editor's corrections to the bishops' Latin.

The translations in this study are entirely my own and so I accept responsibility for any inaccuracies which may have crept in. Some satisfaction may be derived from the fact that this is the first time that the addresses of Clifford have been translated into English in their entirety. Quotations from those speeches are often to be found in histories of the period. These translations, it is hoped, will enable scholars to pass judgement with an eye both to the manner and to the context in which they were delivered.

I would not wish to pretend that the present study dealt with all aspects of Clifford's episcopal career. Some of the issues which could not be encompassed within the limitations of this work are:

- The English Catholic Church and the charitable trusts;

- The Benedictines and their perception of the monastic life;

- 'Archbishop' Arnold Mathew: a former priest of the Clifton diocese who joined the Old Catholics but who at the end of his life was reconciled to the Church by Father C. C. Martindale, S.J. [17]

- Some disputes in Cheltenham over infallibility and whether or not it was involved in the process of the canonisation of saints (Perkins Nevins and Father Wilkinson).

It has to be said, however, that as far as most of the above relate to Bishop Clifford, archival material is not abundant.

---

17   Alan Bain, *Bishops Irregular: An International Directory of Independent Bishops* (Publ. Bristol, 1985), p. 158. For Mathew's reconciliation: Southwark Archdiocesan Archives, Martindale to Bishop Amigo, letter dated 15.12.1915. Mathew died 21.12.1919.

Bishop Clifford was related either by blood or by marriage to many distinguished Catholic families – to the Welds (his mother was the daughter of Cardinal Weld), to the Arundells, to the Vaughans, and to Ambrose de L'Isle Phillipps – all of whom enter the story of one who belonged to an age which was not wanting in ecclesiastics of renown. This study aims to tell at least part of that story.

CHAPTER ONE

The Western District and the Diocese of Clifton (1688 – 1857)

The rupture between England and Rome under Henry VIII and renewed after the Marian reconciliation by vigorous force of law under Elizabeth I, necessitated a reappraisal by the Catholic Church of its pastoral provision for its members in this country. Deprived of the ministry of bishops for many years – the last of the Marian bishops, Thomas Goldwell of St. Asaph, died in exile in Rome in 1585 – the Catholic community was entirely dependent on the spiritual succour provided in secret by the missionary priests ordained abroad.

By 1625 all the Marian priests must be assumed to have died. The remaining body of clergy, for the most part brave and energetic, was nevertheless divided in loyalty between religious superiors (often resident in Rome) and the priest appointed by the Pope to exercise a limited overall jurisdiction in the conduct of the English Mission. This superior, appointed in 1598, was given the title of Archpriest and he was helped in the exercise of his responsibilities by twelve assistants who represented the interests of the various regions. The plan, however, was far from being a success, this being due mainly to the controversies which often flared up between the Jesuits and the secular clergy.

In 1625 Pope Gregory XI appointed a Vicar Apostolic. Although possessing episcopal orders, such a prelate does not enjoy the authority of a diocesan bishop as enacted by the 'ordinary' laws of the Church. For the next 225 years – until 1850 – the English Catholic community was to remain in the charge of Vicars Apostolic. This underlined the fact that in Rome England was regarded as missionary territory and in consequence was given bishops who in their decision-making were very much subject to the Congregation of Propaganda Fide. This is a body of cardinals, bishops and other advisers in Rome whose responsibility it is to govern Catholics in those parts of the world where a properly constituted hierarchy has yet to be established.

For English Catholics the religious climate took a turn for the better with the accession of a Catholic King, James II, in 1685. All the Stuart Queens had been Catholics and there were well-founded rumours that Charles II had been reconciled to the Church on his death-bed.[1] Anti-Catholic tensions were somewhat eased and these factors, together with the virtual impossibility of any bishop adequately ministering alone to a flock which extended from one end of the country to the other, persuaded the Pope, Innocent XI, to increase the number of Vicars Apostolic to four. The Districts were to be designated London, Midland, Northern and Western.

1688 – the year which marked the birth of the Western District – was also to signal the end of the only Catholic reign this country had known since the days of Queen Mary. The subsequent Revolution Settlement, with the invitation to William of Orange and his Queen to sit on the English throne, was indeed a Revolution which saw a radical shift of power from the Monarch to Parliament. It was precisely the tension between these two institutions which had triggered, but was not solved by, the Civil War and subsequent execution of Charles I.

The departure of James II did not signify a loss of royal influence over English Catholic affairs. For many years nominations to vacant Vicariates were channelled to Rome via the Old Pretender's residence in France and it was he and his son, the Young Pretender, who exercised a hidden but very real influence over the course of Ecclesiastical events in England. Indeed, with English Catholics so determinedly giving allegiance to the Jacobite cause, they became their own worst enemies, giving credence well into the 18th century to Elizabeth's contention that to be a Catholic was to be a traitor. This, at least, was the popular perception, and it is to the great credit of John Stonor (V.A. Midland District 1716 – 1756) that he successfully weaned his fellow bishops away from this highly damaging attachment to a more sober and realistic loyalty to the *de facto* succession of the House of Hanover.

---

1   *The Venerabile*, Vol. xv, No. 3, November, 1951,
        Article *'The Master of us all'* by Anthony Kenny.

2   Basil Hemphill, *The Early Vicars Apostolic of England
        1685 - 1750* (Publ. London, 1954), especially Chapter VII.

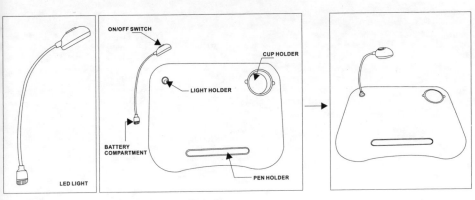

Fig. 1   Fig. 2

AM10092 Laptop Tray & Light

Please read these instructions carefully.
The LED light (Fig.1) is designed for use with tray (laptop or reading) and will not
withstand shocks or vibrations. Avoid contact with detergents.
The LED light is located within the zipped pocket of the actual cushion.
This light easily slots into the light holder (see Fig. 2) which is located to the top
left hand corner of the laptop tray.
The battery compartment is located at the base of the light (see Fig. 2) and can be
replaced by a slight twist to the right and pull. (batteries included)
Please ensure the compartment is secure.
Battery Spec is LR44 x 3.
Do not dispose of battery in fire, do not re-charge.
Keep loose batteries away from children.
Never mix new and old batteries together.

Made in China

Warning small parts -
Keep away from children

Of the four Vicars Apostolic, one was invariably a religious. This was appropriate as a reflection of the contribution being made to the pastoral ministry by the members of the Religious Orders. With one exception – a Dominican appointed by a Dominican Pope to the Northern District[3] – these appointments of religious were to the Western District as the following list shows:

1688 – 1705	Philip Michael Ellis, O.S.B.
(1705	Andrew Giffard, appointed but refused)
1713 – 1750	Matthew Prichard, O.S.F.
1750 – 1770	Laurence York, O.S.B.
1770 – 1797	Charles Walmesley, O.S.B.
1798 – 1808	Gregory William Sharrock, O.S.B.
1809 – 1829	Bernardine Peter Collingridge, O.S.F.
1829 – 1843	Peter Augustine Baines, O.S.B.
1843 – 1845	Charles Michael Baggs
1846 – 1848	William Bernard Ullathorne, O.S.B.
1848 – 1850	Joseph William Hendren, O.S.F.

Why this should have been is not altogether clear although it is possible that the Western District was chosen because of its extreme poverty. Doubtless Rome would have seen an advantage in nominating a religious because, unlike his secular counterparts, he would have been able to look to his Order for financial support, if not for his work, then at least in the matter of his personal maintenance. This would have included travelling expenses which, in a Vicariate covering no fewer than twenty (pre-1974) counties, would not have been insignificant.

In 1840, to meet the pressing needs of the growing Catholic population – resulting chiefly from the immigration from Ireland which was to reach its peak in the years of the Potato Famine, 1845 – 1847, – the number of Vicars Apostolic was increased from four to eight. One of the new Vicariates was for Wales which was now taken from the Western District.

---

3   Benedict XIII appointed Fra Dominic Williams. A Welsh Dominican he was Prior of Bornhem in Flanders at the time of his appointment in 1726. See Hemphill *op. cit.*, p. 123.

Brief notice should be made of some of the bishops listed above. Philip Michael Ellis, O.S.B. was incarcerated within a few months of his appointment. This was on the occasion of the arrival of William of Orange, and the bishop on his release 'foreseeing little prospect of serving the cause of religion in such turbulent times',[4] left England and went first to St. Germains (where the exiled King had taken refuge) and then to Rome. Here the Pope of the day, Clement XI, recognised his talents and in 1708 appointed him Bishop of Segni in the Campagna, an office which he filled with considerable distinction. [5]

Charles Walmesley, O.S.B. was an astronomer of international repute and was consulted by the British Government when at long last it decided to change from the Julian to the Gregorian calendar – a change which had been made by the rest of Europe but was delayed for 170 years (1752) because, in the Protestant mind, the new calendar was too closely associated with the Papacy.

Another Vicar Apostolic of note was Peter Augustine Baines, O.S.B. It would not be an exaggeration to see in his grandiose – some might say, profligate – schemes for the establishment of a seminary at Prior Park on the outskirts of Bath the cause of many of the financial troubles which were to beset the infant diocese of Clifton well into the episcopate of William Clifford. Appointed coadjutor to the Franciscan Bernardine Peter Collingridge, Baines took himself off to Rome in 1826 where he arrived 'in a state of almost hopeless illness' (Wiseman)[6] for a period of convalescence. Some have seen in this sojourn the beginnings of Baines' *illusions de grandeur* resulting from his contact with the spirit and buildings of antiquity. Why could not such a spirit – he might well have asked himself – be rekindled in another Roman city nearer home? Such a move would in its turn help to bring the Catholic community out of its ghetto mentality into the cultured world of literature and the salon.

---

4   George Oliver, *Collections Illustrating the History of the Catholic Religion, etc.* (Publ. London, 1857), p. 295.

5   *The Venerabile*, Vol. xix, No. 3, November 1959, Article '*An English Bishop in the Volscians*' by George Hay.

6   Wiseman writes this in his *Recollections of the Last Four Popes* as quoted by Mgr. James Shepherd in *Reminiscences of Prior Park* (Publ. London, 1894), p. 2. In pages 2 – 4 Shepherd argues that Baines's time in Rome had a lasting effect and resulted in his predilection for things Classical.

On the death of Collingridge in 1829 Baines returned to take charge of the Western District. As Rector of the English College in Rome Nicholas Wiseman had come to know the new Vicar Apostolic well. His assessment of Baines was to be borne out by events:

> '. . . he had a power of fascinating all who approached him, in spite of a decided tone and manner which made it difficult to differ from him in opinion. He had sometimes original views upon a certain class of subjects; but on every topic he had a command of language, and a clear manner of expressing his sentiments, which commanded attention, and generally won assent. Unfortunately, this proved to him a dangerous gift. When he undertook great and magnificent works, he would stand alone: assent to his plans was a condition of being near him; anyone that did not agree, or that ventured to suggest deliberation, or provoke discussion, was easily put aside; he isolated himself with his own genius; he had no counsellor but himself'.[7]

Invested now with the full authority of a Vicar Apostolic and endowed with a personality that would brook no obstacle, Baines proceeded to launch on his impecunious and scattered flock schemes that in financial terms it just could not sustain. The Prior Park Estate of 186 acres was purchased in 1829 for £22,000. In May, 1836 there was a disastrous fire which destroyed the mansion. The estimated cost of the damage was £15,000 which was only partly covered by an insurance of two to three thousand pounds, Baines having already spent £50,000 on buildings and embellishments. The financial worry took its toll of his health but it was not until another seven years had elapsed that Baines finally succumbed.

The only secular bishop amongst the Western Vicars Apostolic, Charles Baggs, succeeded Baines in 1843 but within two years he too was dead at the early age of 39. His successor was William Bernard Ullathorne, O.S.B., certainly one of the greatest of the English bishops of the 19th century. He remained in the Western District for only two years before being translated to the Midlands where in 1850 he became first Bishop of

7   Nicholas Wiseman, *op. cit.*, as quoted by Jerom Murch, *Biographical Sketches of Bath Celebrities. Ancient and Modern* (Publ. London & Bath, 1893), pp. 217, 218.

Birmingham. His two years in the West Country were not uneventful. He purchased land in Clifton and was responsible for the building of a church, dedicated to the Twelve Apostles, which was later intended to become the Cathedral Church of the new Diocese of Clifton. This, however, was not without its problems. Built on the edge of a former quarry the movement of the foundations necessitated the spending of much of the money which had been set aside for the completion of the building. For two years it remained incomplete until money was available for a temporary roof to be put in place and the church was given the status of a Pro-Cathedral. [8]

Joseph William Hendren, O.S.F., who had been Ullathorne's Vicar General, succeeded him as Vicar Apostolic of the Western District in 1848. Two extracts from a letter which he wrote to Ullathorne just before his appointment illustrate the plight of the District at that time. In the course of suggesting possible names for vacant missions he feels constrained to write:

> These are *queer* suggestions, such as I feel almost ashamed to make. But then the District is in such a queer position. As for "catching" priests ready made and fit for work, that is a very difficult feat. I know of no stray game of that sort. There are many such no doubt, but all in other people's preserves. And it would not be fair, nor *gentlemanly*, to decoy them into ours.[9]

The letter continues with a graphic account of Hendren's view of the intolerable burden which Prior Park, vacated by the Rosminians in favour of Ratcliffe and now again up for sale, would place on all concerned:

> I cannot tell you how annoyed I feel whenever your Lordship drops hints on the probability of your being obliged to take P. Park on *your shoulders*. Why, it will crush you! and every man who may be standing near you!

---

8   When Bishop Clifford took possession in 1857 he found liabilities of £3,500 on the church, and the Bishop's House (adjoining) unfinished. He made a donation of £1,000 from his private purse.

9   Clifton Diocesan Archives *Letters of Bp. Hendren.*
Hendren to Ullathorne, letter dated 9.10.1847.

"Grapple with P. Park"! That is, take an enormous load of debt upon yourself, which you would not be able to pay off for 20 years to come, even if you were to *clear* £3,000 every year!

Devote to this *useless* establishment all the available resources of the District for years and years to come Oh! do not talk of being obliged to take up P.P. If you *should* be obliged to do it, surely I will run away, like a coward; or, what will be better, I will surely die ... We can hardly be in a worse condition than was the Jewish Church at the time of the Syrian persecution.[10]

In September, 1850, the Hierarchy was restored to England and Wales. The Western District, as it was reconstituted in 1840, was divided into two dioceses, Clifton and Plymouth, both of which have remained virtually unaltered ever since. Clifton comprises the city and county of Bristol, Gloucestershire, Wiltshire and Somerset – the creation of 'Avon' in 1974 did not affect it territorially – and Plymouth the counties of Devon, Dorset and Cornwall. As might have been expected, Dr. Hendren was appointed first Bishop of Clifton but in fact he remained only nine months, and in 1851 he was transferred to Nottingham where he was again the first Bishop. The key to this mysterious move is to be seen partly in terms of his ill health but more particularly in his continued opposition to the retaining of Prior Park. So total had this been that

> . . . the college authorities decided that his continued presence would be intolerable. They went so far as to send a delegation to Rome to present their case. Grant wrote to Wiseman; "In *confidence*. It would be *cosa grata* if, in suggesting the arrangements for the new bishops, Dr. Hendren could be taken from Clifton." Propaganda at first thought of sending Hendren to Southwark, but, as the cardinal prefect later wrote, it was not known whether Wiseman would have placed his confidence in Hendren, and the proposal never received serious consideration.[11]

---

10   *Ibid.*

11   Richard J. Schiefen, *Nicholas Wiseman and the Transformation of English Catholicism* (Publ. Shepherdstown, 1984), p. 194.

This account of events omits to explain why precisely Hendren went to Nottingham. A confidential letter from Bishop Grant of Southwark (who had charge of the Bishops' dealings with Propaganda) to Bishop Ullathorne furnishes the answer:

Aug 4 (*in pencil*: 1851)

My dear Lord,

....

When he (Hendren) perceived that it was not thought desirable that he should remain at Clifton, he begged not to be placed at P(lymouth) which would still keep him in contact with P(rior) Park. As the S(acred) C(ongregation) was resolved to commit to all the 4 Bishops of the old W(estern) District the care of P(rior) Park, it was clear that he could not be placed at Shrewsbury, which by this arrangement was as much interested in P(rior) Park as P(lymouth) or Clifton . . . three others were open. To Salford he could not be sent when everything proved so clearly that it was the See most suited to Dr. Turner. The S(acred) C(ongregation) thought that it was expedient to place at Southwark a person likely not to interfere in any way with the Cardinal's wishes about St. George's, and for this reason it was thought well that I should go to Southwark.

Nottingham therefore was the only See open . . .

T. Grant[12]

Propaganda had noted specifically that Ullathorne's diocese adjoined Nottingham and that this fact would prove conducive to a continuing of the friendship which had existed between the two men when they worked side by side in the Western District. It was in June, 1851, that Hendren, now in his sixtieth year, was transferred to Nottingham, but again his tenure of office was very short – a mere twenty months. He suffered

---

12 Clifton Diocesan Archives *Letters of Bp. Hendren*, Grant to Ullathorne, letter dated (in pencil) 4.8.1851.

severely from gout and died in November, 1866, at the age of seventy-five.

Hendren's successor at Clifton was the former Prior of Ampleforth, Thomas Burgess. That he should have become a secular priest was apparently due to the strong influence of another monk, Peter Augustine Baines, although this fact is omitted by Oliver in his biographical note on Burgess:

> Whilst still holding that office (i.e. of Prior), in the spring of 1830, he was over-persuaded, with Dr. Rooker and F. Edward Metcalfe, that they would do a better thing to forsake their first love, or vocation to the Benedictine order, obtain their secularization, and concentrate their talents, and energies, and influence, in raising up a new collegiate establishment at Prior-park. Their abrupt withdrawal, as well as of several students, excited alarm, and threatened shipwreck to Ampleforth; but, like a gallant vessel, she righted again, and most prosperously continues her course. [13]

Burgess's short reign of three years was characterised by disputes with the Regular Clergy (e.g. about St. Nicholas of Tolentino, a quarrel which eventually reached the corridors of Propaganda in Rome), the ever-present financial burden of Prior Park and tensions with his own Cathedral Chapter (erected in 1852) which felt that it was not being consulted sufficiently in matters relating to the general well-being of the Diocese.

The minutes of the Chapter Meetings held in the Summer of 1854 make interesting reading. On 31st May it was learned that Bishop Grant of Southwark, a man skilled in ecclesiastical procedure, was visiting Bristol. An invitation for him to address the assembled Canons was hurriedly despatched.

> 'The Bishop having kindly accepted the invitation, gratified the Chapter by giving some interesting information concerning the mode of transacting business in Chapter and other subjects.[14]

---

13   Oliver, *op. cit.*, p. 255.

14   Clifton Diocesan Archives *Acta Capituli Cliftoniensis a die 28 Iunii, 1852 usque ad 1 Decembris. 1860*, 31.5.1854.

The next day the Chapter met again:

> 'The three following questions were proposed to the Chapter and after a secret scrutiny were all carried in the affirmative –
>
> - That the *discussion* on the question of sending a respectful Address to the Bishop praying His Lordship to consult the Chapter on the Affairs of the Diocese *be taken now*, and be not postponed to the next Session.
>
> - That some Canon be appointed to prepare an address to the Bishop from the Chapter.
>
> - That Canon English be appointed to prepare an address for presentation to the Bishop.[15]

(English later became Archbishop of Port of Spain in Trinidad).

Burgess might well have had an intimation of what was afoot as the minutes of the next meeting, held on the 19th July, begin with the following:

> 'The Provost having brought a message from the Bishop requesting the opinion of the Chapter on the cause which has been going on in Rome in regard to the claim of the Augustinian order to the Church of S. Nicholas Bristol. In answer to which it was resolved to collect the declarations of those members of the Chapter and of other persons who were well acquainted with the case'.[16]

A discussion ensued which produced some very practical advice. The Chapter had proved to the Bishop that its counsels could be of immense value – if only they were sought.

Canon English then put before his colleagues the address which he had been charged to prepare in their name for presentation to the Bishop. 'A

---

15   *Ibid*. 1.6.1854.

16   *Ibid*. 18.7.1854.

portion of it was agreed.' –

> 'My Lord. The Members of your Chapter are anxious to draw closely the ties that already unite them with their Head, the Bishop. They are desirous also of rendering their Body one of the most useful institutions emanating from our re-established Hierarchy and they are of opinion that these objects would be materially advanced by your Lordship's condescending to lay before Chapter the actual state of the Diocese. They press this upon your kind consideration with the more earnestness as they are convinced that such confidence would not be misplaced, but prove beneficial as well to your Lordship and the Diocese, as to the Canons themselves'. [17]

They also sent copies of their resolutions in the dispute over St. Nicholas.

In August we again find the Bishop seeking advice from his cathedral chapter:

> 'The Provost brought a message from the Bishop requesting the advice of the Chapter regarding the offer of the Mission of Shepton Mallet which had been made to him by the Provincial of the Jesuits'. [18]

The Bishop's reply to the Address was read at the September meeting of the Chapter. It is almost a *cri de coeur* from a very worried man:

> 'Very Reverend and dear Brothers in Xt. In reply to your dutiful address of the 18th July last I have to assure you of the great consolations it gave me to see you endeavouring to draw more closely the ties that already unite you to your head the Bishop of this Diocese. Had I not been obliged to leave my diocese to solicit the Charity of the faithful, as I have already informed the Holy See, I should have made a more particular visit of my Diocese, and been prepared to give a more exact account of the resources thereof. The

---

17   *Ibid.* 18.7.1854.

18   *Ibid.* 31.8.1854.

Missions in general are poor, and some of the important
ones involved in debt by reason of the great outlay at first.
You have seen from the printed circular giving an account of
the amount of Collections and disbursements, how little has
been done towards liquidating any of the outstanding debts,
and the receipts of the two last half years do little more than
pay the interest of the same. The Bishop has no funds and
found none for his own support, or for the Education of the
Clergy that he can avail himself of. In the midst therefore of
so many overwhelming difficulties, I feel more grateful than
I can express, for this testimony of your good will to help me,
and remain very Reverend Brothers in Xt.

> Your unworthy Bishop
> + Thomas Burgess [19]

The letter was written on 31st August, one day before the Chapter was
due to meet to hear his reply. It reveals a man who had kept everything
in his own hands, not because of arrogance, but because of a
temperament which till then had prevented him from sharing with others
the worries which resulted from so many crippling debts.

On hearing the Bishop's reply a discussion ensued:

'A question was then put "that some further step be taken
with reference to the Bishop's reply just received" which
after secret voting was decided in the negative . . .

The Provost then said that the Bishop wished to have the
advice of the Chapter with respect to his making an
application for pecuniary help to the Society for the
Propagation of the Faith. The opinion of the Chapter was
that such an application is highly advisable. [20]

---

19   *Ibid*. 1.9.1854.

20   *Ibid*. 1.9.1854.

Within three months Bishop Burgess was dead. Oliver wrote: 'Super-human were the efforts of this prelate to rescue Prior-park from its overwhelming incumbrances', [21] while Errington later declared: 'the late bishop fell a victim to the burden he had undertaken'.[22]

The Clifton Chapter met on 7th February, 1855, to submit three names (*terna*) to Rome – Brindle (the Vicar Capitular), Rooker (who had served at Tiverton, Shortwood and Bridgwater) and O'Ferrall, O.S.F. (who had purchased the imposing Irvingite church in the heart of Bristol and dedicated it to 'St. Mary-on-the-Quay'). Rome, however, had other ideas. On the 18th October the canons were summoned to meet in order to accept the nomination of Archbishop George Errington as Apostolic Administrator of Clifton.

This unusual step of appointing an Administrator is taken by the Holy See only in the most exceptional circumstances. These can occur when political considerations counsel delay before making a substantive appointment, when a serious split in loyalties has occurred amongst the clergy of a diocese or when, in the view of the Holy See, some overwhelming problem needs to be urgently addressed so that a new bishop can make a fresh start, unhampered by the decisions of others. Clearly Rome did view Prior Park in such a light. 'At the time, this diocese was almost bankrupt and was probably the most difficult episcopal charge in the country' (Holmes).[23]

By appointing an Administrator Rome was in fact following advice which had been tendered by Wiseman. Propaganda had written to the Cardinal for his comments on the diocese of Clifton in general and on Prior Park in particular, and in his 16 page reply (in Italian) he repeated the advice which he had apparently given on the occasion of the previous vacancy, namely, that unless a definitive solution were found, any new bishop 'would find himself swamped in an abyss of contending parties' –

---

21   Oliver, *op. cit.*, p. 256.

22   Clifton Diocesan Archives *Pastoral Letter*, 30.1.1856.

23   Derek Holmes, *More Roman than Rome* (Publ. London, 1978), p. 92.

... therefore it would be expedient to put the Diocese in the charge of an ecclesiastical administrator who, coming in free from any handicap of prejudice or party, would bring the whole affair to a conclusion, calmly and firmly, and then depart, leaving the field free for a new bishop 'di carattere dolce ma energetico' who would soon get things back to normal. Such a person whom I would propose would be the Bishop of Hexham . . . [24] [My translation].

Wiseman went on to say that he was proposing Hogarth's name only after a good deal of thought. In the event, however, Hogarth did not come. The choice fell on Wiseman's coadjutor, Errington, who apparently came to Clifton 'at his own suggestion'. [25]

In sending Errington to Clifton Propaganda was taking a major step to relieve the tension between him and Wiseman whose coadjutor he had been for only six and a half months. [26] The reasons for this tension stemmed from a clash of personality with Errington complaining that the Cardinal would not infrequently countermand decisions that he (Errington) had taken. This, however, was not the only reason for the move. When Wiseman was Rector of the English College in Rome, Errington had been his Vice Rector and 'through his stern and relentless organisation of the drooping finances, as Wiseman himself admitted, saved the College from bankruptcy'. [27]

Errington was a martinet, and yet in retrospect there can be little doubt that his appointment to Clifton had been providential. He applied the surgeon's knife and got rid of the major cause of the ills of the diocese. Prior Park was sold.

---

24   Archives of Prop. Fide, Rome: *Scritture Riferite nei Congressi 1855 - 1857. Anglia 14*, No. 278, Wiseman to Prop. Fide, Londra 27.4.1855. The Bishop of Hexham and Newcastle was William Hogarth.

25   Schiefen, *op. cit.*, p. 246.

26   Errington was appointed Coadjutor to Wiseman and titular Archbishop of Trebizond on 30th March, 1855.

27   *The Venerabile*, Vol. xv, No. 3, November, 1951, Article "Monsignor George Talbot" by Michael Moore.

One writer has given this verdict on Errington's rule at Clifton:

> (It) was not a pleasant one, and it took him the greater part of
> a year. In addition to closing the college he was involved in
> other diocesan matters. His rigorous enforcement of
> ecclesiastical discipline, coupled with the unpleasant
> negotiations regarding the college, made him unpopular with
> some of the clergy. Wiseman defended his coadjutor: "His
> firmness, prudence, and patience, seems to me beyond all
> praise". A month later, however, he was more reserved: "In
> theory and law I believe Dr. Errington has been right: but I have
> found fault with him for not leaving many things to the next
> bishop, instead of doing them while only an administrator".[28]

This assessment may well be true, but a reading of Errington's
Administration (a diary/minute book of his tenure of office) does show
a pastor who did not court popularity but whose sole concern was to
discharge as quickly and as efficiently as possible a responsibility that of
its nature was bound to call for hard decisions. In addition, he travelled
the diocese, conducted Visitations and Confirmations, and generally
filled the pastoral gaps left by his anxious predecessor.

The former Vicar Capitular, Thomas Brindle, wrote to Dr. Rooker:

Bath 20 Feby 1857

> . . . I begged Canon Neve to send you . . . a Copy of the
> Circular from the Archbishop to all in this Diocese, on
> taking leave of us – What do you think of it? Most of the
> Canons laughed and turned up their noses at it. [29]

The Archbishop departed for Rome to give an account of his stewardship
at Clifton. All was now ready for the appointment of yet another Bishop –
the third Bishop of Clifton and the fourth to have charge of the diocese in
less than seven years. His name was William Clifford.

---

28   Schiefen, *op. cit.*, pp. 246, 247.

29   Clifton Diocesan Archives *Letters 1815 - 1862*, No. 380, Brindle to
      Rooker. Letter dated 20.2.1857.

Coll. Inglesi Roma.
Jan 29. 1857.

Dear Charles.

Mr Talbot has just
announced to me that I am
appointed Bp of Clifton &
that the Pope will consecrate
me himself on Sunday 15th inst.
Pray write a line to Elly,
                    Aunt Lucy & Laura Whyte
Conny, Henry & Watty. and
get what prayers you can for
me — This is all I can say
before Post time
                    Your affate brother
                        William Clifford

WILLIAM CLIFFORD'S LETTER TO HIS BROTHER, CHARLES, INFORMING HIM OF HIS
APPOINTMENT AS BISHOP OF CLIFTON (FEBRUARY 1857)

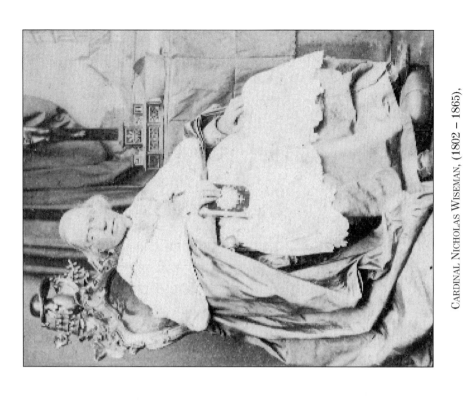

CARDINAL NICHOLAS WISEMAN, (1802 – 1865),
FIRST ARCHBISHOP OF WESTMINSTER

GEORGE ERRINGTON, (1804 – 1886), FIRST BISHOP OF PLYMOUTH.
WILLIAM CLIFFORD SERVED AS HIS VICAR GENERAL

CHAPTER TWO

The Early Years of Dr. Clifford
and his Appointment to the See of Clifton

'The Cliffords claim descent from Robert, third Duke of
Normandy whose grandson came over with his cousin William
the Conqueror and was sent to hold back the Welsh. The family
takes its name from the site of one of the castles he built on the
cliff above the ford overlooking the River Wye at Clifford,
Herefordshire. The ruins of the castle can still be seen'. [1]

Ugbrooke, on the outskirts of Chudleigh in South Devon, is the ancestral
home of the family. 'Thomas, great-grandson of the first Clifford to own
Ugbrooke, became Burgess (M.P.) to Totnes, Lord High Treasurer of
England and Chief Minister to Charles II, the C of the CABAL ministry
and was made first Lord Clifford of Chudleigh'.[2] Writing in 1857 Dr.
George Oliver states:

'This ancient family returned to the faith of its forefathers in
the person of Thomas, the Lord Treasurer Clifford, early in
1672. As late as 17th July, 1671, he had procured Dr.
Anthony Sparrow, the Protestant Bishop of Exeter, to
dedicate and consecrate a domestic chapel at Ugbrooke . . .
[3] What led to his conversion I cannot pretend to discover;
but Lord Shaftesbury had purposely contrived the Test Act
to exclude him and the Duke of York from the Cabinet . . .
To use the words of King James II . . . "This *new Test* had
the effect in ou(s)ting Lord Clifford of the place of Lord
Treasurer of England, and of being any longer a privy
councillor, who, though a *new convert*, generously preferred

---

1   *Ugbrooke*, a publicity brochure issued by the Clifford family
     (no author or date), p.3.

2   *Ibid.*, p. 3.

3   The Deed and Licence hang in the entrance porch of the chapel. The
     present building was designed and executed in 1760 to a plan by
     Robert Adam.

his conscience to his interest"'.[4]

In 1715, the year of the Jacobite Rebellion, Hugh, the second Lord Clifford, was suspected of being a Stuart sympathiser and was 'placed under the surveillance of an officer appointed by the new dynasty'.[5]

The family continued loyal to the Catholic Faith without, apparently, anyone seceding to the Established Church. On the contrary, in common with many of the great families of the period, several holders of the title had large families with some of the younger sons becoming priests and the daughters taking the religious habit.[6] It was not uncommon for those who married to find partners among members of the Catholic families of the district, in particular the Welds of Lulworth Castle, Dorset, the Arundells of Wardour Castle, Wiltshire and the Vaughans of Courtfield.

Arguably the most celebrated of these unions took place on 14th June, 1796. It was between Lucy Clifford[7] and Thomas Weld who, on his wife's death at Clifton 19 years later, became a priest and subsequently titular Bishop of Amyclae on 6th August, 1826, and later cardinal. Dr. Oliver's epitaph is worth quoting:

> 'In the world he was a model to all our Catholic gentry: as a priest, as a bishop, and as a prince of the Church, no panegyric can do him sufficient justice'.[8]

Weld's daughter married Hugh Charles Clifford (later the 7th Baron) on 29th May, 1790 and bore him eight children, the second surviving son of whom was William Joseph Hugh (born 24.12.1823) who became the third Bishop of Clifton. It must be rare in the Catholic Church for a bishop to have had a cardinal as his grandfather.

---

4   George Oliver, *Collections illustrating the History of the Catholic Religion in the Counties of Cornwall, Devon, Somerset. etc.* (Publ. London, 1857), p. 22.

5   Oliver, *op. cit.*, p. 23.

6   Hugh Clifford, *The House of Clifford* Publ. Chichester, 1987), p. 180.

7   Oliver, *op. cit.*, p. 434.

8   Oliver, *op. cit.*, p. 434.

The others who gave themselves to the service of the Church were:

2nd child   Eleanora Mary (born 10.7.1820)

8th child   Walter Charles Ignatius (born 5.12.1830)

Seven cousins or nieces of the future Bishop took the religious veil, while other members of the Clifford family married into the Petre, Stourton, de l'Isle Phillipps and other families of the Catholic aristocracy.

William Clifford was baptised at the Catholic Church at Irnham in Lincolnshire on Christmas Day, 1823. Father James King, missionary apostolic, officiated and the god-parents were William Lord Stourton and Christine Weld. He studied for a time at Hodder, Stonyhurst, and then went to Prior Park. When at this time he was asked whether he had any intention of becoming a priest, he would reply 'I am thinking'.[9] Eventually he did make his intention known and was sent to the Collegio degli Ecclesiastici Nobili in Rome where, in 1840, he came under the notice of Pope Gregory XVI by delivering in his presence, on August 15th, a Latin panegyric on the Blessed Virgin.[10] In July, 1844 he took his Doctorate in Philosophy.[11]

Clifford was subsequently ordained subdeacon at Bruges on 2nd July and deacon on 26th July, 1849. He received the priesthood from Bishop Hendren, Vicar Apostolic of the Western District, in the Church of the Twelve Apostles, Clifton (later the Pro-Cathedral) on 25th August, 1850. He remained attached to the church where he had been ordained for about a year. On September 16th, 1851 he returned to Rome where he took his degree as Doctor of Divinity.

The significance in the public mind of a cleric taking a doctorate is

---

9   Ugbrooke Archives, *Letters to Bp. Clifford, 1865*, Laura de L'Isle to Bp. Clifford, letter dated 26.3.1865.

10   Such formal, and to some extent contrived, occasions of learning were not uncommon at the time. Clifford had a life-long devotion to Our Lady. When he was buried he was clasping not only a crucifix and rosary but also 'a small brass figure of the Blessed Virgin' (Monsignor James Shepherd, *Reminiscences of Prior Park*, Publ. London, 1894, p. 120).

11   Ugbrooke Archives, Official documents belonging to Bp. Clifford.

described in an amusing comment – though hardly intended to be such – in a letter dated March, 1837 from George Clifford in Rome to F. C. Husenbeth (father of the future Provost and Vicar General of Northampton):

> '. . . you have mentioned your pious and good son, for whom I entertain a great regard & respect. I am of opinion that he ought as an act of Duty towards you to obtain his Degree of D.D. and moreover I have witnessed since I have been at Rome how much respect is shown to Clergymen of inferior rank, when they are raised by their own merit to some less dignity or Title in the Church & Titles thus conferred shed also a lustre over our holy Religion which renders it more amiable and more prepossessing in the minds even of those whose early prejudices & indolence prevent them from seeking the truth'.[12]

Dr. Clifford returned to England and in April, 1852, became secretary to the newly consecrated Bishop of Plymouth, Dr. George Errington. This marked the beginning of a friendship which was to last until the death of Errington in 1886. Indeed it was Clifford's wish that he be buried next to his life-long friend in the portico just outside the church at Prior Park.

Clifford later became priest at St. Mary's, Stonehouse and accompanied Errington to the First Provincial Synod at Oscott in July, 1852 at which he was appointed one of its three secretaries. When the Plymouth Chapter was erected on 26th November, 1853 Clifford was appointed a member by his bishop, holding the offices of canon theologian, secretary and treasurer. In this capacity he made a present of the official seal, fashioned from a design by Charles Weld of Chideock.[13]

---

12   Northampton Diocesan Archives, *Letters to F. C. Husenbeth*, Letter from George Clifford in Rome, dated March, 1837.

13   Oliver, *op. cit.*, p. 264.

It was at this time – while Clifford was still in his 30th year – that an invitation was extended to him by John Henry Newman to preach in Dublin:

The Oratory, Hagley Road,
Birmingham. August 18/54

My dear Dr. Clifford,

Would you kindly consent to be one of our University Preachers? It will only take you one day in the year, and you shall have plenty of notice.

Some one said you were rather delicate just now, and would be unwilling to preach. I hope it is not so – but any how, I want your name, if you would kindly give it – and then, if when the time came, you felt unequal to the exertion, which I trust would not be the case, we could postpone your turn . . .[14]

Six months later Newman wrote to Canon J. B. Morris at Yealmpton (Diocese of Plymouth):

Report is . . . that Dr. Clifford is going to Rome to take someone's place.[15]

Errington was appointed Coadjutor Archbishop to Cardinal Wiseman on 30th March, 1855. Clifford was elected Vicar Capitular of Plymouth on 16th May and in this capacity assisted at the Second Provincial Council held at Oscott two months later. The new Bishop of Plymouth was Clifford's cousin and friend, William Vaughan. He was forty-one and at the time of his appointment was in charge of the Pro-Cathedral at Clifton. This was in July, 1855, and on going to Plymouth he immediately nominated William Clifford his Vicar General, but within two or three

---

14   Clifton Diocesan Archives *Letters to Honble. & Revd. William Clifford* (Part I, 1854 – 1874), Newman to Bp. Clifford, letter dated 18.8.1854.

15   *The Letters and Diaries of John Henry Newman* ed. Dessain) Vol. XVI (Publ. London, 1965), p. 381, Newman to Morris, Letter dated 13.2.1855.

months Clifford was on his way to Rome – not, however, 'to take someone's place' but in order to complete a course in canon law.

This period of training was to prove invaluable in his future career. Because of his specialist knowledge, and his fluency in Latin and Italian, he would often be called upon by his fellow bishops to advise on, or even present, difficult cases at Rome. He was to draft and argue the Bishops' case in their controversy with the religious orders, culminating in the publication in 1881 of *Romanos Pontifices*. Most significant of all, in the debates of Vatican I he was to draw the attention of the assembled Fathers to the fact that their deliberations were, in his view, going beyond the terms of reference as laid down in the Bull summoning the Council and were therefore in danger of being invalid. But this was to be in the future.

The Diocese of Clifton had been without a Bishop since the death of Thomas Burgess in November, 1854, although it had had the great advantage of Errington's appointment as Apostolic Administrator. In this capacity (as we have seen) he did a great deal to put the Diocese, poor though it was, on a sound financial footing and taken the one essential step to achieve this, namely, the sale of Prior Park. He had also reached an agreement with the Augustinians over the dispute about St. Nicholas, Pennywell Road, Bristol.

Errington had relinquished his burden and the appointment of a new Bishop was eagerly awaited. Rumours abounded with William Clifford's name high on the list. His younger brother Henry (now aged 30 and an officer in the Army) wrote at the end of 1856:

Court House. Dec. 18th

My dear William

(Perhaps at this moment destined to be "My brother the Bishop"!!)

....

I am most anxiously expecting to hear your fate and you will be a sad loss to –, but I cannot thank you enough for your great kindness to us, so it is no use trying, you have some reward in making both so happy. I shall be <u>very very</u> glad to see you Bishop or not. I almost wish not Bishop, for I long to give you a few good thumps to pay you off for Chuff . . .[16]

Henry had been awarded the Victoria Cross earlier in the year for conspicuous gallantry at the Battle of Inkerman (1854).

However, other names were being canvassed for the vacant See. Mgr. Talbot, the Bishops' Agent in Rome and close confidant of the Pope, had written to Cardinal Wiseman apparently suggesting the possibility of nominating Mgr. Francis Joseph Weld. Weld was aged 37 and was Parish Priest in Isleworth. Educated at Downside his influence in later years was to be felt in the debate over the relative merits of a pastoral rather than a strictly monastic ministry for the English Benedictine Congregation. Parfitt – who is mentioned in the Cardinal's reply – was a convert to the Faith at the age of 20, ministered to the flock at Midford Castle on the outskirts of Bath. In the 1800s he inherited a considerable sum of money from the family at Midford but only after the will had been disputed by relatives in the civil courts.

Wiseman was not happy with the suggestion that Weld be appointed Bishop of Clifton. In his reply to Talbot the Cardinal wrote:

'What you write to me on the subject in part alarms, & in part consoles me. For first you say that Mgr. Weld *desires* to be Bishop, & then that at Rome, there is a propensity in favour of Dr. Clifford. I should dread seeing anyone made a Bishop in England who sought it. It Shows but a poor estimate of the labour & burthen, not to speak of its responsibility anywhere. In fact, though there are few among the clergy Whom I love more than Mgr W. I should be sorry to see him Bp. of *Clifton*. The difficulties, there, will be immense for some time to come, Which will require a steady & strong hand on the reins. This I fear is not W's gift. He is a gentle quiet character, & will be led, but will not lead. Indeed I fear greatly that the wish to have him bishop, & the endeavour, come from another person, Can. Parfitt, who has

16   Ugbrooke Archives, *Letters to William Clifford, 1856*, from Henry Clifford, Letter dated 18.12.1856.

the most complete command over him, and would be the real bishop, if W. be named. Of course I have no right to speak, unless the H(oly) F(ather) & S(acred) C(ongregation) apply to me: but I shall grieve to see any appointment so made, though the arrangement which you suggested of Dr. Vaughan would have been much better, with Mgr W. at Plymouth'.[17]

Bishop Vaughan's years at the Pro-Cathedral in Clifton and as a member of the Chapter made him a strong candidate for a post where it might be felt that a knowledge of the intricacies of recent past history would be an advantage. Wiseman, however, favoured the candidature of Clifford:

'But Dr. Clifford's nomination would, I believe please all, certainly the Bishops. His health seems to me to be the only objection. Nor do I think much of this at Clifton which is a healthy place. He would carry out the Archbishop's reforms, while he himself thinks that he would be acceptable to Mother Margaret, & not perhaps continue all his changes. In theory & law I believe Dr. E. has been right: but I have found fault with him for not leaving many things to the next bishop, instead of doing them while only an administrator'.[18]

---

17   Venerable English College Archives, Rome, *Talbot Letters*, Wiseman to Talbot, Letter dated 26.9.1856. Talbot may well have taken his cue from Parfitt who had certainly written to Propaganda suggesting Weld, but what is of even greater interest is that the previous year Weld had put himself forward for the post. Commenting on this to the Cardinals, the Secretary of Propaganda wrote:

However great may be the qualities which, as alleged by Parfitt, distinguish Mgr. Weld, he does not appear to be very strong in that virtue which is the foundation of all others, since rather inappropriately, he wrote last year to Propaganda requesting the bishopric for himself and putting forward all the points on which – as it appeared to him – he merited it. [My translation]

(*Acta Sac. Cong. de Prop. Fide, Roma, Ab Anno 1857, 221* RISTRETTO CON SOMMARIO Sulla. elezione del Vescovo per la vacante Chiesa di Clifton in Inghilterra., e su qualche provvidenza. da. adottarsi pel bene di quella Diocesi. 28 Gennaio 1857, Articolo I, No. 12.)

18   *Ibid.*

Mother Margaret Hallahan was the foundress of the Congregation of St. Catherine of Siena. In the early days of the Catholic revival in England she had built a Convent and Chapel (later consecrated) adjoining the Pro-Cathedral. Mother Margaret and Errington had been in dispute over the Convent and clearly Wiseman regarded the desirability of good relations with her as being a factor in the appointment.[19]

At this point in the narrative it is fascinating to explore the archives at the Vatican and at Propaganda Fide to discover the tortuous route by which the choice was eventually made.

As a result of Errington's Administration of the diocese the difficulties in the way of appointing a new bishop had been largely removed. The Cardinal Prefect of Propaganda wrote to Wiseman to enquire whether the passage of time had caused him to change his mind with regard to the terna proposed by the Cathedral Chapter in February, 1855, on the death of Bishop Burgess. He replied on 23rd December, 1856, that his reasons for excluding Brindle (Vicar Capitular and Provost) and Rooker (Canon Theologian) were all the more valid because of the part they had played in the controversy over Prior Park. With regard to O'Ferrall, O.S.F. (Missionary Apostolic in Bristol) he had changed his views in the light of the praises ('elogii') expressed about him by Errington. [20]

While these communications were taking place, Errington wrote to the Pope giving an account of the state of the diocese of Clifton now that he had completed his work there as Apostolic Administrator.[21] The *sommario* at Propaganda states:

---

19   Mother Margaret's nuns remained at St. Catherine's until May, 1876, when they moved to Stone in Staffordshire. Bishop Clifford bought the property and from 1881 to 1884 gave refuge to a large community of Franciscan Friars who had been driven out of France by the severity of the laws against religious orders (*Guide Book to the Catholic Conference, Bristol*, C.T.S., Publ. Bristol, 1895, p.43) After the Second World War additional classrooms were needed at the adjoining Pro-Cathedral School, Park Place. These were provided for by adding an extra floor to the roof of the former Convent.

20   Propaganda Fide Archives, Rome (see note 17 above). Articolo I, No. 7. Letter of Wiseman dated 23.12.1856.

21   A summary of Errington's *Report* is in the Diocesan Archives.

Noting the difficulties attached to the names proposed by the Chapter and the probability that the Sacred Congregation would wish to ignore these completely, and perhaps also those proposed by the bishops, it seemed opportune to consult Errington to ask whether in his view he could suggest someone from among the clergy of Clifton.

He replied in the negative. [My translation]. [22]

Meanwhile the Pope himself had been in touch with Wiseman, just six days after the latter had written to Propaganda (see above). Writing in Italian the Pope said:

I have spoken with the Archbishop of Trebizond [Errington] who has conveyed to me an exact account of the diocese of Clifton. I feel very inclined to see there the son of Lord Clifford who at the moment is studying here at the Collegio Pio. (*Italian:* Mi sento malto inclinato di vedere su quella Sede il figlio di Lord Clifford che ora trovassi in questo Collegio Pio.) Mgr. Errington agrees with me and I believe that you too would be of the same mind. The *terna* has already been presented and it does not appear to place an unlimited confidence in the three names suggested: on the other hand the chapter has suggested it might be useful to submit another *terna*? I shall await your verifying this. [My translation] [23]

One would doubt that Wiseman, once the Pope had suggested a preference, would wish to pursue the matter further. At any rate Propaganda was now thinking along the same lines as the Pope and it was thought 'opportune' to put before the Cardinals of Propaganda what Wiseman had written in May, 1855, on Canon Clifford of Plymouth when they were seeking to appoint a new Bishop of Plymouth:

In fact he enjoys the esteem and benevolence of all for the excellent qualities with which he is endowed. [My translation].[24]

---

22   Propaganda Fide Archives, Rome (see note 17 above)." Articolo I, No. 9.

23   Vatican Archives, *Archivio Particolare Pio IX, Oggetti Varii*, No. 30. Letter from Pius IX to Wiseman dated 29.12.1856.

24   Propaganda Fide Archives, Rome (see note 17 above). Articolo I, No. 10.

Talbot was to write later that the appointment of Clifford to Clifton had been made *motu proprio* by the Pope and so it is likely that the Pope had prompted Propaganda to look at Clifford's candidature bearing in mind how close he had been to being appointed Bishop of Plymouth.

On that occasion Wiseman had written to Propaganda to explain why, at the sixth scrutiny for the terna from the Plymouth Chapter, a Canon Woollett had received four votes and Clifford only one.

> Perhaps it will come as something of a surprise to Your Eminence that the latter (Clifford) did not figure among the names proposed – all the more so as on the previous day the Chapter had nominated him Vicar (Capitular) *sede vacante*.
>
> Mgr. [Errington], Archbishop of Trebizond, has advised me that without doubt his name would have gone forward, and probably in the first place, were it not for the fact that he was determined to return to Rome to resume and complete his studies in canon law. This determination of his was already known to the Chapter, and so it was thought pointless to nominate him even though he is loved by all (*a tutti carissimo*) for his piety, wisdom, knowledge and good nature (*amabilità*).
>
> The only thing lacking is good health, and if in the more mild climate of Italy he acquires health and strength – as the doctors have given him reason to hope – he will certainly be amongst the most worthy to find a place on the episcopal bench. [My translation] .[25]

The two candidates proposed by the bishops were:

1) James Aylward (former provincial of the Dominicans and at that time Prior of Woodchester).

---

25   Propaganda Fide Archives, Rome (see note 17 above). Num. IV: *Estratto di una lettera dell'Emo Arcivescovo di Westminster colla quale accompagnava nello scorso anno 1856 la terna per l'elezione del Vescovo di Plymouth*. Letter dated 25.5.1855.

   2) Louis English (Rector of the Collegio Pio in Rome and priest of the Westminster Archdiocese). The Collegio Pio was founded in 1852 for the purpose of training more mature students for the priesthood. It was under the same roof as the Ven. English College. Dr. Clifford was residing there at the time of his appointment to Clifton.

This was Wiseman's view – and also Errington's – in May, 1855. As the latter happened to be in Rome while Propaganda was considering the vacancy at Clifton, it was only natural that he should be approached again on the suitability of Clifford for episcopal office. For those who were asked their views in such cases, it was customary to require that they be expressed under three separate headings. Errington's replies about Clifford were as follows –

Academic qualities

His studies went very well under the Jesuit Fathers; principally in Rome until the Revolution of 1848, then at Louvain, and finally at their theological college of St. Beuno in Wales where he was created Doctor of Divinity 'by public act' in 1850.[26] During the four years (approx.) that he lived in Plymouth, both as missionary and as secretary to the present writer, his ideas in theology and canon law were very precise and clear.

This showed itself in the care and precision in regard to the presentation of the cases and other questions which he was asked to enquire into, and in his ability in the conduct of affairs with which he was entrusted.

When the present writer was translated from the See of Plymouth, the Canon was elected Vicar Capitular and in that capacity took part in the Second Provincial Council of Westminster in which he again fulfilled the role of Promoter.

-----

26   Here Errington clearly differs from Oliver (*op. cit*.,) who says on page 264 that Clifford took his Doctorate of Divinity in Rome in 1851.

He then came to Rome to continue his studies, particularly in canon law, while his health – which was not sufficiently robust to enable him to continue his work as missionary – recovered.

Moral qualities

He has a good head, a firm purpose, a cool temperament, a peaceable nature, is lively and cheerful and has an open manner. He loves the studies and the work associated with the duties of his state, and he places great store by the exact observance of ecclesiastical discipline.

Religious qualities

He has the true spirit of an ecclesiastic and of a missionary. He is pious, simple and zealous, and very conscientious in the exercises which pertain to his own personal sanctification.

A physical constitution which is less than robust (inherited from his mother) is an impediment to the full exercise of the qualities mentioned above, and this in turn gives rise to some concern that these (same qualities) will not bear the degree of fruit on which one might otherwise have been able to count.

It does appear, however, that with each passing year, his health will become less delicate and less of a problem (*critica*), and doctors are of the opinion that after two or three years he should enjoy more robust health.

He is now 33 years of age. [My translation] [27]

---

27   Propaganda Fide Archives, Rome (see note 17 above). Num. VIII: *Monsig. Errington risponde all'interpelazione fattagli da Mons. Segretario sulle qualità del Can. Clifford.* Letter sent from the English College dated 4.1.1857.

In appointing Clifford to Clifton Propaganda also saw a 'bonus' in so far as the loss of Vaughan (to Plymouth) some eighteen months before would in this way be compensated. [28]

On the 25th January, 1857, the eleven cardinals of Propaganda met in General Congregation and appointed Canon William Clifford to the vacant See of Clifton. [29] Clifford's relative youth was apparently not an obstacle. Today such youthful appointments would perhaps be rare but it certainly was not so in the mid-nineteenth century as the following examples – taken only from England – show:

> 1840 Nicholas Wiseman (as V.A.) 37 years
>
> 1851 James Brown (Shrewsbury) 39 years
>
> 1851 Thomas Grant (Southwark) 34 years

Some eighteen months later Mgr. Talbot revealed in a letter to Mgr. Parfitt exactly how the appointment of Clifford was made:

> He was named *motu proprio* by the Holy Father, although afterwards his name was submitted to the Sacred Congregation of Propaganda, which was unanimous in approving of the choice.[30]

----

28   Propaganda Fide Archives, Rome (see note 17 above). Articolo I, No. 11.

29   Propaganda Fide Archives, Rome (see note 7 above). Articolo II, handwritten document (in Latin) inserted between pages 6 and 7.

Rumours about Clifford's possible nomination continued to the very last moment, e.g. Bishop Turner of Salford in a letter to Dr. Rooker asked: 'Is Dr. Clifford to be, as is stated in the papers, Bishop of Clifton? I know nothing.' The letter was dated 30.1.1857 – five days after the appointment but probably before the official announcement. (Clifton Diocesan Archives, *Dr. Rooker's Letters. 1850 - 1857*, Turner to Rooker). Rooker was seeking to leave Clifton and join the diocese of Salford.

30   Ugbrooke Archives, *Letters to Bp. Clifford, 1858*, Talbot to Parfitt, letter dated 23.11.1858.

Talbot, having noted that 'Dr. Clifford is so much liked in your Diocese' added:

> His greatest difficulty will be to raise a fund for the Diocese, which I am afraid has been drained to the dregs. *Money, money* is what is wanted in England to make the Church advance. With money one creates everything, Schools, Seminaries, Colleges, Churches, etc. etc. [31]

The current state of the diocese also worried Dr. Brindle. Writing to his friend, Dr. Rooker, he said

> I hope and trust he (Clifford) will make a good Bishop, and be able to repair the injury to religion, wh. I cannot but think has been unnecessarily caused. [32]

Congratulations, tinged with a certain sympathy, poured in. Cardinal Wiseman wrote to Talbot: 'I am glad about Clifford, and the Holy Father's kind condescension in consecrating him'.[33] In a letter the same day (February 3rd, 1857) to the Bishop-elect the Cardinal said:

---

31   The 13th Lord Clifford in his history of the family, *The House of Clifford*, writes about William's nomination to the See of Clifton:

> . . . it is only fair to add that his appointment was based upon his financial and social position as much as upon his personal intellect and brilliance . . .

> Soon after his installation as bishop of Clifton he gave £1,000 towards the extinction of the diocesan debt. (page 183).

The fact remains that in the records at Propaganda relating to the appointment no mention is made either of Clifford's social position or of his ability personally to help pay off the diocesan debt.

32   Clifton Diocesan Archives, *Letters 1815 - 1862*, No. 379, Brindle to Rooker, Letter dated 5.2.1857.

33   Venerable English College, Rome: *Talbot Papers*, Wiseman to Talbot, Letter dated 2/3.2.1857.

'I have just received your letter, and venture to wish you joy, on your nomination, which I am sure will be for the good of the Church of Clifton, if not for your own comfort.

But especially I congratulate you on the peculiar mark of favour and paternal affection shown you by the H(oly) F(ather) in condescending to consecrate you himself.

Begging a share in your prayers, . . .

N. Card. Wiseman[34]

The theme of commiseration was taken up by Clifford's cousin, Bishop Vaughan of Plymouth, who, more than most, knew the scale of the problems facing the new Bishop. His letter is worth quoting at length:

Lulworth Castle
Feb 8th 1857

My dear Clifford

I suppose a great many will consider that the right thing to do is to *congratulate* you – for my part I think all the congratulations, or at least the larger share of them, may more appropriately be expended on Clifton whilst compassion, and a hearty prayer will be more congenial to your feelings – Well – Take courage – It will not be so hard as you may anticipate – you have the good *wishes*, and what is better you will have the hearty co-operation of all those whose good will is worth having. And as you will take a straight-forward course you will be seen to go ahead, and all will come right. You know what Clifton *was* – and I hope soon to see it like itself again – That spot is the hope as it is the centre of your Diocese – and when you have got all right there you will be able to spread out . . . As soon as I heard of your appointment I sent to the convents to make them all pray stoutly for you – particularly on the 15th . . .

William Vaughan[35]

---

34   Ugbrooke Archives, *Letters to Wm. Clifford, 1857*, Wiseman to Clifford, Letter dated 3.2.1857.

35   Ugbrooke Archives, *Letters to Wm. Clifford, 1857*, Bishop Vaughan to Clifford, Letter dated 8.2.1857.

A very agreeable letter of congratulation came from the Archbishop of Dublin (Dr. Joseph Dixon) who, describing himself as a sincere friend, spoke of Clifford's 'high character for learning, piety and zeal'.[16] Already, it would seem, the new Bishop's reputation was recognised in Ireland as well as in England and at Rome.

The Tablet noted (14.2.1857) that 'His Lordship will be the youngest member of the Episcopal body in England' and in subsequent editions gave accounts of Clifford's episcopal consecration at the hands of the Holy Father himself. As Wiseman had done, so Archbishop Dixon commented on his signal honour:

> 'It will be for ever a source of joy to you to have had the honour and happiness of being consecrated by the Vicar of Jesus Christ. Permit me to say that . . . I share your joy from this source'.[37]

During the ceremony the Holy Father was 'much affected'. The correspondent of *The Tablet* observed:

> 'The Holy Father designed [*sic*] by this consecration to show his affection and interest in the English Hierarchy, and this gracious intention was officially announced in the Roman Journal; but he expressed his particular satisfaction in conferring his honour on the son of Lord Clifford, and the grandson of Cardinal Weld, two English Catholics who have both deserved so well of the Church'.[38]

The long ceremony began at 7.30 a.m. and the Pope was assisted by Archbishop Errington and Mgr. Bailles, Bishop of Luçon. The Cardinals' benches which fill up the Sistine Chapel were removed for the occasion so that the large number attending the ceremony could be accommodated within the screen. Lord Clifford and Major Clifford, the father and brother of the Bishop, were present.

---

36   Ugbrooke Archives, *Letters to Wm. Clifford, 1857*, Archbishop Dixon to Clifford, Letter dated 3.4.1857.

37   *Ibid.*

38   *The Tablet*, 28.2.1857.

'At the conclusion of the ceremony . . . the Bishops, and Chaplains, and the relations of the new Bishop, had the honour of breakfasting with the Holy Father, who afterwards presented Dr. Clifford with a richly bound copy of the Pontificale and Canon, and a massive chalice of rare beauty.[39] In the afternoon Cardinal Antonelli . . . entertained the new Bishop at dinner. The Cardinals of the Congregation of Propaganda, the Bishops who assisted in the consecration, together with many of the English residents and visitors in Rome, partook of his Eminence's sumptuous hospitality'.[40]

A few days later a deputation of English Catholics in Rome[41] had an audience of the Pope who

. . . spoke most touchingly of his interest in the conversions that had taken place in England of late years, and of his own ardent and constant prayer to God that a country whose dominion extended to every part of the world should be brought by grace to acknowledge and embrace the true faith.[42]

Before returning to England, a very proud Lord Clifford wrote to his son:

My Rt. Revd. & Dear Son
Ever since I heard from the lips of H.H. Himself on the occasion of the deputation of Englishmen resident in the Pontifical States that to the best of the knowledge and belief of H.H. He was the *first* pope since S.Gregory the Great who had consecrated with his own hands an English Bishop,

---

39   The chalice is now on permanent exhibition at Buckfast Abbey, Devon (by kind permission of Lord Clifford). The students of the Collegio Pio, where Dr. Clifford had been resident for some eighteen months while pursuing his studies in canon law, presented him with a ring which he wore at his consecration.

40   *The Tablet*, 28.2.1857.

41   Some criticism of the composition of the deputation was voiced in Rome (as reported in *The Tablet* the following week). Apparently some people became aware of its having taken place only after a report appeared in *The Roman Journal*.

42   *The Tablet*, 28.2.1857.

I have had those words ringing in my ears and making them tingle . . .[43]

A year later he was dead. John Henry Newman wrote a letter of condolence to Bishop Clifford, praising the qualities of soul of his late father:

> . . . his extreme humility, gentleness, and kindness; united as those graces were with so self-denying and mortified a life and such a perseverance in acts of mercy and devotional practices . . . it made me very sorrowful to hear of his death, as feeling the loss which it was to us all to have a saint the less in the English Church. [44]

On 3rd March, 1857 – only sixteen days after his consecration the Pope – appointed Clifford an Assistant at the Pontifical Throne. This title is conferred on bishops but is usually given only after a long episcopate of particularly distinguished service.[45]

In the Spring of 1857 when the new bishop returned to England, Lord Clifford – and perhaps others – feared that moves might be made under the aegis of the Ecclesiastical Titles Assumption Bill (1st August, 1851) to prevent him from exercising his office. Furthermore it was thought that a distinction might be drawn between appointment by the Pope - which had been at least tolerated both in the case of the Vicars Apostolic and of those Bishops who were appointed in 1850 and 1851 (January to July) – and actual consecration by the Pontiff. Could this be seen as constituting a wholly new situation?[46] Lord Clifford had given the point some thought and mentioned it in the second part of the letter quoted above:

---

43   Ugbrooke Archives, *Letters to Bp. Clifford. 1857*, Lord Clifford to his son, 28.2.1857.

44   Clifton Diocesan Archives, *Letters to Honble. & Revd. William Clifford, Part I, 1854 - 1874*, Newman to Clifford, letter dated 4.3.1858.

45   Clifton Diocesan Archives, *Papal Briefs, etc. 1779 - 1902*. Pius IX, who was noted for his liberality in conferring honours, is said to have created more monsignori in 30 years than his predecessors had done in almost 2,000 years. (Holmes and Bickers, *A Short History of the Catholic Church*, (Publ. Tunbridge Wells, 1983), pages 240, 241).

'As far as I can form a conjecture if any attempt should be made by the Exeter Hall party to get up a row on account of your considerations, it will be made in the H. of Lords – I am very glad therefore that I cannot be in that house this session as I know myself to be utterly unfit to answer questions *improvised*.

When H. Em. Cardl. Wiseman was appointed Abp of Westminster the Ecclesiastical Titles Act had not received the royal assent.

I particularly wish to point out to your notice the passages in the speeches of Lord Monteagle and of the Lord Chancellor's answer which I have marked in the margin . . .'[47]

What is perhaps of greater interest is the number of bishops – almost half the entire hierarchy – who were consecrated in July, 1851, i.e. only a matter of *days* before the bill became law on 1st August:

Grant of Southwark	6.7.1851
Turner of Salford	25.7.1851
Errington of Plymouth	25.7.1851
Burgess of Clifton	27.7.1851
Brown of Shrewsbury	27.7.1851

---

46   It has to be admitted that no prosecution had been brought against the three bishops who had been consecrated since the passing of the Act, viz. Roskell of Nottingham (21.9.1853), Goss of Liverpool (25.9.1853), and Vaughan of Plymouth (16.9.1855).

47   Ugbrooke Archives, *Letters to Bp. Clifford, 1857*, Lord Clifford to his son. Letter dated 28.2.1857.

With the letter Lord Clifford had enclosed a copy of proceedings in the House of Lords (taken from *The Morning Chronicle*, Saturday, July 26, 1851) in which Lord Monteagle received answers from the Lord Chancellor to four questions which he had submitted in writing relating to the Ecclesiastical Titles Assumption Bill just six days before it received the royal assent. Monteagle's second question was:

> 'If a Roman Catholic diocese bears the same title with a diocese in the Established Church, but is conterminous or identical therewith, is such Roman Catholic diocese "a pretended diocese under sec. 1 of the Ecclesiastical Titles Assumption Bill"? Is the Papal instrument appointing or purporting to appoint to such diocese unlawful and void under such bill; and is the jurisdiction, authority, pre-eminence, or title unlawful and void under such bill?[48]

The reply of the Lord Chancellor was very significant:

> . . . with respect to the second question, the free exercise of the Roman Catholic religion had been allowed and recognised by Parliament; and, therefore, what was necessary for the ordinary exercise of that religion was, he apprehended, not unlawful.'.[49]

Commenting on this extract (which he had marked) Lord Clifford wrote to his son:

> 'It seems evident *to me*, that in the existing *non-intercourse* state between the Holy See and the Throne of England Pope Pius IX cannot be held *in Law* to have any Official cognisance of the Ecclesiastical Titles Act of 1851.

---

48   Extract from *The Morning Chronicle*, 26.7.1851 (in the Archives at Ugbrooke with *Letters to Bp. Clifford. 1857*).

49   *Ibid*.

It seems equally evident *to me* that to the question – Are you Bishop of Clifton, you are *legally entitled* to answer, "I decline answering that question as my answer to it might compromise myself"'.[50]

Certainly the whole question of what was permissible under the Act was a moot point; furthermore no one could anticipate whether a strict or more liberal interpretation would be put on its provisions. In this respect it was not unlike many of the Anti-catholic laws under previous monarchs which, though prescribing fines or imprisonment, were not universally applied in the same way.

For these reasons in the early days of its operation the Catholic Bishops decided to 'play safe'. One such was George Errington, a man of undoubted legal skill, whose first pastoral letter as Bishop of Plymouth began:

GEORGE, by the Grace of God and favour of the Apostolic See, Bishop, etc., To the clergy, secular and regular, and all the faithful of the diocese of Plymouth, Health and Benediction in the Lord and ended:

GEORGE ERRINGTON

Given at Plymouth, this 20 day of August, 1851. [51]

---

50   Ugbrooke Archives, *Letters to Bp. Clifford, 1857*, Lord Clifford to his son, Letter dated 28.2.1857.

51   Clifton Diocesan Archives, *Letters 1788 - 1874*, No. 163. In the same volume (No. 162) is a pastoral letter by Bishop Burgess inscribed as follows:

A PASTORAL
BY THE RIGHT REV. THOMAS BURGESS, D.D. ,
BISHOP, etc. etc. but prohibited by Act of Parliament
15 of Victoria chap. from signing himself Bishop of Clifton

1851

Printed at the Prior Park Press

'but prohibited . . . ' is written in Burgess's own hand. Were all copies of the pastoral so inscribed and so circumvent the law? The pastoral was not signed, although it was dated August 15th, 1851.

Nowhere does he explicitly lay claim to the title 'Bishop of Plymouth' (At the time this was written the Act had been on the statute book less than three weeks).

In the event nobody invoked the Act against Bishop Clifford but it continued to be a matter about which he was studious not to cause offence. The following letter is quoted in full because it shows clearly his attitude had not changed even five years after his consecration as Bishop:

(Jan. 18 1862)

My dear Talbot,

I was going to sign my name to the address of condolence to the Queen,[52] when I was told that my doing so might give offence here in Rome. I come therefore to ask your opinion on the matter. The question is this. I should sign my name and surname simply without any title as I usually do in such cases, but some people think that it would be wrong for me to drop my title of Bp of Clifton here in Rome. This is not my view, but as the question has been raised, and I have been told that I should give offence by signing as I propose I should like to know if you think that is the case.

I should sign the address, because I think Catholics ought always to make a point of showing loyalty when occasions offer, that so it may appear that when they oppose temporal authorities they do it only for conscience sake – On the other hand I cannot of course sign an address to the Queen by a title which is (however unjustly) forbidden by law, and it would seem a most ungracious thing to make use of an address of condolence to pick a quarrel. The grievance we have against the government is not that it refuses to recognise our titles but that it has made it illegal for us to assume them. Government did not recognise the Vicars Apostolic but it did not forbid the use of the title. Still nobody signed himself as such on occasions like the present.

---

52   The first anniversary of the death of Prince Albert.

Even if there had been no ecclesiastical titles bill we should not have asked the government to recognise us.

My own view is that I ought to sign the address simply with my name, but if you think the authorities here will be offended I will abstain from signing altogether.

William Clifford [53]

Talbot advised Clifford to see Barnabo who was 'decidedly of the opinion' that he had better sign the address without assuming the title of Bishop of Clifton

'Because, as he says, if it were an act coming from the Bishops as such, it would not be well for one of them here in Rome to hide his title, but being merely an act of loyalty from Subjects to their Sovereign there is no particular call for *Bishops* to use their titles when they know it gives offence; and it is advisable for us to show our loyalty to the Queen when we can do so, that so it may better appear that when we oppose the laws we do so only because they are contrary to the laws of God.'[54]

Barnabo added, however, that it would be well for Clifford to tell the Pope what he intended to do! Pio Nono could, on occasions, be both impetuous and irrascible [55] and the Cardinal was warning Clifford that for a bishop not to use his title when in Rome, unless he had *very* good cause, might well provoke the Pontiff's ire.

---

53   Venerable English College, Rome, *Talbot Papers*, No. 126, Clifford to Talbot, Letter dated 18.1.1862.

54   Venerable English College, Rome, *Talbot Papers*, No. 127, Talbot to Clifford, Letter dated 19.1.1862.

55   Evidence of this will be seen over the issue of who was to succeed Wiseman at Westminster (Chapter 6), and in the Pope's carpeting of Cardinal Guidi of Bologna who, during the Vatican Council debate on Papal Infallibility, had expressed reservations about the proposed definition. (Cuthbert Butler, *The First Vatican Council*, Publ. London, 1962, p. 355).

The sensitive nature of the issue, even as far as the British Government was concerned, lasted well into the twentieth century. On the Coronation of King George VI in May, 1937, the Home Secretary (Sir John Simon) declared

> 'that he would be unable to submit to the King a loyal address "in which these archbishops and bishops were referred to as the *Catholic* archbishops and bishops and in the signatures to which use is made of territorial designations which cannot be recognised in official communications"'.[56]

Dr. Clifford's first pastoral letter as Bishop of Clifton was greeted as 'faulty' by one canon although on what grounds he does not say.[57] However the new bishop did succeed in making a good start with the Chapter, and just ten weeks after his consecration the *Minutes* record

> The Bishop . . . said it was his intention to lay before Chapter the business of the diocese. That he proposed to make an examination of the property and Trusteeships of the missions, that he would endeavour to promote the efficiency of the Chapter and to lessen its burdens. [58]

Clifford was true to his word and throughout his episcopate there appears to have been no recurrence of the complaints levelled against Bishop Burgess that the real state of affairs in the diocese was not being put before the canons.

---

56   *The Universe*, 21.5.1937.

57   Clifton Diocesan Archives, *Letters 1815 - 1862*, No. 380, Brindle to Rooker, Letter dated 20.2.1857.

58   Clifton Diocesan Archives, *Acta capituli Cliftoniensis*, 30.4.1857, p. 31.

CHAPTER THREE

Association for Promoting the Unity of Christendom

Conversions of individuals from the Church of England to the Catholic Church have been a feature of religious life in this country since the time of the Protestant Reformation. The scale of the numbers involved has of course varied – on some occasions a mere trickle, on others an abundance.

The mid-nineteenth century witnessed a double influx: one during the years 1840 – 1846 at the time of the Oxford Movement, and the other in 1850 after the Gorham Judgement (the Reverend Gorham had applied to be incumbent at the parish of St. Peter, Brampford Speke in the diocese of Exeter. On being examined as to his theolgy he admitted that he did not accept the Christian Doctrine of Baptismal Regeneration, as a result of which, Bishop Henry Phillpotts refused to give permission for his induction. The decision, however, was overturned on appeal by the Privy Council). The latter brought many to a realisation of the truly Erastian nature of the Church of England and signalled in their minds its forfeiture of any claim it might have had to be the true Church of Jesus Christ.

For some, however, individual conversions – no matter how numerous – did not meet the real challenge of the situation and for them some sort of corporate reunion was not only desirable and possible, but also the only practical means of achieving the long-awaited 'Conversion of England'.

One example of each point of view may be cited.

In November, 1840, the Rev. Joseph Rathbone (Catholic priest at Cowes on the Isle of Wight) wrote to Bishop Thomas Joseph Brown, the vicar Apostolic of the newly-created Vicariate of Wales. (In his younger days Brown, a Benedictine, had been a considerable apologist in the Catholic cause, and this would seem to have been the reason which prompted Rathbone to write to him).

> I wish the party, with their supporters, the *Bishops of Oxford and Bangor*, could be brought to a conference, *I mean a friendly one*, in which every effort would be brought about to establish a union with the Catholics. On our side the persons to be selected to carry it on should be, Bishop Baines, Dr. Wiseman, and yourself.

> But alas I fear I am a mere visionary. It is quite clear, and every
> page of my learned correspondent tells *me so, that a large
> party in the Church of England wish* to unite with the
> Church of Rome. He says that he would feel more joy in calling
> the Pope *Father* than His Holiness would in calling him *Son*.[1]

Despite Rathbone's mention of Baines in this ecumenical context, it is
nevertheless true that he entertained no real hope of the Conversion of
England, either in the short of medium term. Bishop Baines had been
Vicar Apostolic of the Western District since 1829,and in 1840 he wrote a
controversial pastoral letter in which he poured soorn on the whole idea
that England would ever be converted to Catholicism. The resulting outcry
led to his having to go to Rome to explain himself.[2] Despite this there were
those who still agreed with his original analysis of the situation. Among
these was Frederick Faber who had entered the Church in 1845.

Undaunted by the hesitations of others, a group of Catholics and
Anglicans banded together to form the Association for Promoting the
Unity of Christendom. The leading protagonists were the Anglican
George Frederick Lee (Vicar of Lambeth) and Ambrose de Lisle Phillipps
(who later styled himself Phillipps de Lisle).

Phillipps was a quite unusual character, described by Cuthbert Butler as a
man 'of inextinguishable faith, optimistic hope and zealous charity'.[3] It
appears that as a young man he had met an Italian mystic who had told him
that he would live to see the Conversion of England. Phillipps believed that
Anglicans were schismatics, not heretics, and his own desire was to work for
the corporate reunion of the Anglican and Catholic Churches. To his mind
something akin to the 'coming together' of the Armenians in Venice might be
seen as a blue-print, pointing the way to a corporate *modus vivendi*.

Phillipps was totally obedient to ecclesiastical authority and at each step
kept Cardinal Wiseman informed and sought to enlist the support and

---

1   Cardiff Archdiocesan Archives: *Letters to Bp. Brown*, Rathbone to
     Brown, Letter dated 4.11.1840. The writer died at Cowes in August, 1841.

2   The story is well described by Dr. John Cashman in his unpublished
     thesis *Bishop Baines and the Tensions in the Western District. 1823 -
     1843* (M. Litt., University of Bristol, 1989), section 3.

3   Cuthbert Butler, *The Life and Times of Bishop Ullathorne 1806 -
     1889*, (Publ. London, 1926), I, p. 335.

win the approval of Propaganda Fide in Rome. Wiseman, however, was wary. He saw Anglicans as still at heart Protestants and therefore for him in any scheme of Reunion the private judgement of each must be seen to be surrendered to the divine authority of the Catholic Church.

Crucial to an understanding of the history of A.P.U.C. is the fact that Phillipps was a distant relative by marriage of Bishop Clifford. Deeply conscious of the *entrée* which such a relationship conferred, Phillipps embarked upon a copious correspondence with his episcopal cousin. But family ties were not the only reason for this. In his own right Clifford was seen to be an influential, highly intelligent, liberal minded figure whose good offices, once secured, would be of inestimable value to 'our great subject'.

Bishop Clifford was consecrated in 1857 and before the year was out Phillipps was writing to him. In the letter Phillipps took the initiative to try to set in motion an interest in his cause and to move things forward by arranging a link whereby Dr. Lee and the Bishop were to enter into correspondence with each other. The tone of this letter – with its enthusiasm about the matter in hand coupled with an optimism about future prospects – is typical of Phillipps's correspondence. Here are two extracts:

> There is certainly a wonderful change going on in the minds of the Anglican Clergy, and it seems specially confined to them, as tho' Providence was preparing them as a class and a Body for some special work – What can that work be but the corporate reconciliation of their Church? . . . it is a certain fact that there are thousands now amongst the Anglican Clergy (to say nothing of Laity) who ardently desire it.

> What a glory for Mary and our Blessed old Saints, once more to be honoured and invocated in their ancient noble Churches! – Well all this Mr. Lee says he thinks will be brought about in 20 years, if only we can agree to work together for this glory, this thrice blessed end! [4]

---

4   Ugbrooke Archives, *Letters to Bp. Clifford, 1857*, Phillipps to
     Clifford, Letter dated 21.12.1857.

Clifford's brief but courteous reply shows us the young bishop learning to be cautious and, in this case, 'applying the brakes' to slow down this early engine of ecumenism which, with such a driver as Phillipps on board, was in danger of running out of control. The Bishop's draft reply, with its significant deletions, was as follows:

> I can have no objection to Mr. Lee's writing to me. Of course Whatever he does write to me on the subject of the Reunion I shall consider strictly private except so far as he may at any time express his ('a' *deleted*) wish to the contrary ('on any point' *deleted*). And I am sure he will observe the same courtesy ('as' *deleted*) regarding anything I may write to him. Perhaps I had better add that I must be guided by my own discretion in answering or not answering any questions which may be put to me by him.
>
> *The following is deleted*: Mr. Lee must also not feel offended ('surprised' *deleted*), if at any time, or on any matter concerning which he may address me, I feel it my duty to use reserve in answering him. I think it best to mention these points simply as a matter of prudence before entering into a correspondence of this nature not as implying ('feeling' deleted) any doubt that Mr. Lee would in any way wish to act otherwise. I do not forget to pray that God may prosper this great work of the Reunion.
>
> *The letter continues*: I offered up my third Mass yesterday for the Reunion ('their object' *deleted*) and I pray for it daily (' in the holy sacrifice' *deleted*), and I feel confident God will in his own good time direct our feet in the way of peace.[5]

The letter, written on December 26th, 1857, makes no reference to Phillipps's prognosis of the future. At the top, however, there is a 'doodle' – a circle divided into sections (presumably a symbol of christendom). One can almost see the 34 year old prelate drawing this as he searched hard for his *mot juste*.

---

5   Ugbrooke Archives, *Letters to Bp. Clifford, 1857*, Clifford to Phillipps, Draft reply dated 26.12.1857.

In his letter to Clifford, Phillipps had referred to 'thousands' among the Anglican clergy who, he said, ardently desired reunion. He was in fact repeating an assertion which he had made some six months earlier in a letter to be found in the Archives of Propaganda Fide. This was written on blue notepaper with a hand-painted heraldic device at the top and a memorable signature at the end: AMBROSE DE INSULA PHILLIPPS. The Latin style is that of Caesar's *Gallic Wars*.

After admitting that the two Anglican Archbishops were hostile to the idea of unity with the Catholic Church, he told Propaganda:

> The ten bishops . . . who have been in favour are Salisbury, Oxford, Chichester, Lincoln, Exeter, Bangor (*sic*) in England – all of these in the Province of Canterbury. The remaining four are in Scotland: the Bishop of Brechin and three others. As well as these bishops there are two thousand priests amongst whom are to be found Archdeacons, Deans and Canons, Rectors of Collegiate Churches, the remainder being parish priests and curates.
>
> To this section of the Anglican clergy must be added a large body of laymen from very wealthy and noble families of this realm. [6] [My translation].

On receipt of this Barnabo wrote to Wiseman to ask for his observations. Propaganda must have viewed the communication, if true, as of the highest interest and importance. Wiseman pointed out that the Bishop of Oxford, Samuel Wilberforce, was in no way sympathetic to Rome and that the list of the ten bishops ' was the most complete illusion in the world'.[7]

Wiseman also took the opportunity of writing to Phillipps on two serious issues connected with A.P.U.C.

> 1) that individuals were being advised not to be reconciled to the Catholic Church on the grounds that, if they remained, they would hasten the day of corporate reunion;

---

6   Propaganda Fide Archives, Rome: *Scritture Riferite nei Congressi, 1855 - 1857*, Anglia 14, No. 1118.

7   Cuthbert Butler, *op. cit.*, I, p. 340.

2) Phillipps had spoken of the three great denominations of
    Christians: Catholic, Anglican and Orthodox. This for
    Catholics was not a correct description of the state of
    things, and was defective in that it lost sight of the
    unique claims of the Catholic Church to be the one, true
    Church founded by Christ. For a Catholic, it is
    Christendom that is divided, not the Church.

The A.P.U.C. had been founded in 1857 and the *Union Review* was seen as
its official mouthpiece. In time, however, it had changed its stance to
outright support for the Branch Theory – a point which Phillipps dealt with
at some length in a letter to Clifford, dated October 23rd, 1864 (see below).

Dr. Frederick Lee, too, supported the Theory as is shown by the following
letter which was passed to Clifford who, on reading it, immediately made
a copy. In January, 1863, a Mr. Gutton of West Aberdeen had written to
A.P.U.C. requesting that, since he had now become a Catholic, his name
be erased from the list of persons praying for the union of Anglicans with
the Catholic Church. Lee, while agreeing to his request, was not a little
surprised at the thinking behind it:

> While informing you – which I have the greatest pleasure in
> doing – that during the past two months 3 bishops and about
> 20 priests of the Latin communion have joined the
> association, I may perhaps be excused for remarking that
> your having elected to become a Roman Catholic in no
> degree weakens the unhappy fact that Christendom still
> remains in a state of actual disunion – one part visibly
> separated from the other; and that, consequently, the
> prayers of all Catholics whether Romans, Greeks or
> Anglicans – are as much needed now as they were before
> you took that step, that God in his great mercy may restore
> to us all a state of peace and oneness.
>
> I trust, therefore that the necessary and charitable work
> you once undertook, may not be given up, lest any should
> imagine – what I am sure you would theoretically deprecate
> – that your former Catholic Sympathies are now narrowed
> to the limits of a local Communion.

Pray allow me still to remain

My dear Sir

Your very faithful Servant
in the Common Lord & Saviour
Frederick George Lee
Sec. A.P.U.C.[8]

The matter was now fraught with difficulty so much so that at the Bishops' Low Week meeting in 1864 it was decided that Ullathorne should lay the whole matter before the authorities in Rome, asking at the same time for guidance as to how Catholics were to be advised. A prohibition from Rome against Catholic membership of the Association swiftly followed in September of the same year.

Phillipps was heartbroken, and in October he wrote a long letter to Bishop Clifford who, he reminds him, 'formerly appeared to view the thing favourably. In it he sought to prove that A.P.U.C. had been misrepresented and hence that the reasons for the condemnation did not apply.

The main points of Phillipps' argument were as follows:

- A.P.U.C. was founded with the approval of the Cardinal Prefect of Propaganda Fide;

- It now had 7,000 members. If condemned by Rome, A.P.U.C. will turn in the direction of the Greek churches. Anglicans – already in negotiations with them – will be alienated from Rome;

- A.P.U.C. did not favour Indifferentism. It aimed at a common Profession of Faith;

- Many individual conversions have taken place. Some names given;

---

8   Ugbrooke Archives, *Letters to Bp. Clifford, 1863*, Lee to Gutton, Letter dated January, 1863.

- If condemned by English bishops, great harm will be done to 'Catholicity' in England;

- He (Phillipps) will obey but will try to get condemnation modified;

- *Union Review*: Faulty articles – but could it be otherwise? It was open to men of all faiths;

- He (Phillipps) swears that he has never approved of any of the principles now condemned by the Holy Office;

- Sole aim of A.P.U.C.: union with Rome and acceptance of all Catholic dogmas.[9]

Clifford's reply to these points is of such critical importance to an understanding of his stance on A.P.U.C. that it must be quoted in full:

Bishop's House, Clifton,
Oct. 27th, 1864.

My dear Cousin – I have only just returned from Belgium, and this must be my excuse for not sending you an earlier reply to your letter of the 23rd inst. about the unity Association.

The letter of the Holy Office has been issued (I believe) on account of what appears to me a new phase in the working of the Association. When first I heard of the association through you some years ago I understood its object to be to get people to pray for unity, without any view being expressed by the association as to how this end was to be attained. So that Catholics prayed for unity in the only way in which they could pray, viz: that those who were not united to the centre of unity might become united. Father Ignatius Spencer used to engage all persons, Catholics and Protestants, to pray for a similar object in this manner. But of late it cannot be denied that the theory of there being

---

9   Ugbrooke Archives, *Letters to Bp. Clifford, 1864*, Phillipps to Clifford, Letter dated 23.10.1864.

three Christian communions, the Roman, the Greek, and the Anglican, all three branches of the true church, but all more or less in error, as regards minor points, has become one of the most prominent of the doctrines advocated by the association. I do not say that all hold it, but by far the greater portion do, and hence the opinion was gaining ground that Catholics who were members of the association held this view to be true, or at least tenable. The Church could not but condemn such a view as heretical. This is what the letter does in the first place. In the second place it forbids Catholics to join the association because by doing so they give scandal, for although they hold orthodox views themselves, still, by belonging to a society which prominently puts forward the aforesaid heterodox view they give just cause for people to suppose that they are not opposed to it themselves.

In the third place the letter says that Catholics by joining the association favour indifferentism. This seems to you a hard saying, but you must observe that this letter is speaking of Catholics, not of Anglicans. As regards the latter, as a rule it is certainly not from a spirit of indifferentism that they join the association. Many a Protestant prejudice and error must be given up before men can conceive a desire to be again united with the Church of Rome, and therefore even if this desire be an imperfect one and mixed with erroneous notions, it is a step in advance, a step nearer to truth, and further removed from indifferentism. But if a Catholic who is already united to the centre of unity adopts the view that other bodies separated from that centre may be equally right, or seems by his conduct to countenance that view, he is moving backwards from truth, and favouring indifferentism.

I fear I have not answered all your points, but I must conclude or I shall lose this post and you will be wondering at my silence. I have no hesitation in saying that I believe that much that we now see taking place amongst members of the Church of England in regard of the movement towards unity is the consequence of graces showered down by God on this land. There is no doubt a mixture of much that is human, and no doubt the enemy of mankind knows how to sow bad seed with the good, still I have no doubt good will come of it.

But when the question is plainly put whether a Catholic may join a society which is the result of these different causes, the answer must be that whereas by so doing he would ally himself to that which is bad as well as to that which is good, he must abstain from joining the society altogether. I remain, sending you my blessing, your affectionate cousin,

William Clifford[10]

Meanwhile moves were afoot to mount an appeal to Rome. The tone of the document from Rome had upset Newman while on the Anglican side Dr. Littledale (the celebrated controversialist) agreed that A.P.U.C. had been misrepresented at Rome and pointed out that it was well known that Catholics could never support the Branch Theory.

The appeal was sent but, with Cardinal Wiseman now dead, Phillipps turned to Mgr. Talbot, the Pope's private secretary and confidant of Manning. The Holy Office asked Manning – soon to be appointed to Westminster – for his comments. The resulting condemnation was thus a foregone conclusion, although in the event it was not quite as strong as Manning would have liked. Cuthbert Butler's wry comment is worth quoting: 'This shows that it had been no easy task to tune the authorities at Rome up to the Manning pitch'.[11]

The two sides of the Association went their different ways with Manning writing his pastoral letter on *The Reunion of Christendom* and Pusey his *Eirenicon* (a copy of which he sent to Clifford). For his part Phillipps maintained his links and continued to write to Clifford with undiminished optimism.

---

10   Edmund Sheridan Purcell, *Life and Letters of Ambrose Phillipps de Lisle* (Edited and finished by Edwin de Lisle), (Publ. London, 1900), I, pp. 402, 403.

11   Cuthbert Butler, *op. cit.*, I, p. 353.

Bishop Clifford issued his Advent Pastoral Letter on November 27th, 1864. He devoted part of it to the question of the reunion of Christendom. The following short extracts give the tone of the letter:

> The multiplication of sects, and diversity of religious opinions, is producing in its turn, a sad harvest of unbelief amongst the people. There are thoughtful men, and their number is greatly on the increase, who, grieving at seeing the sad spectacle of so many of their countrymen ever tossed to and fro by the waves of conflicting doctrines, cast their eyes once more towards that rock, which alone stands unmoved, in the midst of the surging waves.

> We should not be either surprised or alarmed, because the views and aspirations of such persons still fall short of that full submission to the authority of the Holy See, without which, no one can claim to appertain to the one fold of the one Shepherd.

Clifford beautifully illustrated this by referring to the blind man in the Gospel who was healed by our Lord. At first the man said 'I see men as trees walking'. Clifford continued:

> It was only after Christ had again laid His hands upon him, 'That he began to see, and was restored, so that he saw all things clearly'. Still that first imperfect vision was the work of the divine power of Our Lord.

So it was with individuals: 'Many partial graces must precede the crowning grace of conversion'. He concluded the letter by briefly outlining, and then condemning, the two specific errors of A.P.U.C. which had earned the disapproval of Rome: the Branch Theory and the idea that it was legitimate for people not to become Catholics so as to hasten corporate reunion. On this latter point Clifford wrote:

> ... but let the presumed probability of such an event (i.e. of corporate reunion with the Holy See) be ever so great, no person can on that account, be justified in refusing to listen to the voice of his conscience, the moment that, by Divine grace, he sees the claims which the Catholic Church has to

his obedience. As neither attachment to earthly goods, nor the fear of earthly loss, nor the love of friends or kinsmen, can form any excuse for refusing to listen to the voice of God, so neither can the desire of being of use to others justify such delay. As Christ said to Peter, when anxious about his friend, "What is that to thee? Follow thou Me." (Jo. xxi, 22).[12]

On balance Phillipps liked the Pastoral (a copy of which Clifford had sent to him), and noted that he had 'taken a more conciliatory and less polemical Line than your Rt. Rev. Brother of Birmingham [Ullathorne]'.[13] But Phillipps was ambivalent in his attitude to the Branch Theory. Despite his protestations that no Catholic 'who deserved the name' could ever subscribe to it, nevertheless he still felt that the Theory could be of value to members of the Anglican and Eastern Churches who did hold that view:

> . . . it may become to them an argumentum ad Hominem for a return to complete normal Unity under the Primacy of St. Peter – I wonder that an acute reasoner like the Bishop of Birmingham does not perceive this, and that in reasoning against it, as held by Anglicans and Greeks, he is cutting from under their feet the last plank that saves them from utter shipwreck of Catholic belief and that might serve as a raft once more to land them in the Haven of Catholicity.

Phillipps liked the kind tone of Clifford's Pastoral 'after the harsh, dry, repulsive effusion from the Cathedra Birminghamiensis' (*sic*):

> Kindness may do much in such Times as these, while severity will not only prevent a corporate Reunion of separate Bodies, but effectually repel the advances even of individuals.

---

12   Clifton Diocesan Archives, *A Pastoral Letter of the Bishop of Clifton*, November 27th, 1864.

13   Ugbrooke Archives, *Letters to Bp. Clifford, 1864*, Phillipps to Clifford, Letter dated 6.12.1864. The extracts which follow are from this letter.

He (Phillipps), and, he guessed, his fellow countrymen, regarded the recent 'ill timed' censure from Rome, 'obtained on such false grounds', as 'a suicidal blow aimed at Catholic Interests in this country'.

> Forgive me for saying so; I am not the man to say it in print, for I would not wish, even to vindicate my own honour as a Catholic, to say anything to compromise Authority – but to you, as a relative, and as a Bishop, I will regret in a private letter.

Naturally the friendship between Clifford, and Phillipps continued, as did the latter's efforts – though not in A.P.U.C. – to secure corporate Christian reunion. On March 2nd, 1866, Phillipps wrote a long letter to Clifford to thank him for a previous communication and for his encouragement.

> Nothing can be more consoling or satisfactory for me than the encouragement of a Bishop and of such a Bishop as yourself in my humble efforts to serve the Catholic cause and in promoting any measure that may tend to put an end to those unhappy schisms . . . [14]

Apparently in his letter Clifford had warned Phillipps of other efforts being made by Protestants – parallel to A.P.U.C. but working in the opposite direction (i.e. against Reunion with Rome). Phillipps took note of this observation and replied:

> I quite agree with what you say about the force of the movement which is going on by the side of the Catholic Movement, and which of course tends to counteract the Latter – It might even ruin it altogether of course even this dreadful alternative is quite possible – But then there are all the promises of Our Lord, His own Prayer for Union . . . to set against this alternative.

Phillipps proceeds to underline the importance of efforts to seek corporate Reunion, but says that this does not compromise individual conversions – a point on which Catholics in A.P.U.C. had been accused:

---

14   Ugbrooke Archives, *Letters to Bp. Clifford, 1866*, Phillipps to Clifford, Letter dated 2.3.1866. Five more extracts are quoted.

> Because I wish for a kingdom, do I refuse a province, because I try to raise an army, do I refuse a few recruits, or because I claim my entire debt, am I to decline any instalment that is offered?

In a previous letter he had criticised the harshness of Ullathorne in his treatment of A.P.U.C. This time his fire is directed at Manning. Having spoken of the importance of kindness and understanding in all ecumenical endeavours, he seeks to draw a contrast:

> On the other hand take the effect of the discouraging Line, of the harsh Line, of the repelling Line: you can have no conception of the despondency, the indignation, that has been excited in Anglican minds by Dr. Manning's Pastoral agt. Reunion. If anything could crush a chance of England's conversion, it would be the Policy of the Party, which that Pastoral may be said to represent. I am the last man to make any public remark upon any document emanating from so high a Hierarch in the Govt. of God's Church – But as there is a constitutional opposition left even to the most loyal Subjects, so is there a Canonical Limit to Ecclesiastical obedience.

Later he adds: 'We have only to look at the immense effect for good produced by Father Newman's conciliatory Letter to Dr. Pusey on his Eirenicon'.

Phillipps felt that all his efforts were being undermined by Manning: 'The Archbishop upsets them all (i.e. the Anglicans) and cuts off all hope of Reunion'. And the consequences of this cold-shouldering?

> They are now turning to the Greek Church – and as I wrote to Rome . . . if the Holy See does not act very warily, an antipapal League, stronger than any the world has yet seen, will be organised between all the oriental Churches on the one side, and the Catholicizing Anglicans of the British Empire and the American United States on the other.

But that was not all. Phillipps maintained that there were Catholics of the Western Church at Munich, Paris and elsewhere who were for casting away the Filioque, and for re-establishing Catholic Unity on the basis of the (so called) *Orthodoxy* of the East in opposition to the changes and developments of the West.

Looking at the period following the death of Ambrose de L'Isle Phillipps (1878) and of Bishop Clifford (1893) one can see that the Catholic position remained very much the same as it had been during their lifetime, notwithstanding the brave efforts of Cardinal Mercier and Lord Halifax at the Malines Conference (1922 – 1926).

So extreme was the tenor of Pope Pius XI's encyclical *Mortalium Animos* (1928) that one commentator has said that there are Roman Catholic ecumenists of the present day who date their 'conversion' to a new view of ecumenical matters by a reaction from their first reading of the encyclical.[15] The Pope's thinking was reflected, not unnaturally, in the position adopted by the English & Welsh Hierarchy. Two examples will suffice:

> 1946
> 'Catholics are not allowed to attend non-Catholic religious services held in conjunction with Remembrance Day or similar functions. They should be encouraged to attend Mass or services in their own church and only be present at the non-religious part of the public function'. (Statement from the Low Week Meeting) .

> 1957
> *Spreading the Truth* – Pastoral Letter of Archbishop Godfrey of Westminster (Trinity Sunday). Arguing against a form of reunion based on 'Lowest Common Denominator Christianity'.

With hindsight one can see Dr. Lee and Phillipps – encouraged by the kindness and understanding, if not the active support, of Bishop Clifford – and Cardinal Mercier and Lord Halifax as forming an honourable part of that long, patient, yet ever optimistic tradition that paved the way for the Decree on Ecumenism (*Unitatis Redintegratio*) of the Second Vatican Council.

---

15   Bernard and Margaret Pawley, *Rome and Canterbury through Four Centuries*, (2nd ed. Publ. London, 1981), p. 281.

CHAPTER FOUR

The Dispute with Bishop Thomas Brown
of Newport and Menevia

Today's English Province of the Order of Friars Minor is in unbroken line of succession with that body of religious which was in this country at the time of the Reformation. Its fortunes, however, have been varied, and there were times when, because of lack of vocations, the line of continuity became extremely tenuous.

One such period were the years between 1830 and 1840 – a time when financial mismanagement served to aggravate the situation. Since 1834 Father Leo Edgeworth had been engaged in building the grandiose Church of the Twelve Apostles in Clifton, a project towards which he had diverted £5,000 of the Order's funds.

In order to avert the total suppression of the Province and at the same time to unravel its troubled affairs, Propaganda at the end of 1840 had appointed Bishop Thomas Brown, O.S.B. of Newport as Apostolic Visitor.

> It is His Holiness's intention that, as long as you continue in the office of Visitor, all the property of the Province should be under your complete control, to be administered by Your Lordship in the name of the Apostolic See.[1]

Brown was Prior of Downside when earlier that same year he was appointed Vicar Apostolic for Wales. At the time of the present controversy he was about sixty, i.e. some twenty-five years older than Clifford. Brown had lived through hard times and had invariably been a doughty protagonist in public controversy. Probably as a result of this, he had developed a literary style that at times was even pugnacious, as the young Aidan Gasquet pointed out in an obituary notice written in 1880:

---

1   For an account of the background to Bishop Brown's appointment as Visitor see the article by Howard Docherty, O.F.M., 'The Friars Minor in England: Their Historical Continuity' (*The Clergy Review*, June 1952, pp. 332 sqq.). This passage quoted p. 345.

> His writings were of a style and school which now no
> longer exists, and his plain-spoken language reads
> somewhat strangely in these more civilized times; but such
> uncompromising assertions of the truth were a necessity
> of the days when Dr. Brown wrote and spoke, and it was his
> boast that with all the hard knocks and home-thrusts he
> gave and took, he never hurt the feelings of any antagonist,
> and never felt wounded himself. [2]

Even a fellow bishop was not spared this combative style as is seen in his
controversy with Clifford. The argument centred around some books
which allegedly Clifford was about to dispose of but which Brown argued
belonged to the Franciscan Recollects. One of the books involved was of
enormous value: it was the so-called *Hereford Missal* and this had in fact
been sold by Clifford for £300. (In England in the 15th century the
principal liturgies or 'uses' were Sarum, York, Hereford, Bangor and
Lincoln.[3]) Understandably it was this transaction which sparked off a
quite bitter dispute in which Rome was called upon to adjudicate.

In February, 1858, the Minutes of the Clifton Chapter record: 'The
Franciscan Library is given to the Diocese',[4] although by whom, and with
what authority is not stated. Some four and a half months later Bishop
Brown wrote to Clifford:

> Your Lordship will have no difficulty, I trust, in favouring me
> with a Catalogue which I will return safely, in case you have
> such or can procure it, of the Books which were under the
> care of the Rev. P. O'Farrell, and formerly belonged to the
> English Franciscan Province.

---

2   Aidan Gasquet, *Downside Review*, 1880, p. 4. The article is reproduced
     in *Fathers in Faith*, (ed. Bellenger) 1991.

3   T. E. Bridgett, *History of the Holy Eucharist in Great Britain* (Publ.
     London, 1881), Vol. II, p. 74.

4   Clifton Diocesan Archives, *Acta Capituli Cliftoniensis*, 15.2.1858, p. 36.

If there be no such Catalogue, will you allow me to have the books inspected, or a Catalogue taken if I desire it? [5]

Clifford's reply, sent from St. John's Wood, is revealing:

Your letter of the 3rd inst has been forwarded to me here. As regards your request about the books formerly belonging to the English Franciscans, I am obliged to say that, as a question affecting my honour is now pending before the S. Congo of Prop. in the matter of these books, I must refrain from answering any questions except such as are put to me by the Sacred Congregation . . . [6]

Someone – it could hardly have been Brown for he surely would have mentioned it – had reported Clifford to Rome. It might conceivably have been the Franciscans. At any rate it must have caused intense embarrassment to Clifford who was still only in the second year of his episcopate. Brown replied:

I have received your Lordship's letter of yesterday – Allow me to say that it is I who am put upon my trial by your Lordship before Propaganda – and that my defence requires that I be allowed by you to have a Catalogue of the Books in question. Your Lordship has made representations, which I am called upon to reply to – and if I find that my original statements were erroneous, I will candidly offer retractation (*sic*) & satisfaction.

But if your Lp persist in not allowing me to come at the truth – and to fulfil what R.S.C. requires from me, I have no alternative but to submit your refusal to the Cardinal Prefect . . . [7]

---

5   Ugbrooke Archives, *Letters to Bp. Clifford. 1858*, Brown to Clifford, letter dated 3.7.1858.

6   Ugbrooke Archives, *Letters to Bp. Clifford, 1858*, Clifford to Brown, letter dated 7.7.1858 (draft copy).

7   Ugbrooke Archives, *Letters to Bp. Clifford, 1858*, Brown to Clifford, letter dated 8.7.1858.

Five days later Clifford wrote:

> I can have no objection to your stating to the Cardinal
> Prefect of Propaganda what I said in my former letter to you
> viz. that whilst the charge is pending against me, I must
> decline answering all questions relative to it, except when
> put to me by the Sacred Congregation.
>
> I am sorry to see that you think I have put you on your trial,
> when the only paper I have sent to Propaganda has been an
> answer to certain charges sent to me by the Cardinal
> Prefect with the request that I would send in a reply . . . [8]

This letter was dated 13th July, 1858. His reply to Propaganda (to which
he refers) was sent on the 5th June [9] and in it we see the several counts
on which Clifford stands accused and their rebuttal:

1) The books in question were very valuable and Father O'Ferrall,
   O.S.F was unaware of this when he gave them to the diocese.
   Clifford:
   The books had come from Douai and had been added to since.
   They filled a small room and were all in a bad condition. There
   were books of devotion, sermons, etc. A friend valued them at
   £100.

2) Bishop Brown paid Father O'Ferrall £5.00 a year for the safe
   keeping of the books. Therefore there was no intention of
   relinquishing ownership.
   Clifford:
   When Father Edgeworth (with Father O'Ferrall) went bankrupt,
   these books were stored in apartments occupied by the
   creditors. Brown wrote to Bishop Hendren to ensure that they

---

8   Ugbrooke Archives, *Letters to Bp. Clifford, 1858*, Clifford to Brown,
     letter dated 13.7.1858 (draft copy).

9   Franciscan Archives, Forest Gate: Transcript of *Correspondence to
     Propaganda*, Nos. 245 sqq. (Heading states: Bishop Clifford of Clifton to
     Prefect of Propaganda, in answer to letter of May 29, 1858. SRC Anglia
     15 (1858 – 1860). Original in Italian in Bishop's writing).

were not seized by the creditors. They were taken to St. Mary's where they were dried out. Some time later still suffering from damp – they were taken back to the priest's lodging.

O'Ferrall, again in financial difficulty, asked Brown to compensate for money spent on the books. He refused to pay for any past expenditure but would pay for any future outlay. No conclusion can be drawn from these payments.

3) Clifford is accused of starting to sell the books at a great price.

Clifford:
i)   Except for one book (see below) none has been sold.

ii) The better ones have been cleaned and rebound and are to be put in a diocesan/seminary library.

iii) A large number are fit only for the fire.

4) Clifford sold one of the books (*Hereford Missal*) for £300.[10]

Clifford:
A personal friend who was also a considerable expert in this field – William Maskell – recognised the great value of the book and offered to sell it in London. He would not do it for his own pecuniary advantage but did ask Clifford to undertake to spend some of the money for a charitable purpose. The *Missal* was sold to a museum in London and part of the money raised was spent to help a young girl who had been badly burned. Some money had been spent on repairing the roof of the Pro-Cathedral and some in paying off debts. Clifford noted that success in this transaction was due entirely to his meeting the right person who, in turn, was aware that a museum in London was searching for this type of object. Maskell could easily have offered £50 to Clifford and sold it at great profit to himself. Finally, the *Missal* might well have perished like the other books if he himself had not intervened.

---

10   *Ibid.*, Nos. 247 sqq.

Other charges were raised by Propaganda and answered by Clifford. Brown too in his turn replied[11] to Clifford's defence but apparently to no avail as it would seem that Propaganda was content to recognise the status quo. 'Possession is nine tenths of the law' and little was heard of the controversy again.

The dispute does shed light on the character of Brown. He it was who had delated Newman to Rome over his article in *The Rambler*. In a letter written just over a year after the 'books controversy', Clifford said to Brown:

> . . . Can. Neve . . . tells me you are very much engaged about the question of Newman & *The Rambler* and that you consider Newman greatly in the wrong. I read the article in *The Rambler* . . . My own impression was rather favourable to Newman but I will read the article over again with more attention.[12]

Brown's penchant for recourse to Rome surfaced yet again in 1865 when he wrote complaining that Clifford and Grant had ruled themselves out as candidates for Westminster without having first consulted their fellow bishops (Chapter 6). He did, however, see eye to eye with Clifford over the issue of Infallibility and was conscious of the lack of freedom which prevailed at least among some sections of the episcopate (Chapter 10).

William Maskell will be mentioned again in connection with the pamphlet he wrote attacking Manning's view of papal infallibility which he regarded as too comprehensive.

This bitter but short-lived episode over the books affords not only an insight into the character of the protagonists but was also symptomatic of an age and of a way of thinking that is now past. An intense loyalty to

---

11   *Ibid.*, Nos. 250 sqq. Heading states: Bishop Brown to Cardinal Prefect of Propaganda. Undated, but was July or August 1858. His own writing. Pages as numbered in original. Propaganda Archives, *SRC Anglia, vol. 15 (1858 - 1860)*.

12   Clifton Diocesan Archives, *Letters 1858 - 1860*, Vol. 1, Nos. 489, 490, Clifford to Brown, letter dated 3.10.1859.

Rome, which has invariably been seen as the hall-mark of the English Catholic, in those days seems to have triggered an almost instant recourse to the Apostolic See when controversy arose. It was a way of thinking which, at least as far as the diocese of Clifton is concerned, persisted well into the present century. Probably it is to be seen as part of that all-embracing process which came to be known as 'creeping infallibility' – the term is used here in a juridical rather than in a theological sense – and which goaded the Fathers of Vatican II into moves calculated to guarantee its reversal.

CRAFTER FIVE

The Encyclical Quanta Cura and the Syllabus of Errors

The eighteenth century Enlightenment had been a movement which involved both a philosophy and an attitude of mind which was to affect the relations between Church and State for many years to come. Although initially a number of clergy had, paradoxically, been involved in this reaction to the Age of Faith, it later became clear that the enthronement of Reason as the sole arbiter of human behaviour and of public policy would make their position untenable.

The central tenet of this philosophy was that nothing was to be accepted as true which could not be brought before the bar of human reason and there tested. Christian Faith, although rational in the sense that its 'preamble' can be tested through an examination of the historicity and authenticity of its basic documents, would fail such a test because by definition its mysteries could not be verified by human reason. Equally the natural sciences were called upon as the instrument of Reason to prove that to speak of God or of the human soul was to make a statement devoid of all meaning because the terms used were scientifically unverifiable.

Such, briefly, was the background to the onslaught on the Catholic Church led by such figures as Voltaire and Rousseau. The French Revolution which erupted just twenty years after their death exalted the concept of Liberty. By this was meant the granting to, and acknowledgement of, the just rights of every human being except, as the history of the Revolution shows, the rights of those who were in any way associated with the *ancien régime*.

Liberty was seen as meaning freedom from all constraint, particularly that of the Church which sadly had become all too easily identified with the oppressive rule of the French monarchy. Liberty, therefore, meant a wholesale rejection of the dogmatic and disciplinary constraints which the Church, like her Master, had placed on human conduct. The only limitation recognised by the revolutionaries of France were those emanating from Equality and Fraternity – i.e. the rights of one's fellow citizens.

The word 'Liberalism' crept into the debate but unfortunately, like the chameleon, it can assume many guises. The eighteenth and nineteenth century version which Pio Nono sought to condemn in his *Syllabus* has been described as follows:

> The 'Liberalism' of which the Pope spoke had its roots in Renaissance humanism and was developed by Hume in England and by the Encyclopedists in France. It implied the 'liberation' of man from all supernatural authority, and was therefore irreconcilable with Christianity. [1]

The taking prisoner of the Pope and his subsequent restoration to the papal throne by the Emperor Napoleon III not only marked a critical period in the Church's history but also occasioned an extreme reaction in the Pope himself. The Papal States were in his mind very much part of the patrimony of St. Peter and consequently he would brook no curtailing of their previous borders. For him they were indistinguishable from his office as Head of the Church.

One lesson that history invariably affords is that any political lurch to left or to right will produce, sooner or later, a reaction in the opposite direction. The leftward swing which had produced the French Revolution and the expulsion of the Pope from Rome resulted in a papal rule which many branded as reactionary. The Church drew together its various strengths and powers and enshrined them in the one who was the Vicar of Christ. The reaction did not confer these powers. They were seen as being already there by virtue of the office but, it was argued, recent events had caused them to be shamefully ignored.

So extreme was the theological justification, as distinct from the political desirability, for the Temporal Power of the Pope that Cardinal Manning is alleged to have argued that one could not be a true Catholic if at the same time one questioned this particular papal prerogative. [2]

---

1   Arnold Lunn in *Is The Catholic Church Anti-social?* by G. G. Coulton and Arnold Lunn (Publ. London, 1947), p. 177.

2   See Manning's *Temporal Power of the Vicar of Christ* (Publ. London, 1862), *passim*. 'Even Rome questioned his view that the loss of the Papal States would mean the reign of Antichrist in Rome, and he was constrained to modify this rash prediction' (E. E. Reynolds, *Three Cardinals: Newman, Wiseman, Manning*, Publ. London, 1958, p. 174).

The definition by Pope Pius IX of the Immaculate Conception was seen as a blow aimed at the Gallican concept of the Church in so far as the Pope acted 'motu proprio' and not in the context of a General Council. This was in 1854 and the whole process may be said to have reached its nadir in 1870 with another definition – this time in a Council – by the Pope. The definition of Papal Infallibility was a gesture of theological politics as well as an event of Faith.

Over the years successive Popes had issued encyclical letters and other documents to warn the faithful against accepting the sovereignty of human reason, the worship of untrammelled liberty, and the attempt to dismantle the legitimate rights of the Holy See. On this last point classical theology was invoked to portray the Church as 'the perfect society', entitled to all the necessary means to achieve its purpose.

In 1864 Pio Nono issued an encyclical *Quanta cura* which was a compendium of many of the papal documents already published. With it he also published a document which came to be known as *The Syllabus of Errors*. What is ironic is that a prime instigator of this move was none other than Cardinal Pecci, Archbishop – Bishop of Perugia, who later (1878) became the enlightened Leo XIII. Damian McElrath says:

> It was probably Cardinal Pecci, the successor of Pius IX, who first brought to the attention of the Pope the idea of promulgating a document, resembling in very general outline what was eventually to develop into the *Syllabus*. As Bishop of Perugia, taking part in a Provincial Council, he persuaded the Council to address a formal letter to Pius IX seeking an elenchus and condemnation of specific errors against the Church's authority and property. [3]

The *Syllabus* was a negative document listing some eighty propositions which were contrary to the Encyclical and which the Holy Father wanted the faithful to reject. Not a shred of doubt was to be left in the minds of the faithful.

---

3   Damian McElrath, O.F.M., *The Syllabus of Pius IX: Some Reactions in England* (Publ. Louvain, 1964), pp. 11, 12.

But there were doubts in plenty. These arose from the fact that the Pope had transposed the philosophical errors and political abuses of one time and place to the area of abstract thought where he then proceeded to condemn them *tout court*. Put another way: the sort of life and freedom of action which the Church hoped to enjoy in an ideal world was here being described to Catholics and Non-Catholics who lived in a world that was far from ideal. The result was that to neither group did the documents make much sense.

> The condemnation of modern civilisation seemed to them to refer to the telegraph, railways, and street lighting. [4]

The Pope, however, was being misunderstood and two important points need to be made in his defence. In essence he was criticising the concept of the inevitability of human progress. Proponents of this view chose to ignore two factors – God and Original sin – and without taking into account Man's beginning and end, together with his moral weakness, one was failing to see that human progress was not, and could not be, 'inevitable'. *Gaudium et Spes* of Vatican II makes the point very clearly:

> . . . all human activity, constantly imperilled by man's pride and deranged self-love, must be purified and perfected by the power of Christ's cross and resurrection. [5]

And again:

> Earthly progress must be carefully distinguished from the growth of Christ's kingdom. (*Ibid*).

Secondly, one cannot arrive at a true sense of the condemned propositions without first understanding the historical context in which the original papal documents had been written and which had given rise to the accompanying condemnations. The *Syllabus* was a compendium of what had gone before.

---

4   J. Derek Holmes and Bernard W. Biokers, *A Short History of the Catholic Church* (Publ. Tunbridge Wells, 1983), p 242.

5   Paragraph 37.

Something parallel may be seen today when those arguing against the use of the vernacular at Mass cite the example of the Elizabethan martyrs who detested the use of English in the Sacred Liturgy. What is being lost sight of is that theirs was not a hatred of the language as such – nor could it have been since they were using it every day of their lives – but an odium born of its association with the Protestant communion service.

Public perception of the Encyclical and the *Syllabus* was not so discriminating, however. For many devout Christians this was nothing to do with 'the folly of the Cross' but rather the folly of a benighted cleric cloistered in the Vatican. Indeed it was in Rome itself that some of these tensions emerged, and the correspondent of *The Times* was not slow to tell readers what he had heard and seen from 'men of the highest rank, character and position'.

Early in 1865 some foreigners living in Rome, including some Englishmen, took it upon themselves to present an address to the Pontiff on the subject of the temporal power 'consecrated by Divine Providence, and which in its weakness is yet more venerable and stronger than all the Powers of the earth surrounded by force.' *The Times* commented:

> Lord Vaux and his son, Sir John Acton, and many other English Catholics now in Rome were not present, being strongly opposed to the spirit and letter of the address. Thus ends an incident in Roman life which for nearly two months has occupied public curiosity, which has ended virtually in a failure, and has produced a schism among our Roman Catholic countrymen, ranging on one side the friends of progress and enlightenment, on the other the supporters of pretensions as monstrous as any that were ever advanced in the darkest ages of the Papacy. [6]

Eight days later these malcontents were quoted as saying: 'The principles laid down in the Encyclical are opposed to all that we learnt in our youth under Dr. Milner, who was no bad Catholic. [7]

---

6 *The Times*, 2.3.1865.

7 *The Times*, 10.3.1865. Dr. John Milner, Vicar Apostolic of the Midland District (1803 – 1826).

The same paper also took to task a group of Protestants who had knelt to receive the Pope's blessing during a visit to the Pincio:

> . . . at a moment when . . . the liberty of the human mind is disputed . . . let not Englishmen when they come to Rome, and especially English Protestants, forget that by the obligation of their nationality, they should show themselves the friends of civil and religious liberty. [8]

Clearly a monumental task of interpretation needed to be done and its importance could hardly be exaggerated, for *The Times* was surely right when it pointed to the 'growing antagonism between the spiritual head of the Catholic world and the educated laity in every Catholic country.[9] Bishop Dupanloup of Orleans was one of the first to attempt a detailed analysis of the Encyclical. Admirable though it was, it earned for itself a rejoinder from Montalembert who described it as 'a first class verbal vanishing trick'.[10]

The task of interpretation to be done in England was no less urgent. Bishop Clifford felt it his duty to guide his flock through the minefield, not only of what the press was saying, but also of the *Syllabus* itself. This he did with such lucidity and adroitness as to earn accolades from several quarters, including Father Newman. Clearly within the short space of a pastoral letter he could not be expected to deal with all the questions which arose in peoples' minds, nor did he enter into a discussion of the historical context of the original encyclicals, which would have been quite inappropriate, but he contented himself with a clear statement of traditional Catholic doctrine.

After the introduction Clifford deals with some basic Catholic truths and some of the traditional objections to them. The existence of God, Revelation, the supposed opposition between Reason and Revelation, and the Inspiration of Sacred Scripture are all briefly treated, together with Indifferentism and Latitudinarianism.

---

8   *The Times*, 28.4.1865.

9   *The Times*, 21.3.1865.

10   Holmes and Bickers, *op. cit.*, pp. 242, 243.

Those who profess the former 'vainly seek to promote unity, not by drawing men to truth, but by sacrificing truth for unity', while the latter teaches, according to the Bishop, that 'all religions are but various roads, leading more or less circuitously to one end'. In the light of God's having founded One, Holy, Catholic Church neither point of view can be regarded as acceptable by a Christian.

Clifford next turns his attention to the 17th Proposition in the *Syllabus* and deals with it in some detail. The Proposition runs: 'The eternal salvation of all those who are not in any way in the true Church of Christ, may at least well be hoped for'. His reply is four-fold:

i)   The Church distinguishes between those who contumaciously resist the teaching of the Catholic Church, and those who do so in error and in good faith.

ii)   In condemning the proposition the Church means to state that such hope cannot be entertained so long as they remain, as they are, out of the true Church.

iii) Eternal salvation is not due *naturally* to man. It is a wonderful and *supernatural* happiness.

iv)   Who, then, are excluded? Two classes:

a) All infants and adults who have never been baptised. The Church does not teach that they are condemned to suffer pain nor that they are excluded from such happiness as becomes their state; but those unbaptised persons who have known the truth but have refused to embrace it will be condemned with the wicked.

b) Those baptised persons who deny some article of Faith and who refuse to resolve their doubts. 'Such baptised persons, and such only, are altogether out of the true Church'.

The issue of the relationship between Church and State was a matter which not infrequently provoked prolonged, and sometimes acrimonious, discussion.

Gladstone was prompted in later years to raise the issue of the loyalty of English Catholics which he believed had been compromised by the definition of Papal Infallibility, and so the Church versus State debate was an issue to which Clifford would return in a later Pastoral Letter (*Catholic Allegiance*, 1874).

In his present defence of the *Syllabus*, however, Clifford relies on traditional scholastic philosophy. He begins by stating that the Church is a complete society – a concept which, though not rejected, was seen as 'not helpful' at Vatican II and when the resulting new Code of Canon Law was drawn up in 1983. The Authority in its own sphere of the temporal power is derived from God, and man is born to live in society which, therefore, must be properly regulated.

> To these principles of reason and revelation is directly opposed the teaching of those who recognise no other source of power than material strength, or the will of majorities . . .

Here, it should be noted, Clifford is not condemning the notion of democracy. What he is saying is that the will of the majority is not supreme, but that that will must itself operate within the framework of a higher will, viz. the will of God. Such an example today would be The Question of Abortion. This issue has. been debated aod democratically voted upon in Parliament. Catholics, however, do not accept that such a vote is binding because they view Abortion as a flouting of God's law which no democratic vote can ever make right.

Clifford next addresses the thorny question – which is still with us – of rulers who have usurped power 'through violence, cunning, or other unjust means'. Are they to be obeyed? He answers by saying that not infrequently such rulers afterwards use their powers wisely; also, that sometimes to oppose the usurpation would lead to much greater evils to society than the usurpation itself. His conclusion therefore is as follows:

> Governments which owe their origin to violence or injustice may at times become legitimate, and rightly claim conscientious obedience from their subjects; but such right is founded not on the violence which has placed such rulers in power, but on the fact that their rule has become, under

the circumstances, necessary for the good of society, for which object the temporal power was ordained by God. Hence they are truly the ministers of God. It was when the Emperor Nero ruled over the world that the Apostle wrote that "princes are the ministers of God serving unto this purpose" (Rom. xiii, 6).

Clifford continued his defence of *Quanta cura*:

> It follows that the Pope in his Encyclical Letter rightly condemns the doctrine "that in the political order accomplished facts have the force of law from the mere circumstance that they are accomplished". There are indeed cases when an unjust fact having been accomplished, prudence and the interests of society forbid its being undone. But if such fact acquires the force of law it is by reason of the relation it bears to the interests of society, not from the mere circumstances of having been successful.

'A godless state is as unnatural and impious as a godless man or a godless family', wrote Clifford and the state should therefore recognise the Church as the sole depository of all true religion. It is the duty of the state to uphold the Church, but the manner whereby this is effected depends on the nature of the society to be governed. Certainly there must be no compulsion. In the case where a nation professes a variety of religions, he quotes Our Lord's parable of the wheat and the cockle (Matthew, xiii).

> Whence we learn that toleration under such circumstances is commendable, not because all religions are equally good, any more than wheat or cockle are of the same value, but because a contrary course is far more apt to damage the interests of truth than to promote them.

Where, however, there is a country in which both Government and people belong to the true Faith, it would be clearly wrong and – to use a modern term – destabilising for the Government to allow immigrants of a different religious faith the public exercise of their religion. The following passage, in which Clifford staunchly defends the Pope, is of the utmost interest, particularly in the light of subsequent Church documents:

Hence, though strangers frequenting Catholic countries are laudably allowed themselves to practise their own religion, the Pope justly condemns the doctrine of those who say that in such countries it is laudable to allow to immigrants the *public exercise* every man of his religion – (Prop. 78). And the Holy Father further shows the reason why such conduct is not laudable, viz. because the public practice of false worship, and the public manifestation of false opinions, tends to corrupt the minds and morals of men, and leads to indifferentism – (Prop. 79). If we believe St. Paul when he says "Be not seduced, evil communications corrupt good manners", (I Cor. xv, 33), it is impossible to deny the truth of such a statement.

Clifford was a child of his time and what he had written here was a reflection not only of papal teaching but also of traditional scholastic philosophy. The Church's teaching, however, while not changing in the essential foundations and doctrines in which it is rooted, can change in the conclusions which different generations draw from those same premises. This explains the contrast between the passages quoted above – in which Clifford upholds the rights of Religious Truth – with the following passages from Vatican II in which the rights of individuals to practise their religious beliefs are clearly enunciated. The quotations are taken from the Council's *Declaration on Religious Freedom* on the Right of the Person and communities to Social and civil Freedom in Matters Religious (*Dignitatis Humanae*):

In all his activity a man is bound to follow his conscience faithfully, in order that he may come to God, for whom he was created. It follows that he is not to be forced to act in a manner contrary to his conscience. Nor, on the other hand, is he to be restrained from acting in accordance with his conscience, especially in matters religious . . .

However, the social nature of man itself requires that he should give external expression to his internal acts of religion; that he should participate with others in matters religious; that he should profess his religion in community. Injury, therefore, is done to the human person and to the very order established by God for human life, if the free

exercise of religion is denied in society when the just
requirements of public order do not so require. [11]

Clearly in the first instance the Church was pleading here for her own right
to religious freedom. Nevertheless since the argument is couched in such
terms as 'social nature of man itself' and 'the very order established by God'
then logically it is bound to extend to the public practice of all religions.

One commentator on this document has distinguished the *foundation* of
these rights as claimed by Catholics and by others:

> The Catholic Church claims freedom from coercive
> interference in her ministry and life on grounds of the divine
> mandate laid upon her by Christ Himself . . . In the case of
> other religious Communities, the foundation of the right is
> the dignity of the human person, which requires that men be
> kept free from coercion, when they act in community,
> gathered into Churches, as well as when they act alone. [12]

To return to Clifford's Pastoral of 1865: in the peroration there is a summing
up of the respective rights, duties and mutual relationship of Church and
State. At the same time he takes the opportunity to criticise obliquely the
Church of England which at this time was still reeling from the Gorham
Judgement of 1850 and other '*causes célèbres*' before the Privy Council all
of which underlined the Erastian nature of the Established Church.

> . . . he (The Pope) will not admit the Church to be a mere
> function of the State, and denies the power of the State to
> regulate her teaching and her discipline.

---

11   Paragraph 3.

12   *The Documents of Vatican II*, General Editor: Walter M. Abbott, S.J.
      (Publ. London, 1966). The commentary on *Dignitatis Humanae* is by
      John Courtney Murray, S.J. This quotation is from footnote 9, p. 682.
      Clearly there has been a development of doctrine. This was an argument
      used by Archbishop Roberts, S.J. and others when calling on Pope Paul
      VI to change the Church's traditional ban on artificial birth control.
      Vide *The Pill and Birth Regulation*, ed. by Leo Pyle (Publ. London, 1964),
      pp. 87, 88. The Church's teaching over the years on Usury and *Extra
      Ecclesiam nulla est salus* were cited as precedents for a possible change.

There is a word, too, for the temporal power of the Pope which, says Clifford, is held for the good of the Church'.

At the end of the pastoral Clifford defines the nature of true and authentic 'progress, liberalism and modern civilisation' mentioned in Proposition 80. In words redolent of Dupanloup's own pastoral, Clifford says

> With such progress and civilisation the Pope needs not to be reconciled, for he has never been at variance with it.

As Clifford's Pastoral began to be read beyond the confines of his Diocese so the letters of congratulation started to arrive. One of the first was from J. Spencer Northcote, the President of Oscott, and in it he asked the Bishop kindly to send him two copies of his Pastoral. One copy was for a young student – a Catholic? – at Christ Church, Oxford, the other

> I should be very glad to keep myself, & to lend to some of our young *Liberals* in the house . . . [13]

Within the fortnight another and much lengthier communication arrived, congratulating Clifford on 'an able and seasonable exposition of the late Encyclical of the pope'. The writer was Ambrose de L'Isle Phillipps who informed Clifford that he had already read 'with satisfaction' the Pastoral of Dupanloup, Bishop of Orleans 'which takes very much the same line as your own'. He continued,

> Both the one and the other were much needed: for it was not merely the Protestant Public throughout Europe and the world but all the Catholic Powers had given a very different construction, the latter had either refused to accept it or (as in the case of the Emperor of Austria) remonstrated against it. [14]

---

13   Ugbrooke Archives, *Letters to Bp. Clifford, 1865*, Northcote to Clifford, Letter dated 3.3.1865. In 1869 Northcote collaborated with William Robert Brownlow to write *Roma Sotterranea*, a work in two volumes, on the then recent discoveries in the Roman Catacombs. Brownlow was destined to succeed Clifford as Bishop of Clifton (1894).

14   Ugbrooke Archives, *Letters to Bp. Clifford, 1865*, Phillipps to Clifford, Letter dated 12.3.1865. All the quotations are from this letter.

But Phillipps proceeds to argue, as Clifford had done, for a moderate interpretation of what the Pope had written:

> Judging from the antecedents of Pius IX, I have no doubt that His Holiness only intended the Encyclical in the mild and restricted sense which you, and the Archbishop of Paris, the Bishop of Orleans and other Prelates have given to it. But it is nevertheless incontestable that there is a considerable Party in the Catholic Church represented by such papers as the Monde, the Osservatore Romano, the Civilta Cattolica & Co., which give it a far harsher and more extensive construction, and view it as the assertion of unlimited absolute Dominion . . .

He continues by saying that he had read an article to this effect only a week before in *Le Monde*. 'The same article censured in the strongest terms what it termed "The Alternators" of the Encyclical' commented Phillipps, presumably to remind Clifford that his Pastoral would also have its critics.

Finally, Phillipps – always conscious of 'The Enemies of the Church' – makes the point that the same extreme construction of the Encyclical will be put upon it by those who wish 'to derive political capital from it for effecting their favourite project of dispossessing the Papacy of the small Territory it still retains'. For all of these reasons Clifford is to be warmly thanked by all those people who feel that it is high time for the Bishops of Christendom to make their voices heard.

So impressed was Phillipps and his family with Clifford's 'admirable' pastoral that eight days later his wife wrote asking for more copies.

> I should be very much obliged if you could let me have 3 or 4 more copies – even 8 or 10 I should be glad to *buy* as we are so very anxious to distribute it amongst some of our Protestant relations and friends.

She continues:

> All you say about the Pope's late Encyclical is so very satisfactory, that one wishes others who have found such

very great faults with it, to see the explanations given by one of our English Catholic Bishops. The Bishop of Orleans' admirable and most able pamphlet is rather long for ordinary readers who generally wish to get as much information possible with as little trouble as need be. [15]

Probably the letter of congratulation which gratified Clifford most was the following from Father Newman:

I have read it (the Pastoral) with great pleasure, for it is rare that an authoritative explanation is so lucid and so persuasive. It seems to me likely to be of great service to Catholics in two directions – first as removing the perplexities of our people, and the annoyance of Protestants, at the wording of theological statements & the drift and sense of theological judgments, which are not obvious to the unlearned reader – And again, it is of use to Catholics living in the world, and having to converse with Protestants or even to write & publish, who are at a loss to know what they may safely grant, and what they must firmly maintain. [16]

Here it is well to note that Newman said nothing *publicly* or *formally* with regard to *Quanta cura* and the *Syllabus* until ten years later when he published his *Letter to the Duke of Norfolk* [17] in which he replied to Gladstone's allegations that these documents, together with the Vatican Decrees of 1870, compromised the civic loyalty of Catholics.

Other bishops, as well as Clifford, felt constrained to write to their flocks on the *Syllabus* and at the same time to deal with the more wild statements being made in the press. Goss of Liverpool, Brown of Newport

---

15   Ugbrooke Archives, *Letters to Bp. Clifford, 1865*, Laura de L'Isle Phillipps to Clifford, Letter dated 26.3.1865.

16   Ugbrooke Archives, *Letters to Bp. Clifford, 1865*, Newman to Clifford, Letter dated 3.5.1865. It is to be noted that not even Newman dissociates himself from Clifford on those issues on which Vatican II adopted a different stance.

17   Damian McElrath, *op. cit.* p. 127.

and Ullathorne of Birmingham all had their say, but none of them could match Clifford in his painstaking analysis of the more controversial points of the document.

The passage of time has not meant the dimming of the bad reputation of the *Syllabus of Errors*, and, understandably, seasoned critics of the Church in the years since have 'wheeled out' this document in an attempt to validate their Anti-Catholic prejudices. One example of this was the famous debate in the 1940s between Arnold Lunn and G.G. Coulton published in 1947 under the title *Is the Catholic Church Anti-Social?* Here Coulton characterised the condemnation of the final proposition 'that the Pope can and should reconcile himself and make terms with Progress, Liberalism, and Modern civilization' as 'smacking too intolerably of antediluvian Toryism to be defended today'. [18]

To conclude: there were those who, in 1865, were to attach considerable significance to this Pastoral Letter which Clifford had written. Cardinal Wiseman died on 15th February and the Pastoral appeared just eight days later. Its effect on the liberal-minded, anti-Pio Nono faction of Catholics, like Acton, was little short of electric. They had studied the *Syllabus* with a sense of deep foreboding but here was a man who was liberal yet orthodox, whose Pastoral Letter had interpreted the document in such a way as to make it acceptable to both wings of Catholic tradition. He was young and his credentials both in Rome and at home were impeccable.

The sequel to Clifford's Pastoral was that they were to use their influence to secure his succession at Westminster.

---

18   G.G. Coulton and Arnold Lunn, *op.cit.*, p. 88.

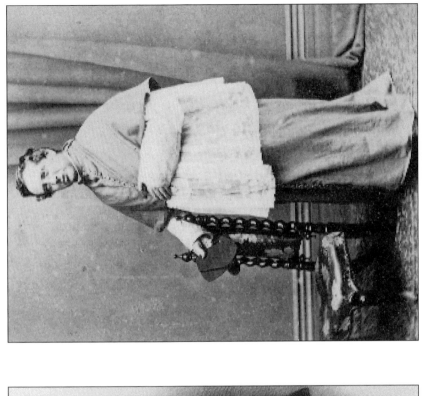

Dr Thomas Grant, (1816 – 1870), first Bishop of Southwark

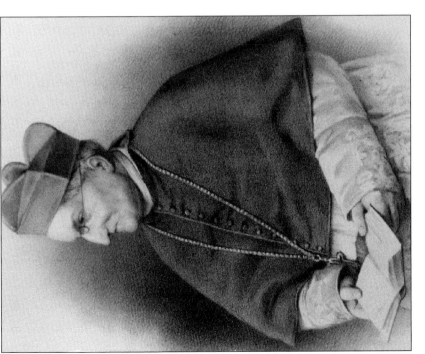

Cardinal Alessandro Barnabò, Prefect of the Congregation of *Propaganda Fide*, Rome

CARDINAL HENRY EDWARD MANNING, (1808 – 1892), SECOND
ARCHBISHOP OF WESTMINSTER

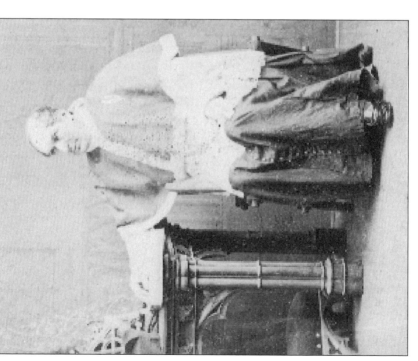

CANON FREDERICK NEVE, (1806 – 1886), PRIEST OF THE DIOCESE OF
CLIFTON AND RECTOR OF THE ENGLISH COLLEGE, ROME

CHAPTER SIX

The Succession at Westminster (1865)

In May, 1860, while staying at the English College in Rome, Bishop Clifford received a letter from Mgr. Talbot, the Pope's Private Secretary and special adviser on English affairs:

> May 29 1860

> Cardinal Barnabo has desired me to write to you today that the H[oly] F[ather] wishes to see Y[our] L[ordship] as soon as you have seen Dr. E [rrington].

> If you have not seen him *yet*, he wishes you to see him as soon as possible.

> As soon as you have seen him, I will let the HF know of it.[1]

This was to mark the beginning in Rome of the moves which were to end in the removal of Errington as Coadjutor to Wiseman in the See of Westminster. Although friends both as students and while on the staff of the English College, and no doubt also as bishops, Errington nevertheless had had serious misgivings when early in 1855 the Cardinal had pressed for his appointment as Coadjutor. Errington knew that the arrangement would not work, and he was right. Indeed it was only a matter of months before the two men parted with Errington going at his own suggestion[2] as Apostolic Administrator to Clifton – a move which, although to the advantage of Clifton, was also calculated to bring a period of respite to Westminster.

Here it should be noted that a Coadjutor (Arch)bishop, unlike an Auxiliary,[3] does have jurisdiction within the diocese of the (Arch)bishop to whom he has been appointed. Clearly, therefore, such an appointment

---

1   Clifton Diocesan Archives, *Letters to William Clifford*, Part 1, 1854 – 1874. Talbot to Clifford, Letter dated 29.5.1860.

2   Richard J. Schiefen, *Nicholas Wiseman and the Transformation of English Catholicism* (Publ. Shepherdstown, 1984), p. 246.

3   *Codex Juris Canonici* (1918), canons 350-355.

presupposes a degree of mutual confidence; but if this should be lacking, or break down, then the canonical entanglements could be considerable. It might be argued that presumption in law would be on the side of the Ordinary (i.e. the Archbishop or Bishop in charge of the diocese), and so in the ensuing dispute between Wiseman and Errington the scales might be viewed as already tipped in the Cardinal's favour.

Further complications arose because of the question of the succession. Usually a coadjutor is appointed with right of succession, but there is provision in law for a coadjutor to be appointed without such a right. This happened, for example, in 1954, when Bishop Edward Myers, Auxiliary in Westminster, was appointed coadjutor *sine iure successionis* during the serious illness of Cardinal Griffin. Indeed such an appointment of Errington – i.e. without right of succession – might well have forestalled many of the problems which form the subject matter of this chapter.

While at Westminster Errington, a well-trained canonist, found that his decisions, properly and reasonably made, were being reversed by Wiseman. At St. Edmund's, the diocesan seminary for Westminster, Errington found a layman (W.G. Ward) lecturing in theology – an arrangement which greatly displeased him. The position in the College of the Oblates of St. Charles, under Henry Edward Manning, also gave him cause for concern because he saw it as giving rise to a form of (canonical) independence within the diocese. When eventually the matter came to a head Errington took the side of the Chapter against the Cardinal. In this he made a grave mistake. As one writer commented:

> 'However sympathetic one may be to Errington's position, he was out of order in assisting both the Westminster and Southwark chapters in a course directly opposed to the superior whom he was assigned to represent in an Official capacity'.[4]

As Coadjutor, Errington was meant to be Wiseman's *alter ego* and in this he had failed. The Cardinal's decision to ask Rome to remove him, and Errington's subsequent determination not to be so removed – because, he argued, he had committed no canonical offence and it was only for such

---

4   Schiefen, *op. cit.*, p. 260.

an offence that he could be dismissed from office – brought Bishop Clifford into the drama. A friend of Errington, yet trusted by Rome, he was an obvious choice to act as go-between in the early years of the controversy, but with the death of Cardinal Wiseman he became only to a slightly lesser degree the centre of controversy himself.

In response to the letter from Talbot quoted at the beginning of this chapter, Clifford duly saw Errington and then was received in audience by the Pope. On 3rd June Clifford told Errington what had transpired:

> . . . he has directed me to write to you and communicate to you his orders, that you send to him two or three copies of the papers you have drawn up relative to the differences between Card W. and yourself. HH bid me inform you that it is not his intention to pronounce any sentence in consequence of these papers. If he should hereafter think it advisable to pronounce a sentence he would in that case first communicate to you the statement made by C(ardinal) W(iseman) and to His Emce the statement made by you in order to give both parties an opportunity of reply.

Clifford ended by offering his help:

> You may either take the papers to HH yourself, or forward them to me for presentation to HH as you judge best. [5]

Errington's important reply to Clifford repeats his plea of innocence. In a letter to the Prefect of Propaganda, written in Italian, the Archbishop – as always – ends on a note of personal respect for the Holy Father. 'Whatever the outcome this will not in any way diminish my appreciation of the great kindness of the Holy Father towards me'. [6] However, in his letter to Clifford, Errington was more forthright:

> I must add that the printed case contains only a portion of the answer I had prepared to the undefined and to a great

---

5   Clifton Diocesan Archives, *Letters to William Clifford*, Part I, Draft of Reply from Clifford to Errington dated 3.6.1860.

6   Clifton Diocesan Archives, *Letters to William Clifford*, Part I, copy of letter in Italian from Errington to Cardinal Barnabo. Undated.

extent unknown charges made by H(is) E(minence) or his friends against me. I had reserved many points to be treated when I should have the charges in precise terms before me in accordance of H(is) H(oliness). [7]

He added that in England any adverse decision would in the circumstances 'necessarily have the force and sense of a condemnatory sentence'.

In the end after a stormy interview with the Pope during which 'those waiting in the antechamber were astonished to hear raised voices,[8] Errington was personally dismissed from office by Pio Nono (March 8th, 1860). Again the succession at Westminster was an open question. Even so, the tragic yet able figure of George Errington – like the ghost of Hamlet's father – continued to haunt the minds of his contemporaries.

In 1863 a priest from the Diocese of Clifton was appointed Rector of the Venerable English College in Rome. Frederick Robert Neve (Eton and Oriel) was a convert, having been received into the Church in 1845, the same year as John Henry Newman. It has been suggested [9] that Neve was sent to Rome because of a certain incompatibility with his bishop, William Clifford. This is not borne out by the tone of the letters which Neve sent at regular intervals to Clifford nor by the confidences which he shared with him. In the Clifton Archives there are over a dozen letters from Neve, and these shed an interesting light on the rumours and counter-rumours current in Rome in the weeks immediately following the death of Wiseman (February 15th, 1865) and preceding the appointment of Manning.

---

7   Ugbrooke Archives, *Letters to Bp. Clifford*, 1860, letter dated.

8   Clifton Diocesan Archives, *Errington Papers*, No. 36, Minutes of audience 8.3.1860.

9   Michael E. Williams, *The Venerable English College, Rome*, (Publ. London, 1979), p. 126 quoting Talbot. It was November, 1865, while Neve was Rector, that the English College gave shelter to John M. Surratt, one of the conspiritors involved in the assassination of Abraham Lincoln, and who was then on the run. (Andrew C.A. Jampoler, "*The Venerable English College and the Hunt for the Last Lincoln Conspiritor*", *The Venerabile*, 33, no. 4, (2007), pp. 33 sqq).

It is significant that even a year before Wiseman's death, when his health was in a state of serious decline, there had been talk of giving him a coadjutor in the person of Mgr. Manning. Writing in February, 1864, Neve told Clifford:

> I have unravelled some of the mysteries of the interferences with the Diocese of Westminster than I knew before. In fact Talbot finding that I differed with him so much on his mode of proceeding would not give me any more information. I asked him if he was planning to get Manning appointed Coadjutor, he denied this so strongly that I supposed that nothing was doing at the Vatican on the subject.

> It is right that you should know that Manning and his people are the offenders and meddlers in everything. When I first came here, I found Herbert Vaughan here who told me that he had been to the Pope to tell him that there was a great fear in London that at the Cardinal's death Dr. Errington would contest the right of succession, and that it was the Pope's life against the Cardinal's which would decide the question. The Pope said that he had thought of it and would provide against it.

> I told Vaughan that I thought that it was not his business to interfere. He however maintained his views and thoughts that either Manning or Dr. Ullathorne ought to be named coadjutor. Vaughan likewise said that his people, the Oblates, ought to have charge of the English College. Then arose in Rome the rumour that Manning was to be named coadjutor on which I spoke to Talbot and he denied that any thing was doing. [10]

This letter from Neve is important as it conveys some idea of the plot and intrigue then current in Rome, even before Wiseman was dead.

---

10   Clifton Diocesan Archives, *Letters to William Clifford*, Part I, Neve to Clifford, Letter dated 13.2.1864.

Speaking of the building of the new chapel (St. Thomas) for the English College, Neve says that 'Manning's ready tongue was of great use, and he has risen high in public estimation by his eloquent advocacy'.[11] Of Westminster Neve quoted Talbot as saying that the Pope was 'determined' that Errington should not succeed, although Neve is careful to add that he (Neve) had heard that Errington had expressed the intention not to contest it anyway.

> It appears next that Talbot has written to the Cardinal and to Dr. Ullathorne saying that the Pope wished the latter to be named coadjutor with the right of succession to Westminster, but that he was not to leave Birmingham before the Cardinal's death. On this the Chapter of Westminster wrote to Propaganda complaining of the invasion of their rights to whom Barnabo replies telling them to mind their own business.[12]

There then follows a passage which, if true, makes one wonder whether the Manning of Purcell and Lytton Strachey was after all so wide of the mark:

> All this has been arranged by Manning who has made use of Talbot to go to the Pope and Propaganda for him. It appears also that Barnabo told Dr. Roskell[13] yesterday that nothing would be done against the Cardinal's will. But there will be no peace as long as Manning is here, he is always scheming – he has schemed for me a complete change in the management of the College . . . he has schemed an English University in Rome . . . I see very little of him now, as I cannot listen to him. [14]

---

11   *Ibid.*

12   *Ibid.*

13   Richard Roskell, 2nd Bishop of Nottingham from 1853 to 1874.

14   *Ibid.*

Neve ends his graphic account of the Roman world of rumour and counter-rumour with a suggestion:

> If ever the Bishops of England can be of one mind, they ought to have an ecclesiastic of high rank here to control all these things, all other nations have one. Talbot from his position about the Pope is unfitted for it . . . More mischief is done by the gossip of the English Priests who come to Rome than can be described.'

– and a hint –

> I have marked this letter private for your Lordship, but you can impart what you please of it to the Bishops.[15]

It would not be reading too much into this to see Neve telling Clifford, and through him the other bishops, that Manning was wielding an immense influence in Rome and that while he (Manning) might not be actively seeking the succession at Westminster, it might nevertheless fall to him unless the bishops, if so minded, presented a united front to stop it.

On New Year's day, 1865, just six weeks before Wiseman's death – Neve was still writing in the same vein about Manning and his intrigues, but this time he included Talbot in his strictures:

> Newman is very unpopular here – The Jesuits do not like his writings – thinking him too liberal – Talbot talks loudly against the Apologia – all the points (?) have been picked out for him by Manning. Talbot has more of the Pope's private ear than anyone in Rome, but I do not think the Pope takes in all that he says violently against anyone . . . I avoid always mentioning names . . . But Barnabo would jump at once at anything I said to show any intrigue of Mannings is Talbots and would work away to oppose it . . . I am quite sure that when Manning is in Rome the Bishops ought to have some one here to watch him. [16]

---

15   *Ibid.*

16   Clifton Diocesan Archives, *Letters to William Clifford*, Part I, Neve to Clifford, Letter dated 1.1.1865.

This letter was written within hours of two others he had sent to Clifford the previous day. In the second of these Neve related that he had gone to Propaganda to see Barnabo about the whole question of the founding of a Catholic university. The Cardinal Prefect told him that although he favoured the idea, he was nevertheless opposed to putting Newman in charge. Neve continued:

> I said plainly that Manning was prejudiced against Newman and that he had Talbot by the nose – as he quoted Talbot as agreeing with himself.
>
> – He said all that was very likely, yet Manning spoke well on the subject. I had not expected this, as last year Barnabo did not consort much with Manning, and there has been no communication between the Cardinal and Propaganda, in fact I was told at Propaganda that there was a mutual coolness.[17]

Two events (the first of which will be treated in greater detail later) should receive brief mention here as they both bring Bishop Clifford into public prominence at a time when it was clear to all that it would soon be necessary to find a successor to Cardinal Wiseman. The first was the issue of the Catholic University and it is germane to the present argument to note that it was precisely at this time, when Wiseman was near to death, that the matter was being discussed in Rome with Manning very much the centre of attention arguing against the idea in general and Newman's part in it in particular. Ullathorne, on the other hand, had a strong sympathy with Newman (a religious of his diocese) and after Manning's elevation was to act as a bridge between the two men. Ullathorne wrote to Clifford in January, 1865:

> Dr. N. and his friends believe, rightly or wrongly, that our friend Dr. M. is at the root of the whole affair and that he moved Rome to move for the meeting. [18]

---

17   Clifton Diocesan Archives, *Letters to William Clifford*, Part I, Neve to
      Clifford, Letter dated 31.12.1864, 2nd letter.

18   Clifton Diocesan Archives, *Letters to William Clifford*, Part I,
      Ullathorne to Clifford, Letter dated 12.1.1855.

The other significant event was the publication of Pius IX's encyclical letter *Quanta cura*, with the appended *Syllabus of Errors*. To say that these had not been well received by the more liberal elements in the Catholic Church, among whom was the historian Sir John (later Lord) Acton, would be a gross understatement. Bishop Clifford issued a Pastoral Letter on the *Syllabus* and was congratulated by many, including Newman. [19] There must have been some who, on reading his treatment of the papal document, saw the sure hand of someone who, while remaining theologically orthodox, could nevertheless command respect among intellectuals both within and beyond the Catholic fold, and for this reason could be regarded by 'Old' Catholics and converts alike as a very acceptable successor to Cardinal Wiseman.

Neve's letters to Clifford – often amusing and always interesting – furnish an insight as to what was happening at the Roman end of events just before and after the death of the Cardinal. On 28th January, 1865, Neve wrote:

> Of course we have all been uneasy about the Cardinal – we have had very little information . . . Manning has not yet come, last year he was in no great favour with Barnabo, now he is at the top of the tree – and because I insisted that he did not always represent in himself the opinions of England I have dropped from Alnantissimo and Carissimo down to Signor Rettore – so I must give Barnabo some more plum pudding to put him into good humour.[20] [Neve had entertained several cardinals to lunch at the English College on the patronal feast of St. Thomas of Canterbury, 29th December].

Wiseman died on 15th February, 1865. Naturally rumours increased both in private and in the press, as to who was likely to succeed him. More importantly, the British Government could not but be interested in the vacancy at Westminster and indeed made its views known in a communication to Odo Russell whom Purcell describes as 'the semi-diplomatic agent or representative of the English Government at Rome'. [21]

---

19   Chapter V, footnote 16.

20   Clifton Diocesan Archives, *Letters to William Clifford*, Part I, Neve to Clifford, Letter dated 28.1.1865.

21   Edmund Purcell, *Life of Cardinal Manning* (Publ. London, 1896), Vol. II, p. 204.

Before considering what that view was and the suggestions which accompanied it, it is of interest to note how over the years various writers have given contrasting accounts of the preferred candidate of H.M.G. :

> EDMUND PURCELL (1896) 'Lord Palmerston accordingly communicated to Mr. Odo Russell . . . the name of the candidate most agreeable to the English Ministry. Odo Russell carried out his instructions and interested Cardinal Antonelli in favour of the candidate suggested by the English Government.

> *Footnote*: The nomination of *Dr. Grant*, Bishop of Southwark, as successor to Cardinal Wiseman, was recommended by the Government, with which Dr. Grant had been in official relations. [22]

> SHANE LESLIE (1921) 'It is not generally known that the British Government supported *Clifford*, or that Newman (not Manning) was one of the proposed. Neve wrote to Clifford (March 25, 1865): "Private. As I expected would be the case, Odo Russell has been instructed to promote your nomination: I lament that you are so misrepresented as a Liberal"'. [23]

> CUTHBERT BUTLER (1926) 'The British Government made a semi-official communication that *Clifford's* would be the most acceptable appointment. [24]

> EDWARD NORMAN (1984) 'The British Government wanted *Grant*, with whom they had had dealings over the provision of Catholic army chaplains during the Crimean War, and an approach on the matter was made to Cardinal Antonelli. [25]

---

22   *Ibid*.

23   Shane Leslie, *Henry Edward Manning* (Publ. London, 1921), p. 151. The letter from Neve is dated March 18, not 25. Her Majesty's Government did not mention Newman's name – at least not initially, if at all.

24   Cuthbert Butler, *The Life and Times of Bishop Ullathorne* (Publ. London, 1926), Vol. I, p. 267.

25   Edward Norman, *The English Catholic Church in the Nineteenth Century* (Publ. Oxford, 1984), p. 260.

The real views of H.M.G. were contained in the following communication from the Foreign Secretary:

F.O. Feb. 20 1865

My dear Odo,

We are rather uneasy here about the succession to Cardinal Wiseman –

A very pompous announcement of a successor might raise a flame here, and be detrimental not only to our design of doing full justice to the Roman Catholic Church, but to the Roman Catholic Church itself. What we should most desire would be that Dr. Grant should quietly extend his spiritual influence over London and Westminster, retaining Southwark in his peculiar district.

But I understand that three names have been already sent to Rome as those of persons qualified to succeed Wiseman.

1st Dr. Grant – 2d. Dr. Clifford brother of Lord Clifford, 3d Dr. Ullathorne now administering the district of Birmingham – Of these three the first is unobjectionable, nor do I know of any valid objection against the second – But Dr. Ullathorne of Birmingham is I understand a very injudicious capable of fostering (?) claims which would arouse resistance and indignation in every part of England.

Lord Palmerston and I are of opinion that by quietly talking to Cardinal Antonelli he would be induced to exert his great sagacity and extreme influence in preventing the flame which burns so fiercely in France from scorching England.

Here are 3 names which we think

1st – Status quo – Dr. Grant

Dr. Clifford – Any other name may cause speedily or at a later date much dissension.

Yours truly

J. Russell[26]

Several comments need to be made:

1) 'A very pompous announcement': This is a thinly veiled reference to *From outside the Flaminian Gate* which broke the news of Wiseman's own appointment to Westminster. The exuberance of the language offended many and this probably explains why Russell twice uses the word 'quietly' in the course of his letter.

2) The writer is incorrect when he says that the three names had already been submitted.

3) Nowhere in the letter does Russell use the title 'Bishop'. The studious avoidance of such illegal terminology shows that he wished to keep strictly within the terms of the *Ecclesiastical Titles Act* (1851).

It is clear from the communication that what Russell wants above all is a quiet transfer of power. In his view this could best be achieved by Grant becoming Archbishop of Westminster while retaining the See of Southwark. [27]

On 28th February Odo Russell reported back to the Foreign Secretary. His account of what he said to Antonelli is almost verbatim what Russell had told him to say.

'Cardinal Antonelli replied that he fully concurred in all I had said with respect to the desirability of maintaining peace and quiet in the interest of the R.C. Church in England and that he would communicate all I had said

---

26   Public Record Office, Kew, *Ampthill Papers*, F. O. 918/45, Earl Russell to Odo Russell, Letter dated 20.2.1865.

27   This is a novel idea and would probably have been unacceptable to Rome.

tomorrow morning to the Pope who would, he felt sure, take it into favourable consideration. – Meanwhile he must explain to me that the Chapter and the Bishops not having yet recommended anyone to the Propaganda to succeed Card. Wiseman the Pope had not yet been called upon to select or decide' . . . [28]

Antonelli continued by making some interesting observations on the names mentioned in the Foreign Secretary's note – names (one must assume) that had been 'rumoured' to him:

'He spoke then highly of Dr. Grant as he had done to me on former occasions and said that Dr. Clifford was also in favour with the Pope. Of Dr. Ullathorne he pretended to know very little, – and of Dr. Manning whose name had been incidentally mentioned he spoke favourably as of a man of learning and eloquence, but added that he would not be suited for a Post like that held by Cardinal Wiseman'.[29]

The audience came to an end with some very illuminating (apparently 'off-the-cuff') remarks from the Cardinal which Odo Russell duly reported back to the Foreign Secretary:

'He said he was glad I had spoken to him and added that now that Cardinal Wiseman was dead he must tell me in confidence that the Pope had been misled by the Cardinal's assurances that the Hierarchy would pass quietly and unobserved in England and would raise no opposition, – had they known the result they would have followed another course, – he merely told me this to show how much he desired peace and quiet in Church matters and in the interest of Religion'.[30]

---

28   Public Record Office, Kew, *Ampthill Papers*, F.O. 918/66, Odo Russell to Earl Russell, Letter dated 28.2.1865.

29   *Ibid.*

30   *Ibid.*

Three days before this report from Odo Russell to H.M.G., Neve was writing from the English College to Bishop Clifford. This was the first of his many post-Wiseman letters giving an account of the whisperings and rumours then current in Rome.

> '. . . pending the arrival of the wishes of Westminster and your Lordships the opinion gains ground amongst those likely to be well informed that the Bishop of Birmingham will go to Westminster and that Manning will be made a Cardinal; but of course this is all premature.' [31]

At this time Cardinals who were not bishops (i.e. the Cardinal Deacons) were required to reside in Rome.[32] This was the reason for Manning's alleged remark many years later when Newman was offered the red hat that he (Newman) would probably wish to decline. In the present instance Neve seems to be saying that it was Manning who would be called to be a 'cardinal in Curia'. Three days later the *Pall Mall Gazette* had a different story:

> 'It is rumoured that Dr. Clifford, the Roman Catholic Bishop of Clifton, will succeed Cardinal Wiseman as Archbishop of Westminster' [33]

---

31   Clifton Diocesan Archives, *Letters to William Clifford*, Part I, Neve to Clifford, Letter dated 25.2.1865.

32   'The cardinals are obliged to reside at Rome and cannot leave the Papal States without permission of the Pope. The violation of this law entails grave penalties, even the loss of the cardinalitial dignity . . . It is otherwise with foreign bishops created cardinals: they retain their dioceses and are not obliged to reside at Rome'.
The Catholic Encyclopedia, (Publ. London, 1908), Vol. III, p. 338, article 'Cardinal'.

It should be noted that Newman was not a bishop and that the requirement concerning residence in Rome has long since been changed.

33   *Pall Mall Gazette*, 28.2.1865.

Four days later it published another story, the alleged provenance of which was Belgium:

> 'The *Bien Public* of Ghent makes the following announcement editorially:-
>
> "The English Catholic Bishop of Clifton, Dr. Clifford, is about to receive the Cardinal's hat, and Bishop Errington will be called to the See of Westminster, vacant by the death of Cardinal Wiseman".[34]

Two days before this appeared (i.e. March 2nd) Neve wrote a long letter, marked 'private to the Bishop', informing Clifford for the first time that his name was now being spoken about openly in Rome. At the time of writing neither the Westminster Chapter nor the Bishops had met to discuss what advice they were to tender to Propaganda, *pace* Lord John Russell's remarks to Odo Russell which Cardinal Antonelli had not been slow to correct. Neve, with his obvious flare for private journalism, assures Clifford that what he is going to tell him 'is not mere gossip but comes from authentic sources'. He alleges that 'a good deal of correspondence principally from England' has been reaching Rome and this, Neve argues, points to a clear division of opinion among the canons of Westminster:

> 'Six . . . will act as one man and so of course will carry the election, as the Holy See will if possible take one of the names – the other five it is expected will vote for various persons. Morris is entirely devoted to (*sic*) Manning and Drinkwater will talk everywhere and writes long letters here in the same sense but it is not likely that the Chapter will send up either Manning or Archbishop Errington's name, as they know that this last wd irritate the Pope. – It is expected as probable that six of the W. Chapter will not send up Bishop Ullathorne's name'.[35]

---

34   *Pall Mall Gazette*, 4.3.1865.

35   Clifton Diocesan Archives, *Letters to William Clifford*, Part I, Neve to Clifford, Letter dated 2.3.1865.

Neve then proceeds to name Clifford as being the preferred candidate of an influential body of people. As with all major appointments, whether of Church or State, the timing of the vacancy is critical and it is often those issues which at the time are perceived as being of paramount importance that sway the minds of those who exercise the right of appointment. Such an issue in early 1865 was the projected opening of a Catholic College at Oxford. Because Clifford was known to be in favour of such an enterprise he attracted the support of the more liberal minded gentry who saw the death of Wiseman as an opportunity to change the status quo and, by getting Clifford appointed to Westminster, hoped to bring the other bishops to a more enlightened frame of mind in the matter of higher education for Catholics.

Neve wrote:

> 'A party called Castlerosse [36] party are urging as far as they can the Chapter to send up your Lordship's name, the reason given is because you were supposed to be favourable to their view of the Oxford scheme'.[37]

An amusing word of explanation is added:

> 'The History of the Castlerosse party (such a man to be the

---

36   Castlerosse, Valentine Augustus Browne, Viscount (1825 – 1905). He
        held the courtesy title from his father, the third Earl of Kenmare, whom
        he succeeded in 1871. He was Member of Parliament for County Kerry
        1852 – 1871, and held appointments at Court, ending as Lord
        Chamberlain 1880 – 1886. (*Letters and Diaries of John Henry
        Newman*, ed. Dessain and Kelly, Vol. XXI, p. 539).

37   *Ibid.*

38   It is difficult to identify this couple though they may have been related to
        Richard Gell MacMullen (1814 – 1895), Scholar and then Fellow of
        Corpus Christi College. On account of his Tractarian views, Hampden
        the Regius Professor of Divinity tried to prevent him from taking the
        degree of B.D. necessary for retaining his Fellowship. In the autumn of
        1846 Pusey sent him to St. Saviour's, Leeds. There he became a Catholic
        on 1st January, 1847. He was ordained the following year, and was from
        1856 to 1880 the priest at St. Mary's, Chelsea (*Letters and Diaries of
        John Henry Newman*, ed. Dessain and Kelly, Vol. XXI, p. 553).

head of a religious party!! and the more dangerous as he is
so intimate with the Government) I believe to be this – Lady
Castlerosse is fascinated by Macmullens[38] forty horse power
of conversation and she has persuaded her husband to
partake of the same fascination – The Ultra liberal party
through Sir J. Simeon[39] have made their way in by this
means and they assume that your Lordship is with them not
only on the Oxford question but on other liberal issues.' [40]

Having said that it is 'evidently the wish of Propaganda' that Ullathorne
should go to Westminster, Neve then admits that he had taken it upon
himself to express reluctance on Clifford's part to the candidature then
being promoted by the Castlerosse Party:

'I have said for you, on being asked, that I believed you did
not wish it, as you were engaged in reforming the finances
of your Diocese, that the work was not yet complete, and
that it would be a great inconvenience to remove you.'

To which he adds with the soberness of hindsight:

'I will not say any more without further instructions'. [41]

---

39   Simeon, Sir John (1815 – 1870): Succeeded his father as third baronet
      in 1854. He was Liberal Member of Parliament for the Isle of Wight from
      1847 to 1851 when he thought it his duty to resign on being received into
      the Catholic Church. His wife too became a Catholic.

      He soon became a friend of Newman and supported him in his efforts to
      found an oratory at Oxford. Among his friends were Tennyson, Jowett
      and Manning. In the sixties his London house was a rendezvous for
      literary and political society. He was re-elected to Parliament in 1865, in
      spite of the intervention of W.G. Ward. Ward, who supported his
      Conservative opponent and was praised for putting party before religion,
      replied with heat that he objected precisely to Simeon's liberal Catholic
      religious opinions (*Letters and Diaries of John Henry Newman*, ed.
      Dessain and Kelly, Vol. XXI, p. 564 abbreviated).

40   Clifton Diocesan Archives, *Letters to William Clifford*, Part I, Neve to
      Clifford, Letter dated 2.3.1865.

41   *Ibid.*

(It is difficult to imagine Neve expressing this reluctance in a matter of such consequence without some prior indication from Clifford himself).

The letter ends with another reference to the projected Catholic college at Oxford:

> 'Your letter to Card. Barnabo was read to the Congregation of Propda and to the Pope. Your remark that a *great body* of the laity were favourable to the Oxford scheme was not much liked, as the result shows that Weld-Blundell[42] and Scott Murray[43] were the only respectable names attached to the Castlerosse Memorial (though of course no one thinks that you had anything to do with that) and of the names not yet withdrawn three are tailors though the address of Tooley Street is not given'.

Neve had obtained his information about the reaction to Clifford's letter from Cardinal Barnabo with whom he was in frequent contact. That Clifford's remarks 'were not much liked' seems to point to the conservative Pope showing his disapproval of the young liberal bishop, and it must surely be arguable that, even if the outcome of subsequent events had been otherwise, Pio Nono would not have been inclined to appoint him to the See of Westminster.

Discussions between England and Rome now take a critical turn with attention being focused on four bishops and Provost Manning:

---

42 Weld-Blundell, Thomas (1808 – 1887), second son of Joseph Weld of Lulworth Castle. Took additional name of Blundell in 1840 on acquiring by bequest a large estate from the Blundell family. He married Teresa, daughter of W. M. Vaughan of Courtfield, and was Sheriff of Lancashire in 1852 (*Letters and Diaries of John Henry Newman*, ed. Dessain and Kelly, Vol. XXI, p. 568 abbreviated).

43 Scott-Murray, Charles Robert (1818 – 1882) of Danesfield, Bucks. was at Eton and Christ Church. He inherited a large fortune and was Member of Parliament for Bucks from 1841 to 1845. He was received into the Church by Cardinal Fransoni in Rome in 1844. In 1846 he married Amelia Fraser, daughter of 14th Lord Lovatt (*Letters and Diaries of John Henry Newman*, ed. Dessain, Vol. XI, p. 356 abbreviated).

Archbishop Errington	60 years	6 months
Bishop Ullathorne	58 years	9 months
Provost Manning	56 years	7 months
Bishop Grant	48 years	2 months
Bishop Clifford	41 years	1 month

(Ages given are as at the time of Wiseman's death, 15th February, 1865). On March 4th 1865, Canon John Morris, the devoted secretary of Cardinal Wiseman, wrote to Mgr. Talbot conveying his thoughts on the succession at Westminster.

'I suppose the choice of names by the Chapter or the recommendations of the Bishops will not affect the matter greatly, for probably the H.F.'s mind is already made up as the Cardinal's death was so long expected'.[44]

In a curious way he was right, but only in the sense that the names put forward led to the Pope making his own choice, though at the time of Morris's letter he had clearly not done so. The writer's antipathy to Errington and the thoughts which might, he feels, be in the minds of some of the canons when they vote are worth noting:

'I only hope and pray that none but worthy names may be sent up, for I should feel thoroughly ashamed if, after all that has passed, Dr. Errington's name were to appear'.

The meeting of the Westminster Chapter was delayed until the 14th, in Morris's words, 'apparently to give time to ascertain how Dr. Errington's name would be taken in influential quarters'.

'The idea of the majority of the Chapter is, no doubt, that Dr. E. was unjustly treated – not that they would say perhaps that the Pope committed an act of injustice, but that he thought well to remove him because of the C's hostility to him, which they think unjust. I look upon it that the idea is a misuse of the power of presenting names to the Holy See;

---

44   Archives of the Venerable English College, Rome, *Talbot Papers*, Morris to Talbot, Letter dated 4.3.1865.

for even with this opinion, that power is not intended as a means of making amends to men who have been treated with injustice, but I hold that each Canon is bound in conscience to vote for the men whom he considers most fit for the vacant see'.[45]

After saying that Clifford's name was 'very likely to make its appearance', Canon Morris next refers to the internal politics then at work to ensure that Ullathorne would not be appointed. Having expressed his view that the Bishop of Birmingham was unlikely to get a single vote, he nevertheless describes the fear of many – the majority? – that Ullathorne might yet succeed by default:

> 'I think it quite possible that if it should occur to the majority that naming Dr. Errington would so offend the Holy Father that he would not look at their other names, but would appoint Dr. Ullathorne, their anxiety to prevent this appointment would lead them to omit Dr. Errington's name. I believe that the majority are working together on an understanding, which of course places the matter of the election entirely in their hands'.[46]

This was to prove prophetic, at least in part, for in the event the Holy Father was so incensed at the naming of Errington that he chose to disregard the other names – but not in favour of Ullathorne.

Surprisingly, neither Grant nor Manning are mentioned by Morris, except to say that the latter's sermon at the Cardinal's funeral was 'a masterpiece'.

A week or so later a curious incident occurred which appeared to indicate that the Pope was going to appoint Clifford. It is related by Purcell[47] and tells of an occasion when the Redemptorist Father Coffin (later the third Bishop of Southwark) had been to see the Pope. The Pontiff asked:

---

45   *Ibid.*

46   *Ibid.*

47   Edmund Purcell, *Life of Cardinal Manning* (Publ. London, 1896), Vol. II, p. 216.

'. . . but who will now be Archbishop?" Father Coffin answered, "Dr. Errington is talked of." Upon this Pius IX cried out, "That would be an insult to the Pope. Non è vero, Padre Generale?" turning to Father General. Then drawing himself up the Pope beat his breast thrice with indignation. After a while he added, "Ma c'è il Mgr. Clifford", and then, as if checking himself, said, "Ma lasciamo tutto al Spirito Santo", and then, "che Dio vi benedica".'

Purcell says that Coffin went away convinced that Clifford was indeed to be the new Archbishop, although his own personal view was that he was too young and not 'ripe enough' for the position. (If the words are quoted accurately, the Pope did not say "è, Mgr. Clifford", i.e. it is Mgr. Clifford, but "C'è Mgr. Clifford" which is translated "there is (always) Mgr. Clifford to fall back on". Neither Coffin nor Purcell seem to have noted this small but important difference).

On 14th March, 1865, the Westminster Chapter assembled and proposed three names (the *terna*) to the Holy See. They were: Archbishop Errington, Dr. Grant of Southwark and Dr. Clifford of Clifton.

Clifford – either before or after the meeting – wrote to Bishop Grant. We do not know the exact contents of the letter but it elicited the following reply from Grant, dated 15th March.

'My Lord,

Your letter makes me think and hope that you and I can help Dr E. more than any one.

In the body of the Bps are some decidedly opposed to him, and all will feel a delicacy in *advocating* his cause.

But, whilst it would look like affectation if you or I wrote to decline the honour in his favour, compose a letter for *both to sign*, showing that as each of us was his subject or pupil, we cannot but know his merits and our unwillingness to be thought of in comparison with him. Also, that he knows the details of Westminster better than any man living. We know our Dioceses and the means of good in them, and would have to *learn* all about Westminster.

Yours in J .C.

+ T. Grant

We may say all this and more less offensively than anyone
else could say it.[48]

In response to this Clifford drew up a draft document to be sent to
Cardinal Barnabo, the Cardinal Prefect of Propaganda. It is only in draft
form in the Archives, but the following are the headings of their joint
argument for appointing Dr. Errington. They preface their remarks by
saying that of course no one has any right to the appointment, that they
(Clifford and Grant) know the pastoral qualities of Dr. Errington better
than anyone, and that it would be 'painful' if Errington were 'postponed
to men younger and inferior to himself'. The five points of the argument
in favour of Errington's going to Westminster were:

1)   'His superior Ecclesiastical knowledge';

2)   'His excellent administrative abilities';

3)   'He has great firmness of character';

4)   'He has made great personal sacrifices';
      'He has always been employed in undertakings which
      . . . were of a painful and thankless nature'; (This,
      among other things, refers to his work as Administrator
      of Clifton when the diocese was on the verge of
      bankruptcy.)

5)   'Dr. E. is well versed in all details of the diocese of
      Westminster'. [49]

---

48   Clifton Diocesan Archives, *Letters to William Clifford*, Part I, Grant
      to Clifford, Letter dated 15.3.1865.

49   Clifton Diocesan Archives, *Letters to William Clifford*, Part I, Draft
      letter in Clifford's hand (no date).

The sending of this letter proved to be the lighting of the fuse. A papal explosion was soon to follow. Not only that, even the other bishops were to protest in writing at what they considered to be a unilateral disregard of recognised procedures.

Meanwhile, on March 18th Frederick Neve wrote to Clifford about a meeting he had had with Cardinal Barnabo:

> '. . . He said that the Pope had been made very angry at hearing that Dr. Errington's name might be sent up. That it would be an insult to him, as if to impute to him that it was simply to please the Cardinal that he was removed from Westminster, and it would be an insult also to suppose that the Pope would not select Errington, in spite of what had passed, if he thought he was the best man for the Post. He said that the highest interests of the Church would only be considered, likes and dislikes of the public would be disregarded, and that if you were selected they would count as nought the difficulties you mentioned.[50] Your being a Roman was in your favour, your youth was against you'.[51]

Neve turns his attention next to the current state of gossip in the *saloni* of Rome and the corridors of power at the Vatican:

> '. . . until the <u>Terna</u> comes, the choice seems to be between Dr. Ullathorne and your Lordship. As I suspected would be the case Odo Russell has been instructed to promote your nomination.'

(This was not entirely true. Although H.M. Government's first choice was Grant, Russell was perhaps trying to indicate that should Rome want either Ullathorne or Clifford, then in the view of his political masters there was no contest – Clifford was their man). Neve adds:

---

50   In the joint letter sent to Propaganda [see note 49] Clifford had written: '. . . and being his [Errington's] friends they [Clifford and Grant] feel greatly that his present position would be rendered more painful by his being put in postponed [*sic*] to men younger and inferior to himself'.

51   Clifton Diocesan Archives, *Letters to William Clifford*, Part I, Neve to Clifford, Letter dated 18.3.1865. The subsequent extracts are from this letter.

'Of course he [i.e. Russell] has no influence over more than
the gossip of the day.'

(But surely Neve, even if unaware of Russell's audience with the
Secretary of State, Cardinal Antonelli, must have known of the semi-
official status accorded to him by Her Majesty's Government?)

The current 'image' of Clifford as perceived in Rome at that time is
described by Neve. The term 'liberal' was not one which endeared itself
to the writer, and when he heard it being applied to his bishop and friend,
he had certain misgivings;

> ' . . . I lament that you are so misrepresented as a liberal, as
> the word means so much now, I know how it has happened,
> which I thought no one knew but myself. People say "that
> some one at Clifton has got round you and taken you in!"'

This may be an allusion to some mystery person. In general, however, it
would not be difficult to find the reasons for Clifford's acquiring such a
reputation. First there was his known attitude in favour of sending
Catholics to a Catholic college or hall at Oxford or Cambridge – a matter
debated by the bishops as recently as December, 1864 [52] and which would
be of considerable interest to the circle gathered in Rome and which
boasted Sir John Acton among its members. Another reason for calling
him liberal – some would have argued – might be deduced from his much
acclaimed Pastoral Letter of Lent, 1865, with its interpretation of *The
Syllabus of Errors*. In this instance it was Clifford's view of a document
which many regarded as supremely reactionary which won him favour
amongst the Catholic intelligentsia and which resulted in their wish to
see him in the See of Westminster. Indeed he would be their preferred
choice – even before Grant.

Frederick Neve, however, had his own particular insight as to why people
were claiming Clifford to be a liberal:

> 'It riles one to hear a man boast of his logical, silent thinking,
> superiorly instructed mind and to hear him drawing different

---

52   Cuthbert Butler, *The Life and Times of Bishop Ullathorne* (Publ.
      London, 1926), Vol. II, p. 10.

conclusions from the same premises according to the company he is seen in, but this I have seen and heard and to the party he belongs to claim you, more, I am sure, from what you have not said than what you have said'.[53]

– a remark which is strongly reminiscent of Canon Morris's 'it appears to me that his (i.e. Clifford's) reputation has been made by silence'.[54]

Neve sums up the fevered pitch of rumour and counter rumour then rife in Rome:

> 'But there are misrepresentations of everybody, and everything that can be picked up about people is being repeated about.'

But the most significant, and in the event prophetic, comment is reserved for the postscript:

> 'Cardinal Barnabo said besides that if Dr. Errington's name came in the Terna – The Pope would upset the whole paper and choose himself'.[55]

On 24th March the Bishops of England and Wales met in Birmingham to choose one name to put forward for Westminster. The result of the meeting was not made public. However, the next day the *Pall Mall Gazette* turned the attention of its readers to what the 'reliable' Roman correspondent of *John Bull* had to say. His account of the frenzied atmosphere in Rome, while confirming Clifford's being appointed to Westminster, differs in other respects from what Neve had to say:

---

53   Clifton Diocesan Archives, *Letters to William Clifford*, Part I, Neve to Clifford, Letter dated 18.3.1865.

54   Archives of the Venerable English College, Rome, *Talbot Papers*, Morris to Talbot, Letter dated 18.3.1865.

55   Clifton Diocesan Archives, *Letters to William Clifford*, Part I, Neve to Clifford, Letter dated 18.3.1865.

'. . . that the Hon. George Talbot . . . who will, notwithstanding, remain ln Rome will be created Cardinal (it being held desirable that at least one Englishman receives this dignity); and that the Right Rev. Monsignor Manning will be nominated Bishop of Clifton, with legatine powers, so that he will rank, after Dr. Clifford, first of the English Roman Catholic Bishops'.[56]

Fleet Street was indeed having a field day as the last prelate to enjoy legatine powers was Cardinal Pole.

By now the *terna* had reached Rome and the news had come out that Errington's name was on the list. Warned about this possibility the Pope, according to Neve, 'rose from his chair and said: "Heu Io Faccio Pio Nono" and that he would disregard the paper'.[57] Very succinctly Neve now reported to Clifford how the fortunes of the candidates had fared since February 15th:

'Before the cardinal's death Manning was at the top – then Dr. Ullathorne – then your Lordship and now that the funeral sermon is published here in Italian, Manning is at the top again'.[58]

What clearly emerges from Neve's letter is the anger aroused in Rome by the suggestion that Errington should be considered for Westminster and Clifford's part in aggravating that anger by sending what was seen as a quite unsolicited letter in his support:

'When I spoke to Barnabo, I did not say that you urged E's appointment because they are so angry about it here. I said that though you knew it was impossible yet that you regretted it, as he was a man so necessary for the occasion, etc. etc. according to your note to me. But have been told

---

56   *Pall Mall Gazette*, 25.3.1865.

57   Clifton Diocesan Archives, *Letters to William Clifford*, Part I, Neve to Clifford, Letter dated 25.3.1865.

58   *Ibid.*

today that you had written to Barnabo to press E's appointment. This version having got about Rome and the fact of Odo Russell busying himself about you have put you down lower in the list'.[59]

Three points are worthy of note:

1) that Clifford, knowing that Neve had the ear of Barnabo, wrote to him (Neve) so that at his next meeting with the Cardinal he might use the occasion to assuage the effect of the joint letter in which the two bishops had pressed the candidature of Errington.

2) Nothing seems to have been kept secret. Whether this was the common practice of the time would only be apparent from a study of the history of comparable appointments. At any rate, in the 1918 Code of Canon Law such discussions were to be placed firmly *sub sigillo*.

3) Neve is still under the impression that Odo Russell was pressing the cause of Clifford. If this were in fact the case, it may well have been a ploy by Russell to deflect attention from H.M. Government's true preference, Bishop Grant of Southwark.

But will the choice fall on Manning? Here Neve relies on rumour, presumably because Barnabo had said nothing either one way or the other about him:

'Unless Talbot is a little in favour of him I have not heard one Englishman here speak with any thing other than dislike of his i.e. Manning being selected. If by chance Talbot sh(oul)d have been named by the Chapter I should not be surprised if he was made to accept it and then perhaps Manning would be made my Protector! which would be a go!!' [60]

---

59   *Ibid.*

60   *Ibid*, i.e. Cardinal Protector to the English College where Neve held the post of Rector.

Clifford took umbrage at being described as a liberal and apparently raised the matter with Neve in his next letter. Neve assured him that it had nothing to do 'with the Westminster business' and that

> ... such a report ... has been set going by Sir J. Acton's party long ago, and has only turned up now In consequence of Odo Russell having supported you. But such an ideal report can do no harm'.[61]

Neve continues: 'No words can describe to you the excitement about the names sent up for the new Archbishop'.

The Pope's view was that

> 'both Chapter and Bishops ought to have ignored the name of a person whom he had removed from the office' (i.e. of coadjutor with right of succession)

and the very fact of their meeting to discuss a successor should have indicated that Errington was no longer *ipso iure* the Cardinal's successor. Those who defended the action of the Chapter were clutching at straws when they argued that, as the late Cardinal had never published the decree about Dr. Errington's removal, the Chapter only knew it officially from his papers found since his death. [62]

The whole business threw Pio Nono into a state of virtual frenzy. It is not generally known that the Pope had suffered from epilepsy, a condition which years before had raised doubts about his fitness even for ordination, and so any stressful situation was almost bound to render him volatile and unpredictable. He was greatly offended and 'wished to act immediately'. When Neve asked what he might be expected to do, he was told 'that in a somewhat similar case in France he once annulled the act of the Chapter and set them a penance'.[63] However, Neve continued,

---

61   Clifton Diocesan Archives, *Letters to William Clifford*, Part I, Neve to Clifford, Letter dated 4.4.1865.

62   *Ibid.*

63   *Ibid.* For the Pope's epilepsy see E.E.Y. Hales, *Pio Nono* (Publ. London, 1954), p. 19.

he was persuaded to allow the matter of Westminster to be considered by a special Congregation of Propaganda Cardinals and a report sent to him, but, Neve added

> 'I am told (on uncertain authority) that the Congregation met to consider not the naming of an Archbishop but how the Pope ought to meet the affront offered to him'.[64]

Warning Clifford that the Pope 'was very much disturbed', Neve said that 'there is very great emotion amongst the Cardinals on this account'. What follows must surely be significant in any appraisal not only of 'the Westminster business' but also of one who was to become the longest reigning Pope in the history of the Church.

> 'In the present critical state of public affairs, the people, official people that is, feel that perhaps their lives and property depend on the next act and very words of the Pope and they have really been quite frightened by his excited manner on the subject. Barnabo was quite frightened and on leaving the Pope after having read your letter he sought immediately for some Cardinals to go to the Pope to calm him. I am relating facts, not accounting for them. You are quite safe now at Clifton. – The paragraph in the *Times* had no foundation in anything that has been thought of here.[65] Individual Cardinals have uttered various opinions in society perhaps but only as suppositions'.[66]

---

64   *Ibid.*

65   *The Times*, 25.3.1865:

> THE ROMISH CHURCH IN ENGLAND – A reliable correspondent, who has recently received direct information from a well-informed source at Rome, writes that it is there reported that the present Bishop of Clifton, the Hon. William Joseph Hugh Clifford, D.D., will be immediately appointed Roman Catholic Archbishop of Westminster in place of the late Cardinal Wiseman.

> The report continued by saying that Mgr. George Talbot would be created a cardinal and that Manning would be nominated Bishop of Clifton 'with legatine powers'.

66   Clifton Diocesan Archives, *Letters to William Clifford*, Part I, Neve to Clifford, Letter dated 4.4.1865.

Now that the Pope seemed bent on ignoring all the names on the *terna*, Neve had no doubts in his own mind as to who would now try to turn the situation to their own advantage:

> 'I think it is probable that the *Legate* has been at work and that extracti statements have been poured into the Pope's ear all along, and that a certain person has been *used* for the purpose'.[67]

(The 'Legate' was Manning and, according to a favourite theory of Neve, Talbot was his tool).

By now Bishop Grant was aware of the repercussions of the joint letter he and Bishop Clifford had sent suggesting that Errington be appointed to Westminster. On 7th April Grant wrote to his co-signatory:

> 'You see our dilemma has come true, and we must only pray that whilst you and I escape, His Holiness may not feel that any insult was really intended, and may see everything in a way not likely to cause pain to his heart, amidst his many other trials'.[68]

On the reverse of this letter Clifford scribbled the following which may have formed the draft of his reply:

> The enclosure was from Canon Fisher [69] and said he had unpleasant news that morning (April 6) from Rome.
>
> Pope angry at Errington's name having been sent
>
> – so said Talbot
> – Martini (?) says all three names are equally objectionable
> – Pope and Barnabo greatly annoyed
> – Rumour says the Pope will appoint an Ap. Administrator for a time and then send Talbot.

---

67   *Ibid.*

68   Clifton Diocesan Archives, *Letters to William Clifford*, Part I, Grant to Clifford, Letter dated 7.4.1865.

69   Probably Canon John Henry Fisher, D.D., President of Saint Edward's College, Liverpool.

Whatever their views about the succession at Westminster, there can be no doubting that Clifford and Grant had a very warm – at times touching – affection for the person of the Pope. For all his imperfections they loved him, the more so because of all that he had suffered at the hands of his enemies. Clifford was very much his favoured son, personally chosen and consecrated by him. It was therefore very clearly not their wish to cause him distress or upset him in any way and yet, equally clearly, this was precisely what their joint letter had unwittingly achieved. Even before the appointment to Westminster was finally announced, Clifford felt that the time had come for mending fences. Accordingly he wrote a personal letter (in Italian) to Cardinal Barnabo, Prefect of Propaganda. After saying that he was in two minds whether to write, he had nevertheless decided to do so lest others be incriminated by his actions.

In his attempt to reassure the Cardinal, Clifford endeavoured to make several points clear:

1) He had not wished to give offence to the Holy Father, the Vicar of Christ, who had conferred on him so many favours including episcopal consecration.

2) The letter from Grant and himself 'fu opera esclusivamente di noi due'. The other bishops neither saw it nor were they aware of their intention of sending it.

3) Clifford and Grant had wished to maintain the practice already established that when the candidates were bishops, no preference should be stated. In this way the whole matter would be left to the judgement of the Holy See.

4) As regards the contents of 'that letter' only those who wrote it were responsible – much less the Chapter of Westminster who had already submitted their three names.

5) In composing the letter they had no intention of obstructing the will of the Holy Father: circumstances were now different from when Cardinal Wiseman was alive. By favouring Errington they were endeavouring to

promote the interests of the Church and of the Holy See.
In so far as the Holy See might view things differently,
they wholeheartedly submitted themselves to that
judgement.[70]

Almost three weeks were to pass before Clifford received a personal
letter of reassurance from Cardinal Barnabo. (The florid language
reflects the Italian original).

In acknowledging your letter of 28th April last which I
made it my duty quickly to lay before the Holy Father at
the audience immediately following, I must inform Your
Lordship that it was with pleasure that His Holiness read
the declaration (which was not made by way of complaint)
to the effect that your fellow bishops in the province had
no part in the letter which you and Mgr. Grant believed it
right to address on the subject of the terna forwarded
by the Chapter of Westminster and sent by the English
prelates to this Sacred Congregation.

As far as any protestation (of loyalty) is concerned that
it might be thought that His Holiness would wish to be
added to the said declaration, there is no reason why
this should be necessary as His Holiness is already in
possession of indubitable proofs given by you on other
occasions of whole – hearted deference and respect
towards the Apostolic See and towards the person of
His Holiness.

In the meantime I pray that the Lord may long preserve and
prosper you.[71] [My translation].

---

70   Clifton Diocesan Archives, *Letters to William Clifford*, Part I, draft of
      letter from Clifford to Barnabo dated 28.4.1865.

71   Ugbrooke Archives, *Letters to Bp. Clifford. 1865*, Barnabo to Clifford,
      Letter dated 17.5.1865.

But the Clifford/Grant saga was not to end there because, although their fellow bishops in the province had had no part in the original letter to Propaganda, they did nevertheless express their considerable unease when eventually they came to hear of it.

Bishop Brown of Newport, in his capacity as senior suffragan bishop of the province of Westminster, wrote a letter to Propaganda which was highly critical of the conduct of Clifford and Grant. (The letter, in Latin, appears in translation in Appendix I). Ironically it was written on the same day as the two Bishops had written their letter of explanation (see above). At the outset Brown makes it clear that each (*'singuli'*) of his colleagues had 'strongly urged' him to write to the Prefect without delay.

As in the case of Clifford's letter, the whole tone of the second half of Brown's communication is of an attempt to deflect the wrath of the Holy Father over the nomination of Errington. The first part, however, is a strong attack on Clifford and Grant for writing independently of their brother bishops in an effort to secure his (Errington's) nomination. Brown gives an account of what happened when the bishops assembled in Birmingham to decide on a name to be forwarded to Rome:

> When the minutes of the meeting of the Westminster Chapter had been read, I asked 'whether it would be right (lawful – 'liceret') for us to pass comment on the candidates?' Each of the bishops gave the same answer, saying that on previous occasions the bishops believed that they should say nothing about those candidates who were already in episcopal orders and that the matter should be left to the judgement of their only superior, the Supreme Pontiff'.[72]
>
> [My translation].

Bishop Brown then gives his reasons for the bishops' practice of maintaining silence when one or more of their number were being considered for a vacant see:

---

72   Birmingham Archdiocesan Archives, B. 4329: *Copy of Bp. of Newport's letter to Prop: on Meeting for designation of Metropolitan,* dated (in pencil) 28.4.1865. It is written in Latin. The handwriting is Ullathorne's.

1) The precedent they had followed, with Cardinal
   Wiseman in the chair, was that when there had been a
   proposal to nominate candidates to be considered for the
   post of Coadjutor Bishop of Beverley. They had discussed
   the relative merits of two priests but not those of Bishop
   Grant whose name had also been put forward.

2) This had been the practice followed by the
   Consistorial Congregation itself.

3) It seemed only right that the Pope himself should be the
   judge (i.e. when the candidates were already bishops).

Later in the letter Brown explains that this was the reason why 'no view
was expressed on the Archbishop of Trebizond.' 'It should not be construed
as an ungracious gesture towards the Supreme Pontiff'.

Brown's letter comes very close to asking the Cardinal Prefect to issue a
rebuke to Grant and Clifford:

> 'So complete was the agreement on this point that the
> Bishops of Southwark and Clifton should not have departed
> from it, nor should they have taken the liberty of discussing
> the merits of their colleagues. Afterwards these two bishops
> chose to send a letter to Your Eminence. In so doing they
> acted completely without our knowledge . . . and we were
> only informed of it when we received a communication from
> the Holy Father. [73]
>
> [My translation].

Not unnaturally Clifford sought to defend himself to Brown although in
his letter he somewhat disingenuously turned the argument and made it
revolve around the issue of a bishop's right to ask the Pope to leave him
in his present post.

> I am sorry that you should think that Dr. Grant and myself
> have given cause of complaint to the Bishops by making

---

73   *Ibid.*

known to the Holy Father our decided opposition to being removed to Westminster: but I think that that is a matter which entirely rested with our own conscience.

It appears to me that in no case has a Bp ever thought it necessary to consult the other Bps about whether or not he should give up his see for another.

The Chapter, and then the Bps may if they think proper, ask for anybody to be made Bishop. But (unless the Pope uses a precept) it will rest with the conscience of the individual whether he will accept or not.[74]

Clifford continues by saying that the bishops had acted correctly in their letter to Rome regarding the appointment itself, and that it was not their custom to comment to Rome about other bishops – a clear reference to their silence about Errington which Rome had not quite understood.

When we consider the many efforts made to keep up the irritation in the Pope's mind against Dr. Errington we need not be surprised at what has taken place.

– an apparent allusion to press reports that, on hearing the name of Errington being suggested for Westminster, the Pope fell into a rage. The letter ends on a conciliatory note. The Bishops, with Brown as their acting leader, are due to send a reply to Rome in answer to a previous communication which sought clarification of their views. Clifford suggests:

I think we should . . . add that since the Holy Father judges one of the nominees unfit, and has accepted the excuses of the other two – we leave the matter in his hands with perfect confidence.

---

74   Cardiff Archdiocesan Archives, *Letters to Bp. Brown*, Clifford to Brown, Letter dated 23.4.1865. This letter is a reply to one not quoted in this study. Nevertheless it is an attempt to answer the points raised by Brown and expressed by him a few days later in the letter to Propaganda.

Eventually an appointment to Westminster was made and the news spread rapidly that the former Archdeacon of Chichester, now Provost Manning, was to be the second Archbishop and Metropolitan. Again what is astonishing is the fact that there had been no attempt to observe secrecy in regard to the other candidates. The *Pall Mall Gazette* was typical of many newspapers and periodicals when it said:

> 'In making this appointment the Pope has, it is said, altogether passed over the nominations of the Roman Catholic Chapter of Westminster . . . Dr. Clifford . . . Dr. Grant . . . Dr. Errington'.[75]

Two days later the *Pall Mall*, quoting *The Times*, was even more specific when it informed its readers that both Grant and Clifford

> 'sent to Rome such a sincere and strong *nolo episcopari*, or rather *nolo archiepiscopari*, that neither of them could be appointed . . . Dr. Manning was chosen as being one of the most accomplished and distinguished men among the Roman Catholic clergy. We are informed that this is the true reason why Dr. Grant and Dr. Clifford were passed over'.[76]

In 1881 *The Whitehall Review* published a series of articles on the current state of the Catholic Church in England. One such contribution was entitled 'Cardinal Manning and His Suffragans'. Re-telling the now well-known story of how Grant and Clifford had declined to be considered so as to favour the cause of Errington, the writer continued:

> 'Pius IX was furious. He sent for Monsignor Talbot and said: "These English bishops cannot know their catechism. They have so far forgotten their respect for my person as to send up to Cardinal Barnabo the name of Monsignor Errington, whom I deposed. I shall be forced by events to nominate Monsignor Manning."

---

75   *Pall Mall Gazette*, 9.5.1865.

76   *Pall Mall Gazette*, 11.5.1865.

Shortly after this incident some English pilgrims had an audience with the impulsive Pontiff, and the conversation naturally turned on the vacant arch-bishopric. Pio Nono jocularly placed the pilgrims in a line like school boys, and asked each one who was the holiest and most learned ecclesiastic in England. The name of John Henry Newman rose to every lip. One young man, however, mentioned Dr. Manning, and the Pope answered with a smile: "I am inclined to send you to the top of the class, my friend: but I am sorely puzzled and must pray for guidance'".[77]

In the Archives at Ugbrooke there are four letters which appear to have lain undisturbed over the years and yet throw considerable light on the appointment of Manning to Westminster and subsequent repercussions. They were written by Neve and by Grant, and two by Errington.

Neve in a footnote calls his communication 'gossip which is at least drawn from authentic sources'. [78]

English College, Rome 9 May 1865

My dear Lord Bishop,

....

Private. So you have got a Metropolitan. Propaganda is delighted, and call him Homo missus a Deo to convert England. The series of events seems to have been as follows, understand *Videtur* at head of each line. When it was rumoured that the Chapter would send up Dr. E's name, people at Propaganda were alarmed and urged that it should be prevented if possible; it was arranged that Fr. Weld should write as an indifferent person (?). Very – Talbot wrote also.

---

77   *The Whitehall Review*, 3.2.1881.

78   Ugbrooke Archives, *Letters to Bp. Clifford. 1865*, Neve to Clifford, Letter dated 9.5.1865.

After the Chapter meeting it seems that Monsr. Franchi
wrote to a Bishop saying that there could be no objection in
recommending Dr. E. (though Nardi is the only person I have
heard to be of this opinion he is looked upon here as less
than –) Before the Bishops letters came, your Lordship was
first favourite and you would have been named, Card.
Antonelli pressing it very much. Everyone amongst the
Romans regretting very much that it could not be so, the
Pope also saying I have known him from a boy, I consecrated
him myself, how could he be drawn into such a mistake –
then the three names were set aside.

For a very considerable time it was certain that it would be
Birmingham, for a very short time Liverpool, and for some
time Beverley – Then at the end of the second week after
Easter the Pope could not put Manning's name out of his
head, and on 30 April Manning was decided on'.

(Shane Leslie quotes the Pope as saying to Manning 'I always heard a
voice saying, "Put him there, put him there"'). [79]

Apparently the news broke in Turin and London before the official
communication had reached Manning. With an apparent sigh of
resignation Neve ends his letter to Clifford:

'Like others I have my own opinion but hope all will turn out
for the best'.

There is some evidence to suggest that Pio Nono was contemplating
disciplinary action against the Westminster Chapter, probably along the
lines of that meted out to the Chapter in France. On May 29th Grant wrote
as follows to Clifford:

---

79   Shane Leslie, *Henry Edward Manning: His Life and Labours* (Publ.
London, 1921), p. 149.

My dear Lord,

I have written to Dr. Errington, trying to dissuade him from writing to Rome, alleging that as the decision of H.H. about the Chapter has not yet been given, any letter on his part will only render such decision more severe in their regard.

I saw a letter last week in which the Propag. still qualifies the conduct of the Chapter as *meno delicata e poco prudente*.

He will not benefit the Chapter by writing again to Rome at this time.

Yours in Xt

+ T Grant [80]

What Propaganda was saying about the Chapter might be freely translated: 'lacking in good taste and short on prudence'. Given the Pope of the day, few would quarrel with that verdict.

The remaining two letters at Ugbrooke were both penned by Dr. Errington. These show a prelate, gracious in defeat, acknowledging the act of self-sacrifice by which both Grant and Clifford had endeavoured to further his nomination to Westminster. There is, interestingly, a gap of ten days between the letters, both of which were sent from Ballynahinch in Cashel.

---

80   Ugbrooke Archives, *Letters to Bp Clifford, 1865*, Grant to Clifford, Letter dated 29.5.1865.

To Dr. Grant he wrote:

May 24, 1865

My dear Lord

> Though I have no direct information on the subject, I cannot
> doubt, from what I hear from friends in Rome, and from the
> newspapers at home that there is substantial truth in the
> reports that you and Dr. Clifford sacrificed yourselves to
> further my restoration.
>
> Though extremely sorry for the result, I must say that I
> never felt so deeply any act of kindness; and were I not sure
> that in whatever you did, you acted from principle, and care
> only as far as this life is concerned for the content which the
> consideration that you did so brings with it, I should much
> regret that in my position at any time of life it would be
> foolish in one to hope for the opportunity of expressing
> otherwise than by thanks and good wishes my appreciation
> of the course you followed.
>
>> Hoping God may reward you
>>
>> I remain
>>
>> Yours sincerely
>>
>> Geo Errington [81]

A lengthy postscript in which he declares his intention of fighting to clear
his name is written as an afterthought.

Having at one time served as his Vicar General, Clifford enjoyed a closer
relationship than Grant with the Archbishop. This probably explains why,
in writing to Clifford, Errington is more forthcoming both as to how he
viewed the appointment of Manning and as to the possible consequences

----

81   Ugbrooke Archives, *Letters to Bp. Clifford, 1865*, Errington to Grant,
      Letter dated 24.5.1865.

which 'that letter' might have for Clifford. There is a sense of bitterness not far below the surface – a sentiment quite lacking in the shorter letter to Bishop Grant. To Clifford he wrote (June 3rd, 1865):

'. . . I cannot tell you how deeply I felt this act of kindness when I first heard it on credible authority during the Sede Vacante; but its value is much greater now that it stands as a testimonial to prevent or rebut the aspersions which the concomitants of the new appointment are calculated to confirm or originate. Though my obligation to your self sacrifice is not lessened, my regret for its first apparent consequence is much weakened by the conviction that you would not have liked the change from Clifton to Westminster; and even if you would prefer a wider field for work you are young enough to see very altered times, and the days when Westminster will present fewer difficulties and disagreeables, if it pleases Providence to call you to it. The 2d result of the course you have followed, viz the dissatisfaction it may have given at headquarters, I should consider more serious, as it might interfere with the wellbeing and business of your diocese on some occasions; but I do not think the dissatisfaction can be real, or, at least, lasting for it has no grounds, and indeed is inexplicable unless we suppose it to arise from annoyance at the onus having been thrown upon Rome of carrying out by force a predetermined appointment which it was hoped to effect sine sensu, and if possible through the regular organisation of appointments. This hypothesis receives additional weight from the reflection that there appears no real, nor even conventional, reason why you or Dr. Grant should not have been appointed if Rome thought fit.

With renewed thanks, and hopes that your kindness may not have any permanent disagreeable results . . .' [82]

---

82   Ugbrooke Archives, *Letters to Bp. Clifford, 1865*, Errington to Clifford, Letter dated 3.6.1865.

To be fair, there is no evidence of there having been any repercussions either for Bishop Clifford or for his diocese. Even so, in reading this letter – as with the letter from Grant in which he speaks of the possibility of action being taken against the Westminster Chapter – the scenario one is presented with is of a style of church government presided over by a Pope who is both volatile and unpredictable. These characteristics of Pio Nono will show themselves again in the Vatican Council, particularly when during the debates voices are raised advising caution in both the extent and the wording of the proposed definition of papal infallibility.

Clifford's reply to Archbishop Errington affords us a summary of his thinking on the whole Westminster affair:

Clifton, June 5th, 1865

My dear Lord

> I thank you very much for your kind letter. Dr. Grant and myself thought that the course we adopted was the only one we could rightfully adopt under the circumstances, and nothing has occurred to make us alter our opinion. The number of those who know the ins and outs of the case are few, but amongst these almost all for whose opinion we should care think we have done right.

> There are indeed some who think we did not act wisely, because there was little chance of Rome restoring you, and therefore the course we adopted could only render the appointment of Manning or Talbot certain. This however is a course of reasoning I cannot adopt – Lord Clifford said to me at once when I told him of what had happened – but surely they could not expect that either you or Grant would do otherwise than refuse to be put in competition with Errington –

> As for any harm that may come to me I apprehend none. Seeing that Rome was angry with the Bishops, I wrote to Barnabo to tell him that the letter written by Dr. Grant and myself was entirely our own act, the other Bishops not having been informed of it, and that we accepted the whole

responsibility of what we had done though we felt confident that his Eminence knew us too well to suppose that by giving our views on such a matter, we intended in any way to oppose or gainsay the Authority of the Holy See –

Barnabo wrote back that he had shown my letter to the Pope and that I need not be any apprehension (*sic*) of my sentiments regarding the Holy see being misunderstood – That puts me right in court, and it must be the interest of the Holy See to conciliate the Bishops now that it has carried its point.

How things will go on time alone can show – but I say *nondum statim finis.*

. . . .

+ William Clifford [83]

It is more than likely that with hindsight Clifford would have agreed with the verdict of history that Manning's going to Westminster was a success. Two things however worried him greatly. The first was the cavalier way in which the Pope, having seen the name of Errington on the list of candidates, chose there and then to disregard all recognised procedures and to act quite independently. The second was that the affair had become public knowledge with some alarmingly accurate reports, notably in *The Spectator*, informing the whole of England, Protestant and Catholic alike, of the very odd way in which Rome chose (at least one of) its Archbishops. Not for one moment would Clifford have questioned the right of the Supreme Pontiff to appoint whomsoever he might wish. The point was that he could foresee the 'image' which the Pope's behaviour would create in the public mind, and the consequent danger of the Holy See bringing itself into culpable disrepute.

These worries were conveyed to Neve even before Manning's appointment had been announced:

---

83 Clifton Diocesan Archives, *Errington Papers*, No. 90, Clifford to Errington, Letter dated 5.6.1865.

> *The Spectator* and other protestant papers have a full
> account of the three names sent up to the Pope and . . . that
> since Errington's name was there he would have nothing to
> do with any of the other names. [84]

Clifford is afraid that this would 'render an impression in the public mind'
that the appointment of the archbishop 'depends not on the merits' of the
individual concerned but on 'feelings' and that

> if these impressions gain ground it will do great damage to
> religion and to the Holy See both amongst Catholics and
> Protestants . . . People on all sides are ridiculing the conduct
> of the Holy See . . . But I earnestly pray God . . . that whoever
> is ultimately appointed archbishop, his appointment may be
> made in such a way as to show the world that personal
> feeling has had nothing to do with it. [85]

When the manner of Manning's appointment became known, and the
events which preceded it, there was a series of 'post mortems' in letters
exchanged between the various parties involved in the affair.

Bishop Brown of Newport was particularly bitter and his long letter of
complaint against Clifford and Grant has already been noted. In
forwarding to Clifford a copy of the official announcement of Manning's
nomination, Brown added a postscript:

> 'I am glad that there are others besides myself who regret
> the resignation of yourself and Dr. Grant without allowing us
> to consult with you. Your resignations were laughed at'. [86]

---

84   Venerable English College, Rome, *Talbot Papers*, Clifford to Neve, Letter
      dated 10.4.1865.

85   *Ibid.*

86   Ugbrooke Archives, *Letters to Bp. Clifford, 1865*, Brown's comments
      are added as a postscript to a copy of the letter from Propaganda, signed
      by Barnabo, announcing to the English bishops that Manning had been
      appointed to Westminster. Date of Propaganda letter: 2.5.1865. Clifford
      noted that he had received the communication 11.5.1865.

Errington, too, was surprised at the inside knowledge displayed by various journals when writing of the appointment:

> 'I have just heard that the writer in the *Pall Mall* on Catholic affairs is a Mr. Higgins who married a Tichbourne – I remember on some former occasion having seen an article in the same paper shewing more Catholic knowledge than I could understand. The outline view is not far amiss if we wash off the Protestant colouring. The errors of detail are annoying, as when he says I was cast upon every count, when in reality, as you may remember, the Pope himself gave his word that no judgement should be passed without intercommunication etc. etc. but appears from the whole piece that the personal part is an affair of no moment, and would not be attended to by the public'. [87]

Turning to the Westminster Chapter and their submission of his name on the *terna*, Errington comments:

> 'I hope to find an opportunity when it will not be dangerous to do so, of shewing that nothing of which the Chapter could take cognizance had occurred from which the Chapter could know that my being named could be offensive to the Pope. I can understand that the Pope in the midst of his troubles could forget, and imagine that he had declared his objections to me on other grounds than those of incompatibility (which ceased with the death of the Cardinal), but Cardinal Barnabo could hardly forget, after all the pains he took to prove to me that the decree of removal ought to be taken as the pure and simple exponent of the Pope's mind'. [88]

What might be seen as Errington's verdict on the whole Westminster affair, and Clifford's part in that, is contained in the final sentence:

---

87   Ugbrooke Archives, *Letters to Bp. Clifford, 1865,* Errington to Clifford, Letter dated 13.6.1865.

88   *Ibid.*

'Thanks to all that has now taken place especially to the
part you and Dr. Grant have acted I now stand well by the
whole affair [it] having assumed a political instead of
personal aspect'.[89]

The friendship between Errington and Clifford lasted until death, and
letters were exchanged when Rome endeavoured to persuade Errington
to accept other dignities. During the celebrated interview with Pio Nono
in 1860 the Pope had offered him the Archbishopric of Trinidad. In 1868
Manning was approached by the Holy See with a view to persuading
Errington to become Apostolic Administrator in Scotland. This would
have involved the laying of the foundations of a new Hierarchy and his
eventual appointment as Archbishop of Edinburgh.

True to character Errington consulted Clifford, but indicated a certain
reluctance because:

1) It would appear as demotion;

2) He sought reparation for his removal from office;

3) Being now sixty-four he felt that his age was against
him. [90]

Clifford and Grant, however, thought otherwise and counselled
acceptance, Grant arguing that if Errington became Primate of Scotland
this would be promotion, and honour would thereby be satisfied.[91]

---

89   *Ibid.*

90   Clifton Diocesan Archives, *Letters to William Clifford*, Part I, Letter
dated 10.3.1868.

91   Southwark Archdiocesan Archives, *Letters to Bp. Grant*, Clifford to
Grant, Letter dated 13.3.1868. It is hard to see why it should be thought
that Scotland might be given a Primate even though none had been
appointed in England. In the event no church leader in either country
has been granted this dignity. As a Primate at the First Vatican Council,
Errington would have taken precedence over Manning who did not
receive the red hat until 1875.

The Archbishop, however, persisted and declined all suggestions that he be appointed to Scotland. He later ministered at Douglas in the Isle of Man and then, when Bishop Clifford re-opened Prior Park, he accepted his friend's invitation to become the Professor of Theology. There he died in 1886 respected and loved by all. A short time after his death Bishop Clifford wrote of his grief to the Father Provincial of the English Jesuits:

> 'I feel his loss very much for we were very great friends and had been so for 34 years'.[92]

It should be noted, finally, that Clifford himself was an unrivalled judge of human character. He knew both Cardinal Wiseman and Archbishop Errington and was able to observe both men closely as he served with them on the bench of bishops. In the funeral oration which he preached at Prior Park during the Requiem Mass for Errington, he gave as it were a thumb-nail sketch of the contrasting characters of these two not inconsiderable churchmen:

> 'One great feature in the character of Archbishop Errington was that he was not only always led by a strong sense of duty, which was with him paramount to all other considerations, but he always went straight to the point; and having once made up his mind as to what in his view ought to be done, he suffered no obstacle to deter him from the course resolved upon. He acquired the name of the "Iron Archbishop". This quality of mind, most valuable in itself, was not always accompanied with an equal appreciation of the difficulties to be encountered and of allowances to be made.
>
> Nobody knew better or more highly valued Archbishop Errington's sturdy character than Cardinal Wiseman. But the Cardinal had a greater feeling for the weaknesses of men, and was more disposed to meet opposition by striving to bend it than to break it. He was also more sensitive of obstacles, and suffered much when compelled to encounter

---

92   Archives of the English Province of the Society of Jesus, Mount Street, *Letters to the Provincial* (Father E. J. Purbrick, S.J.), Nos. 154, 155. Clifford to Purbrick, Letter dated 4.2.1886.

them. The character of these two men both highly gifted, both highminded, and both holding each other's qualities in high esteem – was essentially different. The difference up to a certain point had the effect of making them feel the advantage of mutual co-operation, and so of drawing them nearer to each other; but there was always danger of rupture, and that rupture occurred at last . . . ' [93]

The Archbishop's charity received the following tribute:

'Never was he heard to utter an unkind word in reference to anybody connected with those disputes'.

In a letter to Clifford, Newman said of him: 'He was a most saintly man'.[94]

George Errington was laid to rest in the portico of Prior Park.[95] Next to him is the body of William Clifford.

---

93   *A Discourse Delivered at the Funeral of George Errington Archbishop of Trebizond and First Bishop of Plymouth In the Church of Prior Park College* by William Clifford, Bishop of Clifton on the 26th January, 1886. Clifford used the occasion to state publicly: 'On two subsequent occasions (i.e. after his removal from the coadjutorship of Westminster) the Holy Father offered to appoint him to the government of important Archiepiscopal Sees.'

94   Clifton Diocesan Archives, *Letters to William Clifford*, Part II, Newman to Clifford, Letter dated 23.1.1886.

95   In 1881 Errington had told Clifford that he wished to be buried in Plymouth Cathedral. (Clifton Diocesan Archives, *Clifford Diary, 1881*, December 21st).

PREAMBLE TO CHAPTERS 7 – 11

The calling of the First Vatican Council was the result of a political as well as of a pastoral expediency. A new sense of identity was emerging among the nations of Europe and with it a certain 'flexing of muscles' as they began to test their relationship with the Catholic Church. Gallicanism was the product of an independent spirit within the French Church. The primacy of the See of Rome was indeed acknowledged, but it was felt that the ties which bound a particular church to that See should be kept to a theological minimum. Conversely, the See of Rome, in the face of such nationalistic tendencies, felt it incumbent to underline both its spiritual hegemony and its independence by maintaining its own political identity. This was the rationale behind the concept of the Papal States although there were those who would quarrel with the physical extent of those territories.

For Manning and others, however, the power of the Pope had itself to be buttressed by something far more enduring – a power which was both moral and spiritual and which would be a symbol of papal independence even though the one in whom that power resided might even on occasion be held captive. [1] For this reason the definition by the Council of Papal Infallibility was as much a gesture in the political arena as a proclamation of religious faith.

What is evident In the speeches of Manning and Clifford as they argued their respective positions in the council is their contrasting analyses of the situation then prevailing in England. For the Archbishop, Rationalism was the enemy at the door. This was at the root of his objection to Catholics attending Oxford – the home, as he saw it, of all that was intellectually irreligious. Manning saw it as incumbent upon the Church that she proclaim herself to be that fount of religious certainty for which he believed the people were thirsting. From this it followed that the Pope must be seen as the clear voice of the Church diffused throughout the world.

---

1   Jeffrey P. von Arx, S.J., 'Manning's Ultramontanism and the Catholic Church in British Politics', *Recusant History*, Vol. 19, No.3, p. 332.

'The infallibilist party', wrote Hasler, 'together with the Pope, was hoping to use it (papal infallibility) to change the whole climate of opinion in society. The principle of authority, they thought, would counteract the principles of the French Revolution – the cause of all the contemporary social unrest'.[2]

Clifford, however, viewed the same situation but from a perspective that was quite different. The Pope as tyrant was the view of the man in the street. Witness, he argued, the spirit of Anti-popery which twenty years after the re-establishment of the Hierarchy was still not dead. Any definition of Papal Infallibility – no matter how worded – would do nothing but confirm this popular perception of the Church of Rome and of its leader.

The definition confirmed within the Church a principle that was strongly monarchical, and historians, enjoying the benefit of hindsight, have seen 1870 as the year in which subsequent papal autocracy was legitimised. Pius X (1903 – 1914) and Modernism, Pius XI (1922 – 1939) and the Action Française would be illustrations of this. On the other hand it could be argued that it was precisely this sort of world that the Church of the late 19th century was about to enter – the world of Bismarck, and later of Franco, of Salazar, of Mussolini and of Hitler. Unfortunately some prelates, like Cardinal Innitzer of Vienna, got it wrong and saw National Socialism as a valid political expression of that same principle. Even so, much could be said in favour of the strong papal rule of, say, Pius XI and Pius XII.

Political considerations aside, the First Vatican Council must still be seen as a church-event. General Councils are summoned for the purpose of discussing pastoral problems with a view to suggesting ways in which the Gospel may be more effectively proclaimed. Internal problems must of necessity be very much to the fore and debates took place which dealt with two critical areas of church life – the spiritual well-being of the clergy and the education of the young. On both of these issues Clifford was to speak at some length. In fact it should be noted that his total contribution at the Council far exceeded that of all the other English bishops combined.

---

2   August Bernhard Hasler, *How the Pope became Infallible: Pius IX and the Politics of Persuasion* (Publ. New York, 1981, trans.), p. 52.

At the heart of the whole saga of the Vatican Council is the personality – and indeed the sanity – of Pope Pius IX. Both Hans Kung[3] and Hasler have made the point in trenchant manner with the latter twice quoting Bishop Clifford:

> When Bishops Clifford, Ramadié and Place protested against the highly offensive language the Pope had used in speaking of them at public audiences, he denied the whole thing.[4]

> The Pope's intellectual capacities were deteriorating. "He no longer has any memory from one day to the next", remarked Bishop William Clifford. Many bishops spoke of him as an old man in his second childhood.[5]

Hasler's book on the Council was written some forty years after Cuthbert Butler's *Vatican Council*. It is highly critical – as was Bishop Clifford – of the freedom which should be a pre-requisite of any Council of the Church, but Hasler goes even further and questions whether the subsequent 'reception' of the dogma by the Universal Church was in fact a valid reason for recognising its truth. When writing to Newman, Clifford had argued that for him such reception settled the matter.[6] Theologically, of course, this would be the case, but Hans Kung argues that much of it was under pressure:

> All the books put on the Index, the dismissals, the sanctions and excommunications, all the manipulative and repressive methods used by the Curia and the nuncios, the threats, surveillance, and denunciations, and last of all, the Old Catholic schism and the "interior emigration" of so many Catholics, especially theologians and educated people: All this makes it seem perfectly justified to ask whether the definition of infallibility passed by this Council ever got anything like a free "reception".[7]

---

3   Hans Kung, *Infallibility? An Inquiry* (Publ. New York, 1981, trans.).

4   Hasler, *op. eit.*, p. 12l. No sources given.

5   Hasler, *op. cit.*, p. 124. No sources given.

6   *Vide infra*, pages 196-198, 204.

7   Introduction to Hasler, *op. cit.*, p. 14.

Clifford hinted as much in his letter to Mgr. Bonomi, V.G. (Appendix 5) but his allegations refer to events during, rather than after, the Council.

The political repercussions of the Definition were considerable. Bismarck's *Kulturkampf* in Germany, with its ruthless suppression of Church rights and privileges, drew a vigorous response from Manning in his inaugural address to the Academia in 1873. In this he took 'Caesarism' to task for presuming to demand for the State a supreme allegiance which, he argued, belonged properly to God and by derivation to His Church. The lecture gave rise to a lengthy correspondence with Sir James Fitzjames Stephen in the pages of the *Contemporary Review*. [8]

In England, too, Gladstone envisaged problems which he expounded to the full in his two pamphlets *The Vatican Decrees in their bearing on Civil Allegiance* and *Vaticanism: An Answer to Replies and Reproofs*. Not least of these was the *volte face* which he alleged the Catholic community had performed since the *Protestation* of 1778. [9] For his part, Clifford was to answer the theological issues with some ease, but the objections based on historical fact were to prove a more formidable problem.

The Catholic Church, like its Founder, is both human and divine, and the turbulent nine months during which the Council was sitting served only to make evident the unacceptable (human) face of the Church. But why did Clifford and others like him not secede? The answer is to be found in his Faith which told him that, warts and all, the Catholic Church is still the Body of Christ.

---

8   James Fitzjames Stephen: 'Caesarism and Ultramontanism', *Contemporary Review*, 23, (March and May, 1874).

9   *Vide infra*, pp. 254, 255, 261, 262.

CHAPTER SEVEN

Debate on the Life of the Clergy

The bull convening the Council had given specific directions to the bishops that they were to deal with questions relating to the discipline of the clergy. The world, and with it the Church, had changed considerably in the three hundred years that had elapsed since the Council of Trent (1545 – 1563). The Industrial Revolution had changed the life-style of millions of people and so had the resulting urbanisation of many parts of the countryside. From this the Holy Father had concluded that a General Council would be the most suitable forum in which to conduct a thorough examination of the life and ministry of priests, and in particular of the secular clergy.

An opportune time for doing this came when the schema on Catholic Doctrine was sent back to the Deputation *de Fide* to be recast, taking into account the observations which had been made by the Council Fathers. However, as Cuthbert Butler observed, 'the disciplinary schemata were subjected to the same fire of criticism as the dogmatic schema'.[1] During the fortnight from January 25th to February 8th there were some thirty-eight speeches in the council chamber and they ranged freely over a whole variety of topics – even the wearing of beards – concerned with the life and ministry of the clergy.

Two of the most important addresses, before Clifford spoke, came from Cardinal von Schwarzenberg, Archbishop of Prague, and from the Primate of Hungary, Archbishop Simor. In later debates the former was to prove to be an ally of Clifford and an Inopportunist, but even in this debate there was a clue to his later stand when he complained that in the present schema no indication was given as to the true status of a bishop – i.e. that he was a successor of the Apostles. This was an important point, not only theologically, but also canonically because it meant that much of the present regulatory and disciplinary work of bishops was being carried on using powers delegated by Rome whereas – he argued – bishops already enjoyed them as 'ordinary' powers by virtue of episcopal consecration and appointment. Clifford was to make the same point.

---

1   Cuthbert Butler, *The Vatican Council 1869 - 1870* (Publ. Fontana paperback, 1962), p. 188.

The other significant speech (from the Primate of Hungary) introduced the question of the recitation of the Divine Office and the much-hoped-for revision of the Roman Breviary. This too was a matter about which Clifford would have something to say.

It was on February 3rd, 1870, that Clifford addressed the Fathers for the first time. As we shall see it was a speech which was to be well received. He began by warning the bishops against entering into too much detail in the decisions they took:

> In my view what we must bear in mind above all else is that we are meeting in a general council – not a provincial council, still less a diocesan synod. Therefore the laws which we pass must be such as to pertain to the universal church or else principles from which particular (local) Churches may derive their laws. Therefore it seems to me that things which have been said by many of the Fathers, though excellent in themselves, are not in any way appropriate to what should be said in this council. [My translation. Full text is printed in Appendix 6].

Ironically this was a complaint which was to be echoed by Clifford's successor, Bishop Joseph Rudderham, at Vatican II. He wrote during the discussion on the Sacred Liturgy:

> Mon. Nov. 12
>
> A number of small points were discussed at interminable length . . . have we really come all this way to talk about these minor points?
>
> Tues. Nov. 13
>
> The protracted waffle about trivialities continued – 'again, why ARE WE HERE?' [2]

---

2   Clifton Diocesan Archives, Bp. Joseph Rudderham, *The Second Vatican General Council* (unpublished manuscript), pp. 43, 44.

Clifford's point, however, was more serious in the sense that he was afraid that legislation might be passed which did not take into account local customs and circumstances. He illustrated this by referring to the making of spiritual exercises – 'When?' 'how much' – but with even more point by decrying the suggestion that priests should be forbidden to practise medicine:

> Some have said that we must prohibit priests from practising medicine. In general this is true, but there are seminaries, founded with the authority of the Pope for the work of the foreign missions, in which priests are very definitely taught the principles of medicine because this is necessary for them in their missions. And do we wish to pass a law which would go against this state of affairs? [My translation].

His third example by way of warning against rushing into laws that were too specific referred to females living in the priest's house. Here he made reference to the situation in England where a housekeeper was frequently to be found looking after one or more priests:

> But if the most reverend fathers think that, once a law has been passed prohibiting a priest from having anyone except men in his house, this of itself guarantees the good name of the priest, I know for certain that this is not the case. For it often happens that much greater scandals and more serious difficulties arise from the fact of young people (married or unmarried) living in the houses of priests than if there were living in the house a woman who was respectable and well known among those people where the priest, too, was living. And I am sure that in England, where parents often send their daughters to schools run by Catholics, they would not do so if they were aware that in the priest's house there were also living ordinary young people who looked after the priest. [My translation].

Bishop Clifford's final criticism was levelled against those who wanted to make laws about 'the bigger and richer benefices'. He thought them to be in fact so rare that he chided the Bishop of the Canary Islands: 'In our times it would be difficult to find a golden apple even in the Hesperides.' He continued: 'Were we to pass such a law, I think it would appear more of a harsh irony than a pastoral correction'.

His negative points out of the way, Clifford addressed himself to the fundamental principle that the priesthood is a vocation to perfection – a point made earlier by the Archbishop of Strigonia. But he had misgivings about the use of the term 'secular' as applied to the clergy. He said:

> The fashion grew up of speaking of the *secular* clergy: so much so that often both priests and people think that priests belong to this world and that they are not called to the inheritance of the Lord, not called to perfection. It is wholly necessary, and part of the duty of this council, that priests and people be educated regarding the dignity, the holiness and the perfection of that Office.
> [My translation].

It is hard to understand Clifford's dislike of the term 'secular'. It was of course introduced to distinguish diocesan clergy from the members of religious orders, but was it really true that the term (from the Latin *seculum* meaning age, world) misled priests and people into believing that a secular priest was not only in the world but of it as well?

On incorrigible priests Clifford had much to say. 'It is now a very great evil in the Catholic Church, and it is getting worse from day to day'.

> I am absolutely certain in my own mind that the ancient discipline should be restored. If bad monks are expelled from a monastery, why shouldn't bad priests be expelled from the clergy? Most reverend fathers, what is worse is that if a bad monk, who is a priest, is expelled from his monastery, he does not join the ranks of the laity but the ranks of the secular clergy, and so we are left carrying not only our own ills but also the ills of others.
> [My translation].

He spoke forcefully about the situation in England where a bishop is unable to help financially in the support of a priest in a small mission simply because he may have two or three priests who, though suspended, can still claim '*sustentatio*' from him. They are forbidden to do manual work and yet they use up resources which could help provide a priest in a remote mission.

> I say that when a priest, after many attempts at correction
> does not reform, then, after due process of law, he should be
> expelled from the ranks of the clergy, should be regarded as
> completely secularised . . . in no way should he again
> exercise the office and ministry of priest . . . But we must not
> deprive such good catholics of the means of religion merely
> because he wishes to lead an evil life.
> [My translation].

Clifford added that a prohibition should be issued forbidding other bishops
from readmitting priests in the secular state to the ranks of the clergy.

The *Missa pro Populo* – to be said each Sunday and Holyday – should be
said by all who have the care of souls and not just by parish priests. This
was the mind of the Çouncil of Trent but, conceding that *'finis legis non
est lex'* he pointed out that the law needed to be changed as at the moment
it referred only to parish priests (in the strict canonical sense of that
term). In England until 1907 there were no properly constituted parishes
but only 'missions' and it was the 'missionaries apostolic' (as they were
called) that Clifford wished to see included in the obligation to offer Mass
for their people. In a probable reference to his own diocese he said:

> And certainly amongst ourselves there has been no little
> scandal from the decree which we published in which it is
> stated that priests amongst us are not bound to offer Mass
> for the people: a scandal to both priests and people.
> [My translation].

The Divine Office was the next subject that he touched upon. The bull
summoning the Council referred to the dignity of divine worship and,
Clifford argued, this must mean that the breviary be subjected to
conciliar scrutiny. This is how he saw the problem:

> And we hear priests sometimes saying: I must say it (i.e. the
> breviary) quickly otherwise I shall have no time for prayer.
> How is this? Is not that the very prayer which the Church
> has given you? Is it not true that from the most ancient
> times, even in the Old Law and much more in the New, the
> psalter was the treasure-house for all prayer? Do we not
> read in the lives of the saints that when someone wished to

advance in the spiritual life, the first requirement was that
he should be able to recite the psalter by heart? And indeed
we have been given the whole psalter printed in our
breviary, but in practice no one ever recites the psalter
during the course of a year. [My translation].

His solution, coupled with a proposal that a Pontifical Commission be set
up for the revision of the breviary, was as follows:

We must put into their hands a book which is so ordered that
they can recite the psalter each week, and so arranged that,
without repetitions, they can do it with ease. If we do this
then it is most certain that within a year of ordination, or at
the most two years, all priests will know the psalter by heart:
and this would be of greater assistance to them in prayer
and meditation than any other means that we might provide.
[My translation].

But he was equally concerned that the proposed reform should
encompass other parts of the Scriptures:

If the scriptures were to be so arranged in the breviary that
priests would read the whole bible within a year, then they
would know the scriptures, and by this means it would
become a great assistance to them in prayer, meditation,
spiritual reading and in their preaching.

In the event no revision of the breviary came from the council, but
Clifford's wish to see the entire psalter recited each week was realised in
St. Pius X's reform of the breviary (1911 – 1913).

But even that revised breviary was seen not to meet the needs of the
clergy, particularly of those involved in pastoral work, and so the matter
came up for discussion yet again at Vatican II. Bishop Rudderham,
writing almost a century after Clifford, presents a familiar picture.

Wed. 7 Nov.

De Divino Officio

The main ideas put forward were:

Vernacular with Breviary
– by permission of the Bishop, said some

Psalter spread over longer time than a week
– some wanted 'vindictive' Psalms omitted

Obligation '*sub gravi*' to be limited to Lauds and Vespers

Friday 9 Nov.

Sleepiness was my chief attendant at the start. Anyhow, a
dull discussion on the Breviary. [3]

For Clifford, bishops should be seen to exercise what he saw to be their
'ordinary' powers as successors of the Apostles, and the notion that it
was by virtue of an 'apostolic dispensation' (i.e. from Rome) caused him
some annoyance. Certainly he made this clear when he spoke on the
subject of the title of ordination of the secular clergy. A secular priest
could be ordained with the title either of patrimony or of benefice or of
mission. The reason for such an arrangement was to prevent a bishop
from ordaining more clergy than could be financially supported,
remembering that, if all else failed, a diocesan priest could plead that he
had a right to *sustentatio* from his bishop.

> The title of mission was established originally for the Chinese,
> and then gradually it was given to all missionary areas in the
> Church: and now a considerable part of the clergy of the whole
> world is ordained with the title of mission . . .

And then the central thrust of his argument:

> But what I wish to point out is this that those who are ordained
> *titulo missionis* are not ordained by virtue of the ordinary
> law but only by apostolic dispensation. It follows, therefore,
> that in a great part of the Church where hierarchies have been
> properly constituted the bishop nevertheless has no right with
> regard to the ordination of his own clergy.

---

3   Rudderham, *op. cit.*, p. 41.

This certainly is a considerable anomaly. For if any duty
pertains to the office of bishop it must surely be that of
providing his own clergy, and it must appear as a very great
anomaly that, even where hierarchies have been properly
constituted, a bishop still has no right to ordain clergy
except with permission.

If there were to arise, Clifford argued, a situation in which, because of
some unforseen circumstance, a bishop found that he had more priests
ordained *titulo missionis* than could be provided for, then some
arrangement should be reached in a provincial synod (i.e. a Metropolitan
meeting with his suffragans).

Ten years before, Bishop Grant of Southwark – also a canonist – had
raised with Clifford the question of someone being ordained outside his
own diocese. To us it would seem to be a minor point but clearly it was of
greater significance then than now. Clifford dealt with it as follows:

As regards the *Titulus Missionis*, I do not see why we
cannot get people ordained out of our diocese on that title.
The *Titulus* is not a thing which travels out of the diocese.
All the Ordaining Bishop wants to know is whether the
Ordinandus has a title in his own diocese. If he has a good
title there, all is right. Now we have the right to confer this
title to a certain number in our dioceses, so I don't see why
we should raise any question about the matter. [4]

Although the Council itself took no formal decisions in the matter, the
Curia clearly took note of what had been said during the debate with the
result that the following year Propaganda issued an *Instructio de Titulo
Ordinationis* (April 27, 1871).

In 1885 Propaganda agreed to the transfer of the *titulo missionis* so that
a priest might be moved from one diocese to another, provided that the
bishops concerned agreed. It was Clifford who made the application to

---

4   Valladolid Archives *Correspondence*, Vol. 7, 1846 – 1860, GUEST,
         No. 197, Letter dated 2.8.1860.

Rome, and it would be fair to assume that the thinking behind it in regard to the ecclesiastical province was also his. [5]

Concubinage of the clergy was a grave abuse which had been mentioned in the Council but which the Cardinal of Seville and at least one North American bishop (Savannah) had hoped would not be brought into open discussion. Clifford wholeheartedly agreed:

> It is impossible – as you will appreciate – to imagine what harm would be done in Protestant areas if within a month of the publication of this Council – the proceedings of this Council will be published not only in Latin but also in the vernacular and will be available in the homes of Catholics and Protestants alike, and will be read not only by grown men but also by young girls – it becomes apparent to everyone that the General Council had to consider and deliberate upon this great evil in the Church, namely that of priests living in concubinage. I have no doubt that the scandal will be immense; that many Protestant fathers and husbands would henceforth prevent their wives and daughters from going to Confession as soon as they saw this given publicity in the Council.
> [My translation. Full text is printed in Appendix 6].

Some bishops had argued that it was not the laws of the Church that were at fault but that 'the civil authorities favour such priests and prevent the bishops from applying the ecclesiastical laws against them'. Clifford argued for a 'formula' rather than a law and 'most earnestly requested' that

> we do not publish a law dealing with priests living in concubinage, but that the title should be *Concerning serious Offences Committed by Priests*. For if in treating of priests living in concubinage can also be the occasion of dealing with priests who are drunk or guilty of similar offences, it would be much better to speak in general

---

5   The DECREE, dated 18.8.1885, is quoted in translation by Robert E. Guy, O.S.B., *The Synods in English: Being the Text of the Four Synods of Westminster. Translated into English* (Publ. Stratford-on-Avon, 1886), p. 311.

terms about the more serious offences committed by priests
than if one should read in our proceedings something
specifically on the subject of priests living in concubinage.
[My translation].

Clifford wanted a schema to be produced which would take into
account all the suggestions that had been put forward. Next he spoke
at some length 'of something of greater importance than what I have
said already'. He contended that the Pope had himself, when
convening the Council, laid down in his Constitution *Multiplices Inter*
how disagreements were to be resolved. Clifford emphasised that it
was important that those procedures be adhered to; first, because this
was an instruction coming to them from their Head; second, because
they must be careful not to infringe the rights of their fellow bishops,
and third, failure to do so might well call into question the validity of
their decisions.

Clifford was emphatic: Bishops should *themselves* decide whether
their differences were of a greater or lesser degree (which was a
distinction made by the Constitution itself) and should *themselves*
seek to resolve them. Only as a last resort – and here again he quoted
the Constitution as his authority – should outside help be invoked (i.e.
the matter be remitted to a Deputation). In saying this he was
complaining against the practice of sending all schemata out of the
Council to be resolved by a Deputation.

> I say that we have done none of these things and that we are
> in very grave danger of people saying, and of everyone
> saying, that what we are doing is not in accordance with
> what the Supreme Pontiff has laid down and that as a result
> our decrees will be null. [My translation].

This was an important point. Clifford, who earlier had upheld the rights
of bishops in the matter of ordaining priests for their dioceses, was now
seen upholding the authority of the pope. Indeed the loyalty to Rome of
many of the group which came to be known as 'the Minority' was one of
the features of the earlier debates of the Council.

In this address Clifford the canonist is seen as clear thinking, balanced,
and sufficiently courageous to call into question even the very

procedures which the Council Presidents (all cardinals) had by now been adopting for some eight weeks. 'The entry in Dupanloup's *Journal* for February 2 shows that he knew beforehand that Clifford would bring up the matter of the council rules, the entry for February 3 expressed approval of Clifford's speech' (Cwiekowski). [6]

Bishop Amherst of Northampton noted that Clifford's speech 'seems to have created quite a sensation . . . it was certainly one of the events of the Synod'.[7] Clifford had made his mark. Before February was out he was to be heard again on another topic of practical importance – the Universal Small Catechism.

---

6   F. J. Cwiekowski, *The English Bishops and the First Vatican Council* (Publ. Louvain, 1971), p. 146, footnote 3.

7   *Ibid.*, p. 146.
'Dr. Clifford is, I believe, the only English bishop, who has yet spoken in the Council, and his oratory and Latinity are universally acknowledged to have been of the very highest order.' Odo Russell to Earl Russell, 7.3.1870 (quoted N. Blakiston, ed., *The Roman Question: Extracts from the Dispatches of Odo Russell from Rome 1858 - 1870* (Publ. London, 1962).).

CHAPTER EIGHT

Debate on the Small Universal Catechism

Few would deny the importance of having a small book, in question and answer form, which embodies in concise and simple terms a summary of one's beliefs and which without difficulty can be committed to memory. Such (small) 'catechisms', as they are called, have for centuries held an honoured place in the minds and memories of generations of Catholics. Particularly for the young, the unlettered and the elderly, such a method of learning has proved invaluable as a means of acquiring a knowledge of one's Faith.

Indeed, the efficacy of such small books was recognised by the Chinese during the so-called 'Cultural Revolution' when nearly a thousand million people possessed and committed to memory the contents of the pocket-sized *Thoughts of Chairman Mao*.

Before the First Vatican Council a number of catholic catechisms were in use throughout the Church. The problem to which the Council Fathers addressed themselves was that of variety and lack of uniformity, not only as between one country and another, but also between dioceses in the same country. (One hundred years later, when uniformity is not perceived in such an advantageous light, the situation obtaining in 1870 might well be seen as a positive benefit).

In his address to the Council, Clifford addressed himself to the following points:

1)   Problem: Multiplicity of catechisms

2)   Solution: <u>either</u>   Discard all catechisms
                              and start again

              <u>or</u>   Modify one that already exists

3)   Assuming the latter course:

either   Robert Bellarmine (1542 – 1621;
                                Catechism 1598?)

or   Peter Canisius (1521 – 1597;
                                Catechism 1555)

4)   Clifford favoured Peter Canisius

The problem, argued Clifford, was not of a false or uncertain doctrine that was being propagated nor of the clergy failing in their duty. It was one of variety. Catechisms were being modified between the death of one bishop and the appointment of a successor. Families moving from one part of the country to another were distressed to find their sons and daughters 'being asked to learn new forms of the catechism'.

The first proposal was that all previous catechisms be abandoned and that something new be composed along the lines of Bellarmine's Catechism. Clifford was appalled at the idea:

> I would doubt whether there has ever been in the Church a proposal which so affected the lives of individuals as the removal of the catechisms now in use in the Church. Some catechisms are of but recent origin, but there are others which are held in the greatest esteem among various nations and peoples. For simple folk the catechism is their very religion. They know nothing of their religion except what they have learned from the catechism, and so, if we all too lightly discard all the catechisms of proven worth throughout the Church, we shall not avoid causing scandal and harm to many people. [My translation, full text is printed in Appendix 7].

But even if this were done, he foresaw yet another serious difficulty. Put bluntly, they were tempting providence:

> With the same breath we are told that what those learned men, for three centuries up to the present day, have been unable to do is now to be achieved within a matter of months by some commission.

Speaking frankly to the assembled bishops, Clifford made two very cogent points:

> The wise legislator is one who always keeps that which is good, that which is perfect, in a state of perfection, but eliminates effectively and to the very root only those things which in themselves are bad. In our own day reformers have always followed a rule whereby, when they wish to introduce changes among the people, they invariably first destroy what is already there, and then, having achieved a '*tabula rasa*', they then proceed to put new laws and new institutions before the people. I do not believe that it behoves us to imitate them. It is better for us to improve on what we already have rather than to destroy it only to embark on what is uncertain.

> I take my second point from the circumstances of the time. You will have noticed how everyone speaks of our Council – you know how we read about it every day. The objection has been made to us by Protestants and others, to the effect that the purpose of the Council is to establish a new religion in place of the old. Daily this is what we hear, and not only ourselves but even more so the people, and I do not believe we could give greater credence to this idea than if we were to change all the catechisms throughout the world. [My translation].

Clifford urged that unity should not be imposed but that it be achieved gradually as the result of a natural process, and that Provincial Councils be presented with a model to serve as 'a guide as to how to proceed'. (It is worth noting how he again sees the Province as being a particularly useful structure within which difficulties might be resolved. It will be recalled that in the debate on the Life of the Clergy he had suggested that the danger of too many priests being ordained '*titulo missionis*' might be obviated at Provincial level).

The question now presented itself: which of the contending catechisms – Bellarmine or Canisius – should the Fathers propose as a model for all others? To the chagrin of the German bishops, Clifford, having applauded Bellarmine as the author of many works of controversy, then dismissed him in one sentence:

> There can be no doubt . . . that the teaching of Bellarmine was
> not widely held (*non in multis regionibus evasit communis*)
> for the simple reason that it is more suited to local conditions
> than to the Universal Church. [My translation].

By contrast the catechism of Peter Canisius received a veritable paean of
praise from Clifford, not least because of its remarkable success in
England where it had been in use for many years. (The original
catechism, written in Latin, was first published in Spring 1555).

Clifford said:

> On the other hand since the time of the Council of Trent Blessed
> Canisius has written for this express purpose (i.e. for the
> benefit of the Universal Church) and in fact gave his whole life
> to this one aim: to produce an exposition of christian doctrine;
> first, a simple outline for young children, then something more
> advanced for use in schools, and finally a major work for those
> who are more widely read . . . And I would draw your attention
> to the fact that the (catechisms of) christian doctrine which
> were later to be drawn up, not only in Germany but also in
> England and in many other parts, always used as a foundation
> this exposition of christian doctrine by Father Canisius.
> [My translation. Full text is printed in Appendix 7].

Many translations are listed by Clifford citing Matthew Rader [1] as his
authority – the Council scribe could not quite hear his name –
culminating with one of his customary references to his native land:

---

1   Matthew Rader (1561 – 1634) was Canisius's first biographer. The words
     quoted by Clifford were written in 1615, only eighteen months after the
     Saint's death (James Brodrick, S.J., *Saint Peter Canisius, S.J., 1521 -
     1597*, Publ. London, 1935, p. 241).

2   Father Henry Garnet (1553/4 – 1606), Superior of the Jesuits in England.
     The title of his translation: *A Summe of Christian doctrine . . . With an
     appendix of the fall of man & justification, according to the doctrine
     of the Council of Trent to which is adjoined the explication of certain
     questions not handled at large in the books.* (Allison and Rogers state
     that the translation is only in part by Garnet).

     The first edition was printed privately 1592 – 3. Confusion arose
     because there was another edition, printed at St. Omers in 1622,
     after Henry Garnet's death.

> It was translated into English by Father Garnet [2] who shed his blood for Christ; this doctrine was in use in his time for teaching the catechism.

But Clifford was not alone in his esteem of Canisius. In 1892 the Protestant Dr. Drews wrote:

> The Catechism of Canisius has taken his name through the world and down the centuries. Hardly any other book has had such a huge circulation as this, for 130 years after the date of its first appearance it had gone into nearly four hundred editions . . . The whole plan and lay-out of it is skilful in the highest degree, and the execution a model of lucidity and exact statement, unequalled among Catholic books. [3]

A matter for some surprise must be the following. In 1862 a letter reached Propaganda Fidei in Rome in which it was alleged that the catechism then in use in England was 'Nestorian'. The writer was Father George Montgomery of Wednesbury. Two months later Father Henry Formby, also of Wednesbury, wrote to Propaganda in the same vein. Various continental catechisms (that of Bellarmine, and books in French, Italian and German) were cited to prove the alleged discrepancy of doctrine, and then the offending passage was quoted in full:

Q.   What is the sixth article of the Creed?

A.   He ascended into heaven, sitteth at the right hand of God the Father Almighty.

Q.   What means, sitteth at the right hand of God the Father Almighty?

A.   Not that God the Father has hands, for He is a pure spirit: but that Christ as man holds the next place to God in heaven.

Q.   Why do you say as man?

A.   Because as God he is equal to the Father in all things.

---

3   Brodrick, *op. cit.*, p. 241.

The two priests had written to Propaganda because they had not been happy with the reply they had received from their bishop, Ullathorne. Equally, Propaganda's reply did not afford satisfaction either. In it the Cardinal had argued:

1)   'Next' signified equality: *'aequivoce ut significet talem proximitatem quae cum vera aequalitate consistere possit'*.

2)   The true sense of a word should be understood from its context. [4]

Although apparently no more was heard of the matter, it may have indicated in some small way the need for change.

To return to Clifford's address at the Council: he described the four different age groups for each of whom Canisius had written a catechism but in varying degrees of detail and emphasis so as to meet the educational needs of all.

First of all, an extremely brief account for the very young, secondly one for everyone but in which the creeds and signs and symbols which are used in teaching are introduced, thirdly for the use of those young people who have some familiarity with scholastic thought, and finally a complete work which the more erudite would have at their disposal. [My translation].

Clifford ended by suggesting that the Canisius catechism 'be presented to everyone as a norm, a model which has the approval of this Council' and that 'provincial councils be especially urged to take a close look at the question of how to achieve unity in the teaching of doctrine in their provinces'.

---

4   Propaganda Fide Archives, Rome, *Scitture Riferite nei Congressi*, 1861 – 1863, Anglia, Nos. 745, 746, 747.

Father James Brodrick, the biographer of St. Peter Canisius, has this moving passage about his subject:

> He knew, as must every great reformer, that children are the future, the Church and State of tomorrow. "Win them and the world is won" became his motto, and for the rest of his life he never wearied . . . of revising and improving his gifts to them. One of his last actions on earth, as an old man of seventy-five, was to prepare an edition of the *Shortest Catechism* with the words divided up into syllables, "to enable my dear little children to learn it more easily".[5]

The Vatican Council did in fact recommend that a general catechism be drawn up, but it favoured Bellarmine rather than Canisius with, however, any modifications which local bishops might wish to introduce.

This last point owed something to a contribution made by Clifford on 30th April when he spoke a second time in the debate. His main purpose was to propose an emendation in the proposed schema to the effect that it be stated quite clearly that the Council Fathers wanted a degree of flexibility in the way in which Bellarmine's catechism was to be used.

> In place of what is proposed in the schema I should like to see the following:
>
> 'With the approval of the Council and taking into account first and foremost the aforementioned catechism of the Venerable Cardinal Bellarmine as well as catechisms now widely used among Christian people, not to mention selected works of some bishops in various parts of the world, the new small catechism etc.'
>
> 'I think that those words 'after the model of the aforementioned Venerable Cardinal Bellarmine' should not be put as if we wished to limit those who have to produce a new catechism to such an extent that they follow slavishly all that is contained in Bellarmine's small catechism.

---

5   Brodrick, *op. cit.*, p. 238, 239.

> My view is that we wish to leave it open to the authors to
> take from any catechism whatever seems to be of better
> quality or more useful. [My translation].

Clifford also pointed to two practical difficulties which, he said,
invariably presented themselves to compilers of new catechisms. These
were a) that it looked as though something new was being proposed, and
b) 'that it is extremely difficult to compose a catechism which can meet
the needs of so many different peoples'. (He had tried to address both
these problems in his original speech in which he had argued against the
proposal that the writers start from a '*tabula rasa*' position, and that
Provincial Councils would be an appropriate forum in which to settle
textual problems arising from differences of locality and culture).

Clifford's proposed emendation regarding the manner in which
Bellarmine was to be put forward as a 'model' for any future catechism
was one of the few accepted by the commission (4th May, 1870).[6] On the
other hand the commission rejected the thinking of those bishops
(including Clifford) who had argued for a catechism that would take
children right through their formative years (say, from six to fourteen,
and including any instruction that the priest himself might undertake to
give in church). The commission put the question: What, therefore, is the
small catechism? The answer it gave was as follows:

> According to the mind both of the schema and of the
> Deputation it is understood only to mean those rudiments
> of the Faith which in fact pertain to the basic instruction of
> the faithful.[7]

From such a starting-point it is difficult to see how the argument in
favour of Canisius could be sustained.

The sudden suspension of the Council meant that the proposal was never
brought to fruition, and yet even before that it would seem that the whole
subject was being pushed to one side. Cuthbert Butler comments:

---

6   Mansi, *Collectio Conciliorum* (Publ. 1923 – 1927), Tomus 51, Col. 496, 497.

7   *Ibid.*

... though ready for presentation, it was not brought on at a Public Session for the final voting and enactment. The fact was that the great debate on Church and Papacy had begun and was engrossing the entire attention of all, so that catechism and discipline had faded out of view.

In fact, the proposal of the catechism has remained inoperative, no move ever having been made since the Council to give effect to the idea of a standard elementary catechism for the whole Church. The use of local catechisms has gone on, according to the mind of the Minority bishops at the Council. [8]

(N.B. – Butler was writing in 1930).

England did not suffer unduly from this turn of events. Indeed, the catechism of Peter Canisius as adapted by Bishop Challoner (Vicar Apostolic of the London District 1758 – 1781) continued to form the basis of the *Penny Catechism* which has moulded so many generations of Catholics even to the present day, although now to a much lesser degree than before.

Saint Pius X (1903 – 1914) wrote an encyclical letter on the teaching of christian doctrine (April 15th, 1905). The whole issue of a Catechism for the Universal Church was debated at the Second Vatican Council (1962 – 1965). Later, a Synod was called and "on that occasion, the Synod Fathers stated: 'Very many have expressed the desire that a catechism or compendium of all Catholic doctrine regarding both faith and morals be confessed, that it might be, as it was, a point of reference for the catechisms or compendia that are prepared in various regions.' (Final report of the Extraordinary Synod of Bishops, 7 December 1985). [9]

---

8   Cuthbert Butler, *The Vatican Council 1869 - 1870* (Publ. London, paperback 1962, original edition, 1930), p. 200.

9   The *Catechism of the Catholic Church* was finally published in 1992.

CARTOON FROM "PUNCH" MAGAZINE, (DECEMBER 1869)

MGR. JOHN BONOMI, (1816 – 1872), VICAR GENERAL OF CLIFTON
DIOCESE AT THE TIME OF THE FIRST VATICAN COUNCIL

JOHN HENRY NEWMAN, (1801 – 1890)

CHAPTER NINE

The Definition of Papal Infallibility

To many writers on church history the name of William Clifford signifies someone who was an inopportunist on the issue of papal infallibility or, as Ronald Knox rather crudely expressed it, someone who was 'on the wrong side about infallibility'.[1] The purpose of this chapter is to outline Clifford's thinking on this vital issue which, at least before the definition, so divided the universal episcopate and which even afterwards continued to arouse bitter feelings amounting in some cases to a catalyst which occasioned defections from the Church. Clifford's stance, both in its theology and its respectfully combative style, won the approval of Newman. Indeed, just as the Cardinal is seen in his thinking on the role of the Laity as a forerunner of Vatican II, so by the same token Clifford in his safeguarding of the position of the universal episcopate may be viewed as a figure who would have been much more at home at the later Council.

1867 marked the eighteenth centenary of the death of St. Peter and it appeared to Pio Nono as an apt occasion on which to summon a General Council. In the event the opening was delayed for two years. Nevertheless ceremonies did take place to honour the Prince of the Apostles and it was at one of these that Manning and Senestry (Archbishop of Ratisbon) who were standing next to the Pope took a joint vow that they would secure the definition of the Pope's Infallibility – something they would pursue even to the shedding of their blood.[2] At the end of 1868 and beginning of 1869 Manning – who during his priestly studies in Rome had come to the Pope's attention – was pressing for a definition and one which, he hoped, would receive as wide an interpretation as possible.

Two events took place before the opening of the council which, in the light of what was to happen later, may be seen to have some significance. The first was in 1867 when an address was presented to the Pope requesting that a definition be promulgated. Some five hundred bishops signed, one of whom was William Clifford.

---

1   *Occasional Sermons* (Publ. London, 1960), p. 304. The sermon was
     preached at the Hierarchy Centenary Rally at Clifton, October, 1950.

2   He recalled this in his personal diary, 1881. Quoted in Purcell's *Life of
     Cardinal Manning*, Vol. II, p. 420 and in Cwiekowski's *The English
     Bishops and the First Vatican Council* (Publ. Louvain, 1971), p. 66.

The other was the Pope's expressed hope that the Council would serve to promote the cause of Christian unity, and indeed invitations were sent to Christians both of the Orthodox and of the Protestant traditions. Pusey was one of the latter but his initial reaction of hope soon changed when he realised the influence of Manning and the Ultramontanes in Rome. Nor was he pleased by the Pope's refusal to recognise Anglican Orders. [3]

There was feverish activity on the continent prior to the Council. Not least of people's worries were the fears of men like Acton who saw too wide a definition – or indeed any definition – as being too constrictive of religious thought. Gladstone and others saw any proposed definition as having profound political repercussions in the sense that the civil loyalty of Catholic subjects might be compromised. Here there were seen to be overtones of the infamous 'Bloody Question' put to the Catholic subjects of Elizabeth I. Furthermore Gladstone viewed with dismay the possible repercussions in Ireland which in political terms could well be far-reaching.

As the issues became polarised, so certain other figures came to the fore in their opposition to a definition. Mgr. Dupanloup the Bishop of Orleans was well versed in the subject of Papal Infallibility as this had been the subject of his doctoral thesis some years before. His thinking brought him into opposition to Manning whom he charged with wanting 'a separate infallibility'. [4] (As will be seen, this was precisely Clifford's point when he argued that the Pope's Infallibility should be seen and presented within the wider context of the Church).

Clifford was also in touch with the aristocratic Archbishop of Prague, Cardinal von Schwarzenberg, and with others who went to make up the Inopportunist Party. For a while the Cardinal maintained contact with Clifford even after the Council was brought to an abrupt end. This we see from a letter he wrote (referred to in the next chapter) in which he was enquiring about how the papal definition was being presented and received in England.

---

3   See Cwiekowsi, *op. cit.*, pp. 82, 83, 86.

4   *Ibid.* p. 98.

Although not physically present at the Council, Newman's 'spirit' was certainly felt. His view at that time was that the infallibility of the pope was no more than an opinion, and he failed to see any necessity for a dogmatic definition. The definitions of the past, he argued – for example, the christological dogmas of the early Councils and the Anti-Protestant anathemas of Trent – were a necessity. No such circumstance obtained in 1870.[5] Indeed, as Clifford was to point out more than once, both the fact of having a debate and the resulting definition would serve only to alienate people.

One of the features of the Council was the number of delegations and petitions which came forward arguing either in favour or against a definition of papal infallibility.

Three are worthy of mention, particularly as rumours were circulating in England as to the stance being adopted by individual bishops. Amherst of Northampton, for example, had written to his brother on 1st February:

> I hear the *Standard* has said something silly about me and Clifford, and wants to make out that I signed a petition against the definition. I authorize you to contradict this *in toto* if you hear it mentioned. [6]

On 12th January, 1870, a petition was drawn up signed by von Schwarzenberg, Ketteler and forty-four other bishops, but not by Clifford, asking that the issue of papal infallibility should not be *discussed.*[7] Three days later, Errington, Clifford and twenty-five other bishops signed a petition which said that the proposition should not be defined as a *dogma of faith.*[8] The argument of the latter document was threefold –

---

5 This was the theme of Newman's confidential letter to Ullathorne (28.1.1870) but later leaked by Clifford. Newman: 'When has definition of doctrine de fide been a luxury of devotion, and not a stern painful necessity?' *Letters and Diaries* (ed. Dessain & Gornall), Vol. XXV, pp. 18, 19.

6 Quoted in *Memoirs of Francis Kerril Amherst, D.D.* by Dame Mary Francis Roskell, O.S.B. (Publ. London, 1903), p. 292.

7 Mansi *Acta*, Tomus 51, col. 678 – 680

8 *Ibid.*, col. 681, 682.

1)   Any discussion of the question would clearly show the lack
      of unity 'and especially of unanimity' among the bishops;

2)   It would deter Non-Catholics;

3)   'Interminable strife' would result, 'hindering our ministry
      particularly among Non-Catholics'

Two months later (11th March) when the Council Fathers had already experienced the rush with which some of the business was being transacted and aware also of the far-from-united views on the issue of Infallibility, thirteen bishops – including von Schwarzenberg Cardinal Rauscher of Vienna, and Clifford – requested that more time be given to consider the schemata and also sought a meeting with the Deputation de fide.[9] Feelings were clearly running high as the points of their argument show:

1)   'It is for the Vatican Council to walk in the
      footsteps of the Fathers at Trent. With what diligence
      did they prepare *their* decrees, and what period of
      time did they spend in perfecting them!' [Italics mine]

2)   'When publishing definitions of faith, it is not
      sufficient to have a simple majority. There should be,
      if not a numerical, then at least a moral, unanimity.

3)   The bishops complain about the speed and lack of
      time in which to study the schemata.

On the reverse of the document a secretary had written testily [in Italian]

Why are special meetings being asked for with the members
of the Deputation *pro rebus fidei?* In the first place, there
is no shortage in Rome of distinguished prelates and
theologians with whom difficulties and doubts on particular
points of doctrine can easily be discussed.

---

9   *Ibid*, col. 702, 703.

Secondly, the members of the Deputation could not without difficulty accommodate or find time to attend the meetings that are being suggested as they are already overwhelmed with work.[10] [My translation].

Such a reply goes to show the power wielded by a curia *apparatchik* even over such influential prelates as the Archbishops of Prague, Vienna, Milan and Paris.

Clifford delivered his address to the Fathers on May 25th. It is a model of clear presentation and logical thinking coupled with a due regard for historical precedent. He begins by wryly comparing the inopportuneness, of the late hour in which he was speaking with that of the manner in which they were treating of infallibility, 'namely on its own and separate from the Church (as a whole)'.

Immediately he challenges Manning who had spoken shortly before. This he does by turning the Archbishop's arguments in order to draw a different conclusion, namely 'the necessity of not separating the question of the authority and infallibility of the Roman Pontiff from the question of the authority and infallibility of the Church'.

In his address Manning had quoted a number of secular journals in which it had been argued that the infallibility of the pope was the logical outcome of the Catholic system. From this he had concluded that any holding back now would be a sign of weakness. Clifford, however, takes this argument but uses it as an *a fortiori* for his own position saying that this was all the more reason why the Pope's Infallibility should be presented in a logical and coherent manner, i.e. as part of the overall infallibility of the Church. (A similar situation arose in Vatican II when an attempt to introduce a separate document on the Blessed Virgin Mary was thwarted largely, it is said, through the intervention of Abbot B.C. Butler of Downside who argued that Our Lady's position should be presented within the overall context of the Church).[11]

---

10   *Ibid.*, col. 703.

11   *The Theology of Vatican II* (Publ. London, 1967) pp. 83 sqq. While not mentioning what is said to have been his own contribution, Butler does mention that of R. Laurentin in footnote 16.

Clifford continues:

> And if it really is true, as the most distinguished archbishop
> has said, that things have to be demonstrated logically to
> the English people, certainly in order to be able to convert
> an Englishman to religion then it must in the first place be
> necessary to demonstrate to him that the Catholic Church is
> not despotic. [My translation].

At this point Mansi records 'signs of disapproval' amongst the Fathers,
and from this various commentators (Cuthbert Butler, Cwiekowski) have
concluded that those present were disagreeing with what Clifford was
saying. This is not necessarily the case. Indeed it seems much more likely
that they were protesting against the Church *being seen by her critics*
as tyrannical rather than against the factual accuracy of what Clifford
was saying. An excellent parallel is to be found in Shakespeare's *Julius
Caesar* (Act III, sc. 2) where the murmurings of the crowd are directed,
not against the speaker (Mark Anthony) but against the one to whom he
is referring (Brutus):

> He (Caesar) was my friend, faithful and just to me:
> But Brutus says he was ambitious;
> And Brutus is an honourable man.

. . . . .

> When that the poor have cried, Caesar hath wept:
> Ambition should be made of sterner stuff,
> Yet Brutus says he was ambitious;
> And Brutus was an honourable man.

. . . . .

> I thrice presented him a kingly crown,
> Which he did thrice refuse: was this ambition?
> Yet Brutus says he was ambitious . . .

Undeterred Clifford presses home his point with the following passage
which must be seen as central to his argument:

The whole problem which Protestants have against the
Catholic Church, which they call papistical, is this that they
are always seeking to prove that the Catholic Church is in
fact tyrannical; and these men who will write in these
articles, in these publications, will make every effort with
their arguments so that they will make English people
believe that by this proposed definition what will clearly
appear, what will logically follow, namely that the Catholic
Church is indeed tyrannical and that the Roman Pontiff
truly is the tyrant.

From this, it seems to me, one must come to the unavoidable
conclusion that if we by this definition – whatever form it
may take in the end – wish not to hinder but to help people,
it is necessary that we do not give them a separate
definition which relates to the infallibility and authority of
the Roman Pontiff; but it is necessary that we clearly and
logically demonstrate to them what is the nature and
essence of the Catholic Church, what is the true authority in
the Catholic Church, how the authority of the Church and
the authority of the Pope come together, and how in all these
matters it is neither tyranny nor despotism.

But if, after so many months of labour, we have done nothing
except to put before the people some decree about the
Infallibility of the Roman pontiff – no matter what way the
decree may be worded – this will be the overriding
impression of the people: that we had done nothing other
than to constitute the Pope as a despot. [My translation].

(*Murmurs and signs of disapproval*). Clearly <u>these</u> murmurings were
directed at Clifford.

Clifford now turns his attention to the manner in which infallibility had
been presented to English Catholics over the years.

There was no question among English Catholics on this
point; we have always taught our people in England about
the infallibility of the Church in controversies with
protestants both in writing and in addresses. We used to

teach that the question of whether the final source of
infallibility resided in the Pope alone or in the Pope with the
Church was a matter of theology [*ad scholas*], not of faith;
and in our popular catechisms mention was made only of
the infallibility of the Church. Preachers whom I have often
had in my churches speaking on controversial matters in
the presence of both protestants and catholics, always
explained the matter in this way as presented in the books
which we are accustomed to give to people when we instruct
them in the faith, either catholics, or protestants whom we
wish to convert. [My translation].

When referring to the history of the exposition of Catholic doctrine in
England in regard to papal infallibility, Clifford was acting on a very
important theological principle, namely, that bishops assembled in
General Council are there not only as successors of the Apostles but also
as witnesses to the faith as proclaimed and believed in their respective
dioceses.[12] The ceremony of the ordination of a bishop makes this clear
when at the beginning, after the bull of appointment has been read, the
bishop-elect is examined as to the orthodoxy of his beliefs. At the end of
his life the creed is recited in his presence as a sign that he has
maintained that faith intact.

In pursuing his argument about the transmission of the Faith in England,
Clifford cites the names of Milner, Challoner and Gother but without
quoting them in detail. For our purposes, however, it is important to take
a closer look at these and one or two other authorities in order to see how
the infallibility of the Pope had been treated over the preceding (post

12   William Maskell, however, writing in 1871 turned this principle against
      the Council by saying that there were grounds for arguing against its
      allegedly representative character: . . . and how far the Church at large
      was truly represented where the vote of each member was counted and
      where the proportion of Italian bishops was so immense, and of bishops
      in partibus who could bring no tradition from their people, for they
      have none to rule over. These two classes together formed, it is said,
      more than one-third of the whole episcopate.

      (*What is the Meaning of the Late Definition on the Infallibility of the
      Pope? An Enquiry*. (Publ. London, 1871).

Reformation) centuries. As will be seen, the matter was raised, not only in English Catholic manuals, but also in the rebuttal of objections from Protestant controversialists.

1685 (Gother)   A Papist Misrepresented:

And for this intent, he is assisted with a certain Mysterious Infallibility, such as hides itself, when he (the Pope) is upon his own Private Concerns . . . But when he comes into his Chair to hear any Public Business, then it begins to appear, and protects him from all Mistakes and Errors; and becomes immediately full of the Holy Ghost, though he had the Devil and all of wickedness in him just before.

A Papist Represented:

. . . And this, whether he has the assistance of a Divine Infallibility, or no: Which, tho' some allow him, without being in a General Council, yet he is satisfied, 'tis only their Opinion, and not their Faith, there being no Obligation from the Church, of assenting to any such Doctrine.[13]

1743 (Challoner)

First then 'tis to be observed, that the present Controversy is not concerning the Infallibility of the Pope, or Bishop of Rome for, tho' this be maintain'd by many Divines, 'tis no Article of our Faith, or necessary Term of Communion with

---

13   *A Papist Misrepresented and Represented or A Two-fold Character of Popery* by J. L. (Gother). (Publ. 1685) pp. 21, 22.

us. Mr. R. therefore is mistaken when he says, p. 11 "I take the belief of the Pope of Rome his being the visible infallible Judge of Controversy, together with the Infallibility of the Roman Catholic Church to be the Foundation-Article of our Faith, with which all our other Articles will stand or fall". The Belief of the Infallibility of the Catholic Church is indeed an Article of our Faith; not so the Belief of the Infallibility of the pope. [14]

1749 ('S.B.')

No Catholick, as I know of, will allow the Pope any inherent Gift, or Quality of Infallibility sticking to him like Bird-lime: when Christ's promises to St. Peter were sufficient, viz. that his Faith should not fail: that he would give to him the Keys of the Kingdom of Heaven . . . The Doctor (Chapman) . . . fixes in his (the Pope's) successors, an inherent Gift of Infallibility, which no Body else can understand; nor himself neither; to cast a contemptible Odium on the first See in the World: which King James I owned to be the Patriarch of the Western Church. [15]

---

14   *A Letter to a Friend concerning the Infallibility of the Church of*
      Christ in answer to a Late Pamphlet Entitled an Humble Address to
      the Jesuits, by a Dissatisfied Roman-Catholic (Publ, London, 1743)
      p. 4, The Letter forms part of A Collection of Controversial Tracts
      Published by R.C., D.D. (Challoner), London 1747.

15   *A Modest Enquiry How Far Catholicks Are Guilty of the Horrid*
      Tenets Laid To Their Charge: How far their Principles are
      Misrepresented, or Misunderstood: and what may be alleged in
      DEFENCE of those they REALLY PROFESS, by S. B. (Publ. London,
      1749). pp. 139, 140.

1814 (Anon)

Q When the head of the Church publishes any decree concerning faith or morals, to which he requires submission from all the faithful, is he himself infallible in what he there teaches?

A   This is not proposed as an article of divine faith, nor has the Church ever made any decision concerning it. Great numbers of the most learned divines are of opinion, that in such a case the head of the church is infallible in what he teaches; but there are others of a contrary opinion, who think that his decree is not to be considered as infallibly certain, till the body of Bishops receive it, either by their express approbation, or by their tacit submission to it, by which it becomes a decree of the whole church, whose infallibility is undoubted. [16]

(The writer then proceeds to devote $5\frac{1}{2}$ pages in defending the first opinion and $2\frac{1}{4}$ pages the latter).

1827 (Milner)

In the third place, I must remind you, and my other friends, that I have nothing here to do with the doctrine of the Pope's individual infallibility, (when pronouncing Ex Cathedra . . . he addresses the whole Church, and delivers the faith of it upon some contested article) nor would you, in case you were to become a Catholic, be

---

16   *The Sincere Christian Instructed in the Faith of Christ from the Written Word* in two volumes (Publ. Dublin, 1814), Ch. XII, p. 185.

required to believe in any doctrines,
except such as are held by the whole
Catholic Church, with the Pope at its
head. But without entering into this or
any other scholastic question ... [17]

These quotations suggest the following comments:

1)   Clifford was factually correct in his assertion that in England the
        Infallibility of the Pope had not been a matter presented in such a
        way as to render its acceptance a *conditio sine qua non* of being
        a Catholic, nor had there been any tradition of teaching it as part
        of the *doctrina communis* of the Church.

2)   The 1814 (Anon) quotation, however, does speak of 'great numbers
        of the most learned Divines'. This possibly may not be relevant to
        our present discussion as the work in question was published in
        Dublin and therefore might refer to the situation in Ireland.

3)   The question may still be asked: Why does Clifford apparently give
        no consideration to the possibility of there having been here a
        development of doctrine similar to that of the Marian doctrines of
        the Immaculate Conception (denied by Aquinas, or seen by him as
        at least 'not proven' but defined in 1854) and of the Assumption
        (defined in 1950)? From the evidence available this must
        remain an unanswered question.

Someone Clifford does quote at length is Cardinal Wiseman. Both
extracts are from his *Lectures on the Principal Doctrines and
Practices of the Catholic Church (1844)*, and from the third lecture
Clifford quotes the following:

Suppose there were to arise some question about a
particular doctrine about which no one could agree and no
one knows what is to be thought, what is the mind of the

---

17   *The End of Religious Controversy in a Friendly Correspondence
        Between a Religious Society of Protestants and a Roman Catholic
        Divine, Addressed to the Right Rev. Dr. Burgess by the Rev. J. Milner,
        D.D., F.S.A.*, (Publ. Dublin, 1827), Letter XLVI, p. 130.

Church, and what is prudent and necessary in regard to an enquiry and what is to be done. The method of proceeding is this: a close examination would be instituted of the writings of the ancient fathers of the Church, and so would be known what was held in various regions in different centuries; and thus, having collected the votes of the whole world of all ages, it would not be a new doctrine that would be handed down, but a definition would be made of what had always been held in the Catholic Church. In each case the matter would be dealt with as an historical enquiry, and, so that a right definition would be arrived at, nothing would be omitted; then at last, the decree passed by the Church would be infallible.

Apart from the hypothetical question of how the proposed dogma might have fared had Wiseman been present at the Council – would he have allowed himself to be pressured by Manning whom he might well have taken as his 'theologian'? – this extract was important to Clifford in that it clearly pointed to a *modus procedendi* which would (must?) be followed by the Roman Pontiff before defining a dogma of faith. For Clifford, such consultation was an essential safeguard, and in the letter to his Vicar General (Bonomi)[18] subsequent to the premature closure of the Council he confessed his misgivings that these vital preliminary consultations with 'the Church Universal and Historical' had not been written into the preamble of the definition of Papal Infallibility as being a necessary pre-requisite of any future infallible papal pronouncement.

Clifford proceedes:

We are all agreed in this, and we have instructed our people about the infallibility of the Church along these lines; but it cannot be that this new definition, especially if it is done in such a hurry, without any explanation, can be reconciled with the doctrine of the infallibility of the Church as we have handed it down to them up till now. For many, not only Protestants but also Catholics, it cannot but seem to be a new doctrine. [My translation].

---

18   See Appendix 5.

This was a point which (it will be recalled) Clifford had made in the debate on the Universal Catechism. On that occasion he had said that any sweeping away of all the old catechisms coupled with the introduction of one which was new would be seen by Protestant critics as validating their allegations that 'a new religion' was being introduced. Clifford used the same argument here to urge a cautionary approach to the question of papal infallibility.

Referring to his own diocese of Clifton, he describes the disquiet that was being felt both up to and since his departure for Rome. So important is this passage that it must be quoted in full.

> Indeed, both before I left England and since my arrival in Rome, several priests and lay people have either written or spoken to me to say how much contention there had been among the people and in their families, and how great was their fear that if a definition *de fide* were passed in a hurry, the faithful would defect from the Faith; and names have been given to me not only from recent converts but also born Catholics. To all I have given this one reply: Do not, I said, be worried about what is being commonly put about – things which say that the Council was only summoned for this purpose, these voices, I said, only belong to the writers of journals but have absolutely no authority. I know that Rome does not deal with matters in that way; many wicked things are put about by the enemies of the Roman Church; no one has accused her of being precipitate; Rome must not be judged by the fervent desires of some.
>
> I must confess that things have turned out in a way different from what I was expecting; and indeed the judgment I had made was based on my experience which I thought was in accord with the prudence and dignity of this great City. How very much differently does Saint Augustine teach us to act when he says: "How can this matter, shrouded as it is in so many disagreements, be brought to a clear exposition and ratification by a full Council (*ad plenarii concilii luculentam illustrationem confirmationemque perduci*) unless it has first been debated for a very long time in various parts of the world and is clear from many

discussions and meetings of the bishops?"

> Now we are dealing with a question which is so grave that it radically concerns not only the authority of the Pope but all episcopal authority in the Church. And not only have we not discussed it in any manner "for a very long time", not only have we been summoned here without any prior warning that this matter would be raised in the Council, but furthermore the question was introduced in haste and outside the prescribed order of business and, what is worst of all, on its own, that is without at the same time raising the issue of the relationship which exists between the primacy and infallibility of the Roman Pontiff and also between the authority and teaching power of the bishops. [My translation].

This last sentence, emphasising the crucial role of the episcopate, demonstrates Clifford's concern on a point which he felt to be vital to a balanced theology of the Church. His vindication was not to come until the Decree *Christus Dominus* of Vatican II about a century later. On the more practical level, too, his feeling that the rights of bishops were being somewhat trampled on expressed itself in the debate on the Life of the Clergy. On that occasion he had spoken scathingly of the controls which required that bishops seek dispensations from Rome which he believed they should be able to grant *iure proprio* anyway.

There is a sense of deep foreboding in the next paragraph.

> If the Vatican Council does nothing other than to publish some sort of decree on the infallibility of the Roman Pontiff, saying nothing about the Church, nothing about the Bishops, offering nothing to contain the false views which are going about, then not only can that peace not be hoped for from our labours, but beyond doubt anger and dissension will increase. I cannot help thinking, most reverend fathers, that we are underestimating the difficulties which can arise in many dioceses – as already mentioned by their bishops. [My translation].

Clifford then proceeds to answer those bishops who adopt the line: "If something is true, then it is true and should be proclaimed as such".

Without using the analogy, he sees this as a bull-in-a-china-shop approach whereby all was carried before – but at what cost!

> The Archbishop of Caesaraugusta wants the Church to be ruled by Truth, not by public opinion. Undoubtedly this is most true if it is understood to mean that the Church must not be silent about truth because of the fear of men; that, in other words, it should appear to please God rather than man.

> But if it is understood to mean this: that, although it is the whole truth, prudence in acting is not the most important thing in the running of the Church but everything is to be committed to the care of Heaven; then this pertains rather to Fatalism than to Faith. The church has its unconquered firmness, but it also has its political wisdom. It does not separate the simplicity of the dove from the astuteness of the serpent since it is amongst wolves that it must feed its lambs. It is necessary that the servant whom the Master places in charge of his household should be not only faithful but prudent so that he may give food to all in due time.
> [My translation].

> The Church should not be ruled by public opinion, but nor should she dismiss it out of hand.

Referring to the ravages caused by the Protestant Reformation, Clifford argues:

> There was a time when the Kingdoms of Europe comprised one republic, Christian and Catholic. By a long series of evils it eventually happened that a great part of Northern Europe was torn from the Church: in other regions mobs and rebellions rose up against the Church. The Catholic Church, built on rock, does indeed remain unconquered; but who is there that would not weep over such terrible calamities? Who would say that it is not a matter for the greatest prudence in the Church to ensure that something similar does not happen again?

> If now great men, from wheresoever they come, where the
> enemies of the Church are mixing with her children and
> where men are more easily torn away from the Church . . . if
> these vigilant pastors raise their voices and warn us of the
> grave danger, who will dare to say that one should not take
> them too seriously? Who is it that will persuade himself that
> the business of the Church is only to preach the truth and to
> disregard the signs of the times and public opinion?
> [My translation].

Having drawn attention to the disruption of the past, Clifford next points
to the Church's bright future in the newer nations. In his view that
prospect is going to be put in jeopardy if she does not proceed prudently.

> Can there be any doubt, therefore, that the greatest harm
> would be done to the Church, if, while (still) suffering in
> those areas where Christianity first took root we were to
> give rise to religious difficulties precisely in those places
> where the hope of the Church now lies? Not only would
> difficulties be placed in the way of conversions – we would
> even be giving cause for offence. How therefore can we
> describe as 'small' the difficulties and fears of the bishops
> who come from those places? [My translation].

One speaker had referred rather simplistically to there being either
'good' Catholics or 'bad'. The good will accept, he had argued, and the
bad reject. So what was the problem? Clifford calls this distinction 'both
defective and childish' saying that the 'good' Catholics often had to earn
their living in a Protestant milieu in which they were called upon to
explain and defend their Faith.

> But if the decree on the infallibility of the Roman Pontiff is
> decided in the form in which it has been proposed, without
> any further explanation about the authority of the Church,
> then it is impossible – especially if we think about the
> extreme theories which are going around, fostered by their
> promoters and now in the hands of everyone with no answer
> by way of remedy – that many such men will not be troubled
> and be thrown either into Indifferentism or into a complete
> loss of Faith. [My translation].

As on previous occasions Clifford appeals yet again for a more sensitive approach to the position and feelings of Protestants. He goes even further, saying that many of the freedoms now enjoyed by the Church in the newer countries were due, under God, to the 'persistent efforts of such men devoted as they are to the interests of the Church'.

> In England and America, Catholics – who are in a minority – for the most part are ruled by Protestants, nor are they able to achieve anything for the Church unless they are supported by Protestants. Our laws are made by Members of Parliament who in great part are Protestants; the whole freedom of the Church, the titles of ecclesiastical property, freedom of instruction, the status and liberty of regulars and monks, even the rights of Catholics to hold office as magistrates, in the army or in the law – all these things depend upon the way in which Protestants regard their fellow Catholic citizens. No one can possibly declare, therefore, that it is not a matter of great prudence to the Church to consider whether it is opportune to provoke Protestants in these regions against the Church. Bad times are pressing in upon us . . . we shall have no way of defending the cause of the Church unless we have the help of Protestants and of those ministers of the realm who are well disposed towards us. Our present way of doing business has already alienated many people from us, has weakened our cause, and will alienate many more as the days go by. [My translation].

Perhaps the nearest that Clifford comes to being angry in his address is in the following in which he cites the example of Solomon.

> I cannot but be offended when I hear some dismiss these fears so lightly, fears which several bishops have described of defections or of schism in their dioceses. I have heard many say: "So be it, it is their loss not the Church's; the Church will triumph and in the end will be even more vigorous". This is not the voice of the Catholic Church, the voice of that Church which we confess to be mother as well as teacher. That most wise of kings when judging between two women gave orders that the child was to be cut in two.

> He pronounced that woman to be the true mother who was
> moved to pity over the child. She who was able to say 'let the
> child be divided' was declared no mother at all.
> [My translation].

Prudence continues to be the theme when he turns his attention to the
history of both England and Ireland. In lamenting what had happened he
is at pains to point out that it had been precisely this lack of prudence on
the part of Catholics which had occasioned persecution against them.
Certainly the sentiments contained in the following splendid passage
were not always to be found among Catholic historians of the day, and
here Clifford shows himself to be more of the Louvain-style of unbiased
Catholic historical writing than of the 'My Church right-or-wrong'
defensive stance of many nineteenth century Catholic authors.

> Indeed as I read through the pages of English history I am
> not convinced that those are wrong who are of the view that
> if Queen Elizabeth had been treated with more caution and
> prudence before she ascended the throne and during the
> early years of her reign, then that tragic tearing away of
> England from the Apostolic See with all its horrible
> consequences could have been averted.

> This is even more true of the time of James II. We had a
> Catholic king; more than half the population still held the
> religion of their ancestors, and for the rest the Protestant
> religion was more a question of recent practice than of
> conviction. The more influential people were mere time
> servers, and were easily drawn to the party which appeared
> more likely to win. At that time there was great hope of re-
> establishing the Catholic religion in England. And yet one
> can scarcely credit the blind stupidity of the King's advisers,
> both clerical and lay, who constantly urged on him policies
> that were extreme in matters both political and
> ecclesiastical. King James followed the example of King
> Roboam, and met a fate which, though similar, was worse.

> In the baptistery of this church there stands a monument,
> the work of Canova, on which are inscribed the following
> words: "The last of the Stuarts". What one does <u>not</u> read

there is that hope of restoring the Catholic Faith to England disappeared and that the persecution in Ireland and of the Catholics in England was renewed. If only James II had lent a timely ear to those who warned of the evils which would surely come if, without due consideration, burdens were to be placed on the people which would be more than they could sustain or even understand. [My translation].

All this he contrasts with the benefits which Catholics in England have received at the hands of their Protestant fellow countrymen.

The foregoing passage might well be as much Acton speaking as Clifford. Acton, eminent historian and loyal Catholic, had placed himself completely at the disposal of the Minority while the Council was sitting. His objection to infallibility was more of a moral nature than theological, for he saw any eventual definition as a 'closing-of-ranks' around the Pope and the Curia, giving a seal of approval to all that might in future be enacted. In particular, he distrusted the forays of the Church's 'scholars' into history where first principles appeared to be that the Church in all its doings had been right and that facts had to be subsumed to fit into that overall thesis. Acton describes his own fears on this score as follows:

A contest has arisen, not of dogma, but of a theological opinion against history, that is against truth; the end justifies the means. In order to save the Church and for the sake of souls it was considered permissible to commit what would in any other context have been acknowledged to be sin. Not only was history falsified, but the rules of Christian morality were no longer deemed applicable where the credit of the hierarchy was at stake.

The very sense of truth and error, right and wrong – in a word conscience – was thrown into confusion. Thus, e.g., when Pius V demanded that the Huguenot prisoners should be put to death, he acted correctly, for he was Pope and a Saint to boot. Since Charles Borromeo approved the murdering of Protestants by private persons, it is better to approve it than to call his canonization into question. Many of the leading Catholic writers of this century deny that

> Gregory XIII approved the massacre of St. Bartholomew or
> that heretics have ever been put to death.
>
> This spirit which falsifies history and corrupts morals is the
> crying sin of modern Catholicism . . . [19]

Still in the field of English church history, Clifford now comes to the vexed
question – to which he was to return in a later intervention – of *The
Catholic Protestation of 1778*. In fact this document was to prove a
major source of embarrassment to the English bishops in their defence of
the Vatican decrees against Gladstone (see next chapter). Clifford
recounts how the English Government of the day had refused to
countenance any granting of civil liberties to Catholics until and unless
they took an oath beforehand forswearing any temporal jurisdiction of
the Pope in the domains of the King of England. Chilini (the papal nuncio
in Brussels with responsibility for English affairs) and others argued that
such an oath should not be taken. The English and Irish bishops,
however, took a different view and swore the oath – a decision which later
received the approval both of the Pope and of Propaganda. (These letters,
says Clifford, were in his personal possession). [20]

> An English author [Lingard?] who has written on the
> history of that period, after describing the prudent way of
> proceeding adopted by those church leaders, concludes as
> follows: "It is to these venerable men that we are debtors in
> that we enjoy the free exercise of our religion and the secure
> possession of our property. If at some future date it should
> happen that we can gain further rights, it will be to these,
> before all others, that our success will be due. But when
> such prudence is lacking, alas! how often greater evils have
> befallen us, because the worst enemies of religion are its
> reckless propagators (*quod maximi hostes reliqionis
> sunt immoderati reliqionis assertores*). [My translation].

---

19   Quoted in *Lord Acton and the First Vatican Council* by J. V.
      Conzemius. Article in *The Journal of Ecclesiastical History*, Vol. XX,
      No. 2, October, 1969, pp. 286, 287.

20   They do not appear now to be in the Clifton Diocesan Archives.

And yet again the same warning:

> Just as I have always been sorry that this question had ever
> arisen – nor have I changed my mind in this regard – so now
> I am certain that not only can no good be hoped for from an
> isolated definition of this question (howsoever it be
> phrased) unless at the same time, with the decree on the
> authority of the Roman Pontiff, the whole question of the
> authority of the Church and of the bishops is clearly,
> logically and coherently (*splendide*) explained to the
> people. Unless this is done, strife and disturbances
> everywhere will not decrease but increase. [My translation].

As a canonist Clifford looked for precision of language and clarity of
thought. In the debate he found both to be singularly lacking.

> The more fathers speak the more obvious it is that the same
> words, the same phrases are being used in different senses
> by different people. [My translation].

Finally Clifford returns to the question of the rights of bishops. Some, he
feels, are whittling away those rights for they believe that the bishops are
assembled in council merely to accept a *fait accompli*.

> ... those who assert that, in defending the infallibility of the
> Roman Pontiff, the bishops in a General Council are not true
> judges but only make declaratory judgments (*iudicium
> assertionis*); in other words, they accept that which, even
> before a hearing of the cause, was already held to be judged.
> [My translation].

Just as on another occasion Clifford quoted the Bull summoning the
Council in order to warn the bishops that they were in danger of acting
ultra vires, so he now quotes the same document in order to establish
the true judicial role of the bishops. In no sense are they a rubber stamp.

> From the beginning of this Council nothing more solemnly
> or more clearly was stated than that the bishops would be
> properly seen in the Council as true judges, judging with the
> Pope matters of Faith, and that a strict interpretation was to
> be placed on the words of the first dogmatic constitution:

"with the bishops of the whole world sitting and judging with us". But not only have several whittled down this judgement, but others, including the most reverend Archbishop of Edessa . . . expressly reduce the office of the bishops – even in a General Council – to this, that they provide the Pope with advice, and in so doing puts them in the same category as other theologians. [My translation].

Leaving no one in any doubt as to the conclusion to be drawn, Clifford adds:

Surely you can see that this question touches the very roots of the rights of bishops.

His final comments are to the effect that a round table meeting should be called which would be truly representative of the differing points of view. On this important point Cuthbert Butler comments:

According to the Pope's idea the deputation de Fide should have been such a mixed tribunal; but it suffered incurably from the original sin of its composition, in that the self-appointed international committee of infallibilists had overridden the Pope's intention, and had engineered the election so as to exclude any representation of the Minority. [21]

Lengthy speeches would achieve nothing, Clifford says, but above all the Minority must be given a chance to state their position. Nor was their loyalty to be impugned merely because they had reservations about the proposed definition.

. . . they have never been second to anyone either in writing or in toil or in help to fight the battles of God, and to expose themselves and their possessions to the enemy for the sake of the House of David. There are amongst those, not less than among you, who, like Paul and Barnabas, can speak of what God has done through them for his people; nor should it be thought that if you close your ears against their pleas, whatever the outcome, that history will pass a harsh judgement against them. [My translation].

---

21   *The First Vatican Council 1869 - 1870*, p. 311.

This marks the end of Clifford's main address to the Council. His approach had been both theological and practical, but aware at the same time of the need to satisfy the exigencies of history and the pastoral demands of Catholics living in a world with many Protestant friends and under civil authority which was not unconcerned at their proceedings. 'In his appraisal of the Protestant frame of mind', wrote Cwiekowski, 'Clifford was unquestionably more accurate than Manning, though Manning was without doubt sincerely convinced that his appraisal was the correct one. And certainly Clifford tried to be more eirenic'. [22]

But Clifford and the others in the Minority were reaching an impasse. The request for round table discussions had already been rejected (see above) and a closure motion was passed at the beginning of June in response to a resolution signed by over one hundred and forty bishops (including Chadwick of Hexham and Newcastle and Cornthwaite of Beverley). There were signs of disapproval – not least because, as Clifford told Acton on the day of his address, he felt that the minority were making some headway. On June 4th the committee of the Minority bishops – of which Clifford was a member – met to discuss their reaction. According to the dispatches of Odo Russell, Clifford and his group wanted to leave Rome *en masse* but Lord Clarendon had already intimated to Russell (30th May):

> Gladstone thinks that if the opposition Bishops would leave
> Rome *en masse* it would be a great blow to oecumenicity –
> pray speak to Acton in this sense – it could do no harm
> though the Pope might only laugh at it.[23]

In the discussions of the committee it is evident that some bishops – including Dupanloup and Clifford – were in no mood to compromise. They wished to give public expression to the Council's lack of freedom and even to abstain from further participation except to register a *non placet* at the final session. But other voices prevailed and the majority decision

---

22   *Op. cit.*, p. 249.

23   *Ibid.*, p. 249, f. 5. Clifford's wish to register a *non placet* vote and the
     extracts from *Quirinus* and Dupanloup's *Diary* (quoted below on
     p. 191) are taken from Cwiekowski, *op. cit.*, p. 250.

was that there should be a single written protest coupled, however, with continued participation in the proceedings of the Council. There were eighty-one signatures on the protest, including Clifford and Errington. Acton was indeed right: such a large group of bishops absenting themselves might well call into question the truly ecumenical (i.e. universal) nature of subsequent proceedings of the Council.

For some time now Clifford had been the object of papal attention and his speech in the Council might well have served to confirm the suspicions of the Pope. The first indication is to be found in the anonymous *Quirinus Letters*. These were slight modifications of Acton's letters to Döllinger although the motives of the two men in writing/publishing them were not identical. Döllinger hoped that publication would discredit the Council in advance whereas Acton's motives were rather 'to rouse to the support of the minority the cultivated classes of the laity and the men of government'. [24]

> The letters of *Quirinus* were, before the acts of the Council were published, an extremely valuable, if highly tendentious source of information. Of the value accorded to them at the time, Newman wrote in 1871: "Lady Howard last night said that both Dr. Amherst and Dr. Clifford told her, that *Quirinus* is the most accurate witness of what took place at the Council.

In the light of this remark, it is ironic to read Quirinus telling us what the Pope was saying even in public about Clifford:

> The Pope seems peculiarly annoyed at some of the English Bishops opposing infallibility, probably because Manning had told him that the English above all others reverenced him as the organ of the Holy Ghost.
>
> He lately broke out into most bitter reproaches against Bishop Clifford of Clifton, before an assemblage of Frenchmen, most of whom did not even know him by name,

---

24   Cwiekowski, *op. cit.*, p. 164.

> and accused him of low ambition, saying that he knew "ex
> certa scientia" the only reason why Clifford would not
> believe in his infallibility was because he had not made him
> Archbishop of Westminster. Yet there is perhaps no member
> of the Council whom everyone credits with so entire an
> absence of any ambitious thought. (pp. 657, 658)

Confirmation of these sentiments on the part of the Pope is to be found in
a scribbled note in the *Journal* of Bishop Dupanloup (who might well
have been present at the audience mentioned above):

> "Clifton, Pape: 'Il s'est fait mon ennemi . . . c'est p(arce) que je
> ne l'ai pas nommé Arch(évêque) de W(estminster) . . .
> comment aurais je nommé . . . qui ne sait ni lire, ni écrire . . . Il
> ne s'est pas conduit en gentleman . . . !!! à un prêtre anglais'".

This outburst against Clifford serves to throw more light on the character
of Pio Nono than on that of the Bishop of Clifton. On occasions the Pope
could be extremely volatile and the letter from Mgr. Neve has already
been quoted (Chapter 6) in which he tells how Barnabo had to call in two
or three other cardinals to calm the Pope when the contents of the joint
letter from Grant and Clifford were read to him in which they had
suggested that Errington might be considered as Wiseman's successor at
Westminster. It is interesting that on both occasions it was his undoubted
favourite – Clifford – who was the object of his anger.

It does appear that the reason for the Pope's comments to the French
pilgrims had been some remarks of Clifford which, having been
misunderstood, were conveyed in their 'perverted' sense to the ears of
the Holy Father. To his credit Bishop Amherst of Northampton

> . . . at once enquired into the matter, saw how his friend had
> been wronged, and, being cognisant of the facts, requested a
> private audience of the Holy Father, which, being granted, he
> strenuously and plainly, though with due deference, laid the
> whole matter before the Sovereign Pontiff, adding that the
> Church had no more loyal son than the Bishop of Clifton.[25]

---

25   *Memoirs of Francis Kerril Amherst, D.D.*, by Dame Mary Francis
      Roskell, O.S.B. (Publ. London, 1903), pp. 301, 302.

The speech on the Infallibility of the Pope was Clifford's crowning achievement at the Council. It was extremely well received, gave new heart to the Minority and, although the definition was eventually passed, it is at least arguable that, had the Council not been prorogued, Clifford's deep conviction that the whole matter should be presented within the context of the Universal Church and its Episcopate might well have been realised at a later date.

One incident at an earlier stage of the Council deserves to be noted because it relates to Clifford's passionate concern that Protestants should not be unnecessarily alienated. In the *Letters* of Acton to Döllinger (27 – 29 March, 1870) mention is made of Strossmayer's plea that, in the *proëma* of the Constitution on the Catholic Faith, Protestantism should not be called the source of atheism, pantheism and materialism. The following day other bishops spoke in the same vein but the Deputation indicated that it was unwilling to yield.

Acton's letter tells us what followed:

> A last attempt succeeded. After the mass when all were at attention, a bishop took a page with a few written lines to the presidents. Two of them thereupon left the hall, while the order of the day and the mode of voting were being read. When they re-entered, the decision was made. The proemium would be taken back, to be further improved. The bishop who had this great influence is an Englishman.

Acton's letter to Döllinger on Monday, March 28th, identified Clifford as the bishop.[26]

It is worth noting that as soon as what was to be the final session had come to an end, Acton wrote to Clifford asking to borrow 'any of your speeches, notes, or counsel'. He continued: Your remarks on the state of England, in reply to Manning, are only vaguely known, and it is a pity they should not be actively preserved. They will be of great importance in England'.[27]

---

26 See Cwiekowski, *op. cit.*, pp. 195, 196.

27 *Clifton Diocesan Archives, Letters to Bishop William Clifford*, Part I, Acton to Clifford, 27.7.1870.

CHAPTER TEN

Aftermath of the Vatican Council

Once it had became inevitable that a definition of Papal Infallibility would be passed by the bishops and promulgated by the Pope, the Minority at the Council – now a well-organised and closely knit group – met to decide what their next move should be. It is said that Clifford urged that they enter a *non placet* at the solemn session.[1] Dupanloup, however, disagreed for he saw the move as one which would give scandal on the grand scale. Instead he wanted the group to leave Rome and by absenting itself from the final session in this way register its disapproval.

> It was this plan that won by a vote of thirty-six to twenty-eight. A letter to the Holy Father was drawn up explaining the Minority abstention from the final session. It bore fifty-five signatures. Clifford was among those who signed, but Errington's name is absent. By the eve of the solemn session many of the minority bishops had already departed from Rome and others left as the public session was taking place. Clifford and Errington were quite likely among them.[2]

The subsequent months were ones of considerable turmoil and Clifford, because by now his views were well known, became the centre of attention. By absenting himself from the public session of a General Council in the proceedings of which he had played no small part, he had demonstrated in the most public way possible – short of registering a *non placet* vote – his disapproval of what was being enacted. And yet, as everyone knew and as Bishop Amherst had been at pains to point out to the Pope himself, the Church had no son more loyal than William Clifford. What, therefore, would he do?

---

1   F. J. Cwiekowski, *The English Bishops and the First Vatican Council* (Publ. Louvain, 1971), p. 272.

2   *Ibid.*, pp. 272, 273.

On his return to England the issue was compounded because, unlike his colleagues on the episcopal bench, he neither immediately issued a pastoral letter on the infallibility of the Pope nor did he formally promulgate the Vatican Decrees throughout his diocese. Both Rome and his own flock were watching closely as Clifford argued his position with skill.

The issues under discussion may best be summarised under five headings:

1) Had the Council been truly 'free'?

2) Had there been a 'moral unanimity' among the bishops?

3) Were the decrees as yet binding and should priests refuse absolution to penitents who withheld assent?

4) Was the Council at an end or had it been prorogued only?

5) Was it *necessary* that a Pope should consult the Universal Church before making an infallible pronouncement?

These strands of questioning will be found interwoven throughout the correspondence of this period. Indeed, no sooner had Clifford arrived home than an important exchange of letters took place between Newman and himself on some of these very issues. Newman, having praised the 'noble stand' taken by Clifford and others against 'a violent party', wanted to know whether the Minority bishops had 'openly or tacitly' yielded

> then I should think that the majority represented the whole episcopate, and that the doctrine was really defined . . .

> But if on the other hand I found that there was a concerted and organised protest and stand against it, on the part of a considerable number of bishops of various countries, then I should find it difficult to determine a ground on which it was binding on my faith.[3]

---

3   *The Letters and Diaries of John Henrv Newman* (ed. Dessain and Gornall), Vol. XXV, p. 179, Newman to Clifford, Letter dated 12.8.1870.

This letter was dated August 12th, 1870. Three days later Clifford replied as follows:

> Most of the Bishops of the Minority were of opinion that the only thing to be done at first is to wait the course of events. It is evident that any active steps taken at present by members of the minority would at once provoke action on the part of the violent party, and then schism would be the only alternative which of course is evidently wrong.
>
> On the other hand the Council is not yet concluded, the Bishops have not yet signed, and we are summoned to reassemble on the 11th of Nov. It seems doubtful whether we shall be able to do so. If we do not, probably some measure will be taken to supply the want of signatures, and to publish the Council. The Bishops will then have to decide on their line of action.
>
> If in addition to all that has occurred the signatures of the Bishops should be wanting to the acts of the Council, grave doubts would arise concerning the nature of the Council, but it would be premature for the Bishops to move in this matter at present, 1st because the time for signing has not yet arrived and 2ndly because it would evidently give an advantage to the violent party.
>
> Of course, even if the nature of the Council remained doubtful, still if the doctrines taught by it were generally accepted and believed, that would show them to be part of the teaching of the Church, and so the separate infallibility of the Pope would on that ground have to be accepted as of faith. But this also requires time . . .[4]

It would be true to say that this final paragraph remained the position of Clifford. The 'believing Church' no more than the 'teaching Church' cannot be in error. But his addendum that this acceptance by the faithful

---

4   Quoted *ibid*.

of the infallibility of the Pope could perforce emerge only in the course of time explains his delay in acting. What finally clinched the matter – as we shall see – was when the church (i.e. the diocese) of Rome promulgated the decrees. For Clifford schism was an unthinkable option, and always remained so.

The bishops of England and Wales gathered to discuss various matters concerned with the Council. Bishop Amherst of Northampton raised the question 'Whether a Priest may now absolve a Penitent who refuses to accept the Infallibility of the Pope as of Catholic Faith?' [5] Clearly it was an issue of some urgency and one which was being raised in other quarters, e.g. Frederick Rymer (President of St. Edmund, Ware) asked Newman his opinion, while William Maskell was in correspondence with several of the bishops.

Brown of Newport came away not at all satisfied with what he had heard with the result that he unburdened his problems in a letter to Clifford:

> The conversation I had previously with Your Lordship, whereby I learnt from you that the Protests of the Bishops was deemed equivalent to their utterances of Non Placet – and that many of these held the definitions of a Council not to be finally conclusive until they had been subscribed by the several Bishops at the termination of the Council – also the uncertainty I felt as to whether the proceedings at the Council were compatible with due liberty of judgment & vote, and whether in the face of so many dissentients the Bishops giving Placets could be held to represent as a moral unanimity the whole Council, these considerations caused me to deprecate the discussion, and to hold that it was yet doubtful whether the definition compelled Belief. [6]

As the letter continues so the lack of unity among the bishops becomes more apparent:

---

5   Ugbrooke Archives, *Letters to Bp. Clifford, 1870*, Bp. Brown of Newport to Clifford, Letter dated 26.9.1870.

6   *Ibid.*

One of the other Bishops took the same view, in part at least, & we did not go into the matter, – on which the Archbp decided to allow no doubt. – It was, I suspect, his application to Rome thereon which brought us Card Antonelli's letter.

This letter was not sent us from Propaganda, & therefore I regarded it as the opinion merely of a Cardinal, keeping it in my possession. But your Lordship, we are told, published it throughout your Diocese. If so, do you give to understand thereby that you now consider the definition binding upon Faith? [7]

Cardinal Antonelli was the Papal Secretary of State and his letter had in fact been addressed to the apostolic nuncio at Brussels:

It has been made known to the Holy See that some amongst the faithful, and perhaps even amongst the Bishops, are of opinion that the Apostolic Constitution, which was put forth in the Session of the Ecumenical Council of the Vatican on the 18th of the month of July, will not be of obligation until it has been solemnly published by some further Act of the Holy See. How strange such a supposition is, anyone may easily know. The Constitution in question had the most solemn publication possible on the very day on which, in the Vatican Basilica, it was solemnly confirmed and promulgated by the Sovereign Pontiff in the presence of above five hundred Bishops; for it was then, although such was not necessary in this case, put up with the ordinary formalities in the usual places of Rome; in consequence of which it was, according to the well-known rule, made obligatory for the whole Catholic world without need of any other publication whatsoever.

I have thought it my duty to communicate these brief observations to you, in order that they may be your guide in

---

7   *Ibid.*

the case of any doubts which may from any quarter be brought before you.

With sentiments of marked esteem,

I remain, your affectionate Servant,

JAMES CARDINAL ANTONELLI

Rome, August 11th, 1870. [8]

Clifford had the letter printed and sent copies to all his clergy. A brief covering sentence introduced the text:

Dear Rev. Sir,

I forward to you copy of a letter of his Eminence CARD. ANTONELLI, which will be useful for your guidance.

+ WILLIAM

Bishop of Clifton

(Years later Bishop Burton underlined the words 'perhaps even amongst the Bishops', drew an arrow pointing to Clifford's signature and wrote in the margin 'Oho!')

Bishop Brown also wrote at this time to Ambrose Phillipps de L'Isle informing him that a Colonel whom Manning had received into the Church had returned to the Anglican Communion 'in consequence of the new Definition'. De L'Isle wrote to Clifford:

---

8   Cardinal Antonelli's letter was printed in *The Tablet*, 27.8.1870. As if to emphasise the point, the same journal three weeks later informed its readers twice on the same page that Bishop Clifford had 'circulated through his Diocese the letter upon the binding nature of the Definitions of the Vatican Council' (*The Tablet*, 17.9.1870, p. 366). The second reference was in a news item describing Pontifical High Mass celebrated by the Bishop at Saint Peter's, Gloucester, where Canon George Case, D.D. was Missionary Rector. On Whit Sunday, 1870, he had preached a sermon which was critical of the dogma then about to be defined (see Chapter 11).

But on all sides I hear of cases where People are either
deterred from Catholicity, or driven back after embracing it,
by what strikes them as neither reconcilable with Reason,
Ecclesiastical History, nor the Tradition of the Church. [9]

Brown had shown de L'Isle his pastoral letter which contained a very
restrictive view of Papal Infallibility.

His host replied:

I thought <u>that</u> a very different notion from the Papal
Infallibility of the New Definition – the Infallibility *"ex sese
non autem ex consensu Ecclesiae"* – which strikes me, I
confess, as rank Blasphemy, and as an audacious violation
of the normal form of Councils, as laid down by the Apostles
themselves . . . Here is Pius IX defining his own Infallibility
"adprobante Sancto Concilio" (which by the bye is an
exaggeration, for it was only a majority of the Council):
Whereas in the Days of S. Peter Himself His voice, uttered
during the Conciliar debates, is altogether merged in it's
[*sic*] final Decisions, and Infallibility claimed only for it's
[*sic*] Corporate and conjunctive action. "It hath seemed
good to the Holy Ghost and to *US*". [10]

He sees it as 'a tremendous intellectual difficulty', but comforts himself
with the thought that God Himself 'at last seems to be taking things into
his own Hands, but not exactly in the way Ultramontanism would have
desired or reckoned on'.[11]

Someone else who wrote to Clifford at this time was Cardinal von
Schwarzenberg of Prague. We do not possess the original, but it is
possible that he had written – as he had earlier written to the French
bishops – with a view to keeping the Minority together, particularly in

---

9   Ugbrooke Archives, *Letters to Bp. Clifford, 1870*, Ambrose Phillipps de
     L'Isle to Clifford, Letter dated 27.9.1870.

10   *Ibid.*

11.   *Ibid.*

view of the fact that, unlike Trent, the Decrees of the Vatican Council had not yet been signed by the Fathers. Apparently the French bishops had given him 'short shrift' not wishing

> to embark on any discussion of the ecumenicity of the Council, which might provoke the greatest difficulties and the most deplorable scandals.[12]

Whether or not the Cardinal's letter to Clifford was written for the same purpose, there is certainly no reference to it in the draft reply (in Latin).[13] Even so it does contain some interesting insights. (It is dated 22nd October, 1870 and its crumpled state suggests that it had been rescued from a waste-paper basket).

In Ireland, Clifford says, there was a solemn Mass of Thanksgiving in Dublin Cathedral, followed by a publication of the Acta. Nothing of that sort, however, had taken place in England.

> Archbishop Manning and one or two other bishops have ordered that the decrees be read in public in those churches under their jurisdiction, and they have admonished the faithful there that the decrees are to be received as a matter of Faith under penalty of refusal of the sacraments, but *in several other dioceses (my own included) nothing like that has been done*. [Italics mine. My translation].[14]

The manner of publication of the decrees and the reception given to them had varied. Clifford continues:

> The Bishop of Birmingham and the Bishop of Newport published pastoral letters setting out the Decrees and explaining them in a more moderate manner. The Decrees have been published on private authority in journals

---

12   Cuthbert Butler, *The Vatican Council 1869 - 1870* (Publ. paperback, 1962), p. 421.

13   Ugbrooke Archives, *Letters to Bp. Clifford, 1870.* Draft reply in Latin to von Schwarzenberg dated 22.10.1870.

14   *Ibid.*

with the result that they are known to all, but as far as the ordinary English populace is concerned the question has not in any way been debated. Amongst the better educated, however, and the sophisticated, and in a certain (though limited) section of the clergy, there has been no small amount of excitement. The view of those who have written to me on the subject was to wait and see what the end of the Council would be. [My translation].[15]

He adds that Errington had been visiting several bishops, probably to obtain an overall view of what was happening in other parts of the country, and the letter adds with a personal note of thanks to the Cardinal 'for your great kindness to me in Rome'.

Newman had noted in a letter to Ambrose St. John, dated 21st August, 1870.

Dr. Errington called . . . he said it was not a free Council. [16]

The month of December, 1870, saw Clifford writing some important letters:

1) The first was his reply (in Italian) to Cardinal Barnabo who had asked him where he stood on the definition of Papal Infallibility. Clifford wrote:

I have received your letter in which you enquire as to my faith with regard to the Apostolic Constitution on the Infallibility of the Roman Pontiff when he is defining *ex cathedra*. Since I have always recognised that communion with the Holy See is an essential note (characteristic) of the true Church, and since I have sworn true obedience to the successor of St. Peter, there can be no reason for me to declare my adherence to the said Constitution which has been published with the Pope's authority under penalty of

---

15   *Ibid.*

16   *The Letters and Diaries of John Henry Newman* (ed. Dessain and Gornall), Vol. XXV, p. 192.

anathema. Furthermore, I have notified this to the clergy
and faithful of my diocese. [My translation].[17]

2) On December 7th Clifford wrote to Brown of Newport about his
disappointment that the Minority bishops had 'eaten up their words' so
early and that acceptance could not now be delayed. [18]

3) Two days later he wrote to Father Newman. His letter to Newman in
August (quoted above) had given reasons why some delay in acceptance
could then be countenanced. Much had happened since that letter was
written and Clifford is now informing Newman why he now regards the
definition as binding:

> There is now no reasonable prospect of the Bishops meeting
> again in council for a long time to come, the doctrine has
> everywhere been openly taught without any organized
> stand having been made against it by the Bishops of the
> minority, several of whom have openly expressed their
> adhesion to it. As to the objections raised against the
> Council itself they do not seem to me to affect the real point
> in question. In the history of several of the councils events
> are recorded which we deplore without disputing the
> conclusions arrived at. In this case the main fact is
> undisputed, that the Pope with the approval of a large
> majority of the Episcopate ha.s proclaimed a certain
> doctrine which has then been taught throughout the church
> without any resistance being offered by those bishops who
> opposed it at the Council. Even if opposition were offered by
> a few Bishops, this could only result in a schism. The
> definition therefore must be accepted as the voice of the
> Church and as such, undoubtedly true. [19]

---

17   Cwiekowski, *op. cit.*, p. 302. Clifford to Barnabo, letter dated 3.12.1870.

18   *Ibid.*, p. 305.

19   Quoted in *The Letters and Diaries of John Henry Newman* (ed.
      Dessain and Gornall), Vol. XXV, p. 246.

Acton wrote to Döllinger on 23rd December indicating that Clifford's communication to his diocese was written in the same terms as his letter to Barnabo (see above).

> Clifford wrote to his clergy that his submission to 'the apostolic constitution promulgated in the Council', is proposed as a condition for communion with Rome. The choice of expression shows that he wished to express a truism, and not a statement of dogma. [20]

This may be so, but his letter to Newman of 9th December undoubtedly goes much further.

(Clifford's dealings with his diocese, and in particular with one of his clergy, Canon George Case, and also with the anxieties expressed to him by his Vicar General, Mgr. Bonomi, form the subject of the next chapter).

Someone with whom Clifford had some slight correspondence was William Maskell. He was an Oxford graduate, had received Anglican Orders in 1837 and been received into the Catholic Church in 1850. Maskell had travelled to Rome in 1851 in the company of Clifford and Herbert Vaughan [21] and the following letter, written in 1864, suggests a continuing close friendship between Maskell and the man who had by now become Bishop of Clifton:

> ... I think yours will be an out & out good life to put in:- viz give up your frightful habits of smoking, snuffing, & drinking, & gambling, & I will back you to live for fifty years to come, with a reasonable amt. of exercise: & plenty of priests to "drop into"... [22]

---

20   Cwiekowski, *op. cit.*, p. 304.

21   J. G. Snead-Cox, *The Life of Cardinal Vaughan* (Publ. London, 1910), Vol. I, pp. 31 – 33.

22   Ugbrooke Archives, *Letters to Bp. Clifford, 1864*, Maskell to Clifford, Letter dated 18.5.1864.

In the late summer of 1870 Maskell was writing to several of the bishops asking whether the decrees of the Council demanded interior assent and whether a priest would be right in refusing absolution to a pentitent who continued to withhold such assent.

Clifford's reply was dated 18th August:

> As regards the question you put to me it appears that the decree of a Council duly convoked has a prima facie claim to be regarded as such as soon as it become known. But untill [*sic*] the acts are signed and published, I do not think a man can be charged with sin who withholds interior assent.
>
> If after a lapse of time the acts of the Council were not either signed or published – or the free action of the Council were called into question: still I should hold that if any doctrine were accepted without contradiction throughout the Church such doctrines must be accepted as revealed. Others think as I do on this point, but there are many who teach otherwise. [23]

It will be noticed that this is virtually the same as he wrote to Newman nearly 4 months later (see letter of 9th December, quoted above).

Maskell became embroiled in a dispute with Manning and his secretary. This controversy does not concern us here except to note that Maskell was protesting against the Archbishop's broad interpretation of the meaning of Papal Infallibility. In 1871 Maskell published a pamphlet entitled *What is the Meaning of the Late Definition of the Infallibility of the Pope? An Enquiry.* [24] In it he repeats Clifford's objection made at the Council to the effect that there was no tradition in England of teaching that the Pope alone – as distinct from the Church – was infallible. Clifford had cited Gother, Challoner and Milner. Maskell wrote:

---

23   Quoted in Cwiekowski, *op. cit.*, p. 290.

24   William Maskell, A.M., *What is the Meaning of the Late Definition of the Infallibility of the Pope? An Enquiry* (Publ. London, 1871). 12 pages.

> Again, we shall be told that no Ecumenical Council since the days of the Apostles has ever declared any doctrine to be of Faith which had not been previously . . . taught by many priests and bishops, and often in later times by local Councils, to be already of faith.

> We must own that we cannot say this of the new dogma, as some explain it, and as it is popularly, however wrongly, understood. For where is a single catechism in which people were so instructed? Must we not further confess that such manuals, where they spoke upon the subject at all, distinctly (at least in England and Ireland) taught differently? (pp. 7, 8).

During January, 1871, Maskell was in correspondence with Clifford. We do not have his letters but – perhaps more interestingly – we do have the bishop's replies. Of these, by far the most important is the first: Clifford, in a mood of seriousness mixed with a degree of banter, spells out his reaction to the Maskell pamphlet:

> I am now able to write a little but my wrist is not well yet. –

> I have read your pamphlet & I am not going to knock you on the head with my crosier yet. I shall reserve that vigorous treatment for a future occasion. I have not much fault to find with the pamphlet, except that I don't think it aught [*sic*] to have been written. Cui bono? Men will say it is a quarrel between you & Manning – I do not think that his interpretation of the decree will hold, or that it will be the one finally adopted in the church: but at present men are not in the humor for listening to anything moderate.

> I wish you had sprained your wrist instead of I: it would be so much more comfortable for me, & would decide at once the question of whether you aught [*sic*] to write or not . . .

> When shall we go to Paris again? – or Rome? [25]

---

25   Archives of the English Province of the Society of Jesus, Mount Street, *Proofs, MSS, etc.* 19/1/31, No. 12. Bp. Clifford to William Maskell, Letter dated 18.1.1871.

Five days later he is writing to Maskell:

> I will show you what I wrote to some of my clergy who asked
> for information on some points you allude to. [26]

Though not certain, this could well refer to his lengthy reply to Mgr.
Bonomi, V.G. (see Appendix).

Two days later (January 25th, 1871) a short note which simply asks:

> Where are the letters of *Quirinus* to be found? It is very
> queer, but I have never seen them.[27]

From this one may conclude that Maskell's letter (citing *Quirinus* [28]) had
been Clifford's first intimation of the Pope's outburst against him when
speaking to the French pilgrims (see end of previous chapter). Was
Clifford's reaction one of profound disbelief or of deeply wounded
feelings? We shall never know.

The invasion of Rome by the troops of the Italian Government proved to
be another source of concern to Catholics, but one which produced a
divided reaction. On October 26th Manning wrote to the Bishops
suggesting that a protest be sent similar to that issued by the Bishops of

---

26   Archives (S.J.), Mount Street, *Proofs, MSS, etc.* 19/1/31. No. 13. Bp.
     Clifford to William Maskell, Letter dated 23.1.1871.

27   Archives (S.J.), Mount Street, *Proofs, MSS, Etc.* 19/1/31, No. 14. Bp.
     Clifford to William Maskell, Letter dated 25.1.1871.

28   Quirinus, *Letters from Rome on the Council* (Reprinted from the
     Allgemeine Zeitung), (Publ. London, 1870). After describing the Pope's
     outburst against Clifford in which he accused him of 'low ambition,
     saying that . . . the only reason why Clifford would not believe in his
     infallibility was because he had not made him Archbishop of
     Westminster', the author adds:

     > Yet there is perhaps no member of the Council whom everyone
     > credits with so entire an absence of any ambitious thought. The
     > spectacle of such conduct on the part of the man, who for twenty-
     > four years has held the highest earthly dignity, produces a painful
     > feeling in some, and contempt in others. (pp. 657, 658).

Ireland. He wanted to know first whether they judged such a protest to be 'expedient' and secondly, whether there should be a joint Pastoral by all the Bishops, or whether they should act separately. [29]

Clifford replied that 'several of the Bishops are like myself greatly opposed to joint Pastorals', but that if there was to be one it should be preceded by a meeting of the Bishops. [30] This sentence says much, for it may be assumed that any joint letter would in fact come from the pen of Manning with the result that the Catholic case could be expressed in such extreme terms that some of the bishops would find difficulty in subscribing to it.

But suddenly a plethora of Addresses to the Pope appeared. One was read at Teignmouth bearing apparently the forged name of Lord Clifford (the Bishop's brother)[31] while another circular from the Rev. Alfred Dolman was read before Mass from the steps of Lord Clifford's own chapel at Ugbrooke. It invited signatures, and stated that

> "it is wholly needful that you the Holy Father enjoy the fullness of the Temporal Sovereignty which the wisdom of faithful ages recognised to be God's gift to you"

Lord Clifford was furious and wrote the following to Bishop Vaughan of Plymouth, having first however, submitted it to his brother, William.

> While strenuously maintaining with all Catholics the necessity of the temporal Power of the Catholic Church & the Pope at its Head, which has in fact existed throughout Christendom from the foundation of Christianity; I protest as an English Catholic Layman against a call from the Altar, to support the Territorial *Sovereignty* of the Pope – which is

---

29   Manning to the Bishops, circular letter dated 26.10.1870. A photocopy is
      in the Clifton Diocesan Archives.

30   Ugbrooke Archives, *Letter to Bp. Clifford, 1870*, Clifford to Manning,
      Draft reply dated 30.10.1870.

31   Ugbrooke Archives, *Letter to Bp. Clifford, 1870*, Lord Clifford to his
      brother, Letter dated 30.10.1870.

not coeval with Christianity, has never been exercised actually, except in a small portion of Italy; and has now been abolished even there, by the Italians themselves.

I trust that the introduction of these irritating political topics into our churches does not meet, as it has hitherto not met, with your Lordship's sanction; and reserving to myself the right to publish this protest, if necessary in my own defence. [32]

But Bishop Clifford himself was to be in trouble over the issue. On December 13th the fiery Goss of Liverpool wrote to Clifford:

I have received a letter from Card. Barnabo, as I doubt not you have also, in which he says that it *has been told him* that you & I have denied permission to our respective Diocesans to sign an act of protest against the invasion of Rome & the consequent captivity of the Supreme pontiff, which many hundred thousands of laity & clergy of England this a wonderful impulse of piety have signed (*sic*). [33]

Goss noted that no such permission was necessary and that

my prohibition is exactly the same as yours – for the preface has nothing to do with the substance of my decree – to forbid unauthorised circulars in the Church.

Not unnaturally suspicion falls on Manning as the informant:

I should think it is the Archbp's doing, but Dolman threatened me with an appeal to his & my ecclesiastical superior in the *Tablet* Newspaper –

Ought we not to ask the name of his informant & to be furnished with a copy of the charge? Ordinarily we do not

---

32   Ugbrooke Archives, *Letters to Bp. Clifford, 1870*, Lord Clifford to Bp. Vaughan, Letter dated 31.10.1870.

33   Ugbrooke Archives, *Letters to Bp. Clifford, 1870*, Bp. Goss to Clifford, Letter dated 13.12.1870.

reply to anonymous charges, but Bps have been snuffed out
& editors of journals substituted in their place . . .

We shall probably have a notice in the *Tablet*, in due time,
boasting how certain refractive Bps have been whipped into
order by Propaganda. I shall be guided in my reply by what
you write. Our liberties & our jurisdiction are now surely at
stake. We have an eely foe against us who does not stick at
a trifle, as evidenced by his account of the peaceful &
dignified demeanour of the Council at all times.[34]

One of those to whom the Vatican Decrees were quite abhorrent was
Gladstone. For him they resurrected all the worst fears engendered by
the publication of the *Syllabus of Errors* in 1864, and he even saw the
spectre of the medieval popes stalking menacingly across the modern
world of the 19th century.

The vast new claims were lodged in the reign of a pontiff,
who by the dark Syllabus of 1864 had condemned free
speech, a free press, liberty of conscience, toleration of
nonconformity, the free study of civil and philosophic things
independently of church authority, marriage unless
sacramentally contracted, and all definition by the state of
the civil rights of the church. [35]

. . . Rome has substituted for the proud boast of *semper
eadem* a policy of violence and change in faith; when she
has refurbished and paraded anew every rusty tool she was
fondly thought to have disused; when no one can become her
convert, without renouncing his moral and mental freedom,
and placing his civil loyalty and duty at the mercy of
another; and when she has equally repudiated modern
thought and ancient history. [36]

---

34   *Ibid.*

35   Quoted in *The Life of William Ewart Gladstone* by John Morley (Publ.
      London, 1908), Vol. II, p. 92.

36   *Ibid.*, pp. 90, 91.

Before publishing his challenge to Rome – it took the form of two pamphlets to the first of which Clifford would reply in a notable Pastoral Letter – Gladstone was careful to take soundings from a number of Catholics of varying shades of opinion. The first was Döllinger whose *Quirinus Letters* had done so much not only to alert the world but also to sow mischief as to the possible repercussions of what was being decided at the Council. In a rather curious remark Gladstone's biographer (Morley) says that Döllinger 'was not aware of the purpose of his English friend'.[37] At any rate Gladstone stayed with Döllinger some eighteen days. Morley adds:

> If these strong words (i.e. second passage quoted above) expressed his state of mind before he went abroad, we may readily imagine how the Bavarian air would fan the flame.[38]

In October, 1874, Gladstone invited Lord Acton to Harwarden 'to read as much of the MS. as your patience would endure'.[39] But most interesting of all must be the visit that Ambrose Phillipps de L'Isle paid at about the same time. In welcoming the prospect of a visit by Clifford early in the new year, de L'Isle wrote:

> I am anxious too that you should hear all about my visit to Mr. Gladstone at Harwarden Castle, *which I made to him by his particular request before he published his pamphlet*, as it throws some light on the whole affair – and yet it was a thing I could not write about. [Italics mine].[40]

Gladstone's pamphlet entitled *The Vatican Decrees in their Bearing on Civil Allegiance: a Political Expostulation* appeared in November, 1874. Morley says:

---

37   *Ibid.*, p. 91.

38   *Ibid.*, p. 91.

39.   *Ibid.*, p. 91.

40   Ugbrooke Archives, *Letters to Bp. Clifford, 1874*, de L'Isle to Clifford, Letter dated 20.12.1874.

[It] was meant for an argument that the decree of infallibility aimed a deadly blow at the old historic, scientific, and moderate school; it was a degradation of the episcopal order; it carried to its furthest point that spirit of absolutist centralisation, which in its excesses is as fatal to vigorous life in the church as in the state; it overthrew the principle not even denied by the council of Trent in the sixteenth century, that the pope and his judgements were triable by the assembled representatives of the Christian world. [41]

While not condoning the language, Clifford might well have recognised the sentiment which inspired 'a degradation of the episcopal order'. Morley continues:

The central proposition made a cruel dilemma for a large class of the subjects of the Queen; for the choice assigned to them by assuming stringent logic was between being bad citizens if they submitted to the decree of papal infallibility, and bad catholics if they did not. [42]

Graphically Morley describes the reaction of those who supported Gladstone: Protestant logicians wrote to Mr. Gladstone that if his contention were good, we ought now to repeal catholic emancipation and again clap on the fetters. [43]

By the same token Catholics could not allow such an issue at such a time, projected in such a compelling manner into the public arena, to go unchallenged. Nor were there lacking those who would question Gladstone's motives in launching such an attack on the Church of Rome:

He was accused by some of introducing a Bismarckian *Kulturkampf* into England, of seeking to recover his lost

---

41   Morley, *op. cit.*, p. 91.

42   *Ibid.*, p. 93.

43   *Ibid.*, p. 93.

popularity by pandering to no-popery, of dis-regarding the best interests of the country for the sake of his own restoration to power. [44]

At the beginning of February Gladstone noted that he had just finished reading the twentieth reply to his pamphlet: 'They cover 1000 pages' [45], One such reply would have been the Pastoral Letter of Bishop Clifford issued on 25th November, 1874, under the title *Catholic Allegiance*.

The day before publication Clifford received a cautionary letter from Bishop Brown of Newport who was himself no mean controversialist:

> I am informed that your Lordship is preparing a reply to Gladstone, with much care. It is of great moment that this be done by one who knows how to express Catholic truths in accurate theological language, which Capel cannot be expected to do – for he never went through a course of Theology under a well trained Professor – & I have found him more than once in verbal error.
>
> The *Times* of the two last days yesterday (*sic*) & that I have seen with pain the confirmation from all sides of the fears you uttered at the Vatican Council in contradiction to those put forward by Dr. Manning, as to the likely result of defining the Infallibility of the Pope.
>
> I need not pray you to weigh carefully all you are preparing on the matter, leaving nothing of moment without enabling honest Protestants to judge us fairly. [46]

---

44   *Ibid.*, p. 95.

45   *Ibid.*, p. 95.

46   Ugbrooke Archives, *Letters to Bp. Clifford. 1874*, Bp. Brown to Clifford, Letter dated 24.11.1874.

Synopsis of Clifford's Pastoral 'Catholic Allegiance'

Text: 'Render to Caesar . . .'

Allegiance to Queen and Pope are distinct. Since 1829 (Catholic Emancipation) Catholic and Protestant citizens have lived side by side in harmony.

> But within the last few weeks this harmony has been rudely threatened, and Mr. Gladstone, in whom Catholics not only recognise a great statesman, but one to whom they owe gratitude for his exertions in removing many past grievances, and who is the head of a great party mainly instrumental in obtaining Catholic Emancipation, has proclaimed that, since the publishing of the decrees of the Vatican Council it is no longer possible for English Catholics to pay to their temporal sovereign a full and undivided allegiance. (p.5)

Gladstone: I will not be satisfied with a general declaration of loyalty.

Clifford: Why not? We have Catholic peers, M.Ps., judges, barristers, soldiers . . . We have a claim to be taken at our word.

Gladstone wants a demonstration that the Vatican decrees do not impair the loyalty of Catholic citizens.

Which decrees?   1)   Obedience to Pope in faith, morals, discipline.

                2)   Infallibility of Pope when speaking *ex cathedra*.

On the FIRST decree

Gladstone: There is no human action which does not come within the boundary of morality. Therefore the Pope 'claims power over all'.

Clifford: Correct premise but wrong conclusion.

                     i)   It is not a *terra incognita*. For example, the
                            Decalogue and moral precepts cannot be
                            reversed.

                     ii)   There are separate jurisdictions *within* field of
                            morality:

                            ... the Pope has no more power to assess our
                            taxes, regulate our trade, or interfere with the
                            administration of our law courts than he has to
                            sit and deliver judgment in the Court of Queen's
                            Bench. (p. 9)

                            The Pope may not
                            ... ignore or transgress boundaries already fixed
                            between the temporal and spiritual powers ... (p. 10).

                            This is a question which touches the *Authority*
                            of the Pope, not his *Magisterium*. (p. 10).

                            If a Pope were so to abuse his power as to seek
                            to interfere in that which undoubtedly belongs to
                            the civil authority, Catholics would resist him.
                            (pp. 10, 11).

Clifford proceeds to draw an example from the oath of allegiance
required of Catholics by the Emancipation Act:
                     Catholics owe allegiance to the sovereign. Queen Victoria is
                     the lawful sovereign. Catholics cannot be released from this
                     solemn and lawful contract of allegiance without the
                     consent of the other party.

BUT there are some areas where there is doubt as to the relative
competence of Church and State. The solution?

Protestants: 'We will decide by use of our private judgement'.

Catholics: 'For us the ultimate decision rests with the Pope'.

In either case appeal has to be made to the past, using this as a guarantee of respect for the future.

On the SECOND decree (Papal Infallibility)

Gladstone: . . . prior to the granting of Emancipation, the Catholic Bishops declared "on oath their belief that it is not an article of the Catholic faith, neither are they thereby required to believe that the Pope is infallible". (p. 16)

(This must have touched a sensitive nerve with Clifford as he had mentioned this precise point in his address at the Council as a reason for not proceeding with the definition. In drafting his reply he is constrained to use his forensic skills to the full).

Clifford: 1st – Though the bishops could then declare, and did declare, that they *were not required* to believe that the Pope is infallible, yet they could not, and did not, deny that even then many Catholics did hold, and all Catholics *might* hold, that the Pope is infallible when speaking *ex cathedra*; and if such belief be incompatible with due allegiance to the sovereign, it was no security against a divided allegiance for Protestants to be told that Catholics were not *obliged* to hold it, when at the same time it was certain that a large number of them *did* and all *might* do so. Accordingly it was not required of Catholics to swear that they did not believe that the Pope was infallible, but only to swear that the Pope could not release them from their allegiance. Hence, no guarantee given by Catholics at the time of the passing of the Emancipation Act has been removed. (p. 16)

2nd – If Catholics were regarded as loyal when the Pope was defining in Council, they cannot be accused of disloyalty when he defines *ex cathedra*.

3rd – (not a point raised by Gladstone): Some see Infallibility "like a thunderbolt in the breast of one man", to which Clifford replied that in everyday matters the Church does not operate in this way. Business is transacted through Propaganda.

<u>Conclusion</u>: Neither in the past nor now has the Pope any right 'to oppose in any manner the performance of the civil duties which Catholics owe to the king'. (p. 19).

<u>Gladstone</u>:   What would Catholics think if England, as one of the guardians of the peace of Europe, had to take action against the temporal power of the Pope?

<u>Clifford</u>:   . . . English Catholics, without any imputation to their loyalty, are as free to oppose, by every constitutional means in their power, any measure brought forward by ministers in a sense hostile to the Temporal Power of the Pope, as they are to oppose any other measure of domestic or foreign policy, of which they disapprove; and that as for unconstitutional measures, it would neither be asked of them to have recourse to them, nor would they do so. (p. 20)

Reaction to this Pastoral – as to the one ten years earlier which had dealt with the thorny issue of the *Syllabus* – was over-whelmingly favourable. Lord Belper, however, in a letter to Ambrose Phillips de L'Isle (and forwarded by him to Clifford), while paying tribute to the 'tone and spirit' in which the Pastoral was written, was nevertheless not wholly convinced:

I . . . think that he has been very successful in showing that if we are to judge for the future from the past conduct of Catholics for many years, there can be little cause for apprehension.

But I cannot say that he has in my opinion been equally successful in answering Gladstone's argument with respect to the power & position of the Pope. Indeed in page *15* he seems to admit that the Pope *might* give a decision calculated to impair the allegiance of Catholics, for he says the one "*guarantee*" is that he *has not* given any such decision since Emancipation. But can the fact that certain Popes have, under certain circumstances, adhered to a particular line of conduct for 40 years, be considered a *guarantee* that no Pope, under different circumstances, will hereafter depart from it?

Still less can this be reckoned upon when it is considered that the personal position of the Pope has been materially altered by the decree of the late Council, & that his power of independent action has been greatly increased . . . I think that it may be assumed that the immense trouble, risk & responsibility of holding a General council would not have been incurred unless for the purpose of effecting a *material* & *important* alteration in the Pope's position & Authority.' [47]

Although Lord Belper feels compelled to agree with Gladstone in thinking 'that the present state of the relations of the Roman Catholic Church with the State is most unsatisfactory, & that it is impossible logically to defend such a state of things', he is nevertheless prepared to rely on the 'good sense & moderation' of those in positions of authority. He ends:

For this purpose I cannot do better than hope that you may have many Bishop Cliffords amongst the Prelates & rulers of your Church. [48]

A fortnight later Ambrose Phillipps de L'Isle wrote to Clifford:

. . . from all quarters I hear great commendations of your Pastoral, and I think it will have had a great effect in calming any agitation, that was beginning to spread. [49]

---

47   Ugbrooke Archives, *Letters to Bp. Clifford, 1874*, Lord Belper to Ambrose Phillipps de L'Isle, Letter dated 8.12.1874.

      BELPER, Edward Strutt, 1st Baron (1801 – 1880). Lawyer. M.P. for Arundel and then Nottingham. Chancellor of the Duchy of Lancaster (1852 – 54). (*D.N.B.*, Vol. LV, pp. 63, 64).

48   *Ibid.*

49   Ugbrooke Archives, *Letters to Bp. Clifford, 1874*, de L'Isle to Clifford, Letter dated 20.12.1874.

The same note of gratitude was struck by J. Spencer Northcote, writing from Oscott:

> ... pray accept my best thanks for the copy of your Pastoral, which seemed to me the most English & straight-to-the-point answer that this controversy has as yet elicited. [50]

By now the discussion had widened. De L'Isle, having become embroiled in a dispute with his bishop (Bagshawe of Nottingham), sought advice from Clifford. It concerned an article which de L'Isle had written and which he had shown to Clifford before it was published.

> ... (Bagshawe's) letter received by me today ... shows that he has taken offence at several Passages in it, and even that they are personal to himself. I need not say that this was unintentional on my Part: I was not aware that he belonged to any "Party" in the Catholic Church, or that I was condemning any "Party" as such – What I endeavoured to show was that there were extreme zealots amongst us, who, far more than the Vatican council, were the real cause why so many people, and even Statesmen, cried out agt. that Council making it responsible for their excesses.[51]

This last statement will have reminded Clifford of what he himself had said at the Council: 'The worst enemies of religion are its reckless propagators'. De L'Isle added:

> You will see Bishop Bagshaw affirms the "Deposing Power" to be *an existing Right* still inherent in the Papacy, not what Mr. Gladstone asserted. [52]

---

50   Ugbrooke Archives, *Letters to Bp. Clifford, 1874*, Northcote to Clifford, Letter dated 26.12.1874.

51   Ugbrooke Archives, *Letters to Bp. Clifford, 1875*, de L'Isle to Clifford, Letter dated 11.2.1875.

52   *Ibid.*

What Clifford wrote in reply we do not know, but it made De L'Isle – who had already written a conciliatory letter to Bagshaw – very grateful. He told Clifford:

> Yesterday Mr. Gladstone sent me a copy of his Rejoinder – I conclude he will have done the same to you – I have not time to comment on it today, I will only say it is *tremendously powerful*. [53]

And then a real *cri de coeur*:

> These things, and others that are going on all over the world, tempt me to say (humanly speaking) I wish the vatican council had never been held – It has put us all in a fix that I fear we shall never get out of! [54]

Ironically Gladstone had said precisely the same to Odo Russell over five years before, just as the Council was about to open:

> The odds seem to be that the child yet unborn will rue the calling of this council. [55]

Gladstone's 'tremendously powerful' Rejoinder was published early in 1875, less than a year after his first published attack on the Decrees. The second pamphlet, entitled *Vaticanism: An Answer to Replies and Reproofs* (128 pages),[56] was his defence against those leading Catholics, mostly bishops, who had replied to his *The Vatican Decrees in their bearing on civil Allegiance: A Political Expostulation* (72 pages), and in particular against Manning, Newman, Ullathorne, Clifford and Vaughan.

---

53   Ugbrooke Archives, *Letters to Bp. Clifford, 1875*, de L'Isle to Clifford, Letter dated 26.2.1875.

54   *Ibid*.

55   Morley, *op. cit.*, p. 87.

56   Right Hon. W. E. Gladstone, M. P., *Vaticanism: An Answer to Replies and Reproofs* (Publ. London, 1875).

Gladstone – in so far as his remarks pertain to Clifford – praises the spirit in which the bishop's pastoral letter was written. Even so, he still maintains that none of his critics has really met his objections:

> . . . Bishop Clifford, in a pastoral letter of which I gladly acknowledge the equitable, restrained, and Christian spirit, says I have proclaimed that since the Vatican Decrees were published "it is no longer possible for English Catholics to pay to their temporal sovereign a full and undivided allegiance".

> I am obliged to assert that not one of the writers against me has apprehended or stated with accuracy my principal charge. (p. 7).

> As regards this latter point (i.e. 'loyalty and civil duty') the Pastoral of Bishop Clifford is also everything that can be wished. (p. 13).

> In the train of the Bishops (I except Bishop Clifford) come priests, monks, nay, laymen: Vaticanism in all its ranks and orders. (p. 75).

The strongest arguments deployed in the rejoinder are from history, and here Gladstone virtually makes his own the very points made by Clifford (see Appendix 10) in his attempt at the Council to avert making a dogma out of something which had had but a small part in the faith of English Catholics. Referring to the *Protestation of the Roman Catholics of England (1778 - 9)*, [57] Gladstone says:

> In this very important document there are contained statements of the greatest significance.

> 1. That the subscribers to it "acknowledge no infalliblity in the Pope". . .

---

[57]   *The Declaration and Protestation signed by the English Catholic Dissenters in 1789: with the Names of Those Who Signed It* (Publ. 1791).

Having reminded his readers that the *Protestation* had been signed 'by 241 priests, including all the Vicars Apostolic, by all the clergy and laity in England of any note',[58]
Gladstone continued:

> Thus we have on the part of the entire body, of which Archbishop Manning is now the head, a direct, literal, and unconditional rejection of the cardinal tenet which he tells us has always been believed by his Church, and was an article of Divine faith before as well as after 1870. (pages 45, 46).

At this point it must be of more than passing interest to quote at some length what Ronald Knox wrote about the *Protestation* in 1942 in one of his conferences to the Catholic students at Oxford: [59]

> It is important, then, to examine the circumstances of the time a little. In the first place, the four bishops who then acted as Vicars Apostolic in England only consented to sign the protestation when it was explained to them that the whole paragraph was only meant to apply to the pope's interference in temporal matters, and did not limit his authority in things ecclesiastical; that this had been the undoubted intention of those by whom the protestation was drawn up.

An interesting point, but does it square with the Protestation which states quite clearly (page 4):

> And we further solemnly declare, that We do make this DECLARATION and PROTESTATION, and every Part thereof, in the Plain and Ordinary Sense of the Words of the same, without any Evasion, Equivocation, or Mental Reservation whatsoever.

---

58   Lord Clifford and Charles Clifford were among the signatories, but not Bishop Walmesley (Vicar Apostolic of the Western District).

59   Ronald Knox, *In Soft Garments: A Collection of Oxford Conferences* (Publ. London, 1942), p. 116.

Knox continues:

> In the second place, it is to be remembered that the oath was
> not signed by the bishops, and indeed was twice condemned
> by the bishops, though their grounds for doing so were
> never fully made clear.

> And in the third place, the oath was never actually taken.
> Providence interfered, through the rather unlikely agency
> of the Anglican Bishop of St. David's and the
> emancipation granted in 1791 was secured to Catholics
> on condition of their taking a quite unobjectionable oath,
> similar to that which had already been employed for the
> same purpose in Ireland.

To return to Gladstone's pamphlet: it could not have been any less galling
for Clifford to read the words of one of his predecessors being quoted
against him by Gladstone.

> Finally: it will scarcely be denied that Bishop Baines was, to
> say the least, a very eminent and representative member of
> the Anglo-Roman body. In 1822, he wrote as follows:-

> "Bellarmine, and some other Divines, chiefly Italians, have
> believed the Pope infallible, when proposing ex cathedra an
> article of faith. *But in England or Ireland I do not believe
> that any Catholic maintains the infallibility of the
> Pope." (Defence against Dr. Moysey*, p. 230, 1822) (p. 48).

Again referring to history, Gladstone takes Clifford directly to task on the
origins of the deposing power of the Roman Pontiff:

> Bishop Clifford, indeed, sustains the deposing power on
> the ground that it was accorded to the Pope by the
> nations. It was simply a case like that of the Geneva
> Arbitrators (p. 12) . . . These allegations quiet my fears;
> but they strain my faith; and, purporting to be historical,
> they shock my judgment. For they are, to speak plainly,
> without foundation . . . The doctrine of the consent of
> nations is a pure imagination.

To prove his point Gladstone quotes the Pope himself (*Discorsi di Pio IX*, vol. 1, p. 203):

> "A right which the Popes *exercised in virtue of their authority* when the general good demanded it" .

> Thus Bishop Clifford and Dr. Newman are entirely at issue with the Pope respecting the deposing power. will they not have to reconsider what they are to say, and what they are to believe? (pages 70 – 73)

The *Rejoinder's* final argument against Clifford is to place his words (quoted earlier in this chapter, p. 216) in the context of what Manning had written. Again, Gladstone's argument is compelling.

> In his *'Petri Privilegium'*, iii, 19, n., Archbishop Manning quotes the Bull *In Cena Domini* as if it were still in force. Bishop Clifford, in his Pastoral Letter (p. 9), laid it down that though all human actions were moral actions, there were many of them which belonged to the temporal power, and with which the Pope could not interfere. Among these he mentioned the assessment and payment of taxes.

> But is it not the fact that this Bull excommunicates "all who impose new taxes, not already provided for by law, without the Pope's leave"? and all who impose, without the said leave, special and express, any taxes, new or old, upon clergymen, churches, or monasteries? (sections v, xviii) (p. 90).

Ambrose Phillipps de L'Isle is invariably an interesting correspondent and in a letter to Clifford he sheds light on how Newman was reacting to Gladstone's second pamphlet. Newman told De L'Isle that in his view 'the most important and telling part' of what Gladstone had written

> is that which refers to the discrepancies, real or apparent, between the Councils of Constance and the Vatican – and to Archbishop Manning's contention, that Papal Infallibility even before the Council was always a "Dogma of Divine Faith" – upon this latter proposition Father Newman tells me that he thinks Gladstone "is triumphant in his denial".

For my own part I rather side with the Cardinal Archbishop, and if Gladstone's argument hits His Eminence, it hits the main argument of my article also – and I think that in defending what I asserted I could refute the *substance* of the ex Premier's statements.[60]

Nor is Phillipps averse to conceding a point to Gladstone:

In a letter I wrote a few days ago to Gladstone I acknowledged frankly to him, what I have *always* felt, that the Catholic System has its difficulties, if you will its *seemingly* weak Points, but that these, whatever they may be, are as *nothing* when compared with those that beset any *separated* System of Xtianity, or even Xtiantiy itself, or any system of Revelation such as the Mosaic Dispensation. [61]

As Clifford does not appear to have gone into print on the subject again, one must conclude that for him the controversy with Gladstone was now at an end.

Postscript

In a letter to Bishop Burton half a century later (1924), Cuthbert Butler recalled the impact Clifford's Pastoral had made on him when it was first read at Mass in the Advent of 1874:

I have distant recollection of hearing it as a boy at Downside, & being struck how good it was. It's about the only pastoral I have ever heard in my life that left so clear (an) impression! And in his second Pamphlet Gladstone singled out Newman's & Clifford's – the two Inopportunists! as the two that really met his attack.[62]

A slight exaggeration as when the contest entered the arena of history, a points victory must surely be awarded to Gladstone.

---

60   Ugbrooke Archives, *Letters to Bp. Clifford. 1875*, de L'Isle to Clifford, Letter dated 19.3.1875.

61   *Ibid.*

62   Clifton Diocesan Archives, *Letters 1923 - 24*, No. 306, Cuthbert Butler to Bp. Burton, Letter dated 14.4.1924.

Canon George Case, (1823 – 1883), Rector of the
Catholic Mission in Gloucester

CHAPTER ELEVEN

Canon George Case. D.D.

In treating of the aftermath of the Vatican Council, particularly as it affected the diocese of Clifton, special regard must be paid to the events surrounding a sermon [1] preached in Gloucester by the Rector of the Mission, Canon Case, and to his subsequently leaving the diocese, the priesthood and (apparently) the Church itself. It is a sad story which for Bishop Clifford had an added poignancy. There were several reasons for this:

1) Although there does not appear to have been a close friendship between the two men, it is clear that Clifford had a high regard for Case's intellect. This is shown from the fact of the bishop's having consulted him in 1864 over the possible advantages of Catholics attending the state Universities.

2) Case had expended a great deal of his personal wealth in completing and beautifying his mission church (St. Peter, Gloucester). For this Clifford, presiding over an impecunious diocese, must have felt a great debt of gratitude.

3) Both men had had grave misgivings about the manner in which the definition of Papal Infallibility had come about, compounded it would seem – although Clifford did not say as much to Case – by the pressure ('lack of freedom') brought to bear on the bishops, particularly during the deliberations prior to the solemn definition.

For these reasons, apart from the spiritual tragedy involved, it would not be too much to see the whole episode, coupled with that of the dismissal of Archbishop Errington, as casting the biggest shadow over the whole episcopate of William Clifford.

---

1   George Case, *The Vatican Council and A Duty of Catholics in Regard to It*. A Sermon preached on Whit Sunday 1870 (16 pages), (Publ. London, 1870). Full text is reprinted in Appendix 14, p. 441. Case was Rector of St. Peter's, Gloucester, from 1864 to 1876.

Indeed in some respects there appears to have been a striking similarity between Errington and Case. Both were able men, each with his streak of stubbornness, but how different the outcome!

> George Case was the eldest son of John Deane Case, Recorder of Liverpool. He matriculated at Brasenose College, Oxford, on 9th June, 1841, at the age of 17; graduated B.A. (First Class in Mathematics) in 1845, and proceeded M.A. three years later. He was ordained into the Anglican ministry, and became curate of the 'High' church of All Saints, Margaret Street, London.'

At the time of the Gorham Judgement he became a Catholic, went to Rome as a private student (where he received his D.D.) and was ordained priest. For a while he was at the Jesuit Novitiate in Roehampton but subsequently felt more called to the life of a secular priest. He took charge of St. Mary's, Chelsea and later came to the Pro-Cathedral, Clifton – the reason for the move is unclear – and then became responsible for a Mission in Bristol. [2]

He took over at St. Peter's, Gloucester, in September, 1864. In 1868 we find Clifford praising his work there in a letter to Mgr. Talbot in Rome.[3] This involved building a new presbytery and completing the church to its original design. One of the areas where work was carried out was the Lady Chapel in which he placed a reredos. This was a triptych of the Crowning of Our Lady which had been purchased by Case at the Paris Exhibition. Although several generous donations were made towards the total cost of the work on the church (about £4,000), the remainder had come from Case's private income.

It was on Whit Sunday, 1870, that Canon Case preached his celebrated sermon. The 16 page address was subsequently published under the title:

---

2   Details of Case's early life taken from J. N. Langston, *The Catholic Mission in Gloucester and its Resident Priests (1788 - 1894)*, (Bound Typescript, Gloucester Library), pp. 26 sqq.

3   Archives of the Venerable English College, Rome, *Talbot Papers*, Clifford to Mgr. Talbot, Letter dated 4.3.1868.

The Vatican Council and a Duty of Catholics in regard to it. Inside the cover the reader is immediately presented with a challenge:

> In order to prevent any misconception, the Author takes this means to call attention to these two points:- First, that he has abstained from speaking of the Vatican Council as oecumenical, for the obvious reason that no council can justify its claim to that title until its close. Secondly, that he has spoken of the decision of the Holy Ghost as being made known through the Church's utterance, rather than the Council's, because whatever weight the decrees of a council may have must depend upon its oecumenicity and its freedom.

> Whether the accounts that have come from Rome of the want of freedom of debate at the present Vatican Council are true or not, God now knows, and time will show to the world.

The first point (about the Council's oecumenicity) arose from the fact that some eighty bishops (including Clifford) had departed before the crucial vote was taken and this was to be the subject of a later exchange between Case and Clifford. Rumours about the Council abounded – largely as a result of the secrecy imposed by the Vatican – and the alleged lack of freedom on the part of the participants ran as a *leit-motif* through Quirinus's *Letters from Rome on the Council*.[4] This was published in English in 1870 but Case may well have read them in the original when they first appeared in *Allgemeine Zeitung*. More importantly, Clifford himself (as will be seen) had grave misgivings about the Council's freedom.

The argument put forward by Case in the body of the sermon is as follows:

---

4   Quirinus, *Letters from Rome on the Council* (Publ. London, 1870). The writer is generally taken to have been Döllinger, using material sent to him from Rome by Dr. Friedrich and Lord Acton (Cuthbert Butler, *The Vatican Council 1869 - 1870*, Publ. paperback 1962, p. 224).

1)   The spirit of Truth, given to the Church, operates

    a)   within the Christian soul (holy thoughts, etc.)

    b)   in the teaching of the Church ('Peace In believing')

2)   Yet controversies do sometimes arise within the Church

        (e.g.   4th cent. Divine nature of Christ

                5th cent. Original sin

                9th cent. The Eucharist)

3)   Some controversies affect not substance but 'outskirts' of the
Faith.

Until decided by the Church 'speaking by her rightful organ' no
one person is entitled to condemn another. The present time
presents a controversy as we see bishops, priests and laity
divided. It is Papal Infallibility.

4)   The Church in faith and morals is infallible because

    a)   'Gates of hell will not prevail'

    b)   The spirit of Truth sent into the Church

    c)   'I am with you all days'

5)   <u>Question</u>: What is the rightful organ for this infallibility?

6)   Three main opinions:

    a)   The Pope alone

    b)   General Council with the Pope <u>provided</u> it is

        i) truly ecumenical (i.e. attended by virtually all Catholic
bishops),

        ii) free

    c)   Diffused – i.e. proceedings of General Council do not
acquire full force until accepted by the Universal Church

7)   Alleged failures of Papal Infallibility in the past

      a)   Pope Honorius (625 – 640)

      b)   Usury

      c)   Persecution of heretics

      d)   'Rights of the Tiara over civil governments'

8)   What to do? Wait and see 'in quietness of spirit'.

9)   Unfortunately some self-elected Catholics, 'with a ready pen
      and a printing press at (their) command', 'act as though they
      were the infallible exponents of the Catholic mind'.

10)   He is alluding to 'certain organs of the Catholic press'

      a) Who regard dissentients from papal infallibility as 'heretical'

            BUT i)   What of the *'Declaration & Protestation'*?
                       What of the *Oath & Declaration* of the Irish
                       Catholics, notified by the Irish Bishops in
                       Synod in 1810?

                  ii)   Catholics, even bishops, are not unanimous
                       on the point

                  iii)   In any case, how do these writers know?

      b)   To issue such condemnations is

            i)   against charity as well as against truth

            ii)   to presume to have foreknowledge of the decisions of
               the Holy Spirit

11)   'We will pray and hope and wait for the salvation of God. '

The *Gloucester Journal* commented: 'This sermon gives sufficient
indication that the preacher's position would be critical if the personal
infallibility of the Pope should be decreed. It contains strong protests

against the urgency of the Ultramontane Press in that direction. [5]

Before discussing the controversy which ensued between Case and his bishop, it is worth pointing out that the difficulties quoted by Case from English and Irish history would be cited by Clifford and others during the Council, and although not *theologically* insurmountable, both men would have seen them as *politically* embarrassing when it came to dealings with H.M.G. who might well accuse the Catholic body of bad faith.

It is well known that the case of Pope Honorius (625 – 640) [6] and the other alleged failures of Papal Infallibility did present difficulties at the theological level before the definition, all the more so because there had always been the fear that the final wording would be too comprehensive. In the event the nature of the Pope's infallibility was extremely circumscribed by the Council. One might say that this happened, at least in part, *because* of these cases which would certainly need to be accommodated within the terms of any definition. Typical responses given now, for example, would say that Honorius had not been addressing the whole Church (one of the conditions for an infallible pronouncement) but had been writing 'as a private theologian' to an individual. Other alleged cases can be answered in the same manner, or put down to the decisions, not of the Pontiff himself, but of the Roman curia (e.g. the decision against Galileo).

This is not to minimise the problems experienced by Case and others at the time immediately preceding the definition, but it does serve to underline the vagueness inherent in such an expression as 'the teaching of the Church'. Scholastic theology is in fact a very precise discipline with a whole spectrum of so-called 'theological notes' (e.g. 'defined', 'common doctrine', 'probable opinion') which theologians are accustomed to attach to any theological proposition but which the untutored mind can, as it were, bundle together into the all-embracing expression: The Catholic Church teaches . . .

---

5   Quoted by Langston, *op. cit.*, p.29

6   Honorius was accused of agreeing with the Monothelites who 'taught
        that there was no distinct human will in Christ; that it as absorbed in the
        Divine. In other words, they taught that Christ was not true man'.
        (Sheehan's *Apologetics* 1948, ed. 4, p. 193).

Canon Case's strictures on the Catholic press of the day might well have earned the approval of Clifford. As might have been expected, *'Quirinus'* was particularly scathing on the subject:

> In the English clerical journals, e.g. the *Weekly Register*, the fact has lately several times come to light, that English priests who utter a word against infallibility are promptly reduced to silence by threats of suspension and deprivation. Every infallibilist, who has the power, is also a terrorist, for he feels instinctively that free and open discussion would be the death of his darling dogma. [7]

Case had preached his sermon on June 5th, 1870. It so happened that nine days later a lady wrote a long letter to Newman 'expressing her apprehension about the work of the Council'. Newman recorded on the back of the letter what must have been the substance of his reply: "We must look to see what the Bishops do who have opposed the definition. I advise you to get Dr. Case's sermon on the subject published by Longman & Co.". [8]

What is even more to the point is that Newman wrote to congratulate Case on his sermon, and he replied on 21st June that he had only published it with great diffidence, partly because he feared it might embarrass his bishop, Clifford, "at a time especially when the straightforward and manly course which he is taking necessarily creates for him so many enemies at Rome". [9]

Clifford met Case at the end of August, 1870, and it is interesting to discover on what precise point he would challenge the preacher. In the event it centred around the issue as to whether or not the Council had

---

7   Quirinus, *op. cit.*, p. 359.

8   *The Letters and Diaries of John Henry Newman* (ed. Dessain and Gornall), Vol. XXV, p. 143, Newman to Madam Jacques Blumenthal, Letter dated 14.6.1870.

9.   *Ibid.*

been truly ecumenical. [10] Case replied with a long letter to his bishop. He listed various complaints against the procedure of the Council and, on the basis of the July 13 vote, concluded that the Council could not claim to be ecumenical. It was not free, he charged, and its decrees were not legitimate.

> 'It is a decree of a Council neither free nor ecumenical, made under circumstances when the maximum of unfreedom and non-ecumenicity was reached. And to this decree some 80 bishops, representing in reality a majority of the Council, made a solemn synodal objection, not only by absenting themselves, but lodging at the same time with the Pope a dignified and earnest protest. So that in point of fact, the Council became, then broken up into two councils, contradictory each (*sic*) other, – one having the majority in numbers, the other, if numerically in minority, at any rate not a minority, either in character or learning, or representative weight'.[11]

He adds that for these and other reasons he can neither accept nor teach the infallibility of the Pope.

Clifford had been one of the eighty bishops – and Case knew it. His reply, therefore, is of more than ordinary significance.

> 'I will make two observations on your letter.
>
> 1st Although a Council has not the full stamp of oecumenicity till it is finished, still if summoned as oecumenical it has a right to be considered as such from the commencement till it is proved not to be so, and I do not think that any private individual has a right to call it in question.

---

10   F. J. Cwiekowski, *The English Bishops and the First Vatican Council* (Publ. Louvain, 1971), pp. 296, 297. The author says: 'I have not found any of the original Clifford-Case correspondence'. All the letters by Clifford and Case quoted in this chapter are to be found in the Clifton Diocesan Archives with the exception of those quoted under footnotes 11 and 12. These are taken from Cwiekowski who in turn admits that he has taken them from an earlier work published in 1887; *Der Altkatholicismus* by J. F. Schulte, p. 270.

11   *Ibid.*

It is in possession, and presumption is in its favour; and nothing but some public act of the Church could set it aside. There have been complaints and protests against many things during the council so far, but no act proclaiming it non-oecumenical.

2dly as regard the decree of the 18th July, I think that the statement made by Card. Antonelli in his letter to the Nunzio of Brussels is explicit, and must be accepted as an authentic declaration – viz. – That the Constitution in question was solemnly promulgated by the Pope in the presence of 500 bishops, and was put up in the usual places in Rome. "In consequence of which it was made obligatory for the whole Catholic world without need of any other publication whatsoever". I cannot therefore avoid the conclusion – that all Catholics are bound to accept the doctrine of the decree, as it stands, and all priests are bound to teach it. To do otherwise would be to break off communion with the See of Rome, Which is evidently wrong, whatever difficulties there may be on the other side of the question.

This is all I am able to say on the subject.[12]

But we now know that on one issue Clifford secretly agreed with Case and that he, too, had the gravest doubts about the supposed freedom of the bishops during the Vatican Council. The following forms part of a letter written to his Vicar General (Canon Bonomi) in November, 1870 – when his recollections must still have been very vivid – and which may be regarded as the most important of the Clifford papers in the Archives at Clifton. This fact alone justifies quoting it at length:

---

12   *Ibid.*

. . . I can neither banish from my mind nor ignore the immense pressure put on so many Bishops who were wholly dependant [*sic*] on the Pope. [*The following crossed out*: This is a matter which is partly public though not to its full extent. Many Bishops have signified to me and to others that they dare not vote as they wished as their bread or position depended on it. Others that for this reason they declined to consider the question on its merits, & simply voted as they were told. Of those that voted in the minority more than one said he did so knowing how dear it would cost him. That these fears were not in vain is shown by the fact that one Bishop at least has been punished for his vote].

The fear expressed by so many bishops both to me and to others of what would be the consequences to them of giving a vote not pleasing to the Pope were not without foundation. Even since the Council one bishop at least has lost his place by his vote.

The way Cardinal Guidi was treated, simply for expressing his views freely but most temperately in council, was sufficient to deter any ordinary Italian or Eastern bishop dependent on the Pope, from incurring [*sic*] the Pope's displeasure by an adverse vote. [*The following crossed out*: "I cannot help feeling that such things must have a most serious bearing on the question of the liberty of the Council]. I know what verdict Englishmen would give [concerning similar practices *crossed out*] if it were a question of voting at a parliamentary election . . . I have not written this for publication but you may make use of it to answer those who have made the inquiries you write about'.[13]

The question is: Was Case one of them? and, if so, did Bonomi reveal to him these inner thoughts of his bishop? In the light of this there must be a strong possibility that Case *was already aware* of Clifford's grave misgivings and this in turn provided him with an added incentive when he wrote: 'It is the decree of a Council . . . made under circumstances when the maximum of unfreedom . . . was reached' [see above]. Clifford, for his part, must have been aware of this possibility but would not be drawn. Hence the terse: 'This is all I am able to say on the subject'.

On 31st May, 1871, there was a meeting of the Cathedral Chapter at which eight canons were present, but not Canon Case. The *Minutes* read:

> An address of congratulation to His Holiness Pope Pius IX on the occasion of His Pontifical Jubilee was proposed by Canon Bonomi & adopted by the Chapter and ordered to be forwarded to Rome for presentation to His Holiness before the 17th June. [14]

The following day another meeting was held with Canon Case present. There is no record of any business except the following:

> Canon Case wished his name to be omitted from the list of the signatures of the Canons in the address of congratulation to his Holiness Pope Pius IX.[15]

In April, 1874, almost three years later Bishop Clifford received a communication from Propaganda Fide regarding pastoral advice given by Case both in private and in public alleging non-adherence to the decrees of the Vatican Council.[16]

---

13   Clifton Diocesan Archives, *Letters to William Clifford*, Part I, 1854 –1874. 17.11.1870. In a heated letter to Manning, William Maskell had written: 'Whether the Vatican Council, up to the present day, has had entire freedom of debate . . . these are questions still open to legitimate discussion and 'argument' (*The Letters and Diaries of John Henry Newman*, ed. Dessain and Gornall, Vol. XXV, p. 206, Maskell to Manning, Letter dated 3.9.1870.

14   Clifton Diocesan Archives, *II Acta Capituli Cliftoniensis a die 31 Januarii 1861 usque ad 1 Decembris, 1874*, 31.5.1871.

15   *Ibid.*, 1.6.1871.

16   Clifton Diocesan Archives, *Correspondence 1844 - 1902, Roman*, No. 113.

The complaint had been sent to Propaganda 'da un sacerdote di nota prudenza'.[17] It may be assumed from the tone of Clifford's immediate reply – sent pending a further answer to be drawn up after he had questioned Case – that the enquiry from Rome might also have been a testing of Clifford himself, sent by Cardinal Franchi on behalf of Antonelli ('the chief whip') to make sure that the bishop, despite previous misgivings, was firmly in the 'Aye' lobby and furthermore that his clergy were there with him.

Writing in Italian, Clifford replied on 27th April, 1874.

After saying that he would get the facts of the matter from Case, and moreover that the whole story was news to him anyway, he continued in what can only be described as a defensive mood:

> '. . . 2dly . . . the letter of Cardinal Antonelli was fully published in the churches of the diocese of Clifton, but that independently of this and at intervals of a few weeks there was also published in all the churches (including Canon Case's) my own circular letter advising everyone that the decrees of the Vatican Council, and specifically the decree dealing with the infallibility of the Pope were to be held ['obligatorie'] by all under pain of separation from the Catholic Church. This much I believe it to have been my duty to write without delay to Your Eminence out of fairness to myself ['per mia giustificazione'], and I shall be writing as soon as possible on Canon Case'. [18]
> [My translation].

It is surprising that some nine days were to elapse before Clifford put pen to paper to ask Case about the serious allegations which had been made against him. Even so, they should have come as no surprise to Clifford seeing that he (Case) had already warned him that he could neither accept nor teach the Vatican decrees.

---

17   *Ibid.*, No. 112 (Date in pencil 14.4.1874).

18   *Ibid.*, No. 114, Clifford to Cardinal Franchi, Letter dated 27.4.1874.

May 6th 1874

My dear Case

The following complaint about you has been forwarded to
me from the Propaganda. It is stated 1st that a young man
wrote to you about two years ago stating to you his intention
of leaving the Catholic Church because he could no longer
accept her teaching, especially the decrees of the Vatican
Council, and in particular the decree about the Papal
Infallibility. You are said to have written in reply, that that
was no reason for taking such a step as he intended to take
inasmuch as a person may reject those decrees & still
remain a member of the Catholic Church.

2ly It is stated that when you read in church either the letter
of Cardinal Antonelli, or my circular informing the people
that the decrees of the Vatican Council were binding on all
under pain of being cut off from the church, you added a
declaration, that, though you were obliged to read the
document to the people, you did not accept it yourself.

3ly It is stated that the young man left the Catholic Church
in consequence of hearing such statements from you.

These complaints having been forwarded to me it is my duty
to inquire of you, what truth, if any, there is in the above
statements: and with this object I write you this letter and
await your answer.

. . . . .

+ William Clifford [19]

---

19   Clifton Diocesan Archives, *Letters 1788 - 1874*, No. 420, Clifford to Case,
      Letter dated 6.5.1874.

After eight days – to allow him time to return to Gloucester from Birkenhead – Case defended himself to Clifford:

> 1. As to the first charge – It is true that a member of my congregation some time ago left his religion. It is true also that he wrote to me on the subject, and that I wrote him an answer. He may have mentioned the Vatican decrees as one ground for taking that step; but in point of fact he shewed that his difficulties were anterior to them, and of quite a different order. He had completely lost his faith, not only in the distinctive doctrines of the Catholic System, but also in Christianity altogether; and the Vatican decrees were at most nothing more than an occasion or pretext for his action. I did not think the correspondence worth preserving; and I can only say that, having endeavoured to the best of my power to recall to mind the contents of my letter, I cannot recollect that it contained any such statement as that with which I am charged.
>
> 2. My reply to the second charge is that I never made any declaration whatever to my congregation in connection with either Card. Antonelli's letter or your own circular relative to the decrees of the Vatican Council.
>
> 3. And so of necessity the third charge falls to the ground. It is true, as I have already stated, that the man left his religion; but he certainly did not leave it for the reason alleged.
>
> . . . . .
>
> Geo. Case [20]

Clifford reported faithfully to Propaganda Case's defence of his actions, but the letter (in Italian) contains a gloss or two of some importance:

1)   That the young man referred to was someone 'if I am not mistaken', writes Clifford – about whom Case had previously

---

20   *Ibid.*, No. 421, Case to Clifford, Letter dated 14.5.1874.

spoken as having been 'seduced by the teachings of unbelievers'. This therefore supported Case's contention that the man's Faith had already been in a somewhat precarious state.

2)   Having conveyed to Rome Case's absolute denial of having made any adverse comment in regard to either Antonelli's letter or Clifford's own circular, Clifford adds:

> I recall that towards the end of 1870, I was made aware of various things said by Canon Case *and by others* [italics mine] which smacked of opposition to the Conciliar Decrees, although they did not amount to an (outright) denial, and perhaps one of these instances has been repeated or exaggerated. But these things happened before I sent out the circular in which everyone was warned that the decrees, and clearly that on infallibility, obliged under pain of ceasing to be Catholic. I consider that the publication of the circular by Canon Case, as by the other members of the clergy, was sufficient amends ['riparazione'] for any less-than-correct ['meno retta'] expression used before that date, and I have not taken the matter any further. [21]

A week later the Metropolitan himself (Manning) had joined the hunt. Apparently the news had reached both London and Birmingham and the result was the following vigorous questionnaire addressed to the Vicar General:

> Archbishop's House,
> Westminster,
> S.W.
>
> May 23 1874
>
> My dear V.G.
>
> You remember the case of the young man at Gloucester, whose mother told you that he had lost his faith, are not

---

21   *Ibid.*, No. 423, Clifford to Cardinal Franchi, Copy of letter in Italian dated 16.5.1874 [My translation].

these the facts

1.   that Canon Case told him that he (Case) did not believe it.

2.   that the Mother said her son was losing his faith.

3.   that he did lose it.

4.   that you told all this to the Bp of Birmingham.

5.   that you told it or brought it before the Bp. of Clifton.
      Where is the young man now?

Is his Mother in Birmingham?

What is her name?

Did you ever hear that C. Case after reading the Bps Circular on
the Infallibility said publicly or privately that he did not believe it:
or regard the V. Coun. Oecumenical?

Give me all the information you can as I am called on to use it

You may depend on my secrecy until you release me.

Yours affy.

+ H.E. Abp. W. [22]

The tone of the letter well illustrates Manning's nose for heresy, but by
now Clifford had already dealt with the matter – and far more judiciously.

The immediate consequence of Manning's intervention is not known. But
this was not to be the end of Case's brush with authority over the issue
of Papal Infallibility. At their Low Week Meeting the following year (1875)
the bishops issued a joint pastoral letter on the subject of the Conciliar

---

22   Birmingham Archdiocesan Archives, B.5415, Manning to Vicar General
      (Canon Michael O'Sullivan), Letter dated 23.5.1874.

Decrees. This was largely in response to Gladstone's contention that what had been decided at the Council put the loyalty of Catholics to legitimate civil government very much in jeopardy. Case refused to read the letter.

One year later the *Minutes of the Clifton Chapter* record:

> The Bishop announced to the Chapter Dr. Case's resignation of the Mission at Gloucester. His Lordship said that he had given Dr. Case leave of absence for six months, after which time he must accept work in the Diocese or resign his canonry. [23]

At this point another bishop intervened. This time it was Bishop Brown of Newport. It will be recalled from what he had written to Clifford at the end of 1870 that some at least of his sentiments were not too far removed from those of Case:

'. . . Now from all that I can learn of the proceedings of the latter (i.e. the Council), there was a fatal absence of the characteristics which ought to have existed thereat'. [24]

Certainly freedom, and possibly ecumenicity, were in his mind. He had become concerned about Case and, although Clifford's reply was meant to reassure him, it is nevertheless evident that the ball was now in Case's court as to what his future should be. Clifford wrote:

> There is nothing whatever wrong about Dr. Case. He has been for more than a year pressing me to allow him to retire for a time at least, from missionary work, and considering all he has done for the diocese, I felt obliged to promise him I would do so as soon as I could make arrangements for doing it without injury to the mission.

---

23   Clifton Diocesan Archives, *III Acta Capituli Cliftoniensis* a die 19 Januarii, 1875 usque ad 4 Decembris, 1900, 14.3.1876.

24   Clifton Diocesan Archives, *Letters to William Clifford*, Part I, Brown to Clifford, letter dated 7.12.1870.

Finding myself now in a position to do so I have granted his request of accepting his resignation of the Missionary rectorship of Gloucester, and I have granted him leave to retire for six months from all missionary work, at the end of which period, he will consider what further steps he would like to take. Meanwhile he is simply a Canon resting on his oars, and having no intention to resume work at present. I don't think there would be the slightest use in your making to him the offer you propose. He is spending Holy week with me at Clifton helping in the services and preaching on Good Friday'. [25]

It is interesting to learn from this that Bishop Brown was thinking of offering Case a position (mission?) in his diocese. Clifford's forthright playing down of such a proposal could suggest that he already feared the worst and that, in the light of previous difficulties, it might only be a matter of time before Case would make the final break. After all, they were now living under the same roof and it is hard to imagine that they did not use the opportunity to discuss matters of such common interest.

Clifford ended his letter to Brown by sharing a little banter with him. Referring to the forthcoming meeting of the bishops (and, by implication, to Manning) he wrote:

'I hope this fine weather will set you up and fully prepare you for a strong dose of chaff in Low week'.

On 5th February, 1878, the *Chapter Minutes* record

'A letter was read from his Lordship the Bishop announcing that the Rev. George Case D.D. had resigned his Canonry in the month of December last . . .' [26]

Although the original deadline for Case's decision had been six months (from March) Clifford it would seem had granted him another three months' grace.

---

25   Cardiff Archdiocesan Archives, *Letters to Bishop Brown of Newport*, Clifford to Brown, Letter dated 8.4.1876.

26   Clifton Diocesan Archives, *III Acta Capituli Cliftoniensis* a die 19 Januarii, 1875 usque ad 4 Decembris, 1900, 5.2.1878.

Over forty years later (1918) Mgr. Arthur Russell was asked by Bishop Burton to write of his personal recollection of Case. He replied:

> . . . 1870 The Vatican Decrees upset him. He had correspondence with Döllinger – about 1875–6 he preached & published a Sermon against the Infallibility – the matter reached Rome & Bishop Clifford had to take action and finally require of him a Profession of faith which was not given to satisfaction.
>
> He went to live in London & after an operation died in hospital May 1883, leaving all his money to the Hibbert Society. £20,000 so stated.
>
> I had official correspondence with him & in one letter he expressed his disappointment that tho' he had left the Church, Bishop Clifford when in London had not called upon him. I have always felt that more might have been done to save him. When he was dying Canon Macmullen [27] called, but I heard that Dr. Case refused then to see him. [28]

---

27   Case had been received into the Catholic Church with Richard Macmullen (see p. 112, note 38).

28   Clifton Diocesan Archives, *Canon Case File*, Mgr. Arthur Russell to Bp. Burton, Letter dated 24.5.1918. Russell at that time was living in retirement in Clevedon.

'He died in 1883 leaving an odd and eccentric will. He bequeathed £100 to the Gloucester Infirmary, but £300 to his trustees to be applied at their uncontrolled discretion "for the promotion of the innocent enjoyment and amusement of Sundays for and amongst those who are frequently called the lower orders of the people". The residue of his £22,000 estate . . . was left to the Hibbert Trust to form "The Case Fund", the income to be applied "in the promotion of free thought, unfettered learning, and frank utterances in matters connected with religion, and the development, learning and highest culture of man"'. J. N. Langston, *op. cit.*, pp. 29, 30.

The terms of the will were ridiculed in the *Gloucester Standard*, 24.8.1883.

This letter is one of the very few criticisms levelled at Bishop Clifford, but it must be balanced against Clifford's extreme forbearance throughout the whole infallibility affair. Another criticism – perhaps less justified – came in a letter from Acton to Döllinger: 'Acton said that while Clifford answered the priest's (Case's) charge, he never made an attempt to bring the priest to believe the truth of the definition'. [29]

Furthermore, Acton saw Clifford's oft-repeated position, viz. that acceptance of the decrees is a condition of being in communion with Rome, as (expressing) a truism, and not a statement of dogma'. [30]

But this surely was the crux of the matter. Both Clifford and Case had difficulties, but Clifford was not prepared to go down the road of schism. To what extent George Case was a proud man – 'At Oxford he was called "Jewel Case" and he possessed beautiful rings which were always in evidence on Chapter days' (Russell) – or to what extent he was legitimately following the dictates of conscience, we shall never know. For Clifford, however, the way was clear: 1) Schism was unthinkable; 2) *Roma locuta, causa finita* but his letter to Canon Bonomi betrays a man who had the gravest misgivings as to the manner in which on this occasion Rome had chosen to speak.

---

29   F. J. Cwiekowski, *The English Bishops and The First Vatican Council* (Publ. Louvain, 1971), p. 304.

30   *Ibid.*

CHAPTER TWELVE

The University Question

In an ideal world the English Catholics of the 19th century would surely have wished that, where appropriate, their offspring should be able to attend the Universities of Oxford and Cambridge. The prestige of such institutions was beyond question, and attendance at one or both of them was a *sine qua non* of entry into the professions. The University of London had received its charter in 1835 but sadly was not seen to possess the same kudos as its medieval counterparts.

This was how things would have been perceived in a perfect world. But the Groves of Academe in mid and late 19th century England were far from perfect and the objections of Catholics who would, in other circumstances, have entrusted their children to the Universities were many. First, the rationalistic philosophy then prevalent, especially at Oxford, led many students to a liberal type theology whose tenets were of a very questionable orthodoxy. The Gorham Judgement of 1850 had been seen to be as much an indictment of the Universities as of the Church of England. Indeed, the two were, in this respect at least, indistinguishable.

Secondly it was argued that the exposure of Catholics to this atmosphere of religious free thought would lead to a virulent – because intellectually based – form of Indifferentism. The absolute claims of the Catholic Church would soon give place in the minds of young, impressionable students, to the relativism of the Oxford don. Furthermore, while today Victorian standards of behaviour are judged to have been the very pillars of society at that time, it would be quite wrong to conclude that those standards were all pervasive. Illegitimacy was prevalent and no level of society was unaffected. In a word, the universities were judged to be 'a proximate occasion of sin'.

It was arguments such as these which formed the background to the bishops' prohibition on Catholic students going to Oxford and Cambridge. Furthermore, they were reasons which were well understood and supported by a conservative Curia in Rome – so much so that when eventually a change did come, not the least of the bishops' tasks was that of converting Rome to their new way of thinking.

Finally from 1861 onwards – i.e. for some years before he actually succeeded at Westminster – the *éminence grise* of Manning loomed large over the whole issue. Many have seen this exclusively in terms of the undoubted force of his personality. What is less often noted is that among the English bishops of that period Manning was the only one, apart from Robert Coffin (Bishop of Southwark 1882 – 1885), who had actually been a student at Oxford (Balliol: 1827 – 1830) and this fact alone must have carried weight both with his colleagues and at Rome. Indeed, it was Clifford's successor, William Robert Brownlow, a convert of Newman and a student at Cambridge from 1849 to 1852 who was the only other Oxbridge student to sit on the episcopal bench before the turn of the century.

The overall situation was seen as unfavourable. Nevertheless various practical alternatives suggested themselves during the course of the 19th century. One of the earliest was that of the ambitious Bishop Baines (Vicar Apostolic of the Western District, 1829 – 1843) who in 1834 wished to create an episcopal residence at Prior Park overlooking Bath. His philosophy of English Catholicism was that Catholics were no longer inhabitants of a religious ghetto but that they should be seen to be 'on the map'. Not only therefore did Baines reside at the College but arrangements were made for its students to pursue courses that would lead to a degree at London. (Ushaw, Stonyhurst and other institutions made similar arrangements).

Wiseman too was moved to think along the same lines but not unnaturally he favoured Oscott which he hoped might evolve one day into a university. Indeed, Oscott and Prior Park had much in common. Both colleges were housed in splendid buildings and both could call on people of note to serve as professors. Oscott, however, had two substantial advantages: it was geographically in the centre of England and secondly, unlike Prior Park, it was not burdened with debt.

The Religious Tests were lifted by Oxford in 1854 and by Cambridge two years later. Some hoped, while others feared, that this might mean a general influx of Catholic students into the two institutions. In the event however – as Manning himself noted – in the nine years after 1854 only a dozen Catholics had passed through Oxford with more following.[1]

---

1   Alberic Stacpoole, *The Return of the Roman Catholics to Oxford*, p. 2. Sources there quoted. Contribution to the *Oxford History of Oxford*.

There was also another factor in the equation. Newman had been summoned by the Irish Bishops to establish a Catholic University in Dublin, and so alarmed was he that, following the lifting of the Religious Tests the English Bishops, supported by Rome, might lift their prohibition, he wrote to Propaganda urging that the ban on Oxford and Cambridge should continue lest his own institution be starved of students. The letter (in Latin) is vehement in its condemnation of a University that today is proud to call him its son:

> Since Oxford University has such a splendid reputation which even *lay* Catholics in Ireland gaze at in admiration (I am speaking of the *lay* Catholics of England and Ireland, not of venerable Bishops, nor of priests who, living above the level of ordinary mortals are not deceived by passing fashion, but of *layfolk* who have their own proper business, place, dignity and nobility which has proved to be the very foundation of our new University) the great fear is that if permission be granted to two or three Catholic students to go to Oxford, then the entire Catholic youth – certainly of England, perhaps of Ireland – just like a flock of sheep one after the other either will not seek to enter our Catholic institutions or will leave the sheepfold. They will despise them as being either 'new' or 'not sophisticated' and so will transfer to that most dangerous haven of error ['*in illud periculosissimum erroris tabernaculum*'].
>
> In such pernicious circumstances it will be impossible for our University to prosper for it would be about to lose its best students, nor would its future be in any way clear. [2] [My translation].

In the 1860s both Wiseman and Manning thought seriously about a suitable institution for Catholic students. Newman's University at Dublin had failed and his scheme for the establishment of an Oratory at Oxford,

---

2   Archives of Propaganda Fide, Rome, *Scritture Riferite nei Congressi 1855 - 1857*, Anglia 14, Nos. 473, 474. Newman to Propaganda, Letter dated 12.3.1856. The original Latin text is printed at the end of this chapter.

backed by Ullathorne, was seen as a useful way forward. Initially it would be promoted as a pastoral undertaking, but with Newman at its head the word 'pastoral' would be seen in the sense of ministering to the intellectual, moral and spiritual needs of students attending the University. Clifford was to be a supporter of this idea.

In the meantime, however, Edmund Ffoulkes (Convert, former Fellow of Jesus College, Oxford, and later due to return to the Church of England and become Vicar of St. Mary's) was endeavouring to found a Catholic Hall at Oxford.

What is interesting is the way in which he saw Clifford as a natural ally in his enterprise. Indeed throughout his life – whether it be in the matter of the *Syllabus* or the interpretation of *Genesis* or the admittance of Catholics to Oxford and Cambridge – Clifford is invariably seen to attract moderate opinion to himself. Ffoulkes sent a circular letter to all the bishops, but in writing to Clifford he also enclosed a covering note in order to 'sound out' his views on one whose judgement he clearly valued.

> . . . I am not desirous of attempting anything against authority – My own motives may be summed up in a few words.
>
> I feel that Catholics can never take their proper place in English society till they can finish their studies regularly at Oxford and Cambridge: & I feel that till the popular prejudices wh. exist against Catholics have been broken through at Oxford & Cambridge, there will be no real abatement of them elsewhere –
>
> London University degrees are no distinction at all in good society – on the contrary they serve but to mark our social inferiority – Should your Lordships decide upon founding a Catholic University of our own, I shd. always be ready to withdraw in favour of it: but I submit that it would at least be politic to give Oxford & Cambridge a fair trial first, our laity being at present strongly prepossessed in their favour: & with a Catholic Hall, properly conducted, there could not be anything like

mixed education . . . [3]

Propaganda was well aware of the University problem in England but to its credit, declined to issue another injunction before it had heard the bishops' views yet again. In the event, at their Low Week Meeting in 1864, they took a firm line of prohibition with the rejection both of a Catholic Hall and of a Catholic University and issued an instruction to the clergy urging them to dissuade parents from sending their sons and daughters to either Oxford or Cambridge. [4]

Critical to an understanding of the thinking both of Propaganda and of the bishops on the University Question is the issue of the universities considered as a 'proximate occasion of sin' to the faith, and very probably to the morals, of Catholic students. In the difficult matter of how exactly to evaluate such a danger, Clifford – on his own admission – had recourse to his training as a young student in Rome. His attitude, while firm, did admit of exceptions.

The source of this information is a letter which he sent to Bishop Grant in May, 1867, apparently by way of reply to a question which Grant had posed about the Universities. Clifford writes:

> In the year 1847 when I attended lectures on Moral Theology at the Collegio Romano the text book was "Theologia Moralis Patris Edmundi Voit S.J." – In his treatise "de Fide" 381 he says:

---

3   Ugbrooke Archives, *Letters to Bp. Clifford. 1863*, Ffoulkes to Clifford, Letter dated 8.9.1863. It would seem that Ffoulkes was seldom far from controversy. For example, in 1870 Newman wrote to James Skinner: 'When Mr. Ffoulkes brought out some pamphlets against the Filioque, I heard that priests in London gave him notice that, if he presented himself at the Altar, they could not communicate him'. (*The Letters and Diaries of John Henry Newman*, ed. Dessain and Gornall, Vol. XXV, p. 184, Letter dated 14.8.1870). Later, in 1886, he delated Fletcher of Carfax for heresy in a sermon (Owen Chadwick, *The Victorian Church*, Part 2, publ. paperback London 1987, p. 453.).

4   Edward Norman, *The English Catholic Church in the Nineteenth Century* (Publ. Oxford, 1984), p. 294.

It is lawful in Germany to attend the funerals of Non-Catholics out of sympathy . . . to take a degree in law or medicine in those academies provided that nothing is done or allowed to the prejudice of true Religion. The reason is that here in Germany such activities are not taken to be signs of approval of the Non-Catholic religion.

Furthermore, in a Non-Catholic University <u>it is not lawful</u> to attend lectures in theology or canon law (unless perhaps it is a question of a book dealing with judicial procedures) because these deal with matters of faith and work against the interests of the Catholic Faith.

<u>It is lawful</u> to attend lectures in civil law and medicine because usually these do not embrace matters of faith.

<u>It is more dangerous</u> to attend lectures in Public Law because of the connection this has with matters relating to bishops and to the Church.

Finally, just as it is rare for Catholics to attend Non-Catholic Universities without incurring grave danger to faith, virtue and salvation, so only those would seem to be excused from sin who are strong in their faith, constant in its practice and whose attendance (at university) is purely for the sake of learning.

[Underlining by Clifford. My translation]. [5]

In the light of these principles as enunciated by his professor in Rome, Clifford tells Grant:

This is the doctrine I have been taught & which I have taught others – All communication with heretics is dangerous whether it be in the university, the army, the counting house,

---

5   Southwark Archdiocesan Archives, *The University Question* (Letters to Bp. Grant), Clifford to Grant, Letter dated 19.5.1867.

or at country cousins, and because dangerous therefore sinful if incurred absque legitima causa, & without proper safeguards. The greater the danger, the graver must be the reasons for incurring it.

But as we do not say that it is a sin to enter the army or navy, or take service in a Protestant family, or become partner in a protestant firm, or spend a month on a visit to a Protestant house, or lodge with Protestant fellow students, although all these things are dangerous & *may be* on that account sinful; so neither is it correct to say that to attend the University is a sin, but that it is exceedingly dangerous, & therefore that *ii tantum excusari a peccato videntur, qui fideli custodia muniti, et in fide constantes eo se conferunt discendi causa.*

(. . . only those would seem to be excused from sin who are strong in their faith, constant in its practice and whose attendance is purely for the sake of learning). [6]
[My translation].

This passage is important because it explains the moderate stance adopted by Clifford and serves to throw considerable doubt on the view that he was merely bowing to pressure exerted by a lobby composed mainly of his well-to-do friends.

December, 1864, was a significant month in the long debate. Ffoulkes wrote to Phillipps de L'Isle that he had heard that a special meeting of the bishops was due to be held on the 13th of the month –

Now I have some ground for thinking that the matter in question is that of a College at Oxford & as this has long been my pet subject, I feel a thrill come over me at the very thought of it. [7]

---

6   *Ibid.*

7   Ugbrooke Archives, *Letters to Bp. Clifford, 1864*, Ffoulkes to Phillipps de L'Isle, Letter dated 4.12.1864.

In reality the letter was intended for Clifford for Ffoulkes states as
much –

> Do you think you could . . . submit all this to the Bp of Clifton?
> – If you think so, perhaps you would send him likewise your
> copy of the Novr. No. of the Union with my article, which
> explains the whole subject still more at length in its academical
> bearings, & I will gladly forward you a fresh copy to replace it
> – If I felt sure that anyone of the Bps. was cognizant of the <u>full
> state of the case</u>, I should be quite easy . . .

Ffoulkes's argument was twofold:

> One is that as the law <u>stands at present</u>, a Catholic College
> would be <u>illegal</u> at Oxford, though it might be [legal,
> omitted] at Cambridge provided that the Head of it had
> taken an M.A. degree at that University.

> I am extremely anxious that our authorities should not be
> under any delusion on that head: as, in point of fact, as the
> law stands now , it would [be, omitted] premature for them
> to discuss whether they will or will not have a Catholic
> College <u>at Oxford</u>, where they <u>cannot</u>, till further legislation
> has thrown it open sufficiently for that purpose.

The second part was purely pragmatic:

> I am strongly of opinion that it would be far better to <u>let
> individuals</u> try the experiment, and bear all the chances of
> failure or success in the first instance – If Dr. Newman goes
> there merely with the Oratory, individuals will then have that
> as a rallying point, & as a sure means of spiritual instruction
> & religious worship for their pupils: all in fact that they need,
> to be able to commence <u>unobtrusively</u>,yet under its shadow –

Ffoulkes final paragraph is of special interest:

> I do not like troubling the Cardinal, as I have been urging
> strongly on His Eminence to attempt the carrying out of
> Session XXIII, c. 17 'On Reformation' of the Council of Trent,

by which means employment might be readily found for those clergymen who come over from the Ch of England as married men – <u>Do study</u> the last sentence of that C. if you have the decrees by you – Few people have I think noticed it of late years. [8]

The relevant passage in Trent to which Ffoulkes is referring concerns the restoration of the ancient functions of the Diaconate and of the Minor Orders in those churches where they had fallen into disuse. These were ministries, says the Council, which the heretics had branded useless (*'otiosae'*). The passage continues:

> But if celibate clergy are not readily available to carry out these ministries which pertain to the four Minor Orders, then it would be sufficient (*suffici possint*) to engage for these functions even married men of virtuous life (provided that they have not been married twice) who may wear both the tonsure and clerical dress in church. [9] [My translation].

The point Ffoulkes is making is that consideration should be given to employing convert clergymen in conducting services, presumably along the lines whereby today special ministers of the Eucharist take services in church. However, by raising the issue in the present context he must be seen to be urging on the authorities a whole new vista of ministry whereby former clergymen – for the most part Oxbridge graduates – would also play a major role in the extra-liturgical work of the University chaplaincy. Vatican II thinking even before Vatican I.

This letter (it will be remembered) was addressed to Ambrose de L'Isle Phillipps and it has been suggested that his support for a Catholic Hall was by way of promoting his long term aim of bringing about a reconciliation of Anglicanism and Catholicism. [10]

---

8   *Ibid.*

9   *Canones et Decreta Concilii Tridentini ex Editione Romana* A. MDCCCXXXIV Repetiti . . . edidit Aemilius Ludovicus Richter (Publ. Leipzig, 1853), Sessio XXIII, C. XVII, pp. 208, 209.

10   Edward Norman, *op. cit.*, pp. 297, 298.

Something else happened early in the same month (December), just before the bishops were due to meet. Cardinal Wiseman – who now had barely ten weeks to live – sent out a list of twenty questions to bishops and to others on how they viewed the effect on Catholic students of life at Oxford and Cambridge, assuming that permission were granted for them to attend. What was significant was that the questions were 'loaded', i.e. worded in such a way that Wiseman hoped the whole exercise would vindicate the bishops' prohibiton by exposing what he saw to be the very serious disadvantages if a change of policy were to be adopted.

Clifford, who had had no direct experience of an English University, immediately thought of Canon George Case who had been up at Oxford (Brasenose, 1841 – 45) and who was a natural sounding board for such opinions. At the outset Case made his views known and, although Clifford's letter to him has not survived, it is apparent that both men were of the same opinion about the slant of the questions:

> The questions, as you truly remark, have been drawn up by one who had prejudged the question – They are rather those of an advocate than of one who wished to arrive at the whole truth. But I suppose it wd. be difficult for anyone feeling strongly on the subject not to shew his bias in the questions he set forth. –
>
> There seems to be great confusion in their drawing up . . .[11]

Case made it clear that his sympathies lay with Catholics attending the Universities:

> There is a certain part of education, quite apart from reading, which the English Universities supply in an especial manner. This is the result of the mere friction of men's minds, which imparts a character that cannot be met with in the same degree elsewhere, enables a man to take his position easily in general society, and to preserve his self-respect.

---

11   Ugbrooke Archives, *Letters to Bp. Clifford, 1864*, Case to Clifford, Letter received 11.12.1864 (in time for a meeting on 13.12.1864).

Hence it is the tendency of an University education to make
men more manly, more gentlemanlike, and better adapted to
hold their own in the world. Men even of humble origins, and
belonging to a station in society where they would have little
or no opportunity of intercourse with gentlemen, acquire a
polish, a "savoir faire" by a residence at the universities,
such as they never could have got, except by that means. [12]

Of interest is Case's view that the much-feared 'danger to Faith' would
come, less from unsympathetic Protestant dons than from 'contact with
Protestant companions'.

I believe then, that the danger to faith wd. not be greater to
young men at the Universities than it is to young men in the
Army or Navy, or in any other profession e.g. Law or
Medicine – And I believe that the danger to morals would
rather be less than in any of the above mentioned
professions, or than in life in London. [13]

Question ten shows how weighted some of the questions were while
Case's answer to it is an admission to the existence of some danger over
and above contact with one's peers.

Q.   Considering the present condition of belief in the truths of
       revelation among leading minds in the Universities, do you
       think that the intercourse natural between the learned and
       able men of the Universities with younger minds and
       inexperienced scholars, would not necessarily tend to
       weaken the faith in these?

A.   I think not <u>necessarily</u>. The <u>personal</u> intercourse between
       older and younger men (Dons and undergraduates) was not
       very great when I was at Oxford. I do not suppose it is now.
       – Hence the danger hinted at would arise from attending the
       lectures on religion, or reading the works of heterodox

12   *Ibid.*

13   *Ibid.*

authors. The former danger is obviated by the rules of the University in the case of Catholics – To the latter danger a young man is as open in one place as in another. [14]

Case's reply to the twentieth and final question was in the form of a peroration in which he, as it were, threw back at the questioner the very epithets which it was being suggested would show the body of Catholic young men to be less in stature as a result of their being admitted to the Protestant Universities:

> . . . the result will be the formation of a future Catholic body not less "conscientious", or "orthodox", or "religious", or "devout", or "pure", and much more useful to this country, to religion, to society in general, much more refined, more gentlemanlike, more larger minded, more highly educated, more able to cope with the subjects of the day, more able to hold their own, and more appreciated and respected by their fellow countrymen and by the world at large, "than we can obtain by any other process of education". [15]

Provided that proper attention was paid to the means of religious instruction and 'other opportunities of practising their religion', Case believed that "our successors and the future heads of Catholic families will feel thankful to God, and believe that His Providence has guided and blessed the decision". [16]

There can be little doubt that Clifford would have made use of Case's lengthy reply to Wiseman's questionnaire, but whether it was submitted to the Bishops' Conference unaltered, and in its entirety, cannot at this distance be ascertained. Even if it were not, however, Case's document retains an intrinsic value of its own.

---

14   *Ibid.*

15   *Ibid.*

16   *Ibid.*

The result of the bishops' meeting was that a letter was sent to Propaganda expressing their total opposition to a Catholic presence at Oxford. It was Clifford who drafted the letter and he sent it to Ullathorne for his perusal. [17] Newman, however, although not specifically mentioned in the bishops' decision, felt that the whole affair had been engineered against him. Ullathorne (Newman's bishop) confided in Clifford:

> . . . So soon as Dr. Newman learnt from me the conclusions to which the Bishops had come, he resolved to give up the plan of the Oxford Oratory. His impression is that the London meeting with its consequences were aimed at him – not by the Bishops, but by those behind the scenes, and he feels the whole affair acutely . . .

> I mentioned all this to Dr. Grant, who has written a long letter to Rome in consequence with the object of advising them not to act in any such manner as would seem to aim at, or reflect on Dr. Newman. [18]

The sting was in the tail:

> Dr. N. and his friends believe, rightly or wrongly, that our friend Dr. M. is at the root of the whole affair, and that he moved Rome to move for the meeting. The fact that Dr. M. urged me after the meeting to get Dr. N. to give up the land looks ominous, but it was Dr. N's own act. And for his own comfort, he asked, I think, wisely. It is a fact, and he knows it, that there is not confidence in him at Propaganda. [19]

But had not Newman himself sown the seeds of that doubt when he expressed his own grave misgivings about Oxford in the letter of March 12, 1856 (quoted above)?

---

17   Clifton Diocesan Archives, *Letters to William Clifford*, Part I, Ullathorne to Clifford, Letter dated 12.1.1865.

18   *Ibid.*

19   *Ibid.*

Ullathorne's letter to Clifford concluded by mentioning the serious discontent to be found among the Catholic laity whose interests, after all, were at the heart of the matter:

> In my opinion, it is not only an error against justice, but what some people think a great deal more of, an error against policy, to drive Dr. N. and his friends to extremities, and plant all this discontent without necessity. I saw the other day a letter of strong indignation against both Rome and people nearer, for the supposed way in which Dr. N. has been treated, and that came from one of the most respectable convert families. [20]

But Ullathorne continued to see the whole Oxford venture as a pastoral undertaking and made a second attempt to bring it to fruition. Clifford for his part was not only delighted but even sent Newman a donation of twenty pounds:

> I bless and thank God for thus allowing you, after so many strange events, to gather in with your own hand in gladness some portion of the harvest which long ago was sown by you in sorrow. [21]

The plan failed and Ullathorne again wrote to Clifford:

> It is true that Dr. Newman was authorised to establish an Oratory at Oxford, to be subject to the Birmingham Oratory during his life, but there has been a great outcry, a remonstrance addressed by Talbot to Card Barnabo, and an order came from the Pope that we are to discuss certain points, about preparing youths for Oxford in Dr. Newman's School etc. The Bp. of Newport writes that there is a great deal of excitement and violence in Rome on the part of certain people which he is trying to moderate.

---

20   *Ibid.*

21   Clifton Diocesan Archives, *Letters to William Clifford*, Part I, Clifford to Newman, copy dated 5.2.1867.

I shall privately put before the Bishops a *précis* of this case. Of course I do not look to any point relating to my administration being discussed in our meeting. Dr. N. has been most shamefully treated. It is a long story. [22]

The penultimate sentence about Ullathorne's administration was a timely reminder, though not aimed at Clifford, that Oxford was in his (Ullathorne's) diocese. It should be recalled that since his previous letter quoted above, Manning had become Archbishop of Westminster.

Rome published a rescript and, without issuing a formal prohibition, instructed the bishops to compose pastoral letters the main thrust of which was to be that attendance at a Protestant University was a proximate occasion of sin. [23] Clifford's pastoral on the subject appeared in October, 1867. By the standards of the day it was comparatively short, but even so it succeeded in presenting an adequate exposition of the objections felt both by the bishops and by Rome on the subject of Catholics attending Oxford and Cambridge.

---

22   Ugbrooke Archives, *Letters to Bp. Clifford, 1867*, Ullathorne to Clifford, Letter dated 6.4.1867.

23   The Letter from Propaganda Fide to the Bishops was dated 6.8.1867. They are instructed as follows:

> You will clearly explain in your Pastoral Letter the doctrine of the Church on avoiding the proximate occasions of mortal sin; to which occasions no one without grievous sin can expose himself, *unless under the pressure of grave and adequate necessity, and unless such precautions be taken as shall remove all proximate danger*. And in the present case, where as His Holiness had declared, there is an intrinsic and very serious danger to purity of morals, as well as to faith (which is altogether necessary for salvation), it is next to impossible to discover circumstances in which Catholics could without sin attend non-Catholic Universities.

Summary of Clifford's Pastoral, dated October 27th, 1867 [24]

1.   Religious Tests at Oxford and Cambridge have been removed. It would be wrong . . . to conclude that all objections to Catholics attending have now ceased to exist.

2.   These institutions are essentially Protestant. Furthermore they are attended by young men of an impressionable age.

3.   We are bound to flee sin and proximate occasions of sin. The Universities are for Catholics such occasions of sin.

    <u>Three quotations</u>.

    a)   When great or apparently great temporal advantages present themselves as the consequence of any particular course of action, human nature is but too apt to underrate the spiritual dangers with which that course may be beset. (pp. 4, 5).

    b)   Good Catholics would watch narrowly dangers which threaten morality, but all are not equally keen to the dangers which in these days beset faith. (p. 5).

    c)   Gross infidelity, scoffing at sacred things, irreligion of the school of Voltaire, these are not the dangers to which the faith of young educated Catholics is generally exposed in this country in these days. The danger arises rather from that false liberalism which has so repeatedly been the object of the censures of the Holy Father. (p. 5).

---

24   Clifton Diocesan Archives, *Pastoral Letters of Bp. Clifford.*

Speaking of theological relativism (as opposed to the absolute claims of Revelation as deposited with, and preached by, the Catholic Church) and the dangers perceived to flow from it for those Catholics who are in contact with it, Clifford spells out what those effects might well be:

> Without going to the length of losing their faith, young Catholics easily acquire from the society of such men, a spirit of criticism of sacred things, which gradually weakens that firm hold they had of the Catholic faith, and of matters connected with the faith; which lessens their reverence for authority, cools that practical piety they had acquired during their Catholic education, and renders their whole tone of thought and action less thoroughly Catholic. (p. 6).

He is in no doubt that 'to dangers of this nature young students would be in a special manner exposed when studying in a Protestant University'.

It is interesting to note that Clifford does concede a point in so far as he admits that some might differ 'in their estimate of the gravity and imminence of such dangers' (p. 6), [25] but his response to this is to call for a closing of the ranks with a reminder that the bishops, who are shepherds of the flocks, do see such proximate and imminent dangers and in this assessment have received the support of Rome itself.

The pastoral letter ends by quoting the decree from Propaganda about these dangers. It is not an outright prohibition but is certainly a grave warning to all involved.

Much of the debate about Catholics and a university education has been coloured by the variety of motives projected on the *dramatis personae* by subsequent commentators on the period. For example, one writer's perception of Clifford – as his choice of language shows – is somewhat less than sympathetic.

---

25   We know from a letter to Grant that Clifford was already giving a limited number of permissions (Clifton Diocesan Archives, *Letters to Bp. Clifford*, Part I, Clifford to Grant, Letter dated 19.5.1867). This was in line with his thinking as expressed in the letter quoted earlier in this chapter in which he cited the opinion of a professor at the Collegio Romano.

> Mgr. Clifford, the Bishop of Clifton, was the chief
> representative of the nobled and the well-to-do among the
> Hierarchy . . . As a matter of fact Clifford had never been
> very popular at the Roman Court. It was his custom when in
> the Eternal City to amuse himself among the English
> aristocracy there. Talbot once described to Manning how
> Clifford had 'hired a carriage by the month, and (went) out
> amongst the English every night, eating their good dinners,
> and gossiping at all their parties'. He was considered to be
> Gallican in his ideas . . .
>
> Clifford had been in 1870 the most truculent of the English
> Inopportunists . . . (Clifford's correspondence with Newman
> betrays an enmity to Manning and his policies which is
> almost pathological in its intensity). [26]

Such an overtly critical view of Clifford is surely wide of the mark. It is
always possible to adopt – as Talbot does – an attitude of moral
indignation towards someone who is a welcome guest at the tables of the
well-to-do. However, what makes this quotation (taken from Purcell) all
the more suspect is that it is one of only three references to Clifford which
Purcell makes in a total of 1,534 pages. Nor is the word 'truculent' in any
way an apt epithet for his performance at the Council. In regard to
Manning, Clifford certainly expressed a strong antipathy to his views
before his appointment to Westminster. After that date his dealings were
business-like. Again, 'emnity' is surely too strong a term to describe their
fundamental divergence of outlook.

In a word, Clifford was indeed an aristocrat, but he was also a moderate.
It is difficult to understand why, in any discussion of the University
Question, so much emphasis is placed on his patrician background to the
exclusion of his views – which did in the end prevail.

All this has a bearing on the significance to be attached to a very long
letter [27] which Clifford sent to Manning in 1867. The subject was 'the

---

26   V. A. McClelland, *Cardinal Manning: His Public Life and Influence*
        (Publ. London, 1962), pp. 101, 102.

27   Quoted in McClelland, *op. cit.* pp. 104 – 107.

erection of a place for the Higher Studies, under the Hierarchy and with the concurrence of the Fathers of the Society (of Jesus)'. It also considered the location for such an institution with Clifford arguing the case for Prior Park.

Clifford's letter may be summarised under the following headings:

I		Erection of Institution	(under Hierarchy, with concurrence of the Jesuits)
	1.	House of Jesuits	Compact between Hierarchy and Jesuits to supply 3 or 4 professors
	2	House(s) of Residence	Might later develop into College; and so Rules of discipline
	3	Staff	Initially 6 or 7 professors (3 or 4 of whom S.J.)
	4	Expense	Not less than £2,000 p.a.
	5	Council of University	To include Archbishop and 2 bishops
	6	Degrees	London University to validate
	7	President of University	Responsible to Hierarchy
	8	Appointment	Temporary or permanent?
	9	Finance	Through subscription (not parish collections)

II   <u>Suggests Prior Park</u>, BUT

    1.   Might need extensions.

    2   Might suit initially but move elsewhere might prove necessary. Unhappy about this.

    3.   University might rent the building initially and then take out a lease.

One commentator, in his discussion of this letter, is suspicious of Clifford's motives in writing it. [28] He suggests that the bishop, who had been educated by the Jesuits, was proposing to hand over 'complete control' to the Society. But the tenor of the letter shows otherwise. Clifford speaks about a religious being appointed as Head 'from time to time', the implication of a non-religious Head also being appointed being quite clear. He states unequivocally: 'I feel that we ought to avoid as much as possible from the beginning giving the establishment too much the air of a College of regulars'.

Again, on the suggestion that the University might be housed at Prior Park, Bath, the same writer comments:

> This was in Clifford's own diocese and he would be able to obtain a pincer grip on the new establishment to make sure that it developed along the lines he desired. [29]

This is surely tendentious as Clifford has already outlined a structure which would render the University quite independent – the Council would number the Archbishop and two bishops amongst its members – and subject only to the Hierarchy.

Nor should it be forgotten that, according to Clifford, Manning welcomed the idea. Writing a confidential letter to Father Alfred Weld, S.J., the Jesuit Provincial, in order to sound out his views, he says:

---

28   McClelland, *ibid*.

29   McClelland, *ibid*.

It was with a view of forming some such scheme that I spoke to the Archbishop & to yourself, & the encouragement I have received makes me hope that with God's blessing we may succeed. [30] [Underlining mine].

The scheme however foundered. Various reasons may be suggested for this, one of which may have been financial. Much of Clifford's letter to Weld speaks of rents and of the need for him to move his small school from Prior Park in the event of the University opening there.

Although as far as English Catholicism was concerned the energies of the bishops in the 1870s were absorbed by tho issue of Papal Infallibility and its various ramifications, nevertheless the question of Catholic students at Oxford and Cambridge remained very much on the agenda.

In April, 1872, the bishops met to discuss the issue with Clifford proposing that Rome be approached yet again in view of the changed circumstances resulting from the abolition of the Tests. Such thinking was typical of Clifford who, on any issue on which he felt deeply, would not hesitate to keep pressing his case. Rome, however, again refused but advised the bishops to look for a different way out of the impasse. The Catholic College at Kensington (1874 – 1882) was the result – an enterprise in which Clifford does not appear to have been much involved.

The English bishops returned to the subject at their Low Week Meeting of 1882. The Resolutions repeated the letter of Propaganda of August 6th, 1867, emphasised that the bishops reserved to themselves decisions in this matter as it applied in their dioceses, and instructed all clergy

> that they are bound *sub gravi* not to encourage or to permit Catholics to frequent Board Schools, or to reside at the national Universities for the purposes of education. (Resolution V). [31]

---

30 Archives of the English Province of the Society of Jesus, Mount Street, *Letters of Bishops and Cardinals 1840 - 1891*, No. 142, Clifford to Father Weld, S.J., Letter dated 4.11.1867.

31 *Resolutions of the Catholic Bishops in England at their Annual Meeting . . . Low Week, 1882* (Education). Photocopy in the Clifton Diocesan Archives.

Short of an outright prohibition, the episcopal grip could not have been tighter.

But while in public Clifford supported the 'party line', he was growing uneasy about its inherent justice and about the inevitability of the suspected dangers. His brother bishops, with the exception of Hedley, appeared to be adamant and so a change on that front looked to be out of the question. The laity, however, were becoming increasingly restless and were preparing an appeal to Propaganda to secure a re-opening of the question by the Hierarchy, the main plank of their argument being to question the assertion that a Catholic attending Oxford or Cambridge would be exposing himself to 'a proximate occasion of sin'. Clifford and Hedley were prepared to back this Appeal. Hartwell de la Garde Grissell was the leading protagonist in this move but it is interesting to note that it was Gladstone who tipped off Manning – not the greatest of friends at this time – as to what was afoot. The plan was forestalled. [32]

Unsuccessful on this front, Clifford raised the matter with his fellow bishops at the Low Week meeting of 1883. Sixteen years (he argued) had now elapsed since Propaganda's original prohibition, and so the time was ripe for a reappraisal. In more practical terms, the 'proximate occasion' argument could be obviated by a strong Catholic presence at Oxford. The majority of the bishops found the whole thing too troublesome to be re-opened yet again and although the matter was 'fully discussed . . . ultimately the proposals of the Bishop of Clifton were withdrawn'. [33]

Throughout his episcopate Clifford was the champion, and was seen to be the champion, of moderate opinion. On so many issues, including Papal Infallibility, this was invariably his stance, and to rule out of court any opinion he might have as being due to his upper class social origins would seem to be gratuitous. In the present instance a change did come about,

---

32   This paragraph and the next are based on V. A. McClelland's authoritative *English Roman Catholics and Higher Education, 1830 – 1903*, (Publ. Oxford, 1973), pp. 345 sqq.

33   Westminster Archdiocesan Archives, *Meeting of the Bishops in Low Week, 1883*, ACTA, Thursday, April 5th. XVI Attendance of Catholics at Protestant Universities & Public Schools.

and the possibility for this was due largely to the establishment of a strong university Chaplaincy at Oxford – the very point that Clifford was arguing in 1883.

The end of the story was a recognition by all the bishops that the pressures were now becoming inexorable. The Duke of Norfolk was one of those seeking permission and Bishop John Butt of Southwark – appointed just three or four years before – having granted permission, wrote nervously to Clifford to ascertain whether or not he had done the right thing. [34]

He wrote again to Clifford towards the end of 1889 aligning himself with Clifford in his quest for change. Brief though the letter is, it reveals no small amount of background intrigue:

> I have written to Cardinal Simeoni expressing my entire agreement with the Report on the University question that you sent to Card. Simeoni on Sept. 19th 1883.
>
> The Duke of Norfolk has written to Cardinal Rampolla asking him to procure the Report from the archives at Propaganda and to read it to His Holiness.
>
> The Duke thinks that if any other Bishops are of our way of thinking it would be well that they should write.
>
> Would Shrewsbury do so? [35]

(The Bishop of Shrewsbury was Edmund Knight who at one time had been Clifford's secretary).

---

34   Ugbrooke Archives, *Letters to Bp. Clifford, 1888*, Bp. Butt to Clifford, Letter dated 31.12.1888.

35   Ugbrooke Archives, *Letters to Bp. Clifford, 1889*, Bp. Butt to Clifford, Letter dated 27.11.1889.

Clifford died in August, 1893, less than two years before the embargo was lifted by a decision of the Holy See, dated April 2nd, 1895. [36] In June, 1896, chaplains were appointed to look after the interests of the Catholic undergraduates, and the first chaplain was from Clifford's own diocese of Clifton. He was Monsignor Canon Charles H. Kennard, M.A. whose portrait still hangs in the Oxford Chaplaincy. [37]

Clifford's contribution to the debate about Catholics at Oxford and Cambridge was considerable. His was a quiet persistence in the interests of what he saw to be not only inevitable, but also right. For him the issue was not just a matter of social éclat for his wealthy friends. More importantly it was a matter of social justice because entry to the professions depended on it. Typically all was done within the constraints imposed both by Rome and by the collective responsibility which he owed to his fellow bishops.

36   The decision was printed in *The Tablet*, 27.4.1895.

37   For details of Kennard's ministry as Catholic chaplain, see Walter Drumm, *The Old Palace: The Catholic Chaplaincy at Oxford* (Publ. Dublin, 1991), pp. 37–52.

Prop. Fidei Roma

Scritture Riferite Nei Congressi 1855 – 1857 Anglia 14 473, 474

[Newman to Cardinal Barnabo]

Nuper Universitas Oxoniensis, jubente Parliamento Regni, dedit copiam scholarum suarum omnibus cujuscumque religionis asseclis, ita ut nunc catholici non minus quam Protestantes, studia liberalia, si velint, ibi prosequi prossint.

Probabilis est conjectura, immo certum est, Catholicos quosdam adoloscentes, nisi prohibeantur auctoritate ecclesiasticâ, illuc esse ituros, studiorum causâ, a suis sive parentibus sive tutoribus missos.

Hoc pessimi erit exempli, si rem nostram spectus in novâ hac Catholicâ Universitate Hiberniae.

Nam, cum Universitas Oxoniensis splendidum nomen habeat, et *laicorum* etiam Catholicorum, in Hiberniâ, oculos in se convertos soleat (de *laicis* Angliae et Hiberniae Catholicis loquor, non de venerabilibus Episcopis, non de sacerdotibus, qui, supra hanc quotidianorum hominum orbem viventes, imaginibus saeculi non decipiuntur, sed de *laicis*, qui rem, locum, dignitatem, nobilitatem habent, in quorum gratiâ Universitas nostra nova potissimum stabilita est) vehementissime timendum est, ne, si permissum fuerit uni vel duobus studentibus Catholicis Oxonium adire, universa Catholica juventus, certe Anglia, forsitan Hibernia, tanquam grex ovium, unus post alterm, caulâ Academiae Catholicae aut non quaesitâ aut relicatâ, nostris Institutionibus spretis, tanquam novellis et rudioribus, in illud periculosissimum erroris tabernaculum sint transituri.

Progressus habere non potest, iniquis hisce conditionibus, Universitas nostra, amissura forsitan est optimos alumnos suos; non habitura est plane quos alioquin esset habitura.

Quam ob rem, ignarus prorsus quid de hac re sentiant Episcopi Angliae, dignam eam esse judicavi, qua suis oculis Domine Reverendissime, subjiciatur. Cum tempus brevissimum scribendi datur, de re gravissimâ pauca vix scribo, currente calamo.

Joannes H. Newman
Congr. Orat. Presbry.

die Mart 12, 1856
6 Harcourt Street, Dublin, Via Londra

P.S. Audivi, dum scribo, quod me credere facit, Episcopos Angliae non aliter judicaturos esse in hac re.

Archives of Prop. Fidei Rome
Scritture Riferite Nei Congressi 1855 – 1857 Anglia 14 473, 474

[Newman to Cardinal Barnabo]

Recently the University of Oxford, as ordered by Parliament, has made provision for students of all faiths so that now Catholics as well as Protestants may, if they wish, pursue their liberal studies at the University.

It is probable, nay certain, that some Catholics will now be sent to University by their parents or tutors, unless they are forbidden to do so by ecclesiastical authority. This will afford the worst type of example if our new Catholic University of Ireland is anything to go by.

For, since Oxford University has such a splendid reputation which even *lay* Catholics in Ireland gaze at in admiration (I am speaking of the *lay* Catholics of England and Ireland, not of venerable Bishops, nor of priests who, living above the level of ordinary mortals are not deceived by passing fashion, but of *lay folk* who have their own proper business, place, dignity and nobility which has proved to be the vey foundation of our new University) the great fear is that if permission be granted to two or three Catholic students to go to Oxford, then the entire Catholic youth – certainly of England, perhaps of Ireland – just like a flock of sheep one after the other will not seek to enter our Catholic institutions or will leave the sheepfold. They will despise them as being either "new" or "not sophisticated" and so will transfer to that most dangerous haven of error ("in illud periculosissimum erroris tabernaculum").

In such pernicious circumstances it will be impossible for our University to prosper for it would be about to lose its best students, nor would its future be in any way clear.

It is for these reasons and because I am completely in the dark as to the mind of the English Bishops in the matter that I have thought it right to put the issue before your Eminence.

Time is short and so these few words on a very serious topic have been written in haste.

John H. Newman
Congr. Orat Presby

March 12th 1856
6 Harcourt Street, Dublin, Via London

P.S. I have just heard on reliable authority that the English Bishops will not be of a different mind.

Translation from the original Latin by J. A. Harding.

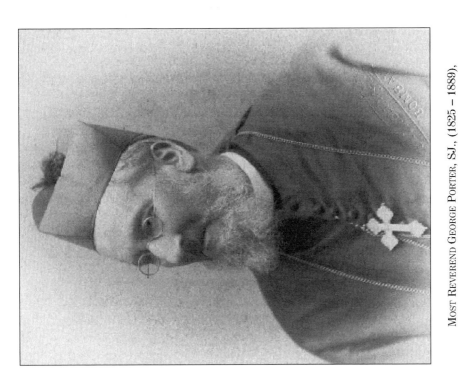

MOST REVEREND GEORGE PORTER, S.J., (1825 – 1889),
ARCHBISHOP OF BOMBAY

FATHER EDWARD PURBRICK, S.J., (1830 – 1914), SUPERIOR OF THE
ENGLISH PROVINCE AT THE TIME OF *ROMANOS PONTIFICES*

CHAPTER THIRTEEN

The Bull *Romanos Pontifices** (May 8th 1881)

Since the reign of Elizabeth I there had been a long-running dispute in England between the Regular Clergy on the one hand and the Bishops and Secular Clergy on the other. It involved claims of privileges contrary to the received common law of the Church. There had been some curtailment of these during the time of Bishop Challoner (Vicar Apostolic of the London District, 1758 – 1781) but still, twenty-five years after the Restoration of the Hierarchy, 'the relations of the regulars with the bishops were not yet fully settled'. [1]

Typical of such disputes were the following:

<u>1730</u> A dispute in which the seculars tried to win back from the Society of Jesus control of the English College in Rome.

<u>1818</u> The opening of a new chapel, run by a secular priest, only a hundred yards from the existing chapel conducted by the Jesuits of Stonyhurst (The 'Wigan Dispute').

<u>1839</u> In June Bishop Baines wrote to Bishop Briggs suggesting that a petition be sent to Rome asking 'that the regulars shall not publish any peculiar indulgences without the express permission of the Bishop'.[2]

<u>1847</u> Writing to Propaganda on the state of the Church in England, Father Luigi Gentili claimed that 'the Benedictines fostered an

---

* (N.B. Bishop Clifford wrote a History of the Bull *Romanos Pontifices* which is now, in typescript, in the Clifton Diocesan Archives. This chapter is an analysis of that account with reference to his Diaries, to the problems as seen by other bishops, and to correspondence in the Archives of the Generalate of the Society of Jesus in Rome. References in brackets in the text are to Clifford's *History*).

---

1 Cuthbert Butler, *The Life and Times of Bishop Ullathorne* (Publ. London, 1926), Vol. II, p. 187.

2 Clifton Diocesan Archives, *Bishop Baines, File No. 15*, Baines to Briggs, letter dated 13.6.1839. Briggs had been Vicar Apostolic of the Northern District since 1836.

anti-episcopal spirit, and were always ready to condemn whatever the Vicars Apostolic did'.[3]

1855   Bishop Goss of Liverpool writing to Clifford in Rome. (The latter was studying canon law and was not yet a bishop). In this diocese it is a subject of paramount importance, for more than one half of the clergy are Regulars . . . Many of the Bps. seem to have made their visitation of the Regulars on sufferance or tolerance, that is, they have visited them as far as no opposition, remonstrance or – was offered. Now this I don't want to do. I want to visit properly and efficiently where and as far as I have canonical right . . . [4]

1868   Bishop Brown of Newport to Bishop Cornthwaite of Beverley:

Some of Missionary Bodies of Regulars in England are taking active measures against all obligation of making known at Episcopal Visitations the income derived by their Missions from the Congregation – and of having to obtain permission from the Bps. for absence from their Missions.

The Prior of St. Michael's starts for Rome this day as Agent for the English Benedictines. He is instructed to claim prescription against making known to the Bp any thing regarding the temporals of a Regular Mission since it had not been required by the Bps.[5]

Such, briefly, was the problem. As stated in Chapter One, all the ten Vicars Apostolic of the Western District with one exception (Baggs) had been members of religious orders, and one is forced to the conclusion that this *de facto* arrangement had been a 'political' decision on the part of Rome in order to give the Regulars at least one voice on the bench of bishops.

---

3   Edward Norman, *The English Catholic Church in the 19th Century* (Publ. Oxford, 1984), p. 86. Norman adds: 'As a member of a different order he might perhaps have exaggerated'. (p. 86).

4   Liverpool Diocesan Archives, *Goss Letter Book June 15, 1855 to May 9. 1857.* Letter No. 24, Goss to Clifford letter dated 8.11.1855.

5   Leeds Diocesan Archives, *Letters to Bp. Cornthwaite*, Brown to Cornthwaite letter dated 5.12.1868. Brandsby Hall, York (1746). Served from Ampleforth (Catholic Directory, 1868).

At the 1877 Low Week Meeting, Manning invited the bishops to consider the expediency of asking the Holy See to frame a Constitution . . . for determining the relations which ought to exist between the Regulars and the Episcopate. (p. 2)

The idea had been given impetus by the fact that *Universalis Ecclesiae*, by virtue of which the Hierarchy had been restored in 1850, had brought to an end the missionary status of the Church in England and restored to it normal government.

The bishops agreed that a Petition be sent to Rome and Ullathorne and Clifford were deputed to draw this up. The two bishops acted with incredible speed for the draft (which had been prepared by Ullathorne, assisted by Clifford) was ready by the end of April, and before May was out, Clifford was in Rome arguing the case on behalf of the bishops. (p. 4) (1877 marked the Pope's Episcopal Jubilee and so it was an appropriate time for Clifford to be there).

In his *History* of the events leading up to the publication of the Bull, Clifford gives a graphic account of the false ideas then prevailing at Propaganda about the issues involved and of how he was able to disabuse the officials of them. This was crucial, for there can be no doubt that Propaganda's 'starting-point' in the argument was that the English bishops were in the wrong and that they were determined to strip the Regulars of all privileges. At Propaganda there were two points at the heart of the controversy:

1)   Cardinal Alessandro Franchi (Prefect pf Propaganda and with whom Clifford was dealing) was under the impression that the bishops wished to interfere in the colleges run by the Regulars. Clifford assured him that this was not the case. (p. 6).

2)   Franchi was concerned – as were the Regulars – about the bishops dividing those missions which were already run by Regulars. (p. 7)

This latter point required a fuller reply. Clifford gave the example of Cheltenham in his own diocese which at that time had some 50,000 inhabitants and yet only one mission (run by the Benedictines). He argued that a time would come when new missions would have to be created but that this would be impossible – in the sense of his being able to put in seculars – if what the Regulars were demanding was granted. (p. 7). What happened next we can read in a letter which Clifford sent to Manning:

> "Well that", said Rinaldini (Secretary of Propaganda), "was a case never contemplated: and, of course, an exceptional case like that would have to be provided against". "But", I rejoined, "so far from this being an exceptional case, it is the very state of things which the Regulars by their new claims seek to establish".[6]

Rinaldini – wishing to avoid a long drawn out tussle, and the involvement of canon lawyers searching into the history of privileges granted to religious – was 'anxious to settle by having a conference' (p. 7). Such a meeting would include the General of the Jesuits, and the Bishops of Southwark and Clifton. The suggestion was put forward on several occasions but Clifford remained adamant saying 'that things had reached such a point that it was necessary to have an authentic declaration of the Holy See on these questions'. (p. 7).

The whole point at issue was the privileges of the Religious – and in particular of the Jesuits – and the rights of diocesan bishops which, in the face of such privileges, often seemed to stand curtailed. Clifford's description (or is it Ullathorne's?) of how things stood is so eloquent and amusing that at least two writers (Snead-Cox and Cuthbert Butler) have quoted it –

> The ignorance which at this time reigned concerning the Privileges of the Jesuits was wonderful. The Jesuits openly made claim in England and elsewhere as if they possessed extraordinary privileges, and quoted the Bulls of Popes granted formerly to the Society, saying that these revived with the restoration of the Society by Pius VII. These claims met everywhere with tacit acceptance.

---

6   Quoted in Clifford's *History*, p. 7.

Among the English Bishops, the Bishop of Birmingham alone had some knowledge that these claims were ill-founded. The other Bishops, though ignorant of the extent of the privileges claimed, took it for granted that the Jesuits had extraordinary privileges: they suspected that they were strained: but nobody knew exactly what they were, and nobody knew how to find out exactly, as it was supposed that many of them were privately given them by the Pope. Clifford thought so too. (pp. 7 – 9)

During the next few months four events were to take place which, each in its own way, were to affect the final outcome:

1)   The claim of the Jesuits to open a college in Manchester against the will of the bishop was decided against them at Rome. (This had been a lengthy dispute between Bishop Herbert Vaughan of Salford and Father Peter Gallwey, the Jesuit Provincial. Each party went into print against the other.)

2)   Ullathorne and Clifford drew up a lengthy statement (a *'Relatio'*) which was then approved by the English bishops. In November it was decided that Manning should go to Rome in order to introduce the case (and then return) and that Bishop Edward Bagshawe of Nottingham and Bishop Clifford should remain in Rome and so be available to answer questions. It is not clear to what extent Bagshawe did in fact fulfil this duty, but certainly Clifford spent many months there. (p. 10). There can be no doubt that his availability – matched by an incomparable knowledge of Italian, of canon law and of curial procedures – paid off in the end. Added to these was his skill as a lobbyist – honed during the controversies of Vatican I – which he also used to advantage.

3)   In February, 1878, Pope Pius IX died after the longest reign in the Church's history. He was succeeded by Leo XIII who throughout took a personal interest in the discussions. This too was to be a factor in the eventual success of the bishops.

4)   Clifford advised the appointment of a lawyer (Sig. Martini) to assist in the presentation of the case on behalf of the bishops. (p. 12).

During his stay in Rome which lasted until 26th March, Clifford wrote with the approval of Manning four papers:

1)   On the dividing of missions in England;

2)   On the elementary schools in England;

3)   On Ecclesiastical foundations in England;

4)   On the conditions required for new foundations by religious orders.

These papers were not for the benefit of Martini only. They were (as Clifford says):

> the means of giving the Cardinals a correct idea of the state of things in England, in regard to the various points of which they treated. These papers proved to be of great practical utility throughout the whole of our case. (p. 14).

A curious turn of events was when both Manning and Clifford noticed that practically all the cardinals who attended the meetings at Propaganda were Regulars. This, they felt, would be bound to prejudice the outcome and so Cardinal Ludovico Bilio – a senior Cardinal and Grand Penitentiary – urged on Manning an approach to the Pope himself in order to ask him to appoint a Commission of Cardinals. This the Holy Father agreed to do. (p. 16).

From the other side there were innumerable delays – and even rumours that the whole matter would be put off *sine die*. Clifford saw the Pope to argue the case against such an eventuality. Not only did Leo agree but he sent repeated requests to Father Ballerini, S.J., who was representing the Regulars, to get his case ready. Clifford was of the opinion that Ballerini was 'playing for time' in the hope that sooner or later the bishops would have to return to their dioceses. 'The resolve of the bishops was not taken seriously'. (p. 18).

In May, 1880, Ballerini's paper was ready. 'It was', writes Clifford, 'voluminous and confused'. (p. 30). More importantly, however, it was offensive in tone with the result that such a document could not but favour the bishops, particularly in the eyes of the Pope. Even so, at this time they were having an uphill task as rumours were circulating both in the press and in private to discredit Manning and his fellow bishops. It was alleged, for example, that the Cardinal had been guilty of invading both the privileges and the property of the Regulars. (p. 21).

Clifford's contribution to the success of the bishops' case was not due only to his being available in Rome. Entries in his *Diary* for this period show the intense amount of lobbying which he did. Many of the figures from the Vatican Council – only ten years before – were still alive. Some of them he knew well and how best to persuade them to the bishops' cause.

Already under strain because of the responsibility involved, he was obliged to return to England in July because of the fatal illness of his brother Charles (8th Baron Clifford) who died on 5th August. The Bishop officiated at his funeral.

One aspect of critical importance (already mentioned) was the attitude of Pope Leo himself. Two entries from Clifford's *Diary* show this clearly:

<u>1880 Dec. 4</u>   He (the Pope) is well up in the case. [7]

<u>1881 Feb. 1</u>   The Pope takes the greatest interest in the matter and has done so all along, seeing everything himself. [8]

Meanwhile at home *The Tablet* was reassuring its readers whose interest had been excited 'by all kinds of false rumours'. Still basking in the comfort afforded by the definition of Papal Infallibility – though the dogma was not here being invoked – the leader writer concluded:

---

7   Clifton Diocesan Archives, *Diaries of Bp. Clifford, 1880*, Dec. 4.

8   Clifton Diocesan Archives, *Diaries of Bp. Clifford, 1881*, Feb. 1.

If . . . we consider that the Holy Spirit is ever watching over
the Vicar of Christ in his government of the Church, we must
rest perfectly satisfied, as good Catholics, that whatever the
decisions are, they will be the wisest and the best obtainable
for the interests of Religion. [9]

The Jesuits, however, appear to have been divided in their view as to
what the future would hold. Father George Porter, was not at all hopeful
in a letter he wrote to Father Torquatus Armellini, the Secretary to the
General in Rome:

Last evening I had a visit from Doctor Smith. Card. Jacobini
told another Card, who told Dr. S. that the Holy Father is
bent on making a new constitution. This means (probably) a
change in the law unfavourable to us.

Dr. S. is very concerned. Wanted your Rev. or myself to post
off to Fiesole in order to confer with F. General & see quid
faciendum . . . I do not see what his Paternity can do, more
than he has done . . .

Meanwhile would you think it well to warn our friends in the
Sacred College of what is in contemplation . . .

George Porter

Think of the powers which ought to be safe A.M.D.G. and may
be in danger – Inform of them and of the consequences. [10]

But two days earlier the General himself had written to Armellini (in
Italian):

9   *The Tablet*, 15.1.1881.

10   Archives of the Society of Jesus at the Generalate, Rome. *Angl. 1014
        Controversiarum inter episcopos Angliae et Societatem Aliosque
        Regulares*, tomus IV, 1850 – 1883, Angl. 14 – VII, 14, Porter to Armellini,
        letter dated 29.1.1881. Cardinal Ludovico Jacobini was not yet fifty years
        of age and had only recently been created a Cardinal (1879).

It augurs well that the other Orders are moving: it is a matter of common concern for the Regulars: the Benedictines are very interested, and Cardinal Petra, in similar circumstances, has been very good to us: then the Holy Father is the organ of God, he by his nature is not against us but rather favourable . . . [11] [My translation].

Eventually the Bull *Romanos Pontifices* appeared. The Pope, it would seem, had taken such great interest because it was to be addressed to the whole Church and was not applicable only to England. Clearly Rome had taken the opportunity afforded by the situation in England to clear up anomalies then existing throughout the Church. Latin scholar of considerable repute, Pope Leo would have had an added reason for scrutinising the final text, but Clifford tells us that the papal involvement went even further:

> . . . The Pope himself directed in great measure the order and form, and a great portion of the language is from his pen, and the whole of it passed under his personal revision. (p. 45).

But part of the Bull came from the pen of Clifford as the following entry from his *Diary* shows:

> On the evening of Thursday 21 (April) Mgr. Masotti called on me and asked me to supply him with some details regarding the progress of religion in England since the establishment of the hierarchy. The information was required for the Bull – The request appeared strange as we had been told that the Bull was all finished – I promised to supply the information next morning. Accordingly I drew up a report of 6 pages foolscap with statistics & details taken from Vaughan's article in Tablet of Jan. 1st and from our Sommarios, & took the report on Friday morning to Masotti at Propaganda. He read it & was pleased & said he would forward it at once to the redattore of the Bull.

---

11   *Ibid.*, Angl. 14 – VII, 13, Beckx to Armellini, letter dated 27.1.1881.

He then told me that the Bull was finished but that on reading it it had been discovered that the Exordium which spoke of the progress of Religion in England since the days of St. Augustine, was almost identical with the exordium of some other Bull. It was therefore necessary to recast it, taking for basis the Constitution of Pius IX establishing the hierarchy, & the progress made in England in consequence. [12]

One cannot but admire Clifford's energy at this time.

Another entry in his *Diary* reads:

> May 14   Bull *Romanos Pontifices* . . . I read it, and made extracts for *'The Times'*, and began a Translation. On Sunday I communicated the decisions to Shakespeare Wood, to telegraph to London for tomorrow's *'Times'*. [13]

As was to be expected, reaction to the Bull was varied. The English Provincial of the Jesuits urged them 'to receive the Constitution in the true spirit of sons of St. Ignatius with hearty and entire obedience'.

> There is no denying that in some points the decision will be found not to be in perfect accordance with our hopes, and some things may not be flattering to our self-love . . .

> It would be well indeed if we could abstain altogether from remark or comment But as absolute silence in the midst of those who will talk freely about the Bull in any and every sense is sure to prove impossible, let me . . . entreat all to keep the most sedulous guard over their tongues . . . [14]

---

12   Clifton Diocesan Archives, *Diaries of Bp. Clifford*, 1881, Apr. 21.

13   *Ibid.*, May 14.

14   Archives of the Society of Jesus at the Generalate, Rome. *Angl. 1014 Controversiarum inter episcopos Angliae et Societatem Aliosque Regulares*, tomus IV, 1850 – 1883, Anglo 14 – VIII, 3, Letter from Edward I. Purbrick, Provincial, to Religious Superiors 'On Receipt of Official News': letter dated 19.5.1881.

Father Purbrick added that he did not wish there to be any criticism of 'any of those persons who have had a part in bringing this event about, or the means employed to secure the result'. By the same token he did not want any one to succumb to the temptation 'either to regret or to express dissatisfaction with the action of our own Superiors in the affair, and to wish that some questions now settled had never been raised'. [14] Obedience to the voice of the Holy Father was to be paramount.

This, too, was to be the theme of *The Tablet*.

It is one of the distinguishing glories of the See of PETER that all disputes and discussions are hushed and ended when PETER has spoken. In no period of history has the voice of PETER been more filially respected and more heartily obeyed than in this brazen age of pride in intellect and of independence and self-assertion. [15]

Bishop Clifford's immediate duties in Rome were now at an end. For some weeks he had been preparing to have an operation but had not dared to undergo surgery in order to ensure his being available to attend to the business in hand. The operation was on the 25th May and, after a period of convalescence and a final audience with the Pope, he left Rome on 22nd June. (p. 45).

Below are examples from the list of 12 *Dubii* submitted by the bishops for solution by the Holy See –

1.   Whether and how far it is lawful for Bishops to proceed in the Division of Missions.

2.   Whether in the establishment of a new Mission, cut off from a Regular Mission, the Bishop is bound to give the preference to Regulars.

6.   Whether and how far the Bishop has the right of visiting Poor Schools, Pious Establishments and Cemeteries in the

---

15   *The Tablet*, May 21, 1881.

Missions served by Regulars.

9.   What particular rules are to be observed between Bishops
and Regulars in the government of Missions? (p. 38).

The happy outcome of the bishops' efforts in their appeal to Rome was to
be an occasion of legitimate pride for Clifford. Bishop Ullathorne wrote to
congratulate him:

We all owe you a debt of gratitude for the patience and
perseverance with which you have worked this cause, and
for the vigilance with which you have protected it from
hostile interventions. [16]

His praise, however, was accompanied by a remark which to Clifford of
all people must have seemed particularly wry:

The episcopal office is strengthened all through the
document, and it gives a complete reply to the objection
raised in the Vatican Council, that the infallibility would
weaken the episcopate. [17]

Five years later a somewhat puzzled Clifford must have wondered
whether all his efforts had been worth it. The entry in his *Diary* for
October 16th reads –ç

On my return to Clifton this evening I heard to my surprise
that the Franciscans have purchased land and are about to
begin to build a chapel at Portishead. [18]

Plus ça change . . .

---

16   Cuthbert Butler, *The Life and Times of Bishop Ullathorne* (Publ.
London, 1926), Vol. II, p. 189.

17   *Ibid.*

18   Clifton Diocesan Archives, *Diaries of Bp. Clifford*, 1886, Oct. 16.

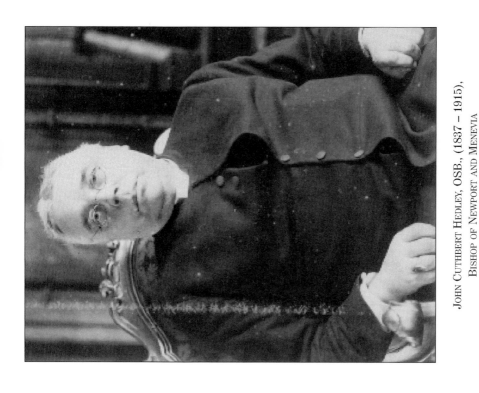

John Cuthbert Hedley, OSB., (1837 – 1915),
Bishop of Newport and Menevia

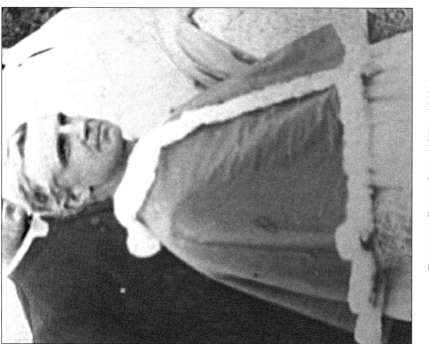

Reverend Daniel Iles, (1855 – 1912),
priest of the Diocese of Clifton

CHAPTER FOURTEEN

The Days of the Week and the Works of Creation

'Bishop Clifford . . . is still remembered for some doubtfully orthodox speculations about the first chapter of Genesis.' (Ronald Knox) [1]

Knox was speaking in Clifton at the celebrations to mark the centenary of the Hierarchy. Sadly some of his comments on that occasion were uncharacteristically facile and even factually incorrect. 'Clifford', he said, 'was on the wrong side about Infallibility.' This was not an accurate nor even an illuminating remark, and one which compounded an error of a few sentences before in which he attributed the well-known achievements in astronomy of Bishop Walmesley (V.A. 1770 – 1797) to his predecessor as Vicar Apostolic of the Western District, Bishop Laurence York (V.A. 1750 – 1770). [2]

Pace Knox, Clifford's views on the first thirty-four verses of Genesis are considered respectable even today. The background to his three articles in *The Dublin Review*, the first of which appeared in April, 1881, was the famous British Association debate some twenty years before when the atheist evolutionist T. H. Huxley debated with Samuel Wilberforce,

---

1   Ronald Knox, *Occasional Sermons*, (Publ. London 1960), p. 304.
In his magisterial work *The Victorian Church* (1829 – 1901) (1970) Owen Chadwick states: 'Bishop Clifford of Clifton caused a sensation when he publicly abandoned the historical truth of the first chapters of Genesis' (II, p. 408) Doubtless Chadwick was reminding his readers that in 1881 when Clifford published his articles in *The Dublin Review*, Anglican divines had been wrestling with the same problem.

In particular, the Bishop of Natal, Dr. J. W. Colenso (1853 – 1883), a mathematician, had sought to demonstrate the impossibility of a strictly literal interpretation of Biblical numbers – the Pentateuch, he claimed, being a clear illustration of this. The 'Colenso affair', (as it came to be known) rumbled on in the Victorian press for many years, complicated by the fact that there was an appeal to the Privy Council. The spectre of another Gorham Judgement (1850) – Church v. State – had returned to haunt the Church of England.

2   *Ibid.*, p. 303.

Bishop of Oxford, the scientific and scriptural implications of Darwin's *Origin of the Species* of the previous year. In 1861 Wiseman, too, had had something to say: 'On science seriously and conscientiously conducted, the Church looks on fearless, but cautious; fearless of facts, but most cautious on deductions', to which proposition he added, with wit: 'How many human skeletons have been announced in pre-adamitic positions'. Yet not one has been admitted as proved'.

The discussion therefore was not new. As Clifford remarked, scriptural literalism had been called into question for at least half a century before he had applied himself to the subject. It was his achievement to combine originality, based on a considerable breadth of learning in the relevant literature of ancient religions, with a loyalty to the Church's teaching on scriptural inspiration, noting always her refusal to dogmatise on any one interpretation of the verses in question, save only the truth of God seen as Creator. The manner in which God had achieved His purpose was clearly a question for the scientist.

Given this premise, therefore, how was the scripture scholar to interpret the opening verses of the Bible? Why was the account in the form in which we have it? Why did Moses (the supposed author) speak in terms of God 'working on six days of the week' and 'resting on the seventh'?

In brief, Clifford's argument was that the verses in question were not to be seen as an historical narrative – which an increasing number of scholars was inclined to accept – but as a Liturgical Hymn in which the different days of the week are set apart for the various works of creation to sing their praises to the Creator.

The idea was a novel one, though not completely so, and one in which it would be necessary to adduce a considerable body of parallel evidence if the theory were to establish itself as tenable.

In the course of his argument Clifford would also find it necessary to discredit the 'Period Theory' in which the 'days' of Genesis were understood as being vague periods of indeterminate length. For many, Clifford's was an interesting interpretation and one which had the added attraction of making Moses's account apparently fit in with the various periods of pre-history prior to the appearance of Man. Increasingly,

Clifford argued, the Period Theory was being called into question and it therefore became incumbent on Christian thinkers to propose something in its place.

Early in 1881 Clifford was in Rome urging the case of the English bishops in their dispute with the Regulars and so he used the opportunity to 'sound out' his theories on Dr. O'Callaghan (Rector of the English College) and Herbert Vaughan (Bishop of Salford). 'They urge me to write them down for the Dublin' says the entry in his *Diary* for January 3rd. The result was three articles in *The Dublin Review*, the first of which appeared in April, 1881, and a very long correspondence in the columns of *The Tablet* in the intervening period. [4]

It is important to see how Clifford presented, and argued, his case and how at the same time he dealt with views contrary to the thesis he was proposing. The following therefore is a *résumé* of the original presentation of his case beginning with his grounds for rejecting the Period Theory whereby its proponents argue that a 'day' is nothing more than 'a vague period of time' during which God brought the various parts of His creation into existence.

Summary of First Article (April, 1881)

1. Failure of Period Theory – Reasons:

    a) Clifford's Objection: Sun and moon created on 4th day although day and night are referred to on 1st day and plants are growing on 3rd.

       Reply: Incandescent mist covered earth and so rays did not reach earth until 4th day although sun in existence since 1st day.

    Clifford: 'Unsatisfactory'.

---

4   The principal contributors are listed in the course of this chapter together with the dates of publication.

b)   Theory first propounded sixty years before. Geology has
        advanced. Pre-history no longer seen as distinct epochs
        with sudden disturbances – hence 'Days' – but there has
        been a gradual transformation.

c)   Alleged 'Direct Revelation from God'.

        Clifford: Nowhere in Bible do we see a
                                       sacred writer receiving direct
                                       knowledge of astronomy, chemistry
                                       or any branch of natural sciences.
                                       All were children of their time. Why
                                       gratuitous exception of geology?

2.   Moses 'learned in all wisdom of the Egyptians'. Implied that
        he belonged to the priestly class and was initiated into the
        mysteries of Egyptian learning. Little doubt he studied at
        Heliopolis.

        Danger that Jews living among Egyptians would copy their
        idolatrous habits whereby seven days of the week were
        dedicated to seven planets.

3.   'It was necessary . . . to make each day tell of one God,
        Creator of all things, in the same way as the heathens had
        made the days minister to the belief that there were many
        gods and many lords. It was necessary to substitute an
        orthodox dedication in place of the idolatrous one which had
        been abolished. Now God is one, and therefore a dedication
        of each day of the week to him would be of no avail to
        distinguish one day from another. But though God is one his
        works are manifold, and these, if classified under separate
        heads, may afford subjects for separate dedications . . .
        Having abolished all reference to the planets, he dedicated
        each day of the week to the memory of some work of
        creation performed by the true God, just as the Egyptians
        had dedicated each day of the month to the memory of the
        supposed actions of false deities'. (pp. 318, 319).

4.   'The worship of the sun being so deeply rooted, both in
        Egypt and in Palestine, Moses, . . . could not fail to take into
        account the danger which any prominent mention of the sun
        might cause to the people. He could not avoid all allusion . . .
        but he was careful to assign to it such rank in the catalogue
        as would indicate that it had no claim to any other title but
        that of a creature of the true God . . . Accordingly he chose
        for that purpose the middle or fourth day of the week; and
        even then he avoided assigning a special day to the sun, and
        classified sun, moon and stars under one head'. (p. 326).

5.   God rested on the seventh day. These words prove ritual
        character of the composition because

        a)   Nothing similar is found in any of the ancient
                cosmoganies and myths;

        b)   No trace of seventh day being kept holy by any other
                race of men except the Jews,

        c)   Nature itself alternates between periods of activity
                and periods of rest (work and sleep; summer and
                winter, etc.).

6.   Conclusion
        ' . . . the first thirty-four verses of the Bible, although they
        stand foremost in the collection of the writings of Moses,
        form no portion of the book of Genesis which immediately
        follows them. They constitute a composition complete in
        itself. They are a Sacred Hymn . . . (p. 330).

This article, and a subsequent reply by Clifford to his critics, prompted
a correspondence in the columns of *The Tablet* which lasted about a
year. First into the field was J.S.V. – of whom more later – who saw
Clifford's theory as 'a vast speculation from beginning to end'. He
argued that it was not a matter of whether Moses had motives for
writing in such a way but whether in fact

' . . . when (Moses) said, "In six days the Lord made Heaven
and Earth and rested on the seventh", he did actually mean
(if not the very opposite) something, at all events, so entirely
distinct from the obvious sense of the words, that we have
had to wait for the present Bishop of Clifton to point it out.'
(*The Tablet*, 30.4.1881).

A writer, signing himself Dies Septimus, accused the Bishop of
'theological untruth', but Dies Primus came to his aid by pointing out
that the interpretation of the passage was an open question. (*The
Tablet*, 9.7.1881).

The Editor of *The Tablet* stepped in with a summary of, and balanced
comment on, the Bishop's article. Speaking of the ensuing correspondence
he said that it had 'elicited many expressions of opinion neither wise nor
pertinent, and some decidedly wanting in respect to the Bishop' to which
he added pertinently' . . . but there is, perhaps, nothing in it of more
importance than the fact that the Bishop's theory has been entertained by
others, and published in Italy without rebuke before his essay appeared'.

This was a reference to Calmet, Cardinal Alimonda and others who had
been mentioned by various correspondents. The Editor expressed some
slight hesitation, but was delighted that 'this courageous hypothesis
should have been broached by one so well known for his ability, sobriety
of judgment, and sound theological training as Bishop Clifford, [which] is
in itself a guarantee that the theory is at least permissible'. (30.7.1881).

Impressed by the 'unusually copious' correspondence which had resulted
from the article, the Editor of *The Tablet* had surmised:

> 'We should not be surprised if he were to reply to some of the
> objections which have been persistently, and in some of the
> cases unbecomingly, urged against his article, and perhaps
> gather up into the lap of his argument some scattered
> observations which confirm his general view'. (*Ibid*).

In this he was correct and in October of the same year a further article
appeared (10 pages in length) in which Clifford endeavoured to counter
the criticisms levelled against both his loyalty to the Faith and the
inherent probability of his thesis.

At this point it is necessary to say something about the organ which published these two articles – and a third some two years later.

'The honour of the first inception of the *Dublin Review* is generally attributed . . . to Dr Wiseman and Daniel O'Connell'. [5] It was a publication which always boasted of its loyalty to the Holy See and consequently of the theological orthodoxy of the articles which it published.

'From the very first number to this, every article has been written or revised under the sense of the most solemn responsibility to the Church, and to her Lord. If we have been reproached, it has been rather for severity in exclusion than for laxity in admission'.[6] Thus Cardinal Wiseman in the last article he ever wrote for *The Dublin Review*. This strict adherence to doctrinal purity occupied much of the attention of W.G. Ward who, at the instigation of Manning, took over the editorship in 1862. 'He (Ward) has stated that all articles passed under the judgement of three censors, who were charged to examine the bearing of them on faith, morals, and ecclesiastical prudence. [7]

In the forty-second year of publication the second series (so-called) of *The Dublin Review* gave way to the third. The proprietor was to be the Bishop of Salford (Vaughan) and the editor Bishop Hedley of Newport & Menevia.

Hedley promised that 'while faithfully adhering to the great Catholic principles . . . *The Dublin Review* will now undergo certain modifications, calculated to render it more widely popular and more acceptable to a larger number of tastes and interests.[8] The strict rule of anonymity, already partially relaxed in the second series, was now to be abolished.

---

5   L.C. Casartelli, Bishop of Salford, *Sketches in History* (Publ. London, 1906), p. 273.

6   Quoted by Casartelli, *op. cit.*, p. 284.

7   Manning quoted by Casartelli, *op. cit.*, p. 291.

8   Quoted by Casartelli, *op. cit.*, p. 295.

Such was the background against which Clifford was proposing his theory. Hence it was recognised that any question which might arise concerning his orthodoxy would be seen as also reflecting on the journal in which those views had been expounded. Hedley welcomed Clifford's second article in which he endeavoured to answer his critics. He supplied the title, '*The Days of Creation: A Reply*', and expressed a liking for what Clifford had written:

> Your excellent paper is in time – and I am much obliged to you.
> It will do good, especially the weighty remarks at the end. [9]

The 'weighty remarks' were words of warning from Clifford to those who wished to stifle all discussion merely because of the novelty of what was being proposed.

> So long as Catholic writers, treating on subjects which come within the limits or touch on the boundaries both of revealed truth and of scientific research, are careful to keep themselves informed of what has been decided in such matters by the authority of the Church, and what has been left open to inquiry by the same divinely appointed guide . . . the discussion of such questions in a scientific Catholic Review can give no just cause for alarm. (pp. 10 and 11).

Other warnings were also made to the effect that:

1) A far greater cause for alarm would be apathy about the burning religious questions of the day.

2) 'Difficulties are not removed and faith is not strengthened by a few flippant sneers directed against scientific men, or by a few platitudes about the liability of all men to err.' (p. 11).

3) The Fathers of the Church can only help in a limited way because 'the objections we have had to meet had no existence in their days'. (p. 12).

---

9   Ugbrooke Archives, *Letters to Bp. Clifford. 1881*, Hedley to Clifford, letter dated 14.9.1881. Hedley had taken over the See of Newport & Menevia just seven months before.

These comments were by way of arguing for the theological legitimacy of the article the main part of which was taken up with dealing with specific objections to his theory.

Having briefly repeated his contention that this was an area where freedom of discussion was perfectly legitimate, Clifford goes into the attack:

> 'A similar mass of evidence has never been adduced in support of any one of the various *other* interpretations which have hitherto been proposed'. (p. 4). [Italics mine].

Meanwhile, his own position is stated with precision:

> 'Since, therefore, the words of Moses may be so interpreted, and since, when so interpreted, they are found on the one hand to avoid all collision with scientific facts, whilst on the other hand they are shown on independent evidence to be in wonderful harmony with the persons, manners, customs, and other circumstances of the time when they were written, there is certainly grave reason for concluding that the proposed meaning is the one intended by Moses himself'. (p. 4).

Conceding that the argument may not amount to a demonstration – indeed, he says is *any* demonstration possible in a question of this nature? – he nevertheless confidently believes that 'the evidence is strong in itself, and certainly stronger than that adduced in support of any other interpretation'. (p. 4).

One of the chief areas in which Clifford had been attacked was in the matter of the Book of Exodus. It was generally agreed, said his critics, that this was an historical book. Since therefore in Chapter xx, 11, we read: 'In six days the Lord made heaven and earth and the sea, and all things that are in them, and rested on the seventh day, therefore the Lord blessed the seventh day and sanctified it', one must conclude that this too is history.

Clifford replied: 'Exodus is indeed an historical book, but it contains other things besides history' (p. 6) and proceeds to prove his case by pointing out that the book also contains passages which are ritualistic ordinances and poetry (e.g. the Canticle of Moses, Chapter xv).

He is, however, prepared to concede a point, although it was on a matter which, in so doing, he strengthened rather than weakened his case. Father Corneli, S.J., Professor of Sacred Scripture at the Gregorian University in Rome, argued in a private letter (which Clifford quoted in his article) that the five books of the Pentateuch were parts of one continuous work 'the arrangement no less than the authorship of which he assigns to Moses' (p. 8). The hymn is therefore seen as a fitting prologue to the whole work.

Clifford then deals briefly with the contention that his theory contravened what had been taught at th Council of Trent, and again throws down the gauntlet by expressing his disappointment that the majority of his critics had ignored the main thrust of his argument, namely, 'that the proposed interpretation harmonises in a perfect way with all that we know of Moses, his office, his mission, his learning, the times in which he lived, and the people with whom he dealt' (p. 9).

To those who were afraid of anything new he warns that since none of the theories of the past has received general acceptance, 'it stands to reason that the true explanation, whenever it shall be forthcoming, must be to some extent a new one' (pp. 11, 12). Had he lived, Clifford would certainly have warmed to the words of Pope Pius XII in his encyclical letter *Divino Afflante Spiritu* (1943) in which he castigates those who criticised all that was new:

> 'The labours of these worthy workers in the vineyard of the Lord [i.e. scripture scholars] deserve to be judged not only with equity and justice, but with perfect charity: and this is a point which all other sons of the Church should bear in mind. It is their duty to avoid that most imprudent zeal which considers it an obligation to attack or suspect whatever is new'. [10]

---

10   *Acta Apostolicae Sedis*, 1943, 319 (On the Sacred Scriptures).

Two letters appeared in succession in *The Tablet* from 'A Student of the Sacred Scriptures'. His argument against Clifford may be summarised as follows:

1)   In the new theory 'an interpretation is put forward which strips them (i.e. the first 34 verses of Genesis) of all geological value. By this he means to imply that Clifford has simply capitulated to Science by emptying the verses of all scientific meaning 'just as Moscow was secured against capture by an invading army . . . it was burnt down'.

2)   There are two undoubted Ritual Hymns by Moses – but they are introduced as such. Why is there no similar introduction in the opening verses of Genesis?

3)   Where does Clifford's interpretation of the verses as, a Ritual Hymn stand *vis-à-vis* Inspiration, for people had been interpreting the words *historically*?

The letter ends; 'An unworthy and most pusillanimous fear of the geological objector can alone have inspired the thought of a recourse to this new interpretation'. *The Tablet*, (5.11.1881).

The second letter appeared ten weeks later in *The Tablet*, (14.1.1882). It continued the attack by quoting authorities on the Continent who had read Clifford's articles:

1)   A French bishop said the theory 'was not well founded'.

2)   A French theologian argued against Clifford's assumption – viz. that Moses adapted a division of time of heathen origin, which he found prevalent in Egypt, to the Israelite people – by saying 'that the week is not in any sense a thing of heathen origin, but a division of time preserved in the Hebrew tradition'.

3)   The theory might have the effect of discouraging attempts 'to discover the true reconciliation of the

Mosaic narrative with the advance made in
geological science'.

4)   How could any student of Science square Clifford's
         interpretation with the Inspiration of Scripture?

J.S.V. – who had written the first letter questioning the new theory –
wrote again in January, 1882. He refers to a fifty page article which had
appeared in the *Revue des Questions Scientifiques* author of which felt
constrained to conclude: 'Son hypothèse . . . nous a paru vraiment
inconciliable avec le silence absolu des témoignages extrinsiques',
adding that the bishop was forcing the text to accommodate his meaning.

So strongly did J.S.V. feel that he contributed a whole article to *The Dublin
Review* a year later (January, 1883) so as to be able to state his case at
length. But who was he? None other than Clifford's cousin, John Stephen
Vaughan who in 1909 was to become Auxiliary Bishop of Salford. At the time
of writing his article he was just thirty years old and on the staff of St. Bede,
Manchester, lecturing on Holy Scripture. During his life he was to publish
some twenty-five titles, many of which were popular in the U.S.A. [11]

The main points of Vaughan's article and of Clifford's subsequent Reply
(1883) may best be summarised as follows:

1)   <u>Vaughan</u>   gives a list of writers who reject Clifford's Theory.

     <u>Clifford</u>   So be it, but noteworthy that not one of them sees it
                 as contrary to the Faith.

2)   <u>Vaughan</u>   What need is there of a new theory? If contradictions
                 seem to exist then this is due to the present
                 embryonic state of geology.

     <u>Clifford</u>   Books putting forward the 'Period Theory' have had
                 to encounter <u>undoubted scientific facts</u> showing that
                 a new approach to Genesis is necessary.

---

11   For further details on the life and character of Bishop John Vaughan see
     Remembered in Blessing: The Courtfield Story by A Mill Hill Father
     (Publ. London 1955), chapter 17; also Brian Plumb's *Arundel to Zabi*
     (Publ. Warrington 1988).

3)	<u>Vaughan</u>	There is no word in Hebrew corresponding with English word 'epoch'. Therefore writer forced to use word for 'day'.
	<u>Clifford</u>	'Nothing of the kind' and quotes two words: 'mohed' (verse 14) and 'het'.
4)	<u>Vaughan</u>	Quotes examples where 'day' means 'indeterminate period'.
	<u>Clifford</u>	Yes, but never where a number has been prefixed. In these instances it means a specific period.
5)	<u>Vaughan</u>	Although light was created on the first day, the creation of the sun is said to have been on the fourth day because it could not be seen (heavy mist etc. over the face of the earth).

	<u>Clifford</u>	i)	This is an arbitrary interpretation. All other creatures were created on the day indicated;
		ii)	If Vaughan is right in saying that sun, moon and stars were in fact created on the first day, then since nothing else is mentioned as having been created on the fourth day, then that makes it a day of rest – i.e. two in one week!

Clifford makes the further point that people long ago ceased to look to scripture in matters astronomical. Why, he asks, should people continue to look there for a solution to questions of geology? The thinking underlying all interpretation of Genesis is that the book is silent on scientific facts – it merely records phenomena as seen, without explanation.

A prolonged correspondence had taken place in the columns of *The Tablet* in the two years which intervened between Clifford's first and third article. Some of the arguments raised were of an extremely technical nature.

What is of more importance is the <u>private</u> correspondence which reached him, much of it from eminent names on the continent.

Vaughan, it will be remembered, was on the staff of St. Bede's at the time of his controversy with Clifford. In November, 1881, 'J.W.' – from the tone of his letter clearly a close friend of the bishop – informed him that there was at St. Bede's a little society of clergy which had been in the habit of meeting to discuss various questions connected with the Sacred Scriptures.

> . . . It may amuse you also to hear that an application has been made to the "St. Bede's (our) Society" inviting us to join in a representation to the Master of the Sacred Palace – if you please – on the subject of your Lordship's heterodoxy.
>
> The applicant, while counting on the satisfaction secular priests might naturally derive from proving a Bishop mistaken, evidently overlooked the disinclination the secular priests would feel to helping a *frate* to prove anybody wrong. [12]

A noted convert and controversialist, T.W. Allies, referred Clifford to a work in German published in 1877. The author was a Father Hummelauer, S.J. who put forward the thesis that

> . . . the passage in question was revealed in vision by God to Adam immediately upon his creation – was communicated by Adam to his posterity, and probably formed part of the liturgical service used on the Sabbath from its institution. Moses received it unimpaired and complete – while copies of it, more or less correct, were spread over the ancient nations. [13]

(Allies was writing in January, 1882).

---

12   Ugbrooke Archives, *Letters to Bp. Clifford, 1881*, 'J.W.' to Clifford, letter dated 8.11.1881.

13   Ugbrooke Archives, *Letters to Bp. Clifford, 1882*, T.W. Allies to Clifford, Letter dated 13.1.1882.

A week later a writer from a learned French Journal, (*Cosmos-les-Mondes, Révue Hebdomadaire des Sciences et de l'Industrie*, Paris) wrote to disagree with the theory put forward. Clifford's footnote to the letter reads:

> Probably we differ widely – but free expression of opinion on matters not decided by Church elucidates truth – Your labours will be appreciated even by those who differ from you – many no doubt accept your views – I make no objection to any fair criticism of views. [14]

Another correspondent from the Continent was a canon of Palermo who had lectured on the subject in Rome. He commended the bishop for 'the deference he had shown to the lights of the natural and historical sciences', and also the independence of judgement which was quite compatible with being a Catholic. He added that he had read in a recent work published in 1881 in Munster 'that some of your ideas are accepted'. [15]

A church student for the Clifton diocese, Daniel Iles, writing from Louvain to Mgr. Williams at Prior Park, said that Professor Leroy 'thought the Bishop entirely in error in his views on the days of Creation . . . His (Leroy's) one great point seems to be that the Egyptians used a period of ten not seven days'. Leroy told his students in class that Clifford's theory might be held 'as it was contrary to no teaching of the Church'. [16]

On May 1st, 1883, a noted Catholic, W.S. Lilly, wrote to express his 'great satisfaction' to the Bishop.

> Living as I do, chiefly with non Catholic men of letters, I have the saddest reason to know how many are repelled from the

---

14 Ugbrooke Archives, *Letters to Bp. Clifford, 1882*, Canon François Marie Moigno, letter dated 18.1.1882. Clifford's reply: 20.1.1882.

15 Ugbrooke Archives, *Letter to Bp. Clifford, 1882*, Salvatore di Bartolo, letter dated 6.8.1882.

16 Ugbrooke Archives, *Letters to Bp. Clifford, 1883*, Daniel Iles to Mgr. Williams, letter dated 27.1.1883. Iles was ordained priest 25.9.1881 went to Louvain the following September and died in February 1912. Bishop Clifford was a friend of the Iles family, who, at the time, lived in Fairford, Glos. (*Memoirs of Mgr. Provost Iles*, Publ. Bristol, 1969, p. 3).

Church by the belief that her teaching is discredited by history, criticism, or physical science. In two somewhat elaborate articles which appeared in the *Contemporary Review* of January and February last, I endeavoured to show, in such outline as the limits to which I was confined allowed me, that this is not so'. [17]

Clearly he saw Clifford's articles as a vindication of his own.

Two days later he wrote again to draw the Bishop's attention to a passage in Newman's *Essay on the Development of Christian Doctrine* (1845). The passage runs –

We are told that God has spoken. Where? In a book? We have tried it, and it disappoints; it disappoints that most holy and blessed gift, not from fault of its own, but because it is used for a purpose for which it was not given. [18]

Mention of Newman leads to reference being made of two letters he wrote to Clifford in January, 1883. In the first he seeks Clifford's advice as to the exact nature of scriptural inspiration. In the second he says:

It rejoices me to see in the Dublin the account given of the criticisms passed on your late Article on Gen i. It shows you have succeeded in opening the door, tho' the critics do not like the particular way in which you have opened it. They seem all to imply, some avow, that you have opened it. We need not to shake ourselves free from science any longer, since you have suggested an interpretation which ignores science altogether. [19]

Clifford's reply to Newman affords an insight as to why he had assumed

17 Ugbrooke Archives, *Letters to Bp. Clifford, 1883*, W.S. Lilly to Clifford, Letter dated 1.5.1883.

18 Ugbrooke Archives, *Letters to Bp. Clifford, 1883*, W.S. Lilly to Clifford, Letter dated 3.5.1883.

19 Both letters in Clifton Diocesan Archives: *Letters to Bp. Clifford*, Part II (1875 – 1892).

this difficult task in the first place:

> What you say about the advantage of having opened the door
> to discussion regarding the relation of scripture to science is
> very true. I shall try and force the question on, for there are
> really a large number of the rising generation to whom this
> question is the chief difficulty as regards faith . . . Everybody
> seems afraid to approach it, but it must be approached. [20]

Two congratulatory letters came from Father F. Mogan, Professor of
Theology at Saint Sulpice, Paris. In the first he said that the Bishop
'disposed finally of Mr. Vaughan and others of his calibre', and that
Clifford's views on the non-historical character of the opening verses of
Genesis 'has commanded very wide favour among those best entitled to
have an opinion on the subject'. Very significantly he added:

> Although it has not been openly stated, much, I believe, of
> the attention – not to say excitement – awakened by the first
> article arose from the apprehension it caused some and the
> hope it gave others that the same system of interpretation
> might be extended to several portions of the ten first
> Chapters of Genesis and ultimately perhaps to other parts
> of the Bible. There is no doubt but that such a method would
> rid us of much trouble. [21]

In his second letter Mogan was able to quote the view of a scientist on
what Clifford had written:

> 'I am sure you will be glad to know that the Professor of
> Geology in the Catholic University, Mons. de Lapparent, who is
> ranked amongst us, especially since his recent book came out,
> as one of the first geologists of the period, is extremely pleased
> with your last article. Though not considering some of the
> theories you rely upon as sufficiently proven, he holds you have
> on the whole taken up an impregnable position and are thereby
> doing a very great and much needed service to Religion'. [21]

---

20   *Letters and Diaries of John Henry Newman* (ed. Dessain and Gornall)
      Vol. XXX, p. 176 footnote 1, Clifford to Newman, Letter dated 5.2.1883.

21   Both letters in Ugbrooke Archives, *Letters to Bp. Clifford, 1883*, Mogan
      to Clifford. First letter dated 4.5.1883; second dated 2.6.1883.

Incidentally one effect of Clifford's articles had been to declare open season for all who had views on the opening verses of Genesis. One such was Bishop Ullathorne who outlined his thoughts in a letter to Canon Estcourt, but in so doing he acknowledged his debt to 'Philo Judeus, Origen, St. Augustine, Melchior, Cajetan, Calmet, and in a recent publication of Rosmini's, which is well and simply explained in Walworth's *Gentle Skeptic*'. 'This view', says Ullathorne, 'is more metaphysical, and therefore more accordant with the action of spiritual power'.

> It assumes that the whole creation was instantaneous, and that the succession described by Moses is the succession of order in which creation was unfolded. Against this, however, I see the difficulty of the human creation, three epocks [*sic*] of <u>positive</u> creation are given in Genesis, the first of chaos, the second of animal life, the third of human life. The rest are developments, at least the language bears this construction. Walworth's Gentle Skeptic is interesting [*sic*] written, and worth reading. He is a convert American priest. [22]

Sufficient has been said to show that Clifford's articles in *The Dublin Review* were a considerable contribution to the debate on the relation of Science and Religion in so far as it impinged on a proper understanding of the Book of Genesis. One would not have expected that his views would receive universal acclaim. Even so, sufficient numbers of people of intellectual calibre did express the view that – at the least – it was a way forward or – at the most – it might even be not only tenable (as Clifford had argued) but also correct. The ensuing correspondence in *The Tablet* also made its contribution to the great debate. Not all the letters, however, displayed the same degree of learning, as Father H.H. Eyre, S.J. of Stonyhurst noted to Clifford:

> It is lamentable to read such effusions as that of "Sacerdos Limericensis" and compeers in ignorance.

---

22   Birmingham Diocesan Archives, *Ullathorne to Canon Estcourt*, B. 8208. Letter dated 3.6.1883.

This he contrasted with the bishop's own contribution:

> It is a treat to come across any letters that show <u>learning</u> in the *"Tablet"*. [23]

One hundred years later and despite the somewhat flippant strictures of Ronald Knox, the views of Bishop Clifford on the Days of Creation are still regarded as worthy of serious consideration.

Postscript

Before concluding this chapter it would be well to see how at the official level the Church dealt with the growing intellectual ferment which was largely the result of an unease among many Catholics in England and on the Continent as to how the findings of Science and the truths of Revelation might be reconciled. As Clifford had remarked, something had to be done.

Many agreed with him in seeing apathy as the danger, and it was felt that even a theory that was wrong could serve as a stimulus for further effort to produce one that would eventually prove to be right. However, while this exercise might prove intellectually satisfying for some, Clifford as a shepherd of souls was only too aware of the tragedies that might occur in the minds of educated Christian men and women who might conclude that there was no answer and so suffer the shipwreck of their Faith.

Huxley, Wilberforce and Clifford were but three in a long line of protagonists in the great debate. With the benefit of hindsight one can see the controversy as a great river dividing into two tributaries: Modernism on the one hand and Fundamentalism (Literalism) on the other – both of which are still with us today.

Clifford may well have foreseen this and certainly neither result would have been to his liking. To its credit Rome stepped into the debate – not, it must be emphasised, by presuming to settle by diktat the

---

23   Ugbrooke Archives, *Letters to Bp. Clifford, 1884*, Eyre to Clifford, letter dated 24.3.1884.

complexities of the issues involved, but by indicating what the state of knowledge at the time would suggest as <u>safe</u>. After all, the study of Holy Writ is not the preserve of academics only. For Rome the pastoral role of the Church is paramount.

Clifford's articles had appeared in the years 1881 – 1883, that is, towards the beginning of the Pontificate of Leo XIII (1878 – 1903). Leo's accession had been generally welcomed as a breath of fresh air and he was seen as a man of more liberal turn of mind than Pio Nono, the Pope of the *Syllabus*.

Some twenty years after the appearance of Clifford's articles, Pope Leo established the Pontifical Biblical Commission 'that Holy Writ should . . . be preserved intact not only from any breath of error but also from all rash opinions' (Apostolic Letter *Vigilantiae*, 30th October, 1902). In 1909 the Pontifical Biblical Institute was founded in Rome by Leo's successor, Pope Pius X, in order to assist the Commission in its work.

It is of crucial importance to understand both the purpose and the nature of the Replies which the Biblical commission issues in answer to the various *dubia* submitted to it for a decision. Père Lucien Choupin, S.J. writes as follows in his *Valeur des Décisions Doctrinales et Disciplinaires du Saint-Siège*:

> 'By such decisions the Holy See wishes to provide for the *safety* of doctrine, to forestall dangers of the faith being perverted, rather than to pronounce a judgement *directly* on the *absolute truth* or *falsehood* of the proposition itself . . . The meaning of a *doctrinal decision* issued by the supreme teaching authority but none the less not guaranteed by the gift of infallibility is this: Given the circumstances, the state of knowledge, it is prudent and *safe* to regard this proposition as true, in conformity to Holy Scripture . . . Or, it is prudent and *safe* to regard this proposition as erroneous, rash, contrary to Holy Scripture . . . ' [author's italics].

The relevance of this point is apparent in the *Reply* of the Biblical Commission Concerning the *Historical Character of the First Three Chapters of Genesis*, June 30th, 1909:

VI   . . . may certain passages . . . be wisely and profitably interpreted in an allegorical and prophetic sense?

<u>Reply</u>: In the affirmative.

VIII   In the designation and distinction of the six days mentioned in the first chapter of Genesis may the word Yom (day) be taken either in the literal sense for the natural day or in an applied sense for a certain space of time, and may this question be the subject of free discussion among exegetes?

<u>Reply</u>: In the affirmative.

Here the Commission is saying that it is safe to hold the 'Period Theory'. It does not say that it is a <u>likely</u> explanation and it was on this latter score that Clifford had rejected it.

On Clifford's own theory that the opening verses were 'a liturgical hymn', VI (quoted above) merely says, by implication, that such an allegorical interpretation is safe.

(A further discussion of these points is contained in the *Letter to Cardinal Suhard of Paris* A.A.S. 40, 1948, 45 – 48).

The Pro-Cathedral, Clifton.

The Romanesque additions on the west side of the building were largely paid for from the personal estate of Bishop Clifford

CHAPTER FIFTEEN

William Clifford – the bishop and the man

William Clifford was born into a close-knit, loving Catholic family. His father was an ardent Catholic who for some time in his later years had taken up residence in Rome/Tivoli and was a familiar figure at the Papal Court. It will be remembered that in the letter appointing Clifford to Clifton, Pio Nono did not mention the prelate by name but said rather that he was sending 'il figlio di Lord Clifford'.

> From the family point of view he (the bishop) is remembered for his correspondence with his brothers, mainly about their father, whom they loved dearly, but whose eccentricities caused them much amusement. [1]

William's relations with the other members of the family remained warm and intimate throughout his life and there are many charming letters in the archives at Ugbrooke which demonstrate his constant interest, particularly in the younger members of the family. Little Lucy, for example, protested at the purloining of her rosary which Uncle William had inadvertently pocketed during a visit to the ancestral home. A grown-up niece excitedly telling her uncle of her forthcoming engagement – she wanted him to be the first to know.

It would be difficult to find a more delightful example of sisterly affection than the following, written by Agnes when she first heard of her brother's elevation to the episcopate.

> Who could have imagined some years back that the young ecclesiastic would have turned into a Bishop. Our brother the Bishop. Our brother the Bishop. When the wonders of nature are so numerous and various, is there more a cause of astonishment in a young ecclesiastic becoming a full grown bishop than the little grub becoming a splendid purple spotted butterfly? [2]

---

1   Hugh Clifford (13th Lord Clifford of Chudleigh), *The House of Clifford* Publ. Chichester, 1987, p. 185.

2   Ugbrooke Archives, *Letters to Bishop Clifford, 1857*, Agnes Clifford to William Clifford, letter dated 25.1.1857.

Or the following mock petition signed by all members of an ever-increasing family seeking episcopal permission to extend their occupation of Court House, Cannington [3] so as to include the apartments hitherto set aside for the bishop's exclusive use:

. . . . .

Your poor Petitioners humbly beg, that Your Lordship will graciously please to take into merciful consideration the state of our large and increasing family and not ijict [*sic*] at this inclement season of the year a mother in a peculiarly delicate condition, a fasting and gouty husband and their tender squalling Children.

. . . . .

That the hereinbeforenamed rooms being commodiously situate and supplied with all necessaries Your Lordship would subject us to great inconvenience by occupying this Your Lordship's Seat –ç

That in lieu thereof your petitioners have caused to be well dusted and aired a certain red room commonly known and denominated the Chamber of Horrors, the which your Lordship's immediate Predecessor of blessed memory did graciously please to pronounce habitable

That if your Lordship will deign to accept the same and confirm the Swop . . . [4]

William Clifford was a man of many parts and it is arguable that, had he so wished, he might well have achieved distinction in the academic world.

---

3   'To help Clifford bear the cost of his peerage, the king had granted him in 1671 the reversion in tail male of the Priory of Cannington . . . ' (Hugh Clifford, *op. cit.*, p. 147).

4   Ugbrooke Archives, *Letters to Bishop Clifford, 1857*, Charles Clifford and family to Bp. Clifford, document dated 12.3.1857.

Fluent in French, Italian and Latin, well-read in the scholarly literature of the day – his was a mind that would have been attuned to the exigencies of life in a university or theological college. His articles in *The Dublin Review* show that he was conversant with fields of literature other than the christian and that in scholarly debate he was able to hold his own.

The true scholar must be a man of balanced judgement and there are many instances in Clifford's busy life which show this side of his character – a quality which in Manning was submerged beneath a single-minded determination which would not allow room for another point of view. His contributions to the debates in the Vatican Council, his refusal when disagreeing with others to adopt a position of extreme dogmatism. his carefully chosen language when making judgements or decisions – indeed, all aspects of his career point to a quiet maturity and soundness of judgement that did not go unnoticed in the varied circles in which he moved. Clifford was the born secretary – secretary to Errington, secretary to the Synods, and finally secretary to the Conference of Bishops. Such posts are normally filled by way of election, and it seems clear that Clifford would have appealed to those around him by those very qualities of judgement and precision of expression which are the hall-marks of the amanuensis.

Such facility, however, does not come easily to everyone. A notable exception was Nicholas Wiseman. His biographer tells us that when he came to write his *Appeal to the Reason and Good Feeling of the English People* he did so without having to modify an expression or even to correct a single word. [5] But such people are rare. That Clifford did achieve a 'quiet elegance' may best be seen in his pastoral letters (e.g. on the *Syllabus*, and on the Vatican Decrees). His private notes, however, and in particular the draft replies to the more important letters he received, reveal a man who had to labour so as to achieve a text in which he said exactly what he meant. For students of history the resulting corrections can be invaluable in indicating a particular train of thought, and in this connection probably the best example is the letter to Bonomi in which Clifford opened his heart on the alleged lack of freedom in the Vatican Council.

---

5   Richard J. Schiefen, *Nicholas Wiseman and the Transformation of English Catholicism* (Publ. Shepherdstown, 1984), p. 191.

Reference to Clifford's private notes suggests a comment about his handwriting. Mercifully it was very legible – a thin, clear stroke with clearly formed letters and clearly identifiable loops. It was not a bold script, but small and precise and used to great advantage in his diaries where, on the blank page provided, he would compose a summary of points made at a meeting and of decisions reached. Such thumb-nail sketches of audiences with the Pope (e.g. with Leo XIII on the question of Catholic schools in England) are of particular interest.

On occasions (e.g. to avoid starting a new page) his script could become extremely small but even so, under a magnifying glass, it is still seen to retain its integrity of form. A graphologist might see in this an interest in detail. Be that as it may, it was a quality which he undoubtedly possessed which, combined with an innate prudence, prompted his bishop (Vaughan) to send him to Rome to pursue a course in canon law. He had just begun his second year of study when he was chosen to be bishop.

Clifford's expertise as a canon lawyer was particularly evident in the correspondence he undertook on behalf of the other bishops who were in the habit of writing to him on difficult or sensitive matters. This unenviable task he shared with another able canonist, Bishop Grant of Southwark, but when he died in 1870, it appears that all then turned to Clifford with their questions.

Early in Clifford' s episcopate Bishop Goss of Liverpool was writing to the Rector af Valladalid (Mgr. Guest) :

> On Dr. Clifford's arrival in Rome I gave him your various commissions, explaining them fully to him, and placing the various documents in his hands. This I did in order to expedite them, for he is better acquainted than myself with the details of Roman business, and from his long residence in Italy is as adequate as an Italian to get through the routine which these things required. [6]

---

[6]   Archives of the English College, Valladolid, *Correspondence (Vol. 7) 1846 - 1860)*, GUEST, No. 198, Bp. Goss to Guest, Letter dated 8.8.1860.

In the public arena this specialist knowledge of Clifford came to the fore on at least two noteworthy occasions. First at the Vatican Council when (as we have seen) he warned the Fathers of the danger of acting *ultra vires* in relation to the Bull convening the Council. A decade or so later he spearheaded the cause of the bishops in the dispute with the regular clergy over their respective areas of competence.

In this, Clifford's contribution was not confined to drawing up and presenting the case on behalf of the bishops. He was very much *persona grata* in Rome, and his diaries show the number of contacts he had both in the curia and in the wider world of Roman society.

It would appear that there were few, if any, cardinals in curia who were not known to him personally. Naturally the Vatican Council had provided the very best forum for such acquaintances to flourish, and the various informal gatherings which took place at that time in private rooms and salons could not have failed to lead to an intimate knowledge of personalities and of the various shifts of power within the higher echelons of the Vatican.

Although a public figure in the world of church politics, Clifford nevertheless would have seen himself as essentially a priest and bishop. This is not to say that the wider issues did not have pastoral implications. Of course they did, and one has to look no further than his three major contributions at the Council to see that what he said was coloured by the fact that he was a shepherd of souls. This is best illustrated, perhaps, by his pleas that a more tolerant view be taken of Protestants.

As Bishop of Clifton, Clifford was caring and efficient. His efforts to revive the fortunes of Prior Park bore fruit and his appointment of Errington to the staff was an inspired move, not only in that it provided a dignified and hospitable solution to the Archbishop's personal difficulties, but also by so doing he put before the students a teacher whose theological acumen and personal example could not but be to their eventual priestly advantage.

When Clifford arrived in Clifton in 1857, he was acutely aware of the lack of a seminary in his diocese – a situation which was aggravated by its having no share either in St. Edmund's, or in Ushaw or in Oscott. [7]

---

7   Robert E. Guy, O.S.B., *The Synods in English*: Being the text of the four Synods of Westminster translated into English (Publ. Stratford-on-Avon, 1886), p. 224.

The Council of Trent had urged bishops to make such provision and in 1873 the Fourth Provincial Synod of Westminster was to echo this. [8]

> At first the Bishop looked at a couple of sites in Clifton. Then he decided to establish a temporary seminary in a house in Berkeley Square, a district reasonably convenient to the Pro-Cathedral. A lease was taken on No. 10 Berkeley Square, and the seminary opened in July, 1865. The rector was Canon Richard Ward with Fr. James Shaker as his assistant. However, the Bishop knew that this could only be a temporary arrangement. [9]

One year later he was to re-purchase his beloved Prior Park. [10]

Although it has been suggested that Clifford's appointment to Clifton was due, at least in part, to an expectation that he would use some of his personal fortune towards the clearance of debts and the furtherance of the work of the diocese, there is no written evidence that this was in fact the case. [11] Even so, it is true that Clifford, once appointed, was extremely generous in using his money on various projects within the diocese. Just three years after his arrival, he described in a letter to the Duchess of Leeds the problem he faced and the policy he had adopted to meet it.

> When I came to this Diocese I found it encumbered with debts to the amount of 12,000 st. and upwards, with little or no provision even towards payment of interest. I had to make myself liable for nearly the whole of this amount. I found no provision for the maintenance of the Bishop, and most of my missions were in the greatest poverty.

---

8   *Ibid.*, p. 236.

9   Dr. John Cashman, *The Clifton Mission, 1830 - 1901* (Bound typescript, Clifton Diocesan Archives), p. 31.

10   For further details on this, in particular the financial arrangements entered into with the Duchess of Leeds, see Cashman, *op. cit.*, pp. 31 sqq.

11   See page 54, footnote 31.

By sacrificing part of my income, by economy, and by the aid
of kind friends I have been able to diminish the debts of the
Diocese by one half . . . [12]

It was economies such as these, coupled with his own generosity, that
enabled him in 1866 to re-purchase Prior Park;

Without touching any of the monies belonging to the
missions or charities of the diocese I have been able to
raise the £22,000 which Raphael demands for the
property. – I have £7,000 from one friend, £5,000 from
another. I add £7,000 of my own, my present Grammar
School premises I value at £2,000 and the timber on the
property is valued at over £1,500, but say £1,000 – This
makes up the whole sum.

– However I have arranged with Raphael to pay down only
£10,000 and to leave the remaining £12,000 on mortgage at
4 per cent so I need not be in a hurry about cutting my
timber or selling my Grammar School . . . [13]

Ten years later he again showed his generosity by adding a section to
the Pro-cathedral which could both serve as a school and at the same
time enhance the church itself. The announcement took the form of an
appeal to the laity to match the Bishop's generosity. *The Tablet* informed
its readers:

. . . the Bishop, from his own resources, has erected at a cost
of £3,000 a building which, for architectural beauty and
superior workmanship, commands universal admiration.
This building, while serving the purpose of a school, forms a
portion of a proposed new front to the cathedral.

---

12   Clifton Diocesan Archives, *Letter Book No. 2* Nos. 12 – 18, Clifford to the
Duchess of Leeds, Letter dated 16.3.1860.

13   Ugbrooke Archives, *Letters to Bp. Clifford, 1866*, Copy of letter to Mgr.
Talbot, Letter dated 21.12.1866.

The next step to be taken is to connect this school with the church by means of an atrium, or antechapel, which will comprise a new porch and afford space, now much wanted, for processions and other ceremonies. The estimate for completing this atrium, and adding a new façade to the church amounts to nearly £2,000. [14]

But Clifford's financial judgement, though not his generosity, could sometimes be subject to criticism. Speaking of St. Peter's, Gloucester, Canon Barron wrote in 1912 to his successor, Father Chard:

Had Bishop Clifford insisted, before allowing the old Presbytery to be pulled down, on a <u>deed</u> being executed leaving at his (Dr. Case's) death sufficient to build a new one and proper schools, I would not have had to pay the £2,000 I had, to make the Mission Buildings complete. [15]

Clifford's *diaries* speak of the usual round of episcopal engagements: attending meetings, opening churches and schools, making suitable clerical appointments and generally representing the Church in all its widest interests. He was willing to supply at Saint Peter's, Gloucester, when during a holiday period they were without a priest. [16] His concern for the welfare of his priests was fatherly – a point which is best illustrated from his dealings with Canon George Case. Loyalty to the Holy See and a sense of responsibility towards the flock in Gloucester might have led another bishop to call for Case's resignation at a much earlier date. While not unaware of these considerations, Clifford still felt compelled to use all his endeavours to save the priesthood of a man who had indeed served the diocese well and with generosity. In this, as we have seen, Clifford's efforts were made all the more difficult by his own unease (of which Case was probably aware) over the alleged 'lack-of-freedom issue' as it affected the bishops assembled in Council.

---

14   *The Tablet*, 1.4.1876.

15   Clifton Diocesan Archives, photocopy of letter from Canon Eustace Barron to Father Chard, Letter dated 26.2.1912.

16   J. N. Langston, *The Catholic Mission in Gloucester and its Priests* (1788 – 1894), (Bound typescript, Gloucester Library), section on Canon George Case.

Someone who, in a moment of personal crisis, turned to Clifford was Mgr. Thomas Capel, dismissed from the Presidency of the Catholic College in Kensington. Allegedly misunderstood both by Manning and, he felt, by the authorities in Rome, he begged Clifford to intervene so that he could obtain justice. His letter begins;

> My dear Lord Bishop,
>
> The kind way in which you listened to me in Rome, and the friendship I have ever met at your Lordship's hands induce me to write and ask your assistance at a grave moment in my life . . . [17]

In education Clifford was not remiss in providing for the children of the diocese. What concerned him greatly was the provision of a Catholic secondary school for boys. In 1890 'St. Joseph's Academy for Young Ladies' had been established in Clifton, and in the same year he wrote that

> 'the Catholics of Bristol in the 1890s desired for themselves the advantages which their co-religionists in other English cities had enjoyed, a Catholic secondary institution of their own'. [18]

On 29th March, full of optimism, he wrote;

> 'There is not a single Catholic Boarding School between Liverpool and Portsmouth, we would have a larger number of boarders from the area'. [19]

---

17   Clifton Diocesan Archives, *Letters to Hon. and Rt. Rev. William Clifford, Part II. 1875 - 1892*, Capel to Clifford, Letter dated 26.6.1879.

18   Brian S. Howell, *The Formative Years of Catholic Boys' Secondary Education in Bristol 1890 - 1918*, with reference to the Christian Brothers' College, Berkeley Square (University of Bristol, History of Education B.Ed. Main study, 1974 – 1975), p. 13.

19   *Ibid.*

This process, initiated by Clifford during the final years of his reign, came to fruition under his successor, Bishop William Brownlow, when in 1896 the Irish Christian Brothers opened St. Brendan's College in Berkeley Square, Clifton. Without Clifford's enthusiasm it is unlikely that St. Brendan's would ever have come into being. [20] The step was to be an important one for over the succeeding years the school was to prove the seed-ground for many vocations to the priesthood (including two bishops) and to the religious life.

Clifford's dealings with Non-Catholics at the local level are particularly interesting in that in his diocese there were a number of Anglican parishes that were centres of so-called 'Ritualism'. This is a generic term and is used, often pejoratively, to describe the liturgical practices of the Anglo-Catholic wing of the Church of England. Ritualist liturgy would involve the use of lighted candles, crucifixes and incense, and place a doctrinal emphasis on auricular confession and on the sacrifice of the Mass. Such celebrations led inevitably to the use of priestly vestments identical to those used by Roman Catholics. Indeed, in Clifford's day, the liturgies of Anglo and Roman Catholics could be indistinguishable save for the fact that one was celebrated in English and the other in Latin.

Among the ritualist centres during his episcopate were Bristol – where in 1877 there were said to be some 24 clergymen of this persuasion [21] – Bath, and in particular Frome, where W.J.E. Bennett exercised a controversial ministry which lasted thirty-four years (1852 – 1886) and which was the occasion, if not actually the cause, of many seeking admission to the Catholic Church. A number of these were received and confirmed by Bishop Clifford, as also was the Rector of Great Elm (Frome Deanery), the Rev. Lord Francis George Godolphin Osborne. [22]

---

20   See Howell, *op. cit.*, pp. 13 sqq.

21   Peter G. Cobb, *The Oxford Movement in Nineteenth Century Bristol* (Bristol Branch of the Historical Association, Local History Pamphlet, No. 68), p. 32.

22   See J. A. Harding, *The Re-birth of the Roman Catholic Community in Frome*, 1850 – 1927 (Thesis for M.Litt., University of Bristol, 1986), especially Chapter 3.

Among former Anglo Catholics who joined the ranks of the diocesan clergy were three men who at one time had been attached to the staff of another ritualist stronghold, St. Saviour's, Leeds. They were Richard Ward, Richard Macmullen and George Case. It says much for Clifford's feelings towards these men that in 1863, three of the four priests with him at the Pro-Cathedral were convert clergymen – Neve, Ward and Case. In Wiltshire a member of the Marquess of Bath's family, although advanced in years, was ordained priest by Bishop Clifford. [23] Lord Charles Thynne had been Vicar of Longbridge Deverill but with his wife and children had been received into the Church during the days of Bishop Burgess (1851 – 1854).

The overt ritualism of people like Bennett and Archdeacon Denison of Taunton led to several demonstrations of Anti-Catholic feeling in the diocese – demonstrations which actually continued with the Kensitites until the outbreak of war in 1914. The point to be emphasised, however, is that the places chosen for such outbursts were almost always those where the Anglo Catholics held sway. Therefore, although ostensibly Anti-Catholic, they were in fact protests at the way the Church of England in a particular locality was seen to be going. This explains why such events took place in a small market town like Frome, the vicar of which had a reputation for High Church practices which was well known even at national level.

Bennett's influence was felt at nearby Warminster. Although only eight miles away it was in a different county (Wilts) and diocese (Salisbury), but there we see feelings running high against the new church, St John's in Boreham Road – dubbed 'the Italian Chapel' – and against the 'monks' and 'nuns' to be seen walking in the streets. [24]

Nearer home in Clifton – less than a mile from Clifford's Pro-Cathedral – is the Church of All Saints. In 1871 Bennett preached a mission there during which he made use of *The Book of the Missions* which recommends the practice of Confession. One local paper commented:

---

23   *The Somerset and Wilts Journal*, 14.11.1885. Readers were informed
      that the 'Lordly Pervert' had been ordained in his 73rd year.

24   J. A. Harding, *op. cit.*, pp. 210 sqq.

Dr. Clifford (Bishop of Clifton) is, I hear, delighted with it, if
only the priests were of the right stamp, instead of being, as
he declares, 'poor shams'. [25]

If true, rather acerbic for Clifford.

Other centres of Ritualism in Bristol were St. John, Bedminster, St.
Raphael, Cumberland Road (where the wife of the Rev. A.H. Ward was
received into the Church) and Holy Nativity, Knowle. Outside the city
there were centres at Clevedon, Wraxall and Barrow Gurney. [26]

An interesting phenomenon of this period was the number of Protestants
who attended the services at the Pro-Cathedral in Clifton. The Anglo
Catholic Mission at All Saints (mentioned above) prompted Clifford to
invite the Jesuits to preach a Mission in his church. Writing to the
Provincial he says:

There has just been a Protestant Mission in this place (in
fact I believe it is not yet closed) which has caused some
stir. There is a large body of Ritualists in Clifton several of
whom come to our services, and more would come to hear
Fr. Humphries. [27]

(Fr. Humphries, S.J. was the missioner who was expected to come).

Just before Clifford's departure for the Vatican Council, *The Universe*
noted:

At the evening service on the same day the church [Pro-
Cathedral] was crowded, as it was generally known that this
would be the last time the bishop would officiate before his

25   *The Somerset and Wilts Journal*, 18.2.1871.

26   Peter G. Cobb, *op. cit.*, p. 2.

27   Archives of the English Province of the Society of Jesus, Mount Street,
      Letters of Bishops and Cardinals 1840 - 1891, Bp. Clifford to Fr.
      Provincial, Letter dated (probably) February, 1871.

departure for Rome to join the General Council. This was a mark of respect to a beloved prelate who well merited the tribute . . . Many Protestants were present. [28]

On his return Protestants continued to come to the church for three days. *The Tablet* informed its readers:

As his Lordship's arrival, as well as a notice that he would officiate on the Sunday and two following days had been announced in all the Bristol daily papers, a large congregation of Catholics as well as many Protestants filled the Cathedral at all the services on the three days. [29]

Here it has to be said that there was also an element of high curiosity which must have caused many of the congregation to be present. Mgr. Bonomi, V.G., said as much three months later in his letter [Appendix] in which he begged Clifford to inform his flock as to where he stood on the papal dogma: 'What is now certain is that your name has been before the world and ln the mouths of both Protestants and Catholics as one of the foremost amongst Bishops opposed . . . to the dogma'. [30]

There can be no doubt that Clifford was held in high regard by people of all faiths as *The Universe* noted at the time of his death:

Popular outside the Catholic faith, he was universally beloved and respected. [31]

Mention should be made here of the *Clifton Tracts*, sponsored by the Society of St. Vincent de Paul, which were published in 1851 just a few years before Clifford's appointment to Clifton. These appear to have been in fairly wide circulation in Clifford's time and were so successful that

---

28   *The Universe*, 13.11.1869.

29   *The Tablet*, 20.8.1870.

30   Clifton Diocesan Archives, *Letters to Bp. Clifford, Part 1, 1854 - 1874*, Bonomi to Clifford, Letter dated 13.11.1870.

31   *The Universe*, 19.8.1893.

they were later published in the United States of America under the auspices of the Archbishop of New York. [32] The tracts are addressed to the 'thoughtful and religious reader' and endeavour to put before him considerations on the two subjects which most commonly occupy the field of controversy between Catholics and Protestants, namely English History and the Bible. They are 'Tracts for the Times' and their aim is to instruct the genuine enquirer while at the same time answering the attacks then emanating from a crude Protestantism. Among the contributors were Northcote and William Gillow who for many years was President of the S.V.P. in Bristol.

The Diocesan Synod (presided over by Bishop Burgess in December, 1853), had issued an instruction

> That each incumbent should strive to induce the Mechanics, etc. of his Flock to take, in place of Protestant Periodicals, Catholic Periodicals, such as the *Lamp*, the *Clifton Tracts* etc. [33]

Some thirty years later, when the tercentenary of the birth of Martin Luther was being marked by articles in the press, a letter appeared in the *Somerset and Wilts Journal* advising its readers that if they really wished to know the truth about Luther, they should read the *Clifton Tracts*. [34]

A personal style is adopted throughout and is on the whole effective. On the other hand, the Church in which the reader might well have been nurtured is referred to in terms which today appear truculent, if not positively rude:

---

32   Publishers: P.J. Kenedy and Sons, New York. No date.

33   Clifton Diocesan Archives, *Synodus Diocesana* habita in Ecclesia *Cathedrali S.S. App. Cliftoniensi, Diebus xiii et xiv Dec.bris, 1853*, p. 7.

34   *The Somerset and Wilts Journal*, 8.12.1883.

. . . It may be but the fault of the religious system in which
you have been brought up, and of that faithless communion,
the State-Church of this country, which as good as
renounced the worship and the knowledge of Jesus when it
revolted against the spiritual kingdom He had set up on
earth, and submitted to the supremacy of the civil power.

(No. 12, p. 9).

There is also a very tendentious line of reasoning in four pamphlets dealing
with various aspects of 'The Kingdom'. The argument starts quite properly
with an exposition of the Church seen as a Kingdom ('The Kingdom of God'
as foretold by Daniel and described by Christ) from which it then proceeds
to argue to the Kingship and temporal power of the Pope!

In supporting these tracts in their stated purpose of presenting Catholic
truth, we see Clifford in his essential stance as defender of the faith.
Although essentially loyal to Pope and Church it is evident that this must
have cost him much when he came to pen what came to be his more
outstanding pastoral letters. This is not to suggest that he was in any way
hypocritical or inwardly disloyal. It is to underline, however, that he was
prepared to defend publicly policies with which he could not privately
concur and which he felt that the fullness of time would indeed see altered.

Although his defence of *The Syllabus* was adroit, he must have felt that
Pius IX was out of date and that a more modern, though still consistent,
policy could still be worked out. (The term *'aggiornamento'* was not then
in vogue, though had it been it would surely have found favour with
Clifford). Perhaps in this he saw a parallel with his own attempts to
present an interpretation of Genesis which modern man would find
acceptable and yet without doing violence to the sacred text.

Between this and his next great pastoral letter, there occurred the
Vatican Council. Here his hesitations found explicit expression in his
address on Papal Infallibility in which he made it clear that he wanted a
more balanced view to prevail which would take into account the position
of the Universal Episcopate. This was why – as he wrote privately to
Bonomi [35] – he hoped for the reconvening of the Council. For him it was
very much at the heart of the 'unfinished business'.

---

35   Clifton Diocesan Archives, *Letters to Bp. Clifford, Part I, 1854 - 1874*,
      Clifford to Bonomi, Letter dated 17.11.1870.

As with the *Syllabus*, so with the university question, one feels that Clifford must have acknowledged, at least inwardly, that to hold Catholics back from the universities was to fight a losing battle. He could not have been unaware that already there were young men – supported by parents, some of whom were influential in the Catholic community – who were already acting in defiance of the bishops' wishes. Such being the state of things, one is forced to the conclusion that the solution which ultimately prevailed – i.e. of having a Catholic chaplaincy and, eventually, a hall of residence – must have presented itself to Clifford's mind or, if not, have been suggested to, and discussed by, the bishops in private gatherings when Manning was not present. There was an increasing groundswell of opinion that the policy being pursued was obscurantist and that far more was being lost in terms of exclusion from the professions than could possibly be gained.

It is in this sense, therefore, that one must see the hesitations of the ever-loyal Bishop Clifford. He did not wish to break ranks. For a bishop to have done so in the late 19th century would have meant scandal. Nowadays this occasional phenomenon is less remarkable, but in the days of Pio Nono and Antonelli for whom loyalty in all things was a necessary condition of being a bishop, Clifford would certainly have incurred the wrath of Rome. In national policy making bishops, like cabinet ministers, share collective responsibility and, given the strong personality of Manning, there was no alternative other than to wait for a change of leadership. When eventually this did occur (1892), the question of Catholics going to Oxford and Cambridge received a more enlightened response from the hierarchy.

The *Syllabus of Errors* was gradually eroded by time – some, like Acton, would say 'even while it was being written' – and finally received its *coup de grâce* with the document on Religious Freedom ('*Dignitatis Humanae*') which emanated from Vatican II. This was the Council which also accorded the Universal Episcopate its proper collegial position in the Church as envisaged by Clifford in the debates of a century before.

As a speaker Clifford was more renowned for what he said than for the manner of his delivery. 'Preaching was not amongst his accomplishments, in consequence of a slight physical hesitancy', wrote someone who knew him, adding: 'It has been even said that Bishop Clifford could preach well in Italian though not in English'. [36]

Be that as it may, Clifford was called upon to deliver the eulogy on his friend and former superior, Archbishop Errington.[37] In accepting the challenge inherent in such an invitation, the preacher presented a balanced and well-formulated assessment not only of the deceased but also of Wiseman, drawing out for his hearers the strong personal traits of each. Clifford argued that, given two such autocrats and given that their single-minded service of the Lord was being exercised within the close confines of the same diocese, a serious clash of personalities was inevitable. A preacher of lesser calibre might have tried to eschew the subject completely – and failed.

Clifford's sermon at the funeral in 1890 of John Henry Newman drew widespread praise. [38] It must be remembered that this was in the days when those who listened to a panegyric expected to hear a literary as well as an homiletic *tour de force*, and for someone to try in this way to encompass the genius of a colossus like Newman must have seemed to many the most daunting challenge of all. In the cardinal's case, there was of course the added dimension of his having been a priest of the Church of England.

---

36   Jerom Murch, *Biographical Sketches of Bath Celebrities* (Publ. London and Bath, 1893), p. 226. Contrast this with his recollection of Bishop Baines:

His great power was in his delivery, in voice, in tone, in look and gesture. His whole manner was full of pathos, sometimes more even than the matter justified; there was a peculiar tremulousness of voice, which gave his words more than double effect . . . (page 218).

37   William Clifford, Bishop of Clifton, *A discourse delivered at the Funeral of George Errington, Archbishop of Trebizond and First Bishop of Plymouth*, in the Church of Prior Park College on the 26th Day of January, 1886 (Publ. Bristol, 1886).

38   William Clifford, Bishop of Clifton, *sermon preached at the Funeral of His Eminence John Henry Newman, Cardinal of the Holy Church* (Publ. London, 1890). Full text is reprinted in Appendix 5.

Bishop Clifford rose to the occasion and the family wrote to Father William Neville, the superior of the Birmingham Oratory, in the following grateful terms:

> 'I wonder if I may say that I felt especially grateful for the respectful terms used by the Bishop in his sermon, in speaking of the Communion the Cardinal had left in joining your Church – one could ill have borne to have harsh words spoken at such a time – but there seemed no fear of that from the tender-hearted Bishop'. [39]

It must have been passages such as these which so impressed his Non-Catholic hearers:

> [Speaking of Newman's thirty year connection with Oxford] it was a most eventful period, and fraught with the gravest consequences to him and to the Established Church. It was not without its effect on the Catholic Church in England, and in the events which then took place we may well admire the merciful hand of God leading the just man through right paths till it showed him the Kingdom of God.
>
> . . . we cannot fail to remark his earnest desire for truth. I remember how, at the time when these events were passing, Catholics, both in England and abroad, used to grow impatient and wrathful at the long delay which took place before Newman submitted to the Church. They used to say that he was not sincere, that he must be keeping back from selfish and unworthy motives. And yet how different is the truth when we come to know it. Never was a man so earnest and sincere in his search after truth as he, Newman, was at that time. (p. 8).

The family's sentiments of gratitude were echoed in a letter from Father Neville to the Bishop at about the same time;

---

39   Ugbrooke Archives, *Letter to Bp. Clifford. 1890* copy (in Clifford's hand)
       of letter from Fanny Mozley to Father William Neville, Letter dated
       21.8.1890. (p. 5).

I am told that many Protestants hereabouts speak of your sermon expressing a great wish to have it, and it pleases the Fathers much that they should be thus joined in their wish that you should print the Sermon for circulation, and they ask me to say how completely it was just what the Cardinal would have wished. [40]

During the crucial years of his episcopate, and, particularly during and after the stressful events of the Vatican Council, Clifford had been ably and loyally supported by his Vicar General, Mgr. John Bonomi. [41] On the Bishop's return from the Council a reception was held in his honour but the opportunity was also taken to propose the health of the Vicar General 'who briefly thanked the clergy for the support and good-will they had continued towards him during the Bishop's absence from the Diocese'. [42]

Bonomi's task had by no means been an easy one. In a situation of extreme delicacy he had endeavoured to sustain the belief of the clergy in the new dogma while at the same time maintaining a sensitive loyalty to the one whom he represented and yet who – as everyone knew – had openly called it into question during the Council and who had, since then, not been as completely frank as many would have wished. In very measured terms Bonomi stated the problem to his bishop:

The Clergy of your Lordship's Diocese with perhaps one or two exceptions believe explicitly in the dogma of Infallibility . . . The letter of Cardinal Antonelli which your Lordship circulated informs them of this, (i.e. that it is a belief to be held *sub gravi*) if even before, any of them had hesitated.

---

40   Ugbrooke Archives, *Letters to Bp. Clifford. 1890*, William Neville to Clifford, Letter dated 24.8.1890.

41   John Bonomi: Born 9.6.1816; ordained 21.5.1842; died 1.9.1872. New stations of the cross were erected in his memory in the Pro-Cathedral. The previous stations had been donated by William Maskell.

42   *The Tablet*, 20.8.1870.

By giving it to the Priests as their rule in the teaching of others both outwardly (and) *in foro conscientiae* yr Lordship has indicated to them in part at least your mind on the matter: but you have not I very humbly suggest, done this as completely or as openly in your words as you might have done.

Hence from the very beginning have arisen anxious inquiries, hesitation and doubty questions and controversies between the clergy and laity. From the very time you left Rome till now, I have been perpetually consulted and questioned about you. The clergy have urged me to speak to you and try and induce you to give them the consolation by some writing of your own on this very grave subject. It is not a matter that slumbers now; it is more than ever before us in proportion to the opposing assertions made perpetually about you.

The foremost priests in the Diocese have entreated me to represent the affair to you. Everyone says that in the confessional and out of it, they are perpetually asked what the Bishop believes and they declare that the letter of Cardinal Antonelli is not sufficient answer to the minds of the laity on the matter: they want to hear the Bishop's voice, to hear his own words and until you speak no body will fully convince himself that your assent is hearty and sincere and that you may not have some mode of explaining away the doctrine as binding under pain of eternal loss. [Extracts] [43]

Clifford's reply to his very serious representation on the part of his Vicar General has already been referred to in large part in Chapter 11 on Canon George Case, D.D. [It is printed in full in Appendix 5] His grave misgivings about the liberty of those voting In the Council, his theological difficulties in regard to matters of consultation with the Universal Church prior to any future infallible pronouncement, and the more immediate

---

43   Clifton Diocesan Archives, *Letters to Bp. Clifford, Part I, 1854 - 1874,* Bonomi to Clifford, Letter dated 13.11.1870. Full text is reprinted in Appendix 5.

issue of whether or not the Council could be re-convened thus providing an opportunity for matters to be discussed further and for the Decrees to be signed – these were all issues in Clifford's mind. But one point Clifford makes absolutely clear:

> The Pope has published the decree on Infallibility and I conscientiously bow to his authority. More than this: in the sense in which I have explained it, the decree presents to my mind no serious theological difficulty. But as regards the means made use of to secure the votes of the Bishops, my opinion remains unaltered. [44]

Such a frank yet respectful exchange affords us a picture of the state of turmoil in the diocese consequent upon the stand which Clifford had taken at the Vatican Council. His reassurance given to Bonomi (quoted above) coupled with the Pastoral Letter he wrote defending the Vatican Decrees against Gladstone would have helped to dispel from the public mind any doubts that may have remained. The tragedy of Canon Case too would not have been without its salutary effect. 'Lord, to whom shall We go? . . .' is very much a Catholic sentiment when faith is assailed. But Clifford's own loyalty, despite his difficulties, would have had the greatest impact of all.

Turning now to Clifford's interests as an antiquary, one finds in his correspondence and in the Minutes of local Antiquarian Clubs to which he belonged how much both his judgements and his presence at their meetings and outings were appreciated. In 1876 the noted writer Prebendary W. H. Jones (whose investigations eventually led to the excavation of the celebrated Saxon church at Bradford-on-Avon) entered into correspondence with the bishop 'touching the original position of a High Altar at Salisbury'. In thanking Clifford for his letter, Jones writes:

> I candidly confess that it throws much light on a subject that has always had a little difficulty for me . . . I admit however (I repeat) that it is to my mind a most probable one. [45]

---

44   Clifton Diocesan Archives, *Letters to Bp. Clifford, Part I, 1854 - 1874*, Clifford to Bonomi, Letter dated 17.11.1870.

45   Ugbrooke Archives, *Letters to Bp. Clifford, 1876*, Prebendary Jones to Clifford, Letter dated 4.9.1876.

The Bishop of Bath and Wells (Lord Arthur Hervey) offered Clifford the hospitality of the Bishop's Palace during his visit to Wells for the meeting (lasting several days) of the Somerset Archaeological Society in August, 1888:

> It will give Lady Arthur and myself much pleasure if you will come to us on Monday the 27th and stay till the close of the meeting. [46]

This kind invitation has to be seen against a background of vicious polemic then being waged by both sides of the Catholic/Protestant divide. This can best be illustrated by a comment in *The Universe* just four months after Clifford had been regaled at the Bishop's Palace in Wells. The Anglican prelate, faced with problems from the ritualists in his flock, had been calling for 'a wide and liberal and yet stringent discipline' in his church. The Catholic paper retorted:

> The so-called Bishop of Bath and Wells is not remarkable either for historical accuracy logical acumen.
>
> These defects in the character of this prelate have been subjects of complaint urged against him by his own clergy for many years. As long as fifteen years ago the Anglican journals complained of the 'Intemperate and ignorant theological utterances of Lord ARTHUR HERVEY, Bishop of Bath and Wells' . . .
>
> We respect age as reason, humanity, and the true religion teaches us, but not age when it drivels. [47]

To return to Clifford's Antiquarian activities: he hesitated from airing his learning in public as this moving tribute written in the *Athenaeum* after his death clearly shows:

---

46   Ugbrooke Archives, *Letters to Bp. Clifford, 1888*, Lord Arthur Hervey to Clifford, Letter dated 19.5.1888.

47   *The Universe*, 15.12.1888.

If archaeology was a pastime for Clifford, it was at the same time a serious study. In Wilts and Somerset he brought much research to investigations in local topography, especially as to the sites of battles between King Alfred and the Danes. He was an enthusiastic member of the archaeological societies of Somersetshire and Gloucestershire; but beyond a few papers read at the meetings of these and similar societies, he has left no written records of his opinions and researches. Few modern bishops have produced less 'copy' of any kind. [48]

The writer then goes on to widen his comments in a most interesting way:

He fought shy, if he could, of that sort of extended 'imprimatur', in the form of an episcopal preface to a pious volume, which the modern Roman Catholic author appears hardly to be happy without. When religious controversies raged, Bishop Clifford seldom ranged himself as a champion of the opinions he was well fitted by his sense of courtesy and tolekation to defend with effect. In 1874, when he published a reply to Mr. Gladstone's anti-Vatican pamphlets, he did so in the form of one of the pastorals which every Roman Catholic bishop is expected to address to his flock at stated seasons of the ecclesiastical year; and this, perhaps, will remain as a standard little treatise on the civil allegiance of the spiritual subjects of the Pope. [49]

As was noted in Chapter 2, Clifford's health was a matter of concern to a number of people. It was felt by both Wiseman and Errington to be the only obstacle to his appointment as bishop, although the opinion of doctors was that, given the passage of time, there was every hope that his health would become more robust. Despite the fact that his *diaries* for the period 1856 – 1879 (inclusive) are missing, some slight picture from a variety of sources can still be presented.

---

48   Quoted by Jerom Murch, *Biographical Sketches of Bath Celebrities* (Publ. London and Bath, 1893), pp. 227, 228.

49   *Ibid.*

<u>1854</u>   (Clifford was priest at Stonehouse in the diocese of Plymouth. His
        entry for <u>Jan. 7th</u> reads: Deaths from cholera during the past
        week 14. Cases still remaining).

        March 4th   Ill in bed

               12th   Communion in bed

               22nd   Out for the 1st time for a drive

               26th   Did not go to Com. as I expected to be well
                      enough to say mass in a day or two – Felt worse
                      in the evening. Obliged to go to bed – I had
                      attempted too much which threw me back.

        April 1st   Today I began to rally

               2nd   Communion

               4th   Walked out after dinner with Agnes, Charles . . .

               7th   Said mass for the 1st time since 1st Sund. in
                     Lent (March 5th). Felt rather fatigued

               8th   Felt rather unwell

               9th   (Palm Sunday). Rather unwell could not say
                     Mass nor go to Communion

(By 12th recovered drove over to Taunton)

               26th   I did not say Mass this morning. [50]

<u>1860</u>   Aug. 2nd   I have been in bed ever since I saw you last but
                          I am better today. [51]

---

50   Diocesan Archives, Bishop Clifford's *Diary*, 1854

51   Archives of the English College, Valladolid, *Correspondence (Vol. 71
       1846 - 1860*, GUEST, No. 197, Clifford to Bishop Grant, Letter dated
       2.8.1860.

	8th	He (Clifford) is unwell at the present moment. [52]

<u>1862</u>   June   ... the Pope with all the bishops (except Clifton in bed) ... [53]

<u>1864</u>   Feb. 15th   If he (Clifford) has not yet done so it is because he is still laid up with fever and cold – for in reply to my letter he tells me that he has been so laid up all last week. [54]

<u>1870</u>   May 25th   It grows hotter and hotter and Bishop Clifford is getting very thin. Dr. Manning asked Amherst whether he and Dr. Clifford had not better go home. [55]

On July 26th, 1893, Clifford went to Prior Park for an operation, possibly for cancer. Mgr. James Shepherd gives a poignant description of what was to follow:

> The blow was in some respects sudden. The bitter chalice of death was placed before him in the form of a dangerous operation. There was a chance of life, but he prepared for death by receiving the last sacraments, in full consciousness of what was before him.
>
> He walked from his sick-room into the small oratory in the Mansion Chapel, and himself directed the ceremony of the last anointing. He made his profession of faith, and said

---

52   *Ibid.*, No. 198 Bishop Goss to Guest, Letter dated 8.8.1860.

53   Wiseman to Manning, Letter dated 17.6.1862. Quoted by Cuthbert Butler, *The Life and Times of Bishop Ullathorne 1806 - 1889* (Publ. London, 1926), Vol. I, p. 247.

54   Archives of the English College, Valladolid, *Correspondence (Vol. 8 1861 - 1868,* GUEST, No. 83 Richard Ward to Guest, Letter dated 15.2.1864.

55   Ullathorne's *Diary* of the First Vatican Council. Quoted by Cuthbert Butler, *The Vatican Council 1869 - 1870* (Publ. London 1930, paperback 1962), p. 328.

prayers aloud suitable to the occasion. It was a most edifying and impressive scene, and I may say unprecedented. The ceremony finished, he returned to his room to pass through the fearful ordeal. I myself was present on the occasion, and Monsignor Williams administered the Extreme Unction, assisted by the Bishop's constant friend and secretary, Canon Russell . . .

The operation, performed by Dr. Fenwick, a specialist from London, was as successful under the circumstances as it could be . . . [56]

During his final illness the bishop was nursed by his sister, the Hon. Mrs. Kavanagh and by two sisters from Clifton Wood Convent. [57] Canon Russell noted that Clifford had a relapse on August 9th. Two days later he went to Prior Park and found that the bishop was dying. His death took place at Prior Park on August 14th, 1893, at 1.30 p.m. [58] Clifford was in his seventieth year, and he was universally mourned.

The funeral was held on August 18th, 1893, in the Chapel of Prior Park. This was most appropriate as the bishop always had a great affection for the College which had played such a major role both in the history of the diocese and in his own life. The chapel, too, meant much to him; it had been completed with donations from the faithful as a token of affection to mark his episcopal silver jubilee.

The Eulogy (printed in Appendix 18) was preached by Dr. Hedley, Bishop of Newport and Menevia and was based on the text:

'O Lord, Thou hast tried me and known me'. (Psalm 138, 1).

---

56   James Shepherd, *Reminiscences of Prior Park* (Publ. London, 1894) pp. 116, 117.

57   *Ibid.*

58   Clifton Diocesan Archives, *Catholic Directory, 1893*. Copy belonging to Mgr. Arthur Russell.

<u>Figures to show the growth of the Diocese during William Clifford's episcopate</u> [59]

	<u>1857</u>	<u>1893</u>
Priests (total)	50	111
Churches, Chapels, Stations (total)	39	67

---

59   Statistics taken from the *Catholic Directories*, 1857 and 1893.

CHAPTER SIXTEEN

The Influence of Bishop Clifford at the
First Vatican Council and on the English Catholic Church

William Clifford was a bishop for thirty-six years. By any standards this must be considered to have been a long reign. Any attempt to describe his place in ecclesiastical history must first place his episcopate in context, and secondly delineate those personal qualities by which he sought to influence the course of events.

By the year 1857, when Clifford was consecrated, the English and Welsh Hierarchy had not yet been in existence for seven years. This meant that in a whole variety of matters it was still 'feeling its way' – and this, not only in regard to governments and the Catholic laity and all that pertained to them, but also in terms of the relationship of the bishops among themselves.

'Begin as you hope to continue' is an adage which would seem to have inspired Cardinal Wiseman, for in him we see someone who is trying to establish a *modus agendi* both for himself and for the Archbishops of Westminster of the future. The difficulty, it would seem, was that Wiseman tried to play the Primate and to act without consulting his brother bishops. Even when they did meet, the expected formality and business-like nature of the occasions were totally absent. 'As far back as 1855 Ullathorne, at the instance of some of the bishops, had made a remonstrance to Wiseman on the informal and haphazard manner in which the Low Week meetings were held, so as to be general conversations rather than business meetings'. [1]

It has to be noted that the Holy See in setting up the Hierarchy in 1850 had studiously avoided making the Archbishop of Westminster Primate. Before the Reformation (and even today) the Archbishop of Canterbury is known as the Primate of all England, and the refusal of the Holy See to confer a similar title on Wiseman and his successors can only be seen as

---

1   Cuthbert Butler, *The Life and Times of Bishop Ullathorne, 1806 - 1889* (Publ. London, 1926), Vol. 1, p. 240.

indicating a desire to limit jurisdiction. Indeed when the other Archbishoprics of Birmingham and Liverpool were created in 1911 (and of Cardiff in 1916) the title conferred on Westminster was that of *coetus episcopalis praeses perpetuus*. He was to be no more than a Chairman.

It was this side of Wiseman's character which so infuriated the other bishops. Clifford, normally a patient man, occasionally breaks out in his letters with sheer exasperation. Writing to Bishop Brown of Newport over the way in which the Bishops' views on the Charitable Trusts Act had been misrepresented by Wiseman to Propaganda he said:

> I have no doubt that the Cardinal's health has much to do with his present conduct but there is no doubt that he will now cause no end of misery to us all in England if things go on much longer this way. [2]

Within the same week two other bishops had written to Brown – the senior suffragan – in the same vein:

Bishop Brown of Shrewsbury

> We have all, save Dr. Grant, got a pretty good snubbing (i.e. from Propaganda) – and we may thank our Archbishop for it. [3]

Bishop Amherst of Northampton

> . . . should we not have a clear understanding as to our relations with His Eminence? viz. whether we are to be allowed liberty of opinion, or whether we are to submit our judgement simply and entirely to his? [4]

---

2   Cardiff Archdiocesan Archives, *Letters to Bishop Brown*, Clifford to Brown, Letter dated 1.9.1861.

3   Cardiff Archdiocesan Archives, *Letters to Bishop Brown*, Bp. Brown of Shrewsbury to Brown, Letter dated 4.9.1861.

4   Cardiff Archdiocesan Archives, *Letters to Bishop Brown*, Amherst to Brown, Letter dated 2.9.1861.

The letters just quoted refer to the occasion when the Hierarchy had met at Low Week, 1861, to discuss the implications for Catholic Charities of the Roman Catholic Charities Act. Wiseman, afraid that monies to be used for Masses were in danger because of the 'superstitious purposes' to which the law saw them being put, was for disobeying the law whereas the remainder of the bishops, possibly all, were for obeying on the grounds a) that to disobey would be to risk serious legal entanglement and b) legal advice was to the effect that monies set aside for Masses would in fact be in no danger of forfeit.

In Wiseman's absence the Meeting adopted the proposals of the majority and asked Ullathorne and Clifford – the latter's training as a canon lawyer here being duly acknowledged – to look into the matter more fully and to report back to another meeting in a month's time. After this meeting a letter was sent to Propaganda giving the views of the bishops, but at about the same time Wiseman too wrote giving his own (different) opinion. Propaganda replied with a letter which contained a rebuke for the bishops for daring to differ from their metropolitan.

It was this which led to the exchange of letters between the bishops themselves in which they not only referred to their proper rights but also – and this was Clifford's view – that such a rebuke from Rome could have been occasioned only by a misrepresentation of their views in the first place. For this he blamed Wiseman.

The following extracts show that even Clifford was beginning to lose his patience with Wiseman. Both letters were addressed to Grant.

> I send you a copy of the letter I have received from Card. Barnabo in answer to the letter sent from our meeting.

> The Cardinal must have given a very strange account of what took place there, for the letter speaks of all the bishops having joined in opposing the Cardinal & yourself. What this refers to I cannot imagine. – The Card. Prefect also lectures the Bishops for not having attended to the Cardinal's advice, & seems to suppose that we had passed some resolution to take the initiative with the Committee of inquiry, & not to consult the Holy See in these matters. I am quite puzzled by it.

> If our meetings are to be judged of not by the resolutions we
> come to, but by such an account as the Cardinal may send of
> them I think it is better there should be no meetings at all. [5]

Writing from Rome almost six months later, he was still of the same mind.

> I am fully alive to the mischief which results from the Card.
> [*sic*] mode of acting with the Bishops, but I do not at present
> see the remedy. Even if we get the Synod confirmed I fear that
> fresh disturbances must arise unless the Cardinal enters into
> the spirit of it & does not interfere with the freedom of the
> Bishops. He may possibly do so, but I fear very much that it is
> a case of nature & the pitchfork-*usque redibit*. [6]

The government of ecclesiastical colleges had also been a source of
friction between Wiseman and his suffragans. Wiseman had wished to
retain a controlling interest in the seminaries whereas the other bishops
– particularly those in the North of England – were insistent that such
control be In the hands of the local bishops. Underlying everything,
however, was the simmering discontent caused by Wiseman's
authoritarian manner. As Clifford pointed out, ill health was bound to
have been a contributory factor; other factors were the increasing
influence of Mgr. Manning whose hand was often perceived to be behind
many of the Cardinal's decisions, and the fact that a number of the
bishops – though not Clifford – had been students of Wiseman at the
English College in Rome when he had been Rector. The fact that they now
wore mitres counted for little.

Two factions emerged with the sending of two delegations to Rome. Their
purpose was to seek advice on the Roman Catholic Charities Act, on the
issues relating to the colleges, and also (in the case of the suffragans) to
report Wiseman for his high-handed attitude and to get Propaganda to
order Wiseman to consult more.

---

5   Southwark Archdiocesan Archives, *Bishop Grant - Catholic Charities
     File*, Clifford to Grant, Letter dated 28.8.1861.

6   Southwark Archdiocesan Archives, *Bishop Grant - Synods File*,
     Clifford to Grant, Letter dated 8.2.1862.

Ullathorne and Clifford arrived in Rome on November 1st, 1861 to be followed three or four weeks later by Manning who was acting as Wiseman's agent. Ullathorne left Rome at the end of February, 1861, leaving Clifford to conclude the unfinished business. All the English bishops came to Rome in May, 1861, to be present in St. Peter's for the canonization of the Japanese Martyrs.

Clifford was ill in bed when the English bishops, with Wiseman, had an audience with the Pope. It was a solemn affair with Pio Nono giving them 'a ticking off'. Referring to their differences he told them

> to take the highest and largest mountain in the Alps and put it over all past questions and dissensions without any tunnel through to get at them. They were never to be referred to again or brought up under any circumstances. [7]

The warning was heeded and peace returned.

The detailed discussions of the issues raised had proceeded slowly with the final decisions reflecting great credit on the skills of Clifford as a canon lawyer – skills which were again to triumph some twenty years later with the publication of the Bull *Romanos Pontifices*. Briefly the decisions reached were as follows:

1) <u>Meetings of the Bishops</u>: There is to be an agenda; there is to be a free discussion; matters to be settled by a majority of votes; where there is no majority, the Holy See to decide. [8]

2) <u>Government of the Colleges</u>: Wiseman was defeated. The local bishops to have control.

3) <u>Charitable Trust Act</u>: Each bishop to decide how he will proceed.

Wiseman had lost on all three counts, and the Suffragans, with Clifford pleading their cause, had won a resounding victory. To be fair to Clifford,

---

7   Cuthbert Butler, *op. cit.*, p. 247.

8   Cuthbert Butler, *op. cit.*, p. 248. The other decisions are discussed in the following pages.

however, he would never have seen the result in those terms. He was not that sort of man. His only wish was that right should prevail.

Two quotations will conclude this unhappy saga. The first is from a letter of Bishop Goss of Liverpool to the Cardinal when relations were at a low ebb:

> As circumstances do not allow me to be in London on that occasion I shall not have the pleasure of meeting my brethren or the <u>honour</u> of dining with your Eminence. [9]

The other is from Bishop Clifford's *Lenten Pastoral* written a few days after the death of Wiseman in February, 1865:

> For generations to come his memory will be as sweet as honey in every mouth. [10]

One matter which in the early days of the Hierarchy troubled many of the bishops concerned Catholic reformatories and the legal requirement that they be open to inspection by government officials. The resulting tension has been described as follows:

> The sisters were torn between the need for public recognition in this world and the need to establish themselves as primarily concerned with the other world. [11]

The sisters referred to were of the Good Shepherd Order which had opened a Girls' Reformatory at Arno's Vale in Bristol in July, 1856.

---

9   Cuthbert Butler, *op. cit.*, p. 241. Extracts of letters from Goss to Clifford, complaining about Wiseman, are in Appendix 1.

10   Clifton Diocesan Archives, *Pastorals of Bishop Clifford*, Lenten Pastoral dated 23.2.1865.

11   Peter E. Hughes, *Cleanliness and Godliness*: A sociological study of the Good Shepherd convent refuges for the social reformation and christian conversion of prostitutes and convicted women in 19th century Britain (Unpublished thesis for Ph.D., 1986, Brunel University), p. 247.

Although, as the same writer has observed, such inspections had 'settled into an amicable working arrangement', there was nevertheless at the start 'considerable dissension between the Home Office and the R.C. authorities as to the extent of the inspection'.[12] Clifford confronted the problem head on and, writing on behalf of the sisters in Bristol, expressed his unease that such a vital issue should be left to the good sense of individual inspectors:

> Suppose an Inspector is authorised to inspect Catholic children, and suppose a difference of opinion to arise between the Inspector and the Catholic Chaplain as to what belongs to religion and what to secular instruction . . . the government would claim a right to settle such points through the Inspector or otherwise – and differences might perhaps be avoided through the moderation of individual inspectors, but Government would still claim the <u>right</u> then to interfere in religious questions, even if the Inspector refrained from <u>using</u> it. This is what Catholics object to . . . [13]

It was a struggle which was to continue for many years to come, but Clifford had laid the ground rules upon which the Catholics would take their stand.

The other great event during Clifford's time as bishop was the First Vatican Council. To understand his influence at the Council one has to examine the personal qualities which he brought to bear not only at that great gathering but also on other occasions. Careful and thoughtful in manner, his competence both as theologian and canon lawyer could not be doubted. As a theologian he was seen at his best in the lengthy debate on Papal Infallibility. The exacting issues which he confronted some twelve years later in his articles in *The Dublin Review* on the Days of Creation demanded the same theological acumen. In the Council his training as a canon lawyer showed itself in his warning to the Fathers not to exceed the terms of the Bull convening the Council and in his general comments on the Life of the Clergy.

---

12   *Ibid.* p. 248.

13   Clifton Diocesan Archives, *Letter Book*, Vol. 1, p. 274, Clifford to the Rev. Sydney Turner, Inspector of Reformatory Schools, Letter dated 10.12.1858.

But over and above this there were two qualities which appeared to colour his whole outlook. First, he was intensely loyal but never slavishly subservient to the Holy See. Secondly, he never lost sight of the fact that English Catholics lived in a Protestant country.

To take the first point: his loyalty to the Holy See was additional to, and quite distinct from, his loyalty to the person of Pio Nono. Loyalty to the Holy See was a necessary condition of being a Catholic. This he made clear to Antonelli when he (the Secretary of State) wrote asking whether the Decrees of the Council had been promulgated in the Clifton Diocese. It was also very much in his mind when dealing with those who would continue the debate over Infallibility <u>after</u> the Definition. Again it was that same loyalty which overcame the very misgivings which he had about the 'lack of freedom' amongst the bishops and which he conveyed so movingly in his private letter to Bonomi. Finally, it was the same loyalty which, no matter how much he might have sympathised with Canon Case, would not allow him to go down the path of Apostasy and Schism.

Distinct from this was his very real affection for Pio Nono. The Holy Father had nominated him personally as bishop, and consecrated him, and it caused Clifford much distress when the Pope totally misunderstood the purpose of the joint letter sent by himself and Grant in which they had urged the appointment of Errington to Westminster in 1865. In putting forward Errington's name they were in no way criticising the Pope who had earlier removed him from the coadjutorship. They were saying only that the conflict which had brought that removal about was no longer a consideration as one of the parties to that conflict (Wiseman) was now dead. The reply of Clifford and Grant to Barnabo (Chapter 6) was a *cri de coeur* of genuine sadness at the thought that the Holy Father had been hurt by their letter.

Loyalty to the Holy See, however, did not amount to a subservience whereby everything that was done at Rome commanded acceptance. In his address at the Council he spoke critically of the Curia and of the way in which it delegated to bishops what Clifford believed they enjoyed already – i.e. the right of ordaining sufficient clergy for their dioceses. Although he opened his mind in private to Bonomi over the pressures to vote for Infallibility, nevertheless, like his friend Ambrose de L'Isle Phillipps, he would never dream of 'going public' and so cause the Church to draw to itself public opprobrium or ridicule. Again, this was what had worried him over the manner of the appointment to Westminster. He felt deeply that the image of the Church would suffer if ever it became known exactly how this Archbishop had come to be chosen. Pius IX was already known to be volatile and such an event as this, if known, would greatly tarnish the Papacy.

Not wanting to 'go public' was one of the ways in which Clifford differed from Canon George Case. He had preached and published his difficulties. Clifford would never have done that. Indeed, it seems to have been fairly well known that Clifford had difficulties over Papal Infallibility, and yet his loyalty – in which the option of schism was completely ruled out as being no option at all – must have had an influence on many who vacillated.

There was in Bishop Clifford an ever present awareness that the English Catholic Church lived, and hoped to thrive, in a Protestant country. As the majority of the bishops at Vatican I were from Catholic countries, Clifford felt it necessary on a number of occasions to draw their attention to the delicacy of the situation in which the minority found themselves and to warn against any hasty or 'provocative' pronouncements. It will be useful to recall some of those occasions:

- Small Catechism: Protestants are saying we have met to start a new religion (see above, p. 189).

- Concubinage of the clergy: Protestant husbands and fathers would react to protect their wives and daughters (see above, p. 182).

- Papal Infallibility: In England bishops would be seen to renege on guarantee given to H.M.G. in the *Protestation* of 1789 (see Appendix 11 b, p. 470).

- 'Protestantism is the root of all evils': Clifford wanted this provocative statement deleted. (see above, p. 228).

On the other hand, Clifford wished to instruct and protect his flock against unwarranted attacks from Protestants and his Pastoral Letters were widely acclaimed in this regard –

Advent 1864	He wrote against the 'Branch Theory' of the Church
Lent 1865	He defended *Quanta cura* and *The Syllabus of Errors* against Protestant attack
Advent 1874	*Catholic Allegiance* – a Reply to Gladstone's attack on the loyalty of Catholic subjects.

In regard to what is now known as 'Ecumenism', it would have to be said that Clifford was a product of his time. Indifferentism – 'one religion is as good as another' – was always perceived as the great danger. Clifford sincerely believed this, as did the authorities in Rome, with the result that no change ever came from the Official level – apart from the semi-official Malines Conversations – for nearly a century (at Vatican II). Indeed there are some today who would argue that since Vatican II, though not necessarily because of it, that danger of Indifferentism has to some extent been realised in the minds of not a few Catholics.

Furthermore Clifford would probably have argued that, given the unique claims of the Catholic Church, there was probably little room for manoeuvre anyway. He was invariably sympathetic to Ambrose de L'Isle Phillipps, but there is no evidence that he saw any realistic hope for corporate reunion.

And yet Clifford did enjoy unofficial contacts with Anglican clergy mainly, it is true, through their common interest in matters historical and archeological. He had been the guest of the Bishop of Bath and Wells (Lord Arthur Hervey), and had been in correspondence with the noted scholar Canon W. H. Jones of Bradford-on-Avon and with the Bishop of Exeter. Although theologically correct in his ecumenical contacts, it could still be said that Clifford was warmer than most. Certainly he would have been prepared to listen.

It was precisely because he would not gratuitously offend Protestants and because he was both willing and able to express his Catholic Faith in a liberal, yet totally orthodox, manner that earned him so much appeal in the minds of liberal Catholics like Sir John (later Lord) Acton. Although he could not have known it at the time, it was his interpretation of the Encyclical *Quanta cura* and its accompanying *Syllabus of Errors* which led him to be their favoured candidate for Westminster. Here was a young bishop – able, popular, acceptable at Rome yet liberal in outlook – who would ideally fit the role of head of the English Hierarchy.

Largely (as we have seen) through Clifford's own efforts it was not to be, but that is not to say that he would not have been a very successful Archbishop. But another Manning he would not have been.

One of the ways in which he would have differed would have been over the question of Catholic students attending Oxford and Cambridge. His aristocratic friends, and others, advocated change, and had Clifford become Archbishop there seems to be little doubt that such a change would have been achieved, although to alter the stance of Rome in the matter might have proved no easy task. In the days of Pio Nono it would have been impossible, but Leo XIII (elected 1878) might have been persuaded to act earlier than he did.

Although Clifford differed from Manning on this and other issues, his relations with the Cardinal, though never warm, were invariably businesslike. Clifford found Manning's Ultramontanism irksome just as he did Wiseman's autocratic manner. In neither case, however, did he publicly break ranks.

It is important, however, to understand Manning's position. For him Papal Infallibility had a psychological as well as a spiritual perspective in that he saw the definition as the culmination of a whole process by which the Church finally declared herself free and independent of all state interference and supremely competent to judge for herself matters affecting faith and morals. It was a battle which, with others, he had fought years before when reacting so strongly against the Erastianism of the Church of England. In this Clifford would undoubtedly have concurred, but being of a moderate temperament he would have been conscious of the extremes which can sometimes be bred of any reaction.

Clifford's relationship with the other bishops was invariably one of warmth and understanding, and as the years went by he eventually became a 'father figure' in whom they would confide. However, in his early years as bishop he found Brown of Newport difficult, but later the relationship warmed as when, for example, he wrote to Clifford expressing his satisfaction that he was preparing a reply to Gladstone.

Brown was one with Clifford in his verdict on how the bishops had been treated during the Council. Writing in November, 1870, the Bishop of Newport – who was never one to 'pull his punches' – said:

> Doings at the Council were the most discreditable, as against liberty of judgement & utterance that I ever read of in any previous General Council, or even any council of Catholic Bishops. [14]

His comments on Clifford's position at this time in the English Hierarchy are also worthy of note:

> Now that good Bp. Grant is removed from us, you must bear to be troubled with questions on the sense of Roman instructions, *as alone amongst us*, being experienced therein. [15] [Underlining mine].

Ullathorne wrote to Clifford on a number of occasions and they travelled together to Rome when asked by the other suffragans to represent their interests in their disputes with Wiseman. Clifford found Ullathorne a useful ally, particularly as he was a religious, when it came to drawing up the bishops' case which ultimately led to the publication of *Romanos Pontifices*.

Grant of Southwark and Clifford corresponded as two canonists on a variety of issues, with Clifford assuming his mantle in presenting cases to Rome when Grant died in 1870. However, it would be wrong to assume from this that Clifford had not been involved before that date in preparing cases for consideration by the Roman Curia or in giving solutions to various *casus* that had arisen in the dioceses and which the bishops felt demanded an expertise that they did not themselves possess.

Goss of Liverpool, for example, had a high regard for Clifford and even wrote to him before his appointment as Bishop of Clifton and while he was still residing at the Collegio Pio studying canon law:

---

14   Ugbrooke Archives, *Letters to Bp. Clifford. 1870*, Bishop Brown to Clifford, Letter dated 7.11.1870.

15   *Ibid.*

I enclose you another copy of my visitation questions, as I
want to know your deliberate opinion thereon after you
reach Rome. I send you also, for a like reason, our Moral
Cases, and I shall be glad if you will give me, after your
arrival in Rome, an example of the manner in which I
ought to forward a solution of them to the different
conferences . . . [16]

The letter is dated November 8th 1855. In it Goss also describes the
problems he has in identifying his rights as bishop when visiting the
religious houses of his diocese. It would seem from the tone of the
letter that Goss, who had probably become aware of the young priest's
talents when the latter was secretary of the Synod, had 'latched on to
him' as a ready source of canonical wisdom. Apparently Clifford, ever
patient, did not object. In later years Goss confided in Clifford – as
Clifford had confided in Bonomi – over the alleged pressures on the
bishops at Vatican I.

Errington and Clifford were close – in so far as closeness was possible
with a man like Errington who to so many presented the image of the
martinet. Clifford spoke in terms of warm admiration for his erstwhile
superior whom he had served as Vicar General in Plymouth and at whose
obsequies he preached. Above all we see this relationship bearing fruit in
the way that Clifford welcomed the Archbishop back to the diocese which
he had served so well in the days when he was Apostolic Administrator.
There can be no doubt that Errington enjoyed his time as professor to the
young church students at Prior Park and it appears that at his death he
left some of his personal possessions to Clifford, including his bull of
appointment as Archbishop which is still at Ugbrooke.

Errington and Clifford had been friends for many years. So too had
Newman and Clifford, and it is a tribute to Clifford's personality that he
could accommodate two such widely differing spirits. Newman and
Clifford had known each other in Rome and there was a steady
correspondence between them over the years.

---

16   Liverpool Archdiocesan Archives, *Goss Letter Book June 15, 1855 to
       May 9, 1857*, Letter No. 24, Goss to Clifford, Letter dated 8.11.1855.

When the year after his consecration the bishop's father died, Newman wrote a delicately worded message of sympathy, while earlier, in 1854, he had written to invite Clifford to preach the University sermon.

In 1865 Newman wrote his *Letter to Dr. Pusey*. The letter was critical of the position of the Ultramontanes and in it he refused to see their theological views and Marian devotions as being necessarily and essentially those of the Catholic Church. Controversy ensued and while some liberal minded Catholics welcomed it, to others it appeared to be a slur on the Catholics of other nations and to be somewhat 'Protestant' in tone. Ward wrote a reply to Newman's *Letter* and Herbert Vaughan (editor of *The Tablet*) wanted Clifford to be a censor of the article. This was in accordance with the practice of the day which required that articles and books of a theological or scriptural nature should be read beforehand by a duly authorised censor so as to assure the reader of the orthodoxy of what he was reading.

Clifford refused Vaughan's request arguing, initially, that he was 'unqualified', but later, and in franker mood, confessing that he had found nothing to criticise in what Newman had written.

> . . . The article (i.e. by Ward) is written you inform me "in order not to let that letter pass without any notice of the stigma cast upon the Catholic practices of other nations, & of two or three other uncatholic passages" – Now I have the greatest admiration for Newman's letter, I have carefully & repeatedly read it, & I have failed to discover in it either "uncatholic passages" or "a stigma cast on the Catholic practices of other nations". Much less do I see, what you say others have seen, any Protestantism in the letter. [17]

But Clifford's letter is not just negative in the sense that he finds nothing to criticise. He tells Vaughan that he actually applauds what Newman has said to Pusey:

---

17   Ugbrooke Archives, *Letters to Bp. Clifford, 1866*, Clifford's draft reply to Vaughan, dated 9.3.1866.

Cardinal Wiseman's sermons on OB Lady in his "Sermons on our Lord & the B. V. Mary" and this Letter of Fr. Newman are the only recent works (which I have read) which have added to my stock of devotion to Our B. Lady. They really enlighten the understanding as to her prerogatives, & inflame the heart with love for her. [18]

Newman sometimes wrote to Clifford to congratulate him on his *Pastoral Letters* and they were in correspondence at the time of Papal Infallibility – their position differing only slightly though arrived at independently. The unfortunate incident of the divulging by Clifford of a private letter from Newman to his bishop, Ullathorne, was never allowed to sour their relationship.[19] Indeed, it is not without significance that it was Clifford who served Newman's first Mass, [20] who read the *biglietto* on his elevation to the cardinalate, [21] and who preached the Eulogy at his funeral.

Newman is frequently referred to as a Vatican II figure. One reason for this is the emphasis which he placed on the role of the laity, especially an educated laity, in the life of the Church. This aspiration of his, rooted in theology, reached fruition in the document on the Church and the Modern world (*Gaudium et Spes*) of that Council.

By the same token one might argue that Clifford was before his time and that he too would have felt at home at the later Council. For him it was the role of the Universal Episcopate that he was anxious to see safeguarded and enhanced, and his fear at Vatican I had been that the definition of Papal Infallibility – with so many questions like the issue

---

18   *Ibid.*

19   What exactly happened is described in the Introductory Note to *The Letters and Diaries of John Henry Newman* (ed. Dessain and Gornall), Vol. XXV, p. xv sqq.

20   Newman said his first Mass on the Feast of Corpus Christi (30.5.1847) in the Jesuit Chapel at Propaganda Fide in Rome. Sheridan Gilley, *Newman and His Age* (Publ. London, 1990), p. 252.

21   12.5.1879. Sheridan Gilley, *op. cit.*, p. 401.

of prior consultation, not even addressed, leave alone answered – might disturb that fine theological balance which exists between the chief bishop, the successor of Saint Peter, and the other bishops who are successors of the Apostles.

It is interesting to note that the influential *Clergy Review*, in the period leading up to the Second Vatican Council, published an article in which the writer made the same plea that Clifford had been making some ninety years before at Vatican I:

> The very important truth is that in the fundamental constitution of the Church, as revealed in scripture and apostolic tradition, the monarchical principle, as represented by papal supremacy and infallibility, co-exists – or, rather, is organically integrated – with the collegiate or episcopalist principle and with the *Sorbonost'* (fellowship, *koinonia*) principle. This fact, however, is to some extent obscured by the premature prorogation of the first Vatican Council owing to the outbreak of the Franco – Prussian War at the very moment when the Council was proceeding to define the place of the bishops in the Church. Legal definition has yet to catch up with fundamental theory. [22]

(While one must accept the main thrust of the argument just quoted, two reservations should be stated: The leadership of the Church in the early centuries must not be lost sight of, as witness the *Letter of Clement* to the Church at Corinth which is dated as early as A. D. 95. Secondly there appears to be no evidence that the bishops at Vatican I had any intention of defining their place in the Church – nor that Pius IX would have acceded to a request for a definition. In any case, such a definition would have to have been so lengthy and unwieldy as to have been practically impossible).

In the event the Bishops at Vatican II did state unequivocally their collegial role in the governance of the Church and in so doing vindicated Clifford in his plea that the primacy of Peter's successor be

---

22   The Rev. A.A. Stephenson, S.J. in an article entitled The Ecumenical Question (*The Clergy Review*, January, 1961, p. 9).

counterbalanced by a recognition of the non-delegated authority of the successors of the other Apostles. The speeches of Clifford at Vatican I foreshadowed *Christus Dominus* of Vatican II. [23]

Bishop Clifford had his shortcomings, though they appear to have been few. One was his handling of the allegation by Bishop Brown of Newport that he had had no right to dispose of the valuable *Hereford Missal*. His reply to Propaganda seems to place more emphasis on the expertise of William Maskell who had recognised the true value of the Missal than on his own right to dispose of the book, which was the point at issue. Again, Clifford appears a little too disingenuous when in 1865 Brown had complained that Clifford and Grant had no right to inform Rome that neither of them wished to be considered for the See of Westminster without having first consulted their brother bishops. After all, he argued, leadership of the Hierarchy was a matter which concerned them all. Clifford's reply was weak, his argument being that any bishop had the right to tell Rome whether or not he wished to be moved from his See. (see appendix 2, p. 470).

Clifford's contribution to English Catholic Church life was to be a voice of reassurance to the more liberal-minded Catholics particularly while Pius IX was Pope and Manning was at Westminster. This was a mantle that would be worn in later years by John Cuthbert Hedley, O.S.B. (Bishop of Newport and Menevia 1881 – 1915) and Louis Casartelli (Bishop of Salford 1903 – 1925). Clifford's articles in *The Dublin Review* which attracted so much national and international attention, and his activities locally as a member (and sometimes President) of Historical and Archeological Societies helped to dispel the suspicion, still prevalent in some quarters, that the Church of Rome was obscurantist and benighted by error. In Church politics he was eminently successful in his efforts to bring an end to the long-standing rift between regulars and seculars. *Romanos Pontifices*, while acknowledging the due rights of the regular clergy, was very much a 'bishops' document' and for this they owed much to William Clifford.

Wiseman, Manning and Newman in their different ways helped to mould the English Catholic Church of the second half of the nineteenth century. Behind them were two other figures – Clifford and Ullathorne – and it fell to them to build the bridges that would span the wide river of English Catholic thought and identity. The three Cardinals, and Ullathorne, have to varying degrees been well served by their respective biographers but, for some curious reason, no one has yet come forward to render the same service to WILLIAM JOSEPH HUGH CLIFFORD who was one of the ablest – and arguably the nicest [23] – of all the English prelates of the nineteenth century.

---

23   Cuthbert Butler, who knew Clifford, says that 'he was famous for his hearty uproarious laugh' (*The Life and Times of Bishop Ullathorne 1806 - 1889*, Vol. I, p. 237, footnote 1).

POSTSCRIPT

Much has happened in the twenty years that have elapsed since this study was first submitted as a dissertation for the degree of Doctor of Philosophy at King's College, London.

Two of the leading, but contrasting, figures who feature in the narrative of nineteenth century church politics – Pope Pius IX and Cardinal John Henry Newman – have been enrolled among the *beati* of the Catholic Church, the latter in the course of a memorable state visit to this country, made by Pope Benedict XVI in September, 2010. During the preceding period many books and studies appeared so as to bring the thoughts and achievements of this nineteenth century colossus to as wide an audience as possible.

Another close friend and confidant of Bishop Clifford – William Bernard Ullathorne – has been the subject of a much acclaimed biography, [1] while the wider background and context of the 150 years since the restoration of the Catholic Hierarchy has been described in *From Without the Flaminian Gate*. [2]

Fresh nuggets of information have emerged in the wholly engaging story of William Clifford. Pope Pius IX, for example, was not historically correct when he said, on the occasion of a deputation of Englishmen resident in the Papal States, that to his best knowledge and belief

> . . . he was the first pope since S. Gregory the Great who had consecrated with his own hands an English bishop . . . [3]

In fact, Stephen Langton, Archbishop of Canterbury (1207 – 1228) was consecrated bishop by Pope Innocent III at Viterbo, June 17th 1207. [4]

---

1   Judith Champ, *William Bernard Ullathorne (1806 - 1889): A Different Kind of Monk* (Leominster, 2006)

2   M. Hodgetts and V. A. McClelland (eds.), *From Without the Flaminian Gate* (London, 2000)

3   See text, pages 46 – 47 (Lord Clifford to his son, 28.2.1857)

4   A. E. McKilliam, *A Chronicle of the Archbishops of Canterbury* (London, 1913), p. 193

In a news item that has a certain modern ring about it, *The Universe* of Christmas Day 1869, informed its readers:

> The Bishop of Clifton has unfortunately lost all his luggage
> *en route* for Rome.

Clifford was travelling to take part in a General Council of the Church during which he was to argue strenuously for the rights of bishops – a theme very much championed by others a century later at Vatican II (1962 – 1965).

Today collegiality – 'Peter and the Eleven' – is a key element in contemporary Catholic thought. Indeed, hardly a week passes without criticism being aired at what is perceived to be the centralised power of the Vatican curia.

Others, however, see things differently, and in this there has surely been no character more colourful than Cardinal Silvio Oddi (1910 – 2001) –

> In 1964, when collegiality was being discussed at the Second
> Vatican Council, Archbishop Oddi quipped that he could find
> only one biblical citation supporting the notion – the
> occasion during Christ's passion when the apostles "all
> forsook him and fled".[5]

On Sunday, 10th November 2002, Bishop Declan Lang was installed as an ecumenical prebendary at Bristol Cathedral. Referring to Bishop Clifford by name, the Dean (Very Rev. Robert Grimley) spoke of the courage which had prompted the Bishop's Victorian predecessor to champion a cause that he believed in, despite its unpopularity at the time.

The unexpected reference was not lost on the congregation. Just six weeks before, Bishop Declan had presided at a service in Clifton Cathedral to celebrate the ministry of women. It was an ecumenical occasion during which the address was given by Dr. Margot Kässmann, the Evangelical Lutheran Bishop of Hannover.

---

5   *The Daily Telegraph*, 11.7.2001, obituary notice.

The event had caused not a few ripples, attracting such newspaper headlines as

Clifton Invites Woman Bishop To Cathedral

(*Catholic Herald*, 4.10.2002)

followed two weeks later by an article asking

Does He Or Doesn't He Support Women Priests?

(*Catholic Herald*, 18.10.2002)

Bishop Declan defended the decision he had taken. Quite apart, he said, from its main purpose to celebrate the ministry of women both through the family and through work, the occasion recognised that in some Christian traditions women are ordained as clergy. Hannover was twinned with the city of Bristol; the previous Lord Mayor had, through her chaplain, requested the service.

So the Dean of Bristol's message was clear: Bishop Clifford and Bishop Declan Lang were both men of an independent frame of mind and as such were to be applauded. [6]

At the end of the decade and in a radical proposal that took many by surprise, Pope Benedict XVI invited Anglicans and others unhappy about the liberal tendencies of their religious leaders to join the Catholic Church. It was a call to those who wished to retain their legitimate liturgical forms of worship ('patrimony') to act collectively and, with his approval, to become a canonical entity ('ordinariate') with one of their own, duly ordained, exercising episcopal oversight. *Anglicanorum Coetibus* (published November 2009) is still in process of taking shape in the diocese of Clifton, with many practical details yet to be finalised.

---

[6] In a similar vein, *The Guardian* newspaper had read into the 'unexpected strong conclusions' of the critical report of the panel set up by Bishop Mervyn Alexander to look into the Neo-Catechumenate in his diocese 'a direct challenge to the Vatican'. (8.11.1996)

The whole concept, however, though not new, inevitably gives rise to those 'what ifs?' of history – the reaction (no doubt favourable) of Bishop Clifford, Blessed John Henry Newman and, most of all, Ambrose de Lisle Phillipps, a man who so fervently espoused the cause of corporate reunion.

August 14th, 1993 marked the centenary of the death of Bishop Clifford. [7] Lord Clifford welcomed a suggestion that there be a special Mass at Buckfast Abbey, attended by members of the Clifford Association. The Abbot graciously agreed, and the Mass was celebrated by Bishop Mervyn Alexander of Clifton and other clergy using the chalice which had been given to the newly consecrated bishop by Pope Pius IX in 1857. A large congregation, a fine summer's day, the Gospel *'Thou art Peter'* (Matthew xvi) and homily – all conspired to celebrate with joy both the memory and the prophetic achievements of someone who in so many respects was ahead of his time.

---

7   Bishop Alexander also died on August 14th (2010).

THE FIRE AT PRIOR PARK (1836)
FROM A CONTEMPORARY LITHOGRAPH IN COLOUR

APPENDICES

I. **Correspondence**

II. Bishop Clifford's Addresses at the First Vatican Council

APPENDIX 1

Bishop Goss Complains to Bishop Clifford
About Cardinal Wiseman

- Meeting at Oscott would avoid the embarrassment of being the Card's guests.

  (*Goss Letter Book 15.2.1859 to 9.2.1861*, No. 453, dated 21.1.1861)

- By this post I send direct to Card. B. a Memorial from my Vic: Gen: complaining that he has been misrepresented to Prop. by Card. W. who pleads as an excuse for not giving him an opportunity of justifying himself that the letter was confidential.

  In the same letter he states of me and my clergy things which are not true. I have the letter he misrepresents copied not by hand, but by machine, which cannot err. It is too bad that Bishops should have to contend not only against his overwhelming influence, but against misrepresentation that on account of its secret character must generally remain hid . . .

  Mgr. Manning has sent me an explanation about some cards, but he much mistakes me if he thinks that such matters influence my opinion: I should not because I could not in conscience act differently if the Card: were yearly to present me with a hogshead of wine . . .

  I send you a Pastoral by book Post. Many thanks for yours: I am going to preach it on Sunday. I write freely & openly because confidentially.

  (*Goss Letter Book 1861 - 1865*, No. 278, dated 7.3.1862).

- . . . Our attitude [to Card. Wiseman] is entirely one of self-defence . . .

  (*Goss Letter Book 1861 - 1865*, No. 292, dated 21.3.1862).

•   . . . I have this morning received a summons to attend a meeting in Low Week, but I have no intention to go to London, yet before returning an answer will wait to see if any joint action is proposed. Our meetings have been too much absurd to consider it honourable to continue to attend them: for H.E. using the privilege of honour attends or absents himself at pleasure: then pleads the fact in Rome in mitigation. Besides before our last meeting I was assured that nothing affecting my feelings would be discussed, & I found an entire day taken up with a covert attack of my procuratorship . . .

(*Goss Letter Book 1861 - 1865*, No. 301, dated 16.4.1862. Liverpool Diocesan Archives).

APPENDIX 2

Bishop Brown Complains to Propaganda About the Joint Letter Sent by Clifford & Grant

Most eminent and worthy Lord Cardinal:

Because a meeting of the bishops cannot easily be summoned, each ['singuli'] of them has strongly urged me as the senior member to write this letter to you without delay and to ask Your Eminence kindly to lay before the Supreme Pontiff these tokens of the love and respect in which he is held by the Hierarchy which he himself restored.

These proofs will show to the Holy Father in the most suitable and fundamental way our common regard for him, the spirit of deep affection which we all have – and which in its turn is a source of comfort to us – and the homage of filial obedience which comes from the hearts of us all.

It was precisely these proofs of our obedience which we wished to demonstrate when we met in Birmingham to consider the three names to be put forward for the vacant Archbishopric. When the minutes of the meeting of the Westminster Chapter had been read, I asked "whether it would be right [lawful] for us to pass comment on the candidates?" Each of the bishops gave the same answer saying that on previous occasions the bishops believed that they should say nothing about those candidates who were already in episcopal orders and that the matter should be left to the judgement of their only superior, i.e. the Supreme Pontiff.

When, for example, there arose the question of proposing a Coadjutor for the Bishop of Beverley, the names of two priests were put forward together with that of the Bishop of Southwark. The bishops, and their chairman (Cardinal Wiseman), were in agreement that absolutely nothing should be said with regard to one who was both their colleague and equal. In like manner the example of the procedures followed by the Consistorial Congregation was quoted in which it was customary to mention the qualities of priests being considered for promotion to vacant sees, but on the other hand in the case of candidates who were already bishops reference was made to the testimonials drawn up at the time of their promotion to the episcopate. It also seemed right to us that we should leave the merits of the candidates to the careful consideration of the Supreme Pontiff, guided by the light of the Holy Spirit.

So complete was the agreement on this point that the Bishops of Southwark and Clifton should not have departed from it, nor should they have taken the liberty of discussing the merits of their colleagues. Afterwards these two bishops chose to send a letter to Your Eminence. In so doing they acted completely without our knowledge both in regard to their intention and the deed itself and we were only informed of it when we received a communication from the Holy Father.

From this sequence of events it will be clear to Your Eminence that the bishops – as they were aware – should have followed to the letter the precedent of previous meetings in which both Cardinal Wiseman and they themselves remained silent when the matter concerned a candidate already in episcopal orders; it will also be clear that we had no wish to favour, either actively or passively, any of the candidates; much less that our silence about all three – taken under religious obedience and faithfully and sincerely maintained ever since – should be construed as an ungracious gesture to the Supreme Pontiff on the grounds that no view was expressed on the Archbishop of Trebizond [Errington]. We wanted to leave the matter entirely to the judgement of the Pope who would appoint an archbishop who was not only suitable but would also enjoy the confidence of the Holy See. One thing only we seek and desire: that the Holy Father be convinced of the great devotion he enjoys among the bishops and clergy of England who have the utmost confidence in his wisdom and prudence and have not the slightest doubt that he will put in charge of this Province someone who is most suited to our times and whom we ourselves will welcome with the greatest respect.

28th April, 1865

[My translation from the Latin J.A.H.]

(Birmingham Archdiocesan Archives, copy of Bishop of Newport's complaint to Prop. Fide. B. 4329).

Note: The relevant part of Clifford's reply to Brown's accusation is printed in Chapter 6.

Bishop Brown of Shrewsbury to Bishop Brown of Newport on How He Views Either Manning or Talbot Being Appointed Archbishop of Westminster

Newport,
Salop April
24/65

My dear Lord,

. . . . .

I most sincerely hope that neither Talbot nor Manning will be appointed. We should not get on well with either. For my part, I feel no confidence in either – Talbot is a man of very limited mind and Manning essentially a schemer and [despotical?] – *Liverpool* would soon come out strong if either were named.

I was, and still am, of opinion that Dr. Clifford would be, all things considered, the best man – and I quite agree with you that he and Dr. Grant, should not have written to decline without letting us at least know that they intended to do so – Had they ascertained the wishes of their confreres perhaps they would have reconsidered their determination.

. . . . .

+ J. Brown

(Cardiff Archdiocesan Archives, Letter to Bp. Brown).

Letter From Mgr. John Bonomi. V.G. to Bishop Clifford Regarding His Alleged Silence Over Papal Infallibility

Clifton
Nov. 13. 1870

My dear Lord,

Having occasion to send you unopened letters from F. Larive & the Abbess of Woodchester I add a few lines, though, as I have told you, I am going to Bath tomorrow & I very possibly see you at Prior Park.

I have long had on my mind & conscience a matter that has given me great trouble on my own account and on account of the relations in which I stand towards you as your V.G. A recent circumstance as well as the approaching period for your Pastoral and also your own expressed intention of ordering a triduo for the Holy Father seem to compel me to address you on the subject in question. Your Lordship knows better than I can ever know, what were the reasonings & what were the causes of your opposition in Rome to the dogma of Infallibility. With all this of course I have nothing to do. What is now certain is that your name has been before the world and in the mouths of both Protestants & Catholics as one of the foremost amongst Bishops opposed at all events reluctant to refer in any way to the dogma & reticent on the subject in your public capacity as the Bishop of Clifton. To all this no doubt your Lordship will at once answer that it does not behove you to notice strictures of newspapers & writers of reviews in that every man in an official position must inevitably look forward in the course of his life to being misunderstood or misrepresented.

This I grant: but then another question far more serious arises, it appears to me, & that is, whether a Bishop ought not to illumine & clear up matters of doctrine for the souls of those who are under his immediate & direct guidance & for their sakes must he not speak out & be instant in season & out of season with the word of God.

Here then are the facts, my dear Lord. The Clergy of Your Lordship's Diocese with perhaps one or two exceptions believe explicitly in the dogma of Infallibility & the writings of Bishops & others convince them, that it does not require the signing of conciliar Decrees & closing of the Ecumenical Council to make the belief one as much *sub gravi* as the doctrine of the Trinity or any other dogma. The letter of Cardinal Antonelli which your Lordship circulated informs them of this, if even before, any of them had hesitated. By giving it to the Priests as their rule in the teaching of others both outwardly [and] *in foro conscientiae* yr Lordship has indicated to them in part at least your mind on the matter: but you have not I very humbly suggest, done this as completely or as openly in your words as you might have done.

Hence from the very beginning have arisen anxious inquiries, hesitation & doubty questions & controversies between the clergy & laity. From the very time you left Rome till now, I have been perpetually consulted & questioned about you. The clergy have urged me to speak to you & try & induce you to give them the consolation by some writing of your own on this very grave subject. It is not a matter that slumbers now; it is more than ever before us in proportion to the opposing assertions made perpetually about you. The foremost priests in the Diocese have entreated me to represent the affair to you – Canons Clarke & Parfitt, Fr. Sweeny, Fr. Worsley, Can. Maes & several others. Everyone says that in the confessional & out of it, they are perpetually asked what the Bishop believes & they declare that the letter of Cardinal Antonelli is not sufficient answer to the minds of the laity on the matter: they want to hear the Bishop's voice, to hear his own words & until you speak nobody will fully convince himself that your assent is hearty & sincere & that you may not have some mode of explaining away the doctrine as binding under pain of eternal loss.

I began by telling you that a recent circumstance operated as a further inducement to address you on this very serious point. It is this, the day the meeting was held at your house Frs. W & S came & asked to see me privately & the latter produced a letter he had received from Oxford from a person joining the Church there, who demands an answer in explicit terms whether Dr. Clifford Bishop of C. did or did not hold the dogma of Infallibility on the footing of all dogmas of the Church, or some words of the same purport. Of course if Fr. S. had had positive evidence from a pastoral or other public announcement that you did, it would have been losing time to ask me. I really could not tell him the precise state of your mind on the matter for I had noticed on two or three occasions that the subject was distasteful to you & that you had tried to avoid entering on it.

What I said to him was this: Fr. S. The Bishop I know has a high esteem for you & a very just opinion of your learning as a theologian & as a controversialist, Why not then ask him point blank yourself. I know from others that you have long regretted his silence, that you have been persuaded he ought to speak out, that the Catholics of the Diocese look for an expression of his Faith & in fine that his Bishop will treat with consideration & great forbearance anything that you might say to him.

To this Fr. S. replied, that if anyone, ought to know the mind of the Bishop & as a duty ought to address him it was his V.G., that whatever I said, he knew you would receive as from the proper source & would attend to.

Feeling very much embarrassed by his letter & (if I may judge) unhappy that you did not enlighten us & put in our mouths words of consolation to the inquirer & of conviction of your own Faith to the wary who now call it in question, he left my room. I then inwardly resolved, that I would try & induce your Lordship to say *something* at least in your forthcoming pastoral that would set all doubts at rest & give peace of mind & satisfaction to the laity as well as the Clergy; send for Fr. S. if you wish it & he will, I assure you tell you more than I have told you, or ask any of the Priests I have named, or if you fear, that I exaggerate, arrive at the truth on this subject with regard to the general feeling about you on the question of Infallibility.

If your Lordship ordains in a public Pastoral at this juncture a 3 days' prayer for the Pope, I don't see how you can avoid the question uppermost in men's minds & leave it quite unnoticed.

It is useless to add, which I am sure you will at once ascertain, that I have no other motive in writing to you but the motive of conscience & the duty I owe you, in the intimate official relations between us, & which to the best of my judgment directs every word I have placed before you.

Thinking you may not see *The Tablet* at Prior Park & would like to read in the supplement the Archbishop of Mayence's answer to Lord Acton I send it to you by this post. Everyone must be convinced by it of his faith & rejoice.

[No signature, presumably because it was a note forwarded with other items].

(Clifton Diocesan Archives, *Letters to Bishop Clifford*, Part I, 1854 – 1874).

Bishop Clifford's Reply to Mgr. Bonomi. V.G.

Nov. 17, 1870

My Dear Bonomi,

I have received your letter of the 13th inst[ant] in which you express to me the uneasiness caused in your mind & in that of several of the clergy of the diocese by my not publishing anything regarding the Infallibility of the Pope. You have done quite right in writing that letter. Personal friendship would of itself have justified your doing so, but in your position of Vicar general it is moreover natural that members of the clergy should wish to address to me through you questions which they may have a delicacy in putting personally to myself. Whilst therefore I have not thought it advisable to treat these matters in a pastoral, I have here stated for your information the chief motives which have influenced my line of action.

The decree of Papal infallibility asserts two things.

1st that the Pope is infallible "when he speaks *ex cathedra* i.e., defines matters relating to faith & morals in discharge of the office of Pastor and Doctor of all Christians".

2dly that he is under those circumstances infallible "in virtue not of the consent of the Church" but "of his supreme Apostolic authority, by reason of the divine assistance promised to him in B. Peter".

To speak first of the second of these propositions: A person in authority derives his powers either from a higher authority, or from the community itself over which he presides. St. Peter received his authority not from the Apostles but directly from Christ; hence the Pope his successor, derives his supreme authority both to rule and to teach, & so his infallibility, not from the consent of the Church but from Christ through St. Peter.

But the question further arises, not as to what is the source whence the Pope derives his authority to teach infallibly, but as to what are the circumstances in which the special assistance which preserves him from falling into error, has been promised to him; and more especially whether those circumstances comprise a previous research by some means or other not only into past traditions but into what is the actual teaching of the universal Church in the present day. Must the Pope, in order to ascertain the truth he wants to define, in some way or other, *uti adjutorio Ecclesiae?* That he has done so in times past (sometimes by means of general Councils, sometimes by consulting the Church scattered, and sometimes by other means) is stated in the decree; nor could it be said that on that account he derived his authority or infallibility from those councils or from the Church scattered, or from any other source than the divine assistance promised to him. But was this done from free choice, or was this necessary in order to insure that divine assistance without which his decisions would not have been infallible? The statement that the pope is infallible "*non ex consensu Ecclesiae*" does not touch this question, but so far leaves it open.

The circumstances in which, and in which alone, the promise of infallibility was made to St. Peter and his successors are laid down in the first of the two statements mentioned above. The Pope is said to be infallible when he speaks *ex cathedra* and this term is explained to mean, not only that the infallible decisions of the Pope are restricted to those cases where he "defines questions relating to faith and morals", but further still, to those, only when he is "teaching in discharge" of the Office of Pastor and Teacher of all Christians. Now when is he properly said to be discharging that office? Is it then only when he addresses himself *Urbi et orbi?* Does it comprise addresses to particular Churches regarding matters which effect the universal church? (as for example, the letter of Eugenius to the Bulgarians). The decree states that the commission given to the Pope is that of "expounding the revelation or deposit of Faith delivered through the Apostles". Can the Pope be said to be doing this, & so to be discharging the office of Pastor and teacher of all Christians if he omits to inform himself before hand as to what is the Deposit of faith held in the Universal Church?

The decree does not solve these questions, they may therefore still be considered as open. More than this: their right solution must depend in no small degree from that of two other questions still pending before the council, vis. 1st what is "that infallibility with which the divine Redeemer willed that His Church should be endowed for defining doctrine" and 2dly what is the real position of Bishops in the Church. For if the Bishops as successors of the Apostles are depositaries of the faith delivered to the Apostles, it could scarcely be said that the Pope is discharging the office of expounding that deposit, if he omits to inform himself beforehand concerning the teaching of those who are charged with the custody of the same. It would be otherwise if the Bishops derive their commission only indirectly from the Apostles through the Pope. Now a distinct promise was given to the Bishops that these two points should be treated immediately after the question of the Pope's infallibility had been settled. A Roman cardinal told me that he had voted Placet on the ground of this promise – and other bishops did the same. If the Council had met this winter these subjects would have been treated and now they are only postponed as the Council is only prorogued not closed.

Now do I not think it advisable for me to treat these subjects in an official manner, knowing as I do that many take a very different view of the meaning which aught [*sic*] to be attached to the decree. But especially I do not think it right to urge at this time explanations the correctness of which is dependent on the solutions of questions which are still pendent before the Council. I carefully guarded myself last year from giving any official statement of my views on the matters which it was then supposed might be treated in the council. I follow the same course now, until circumstances oblige me to act otherwise.

But there is a further reason why I refrain from treating

before the public questions connected with the Council. The Pope has published the decree on Infallibility, & I consciously bow to his authority. More than this: in the sense in which I have explained it, the decree presents to my mind no serious theological difficulty. But as regards the means made use of to secure the votes of the Bishops [" induce the Bishops to vote" crossed out], my opinion remains unaltered. Dr. Ullathorne in his pastoral gives a very favourable description of the Council. With some of his statements I cannot ["fully" crossed out] agree but it is not so much to his statements as to his omissions that I object ["with what he omits that I find fault" crossed out]. I can neither banish from my mind nor ignore the immense pressure put on so many Bishops who were wholly dependant [*sic*] on the Pope. [The following crossed out: "This is a matter which is partly public though not to its full extent. Many bishops have signified to me and to others that they dare not vote as they wished as their bread or position depended on it. Others that for this reason they declined to consider the question on its merits, & simply voted as they were told. Of those that voted in the minority more than one said he did so knowing how dear it would cost him. That these fears were not in vain is shown by the fact that one Bishop at least has been punished for his vote"].

The fear expressed by so many bishops both to me and to others of what would be the consequences to them of giving a vote not pleasing to the Pope were not without foundation. Even since the Council one bishop at least has lost his place by his vote. The way Cardinal Guidi was treated, simply for expressing his views freely but most temperately in Council, was sufficient to deter any ordinary Italian or Eastern bishop dependent on the Pope, from incuring [*sic*] the Pope's displeasure by an adverse vote. [The following crossed out: "I cannot help feeling that such things must have a most serious bearing on the question of the liberty of the Council"]. I know what verdict Englishmen would give ["concerning similar practices at" crossed out] if it were a question of voting at a parliamentary election. To what extent this may affect the liberty of the Council I do not

pretend to say; but it certainly prevent [*sic*] my speaking of
the Council in the only way I should wish to speak of it. I have
not written this for publication but you may make use of it to
answer those who have made the inquiries you write about.

I remain

My Dear Bonomi,

Yours most sincerely,

+ William Clifford

Note: This text, with its important deletions, is taken from F. J.
Cwiekowski, *The English Bishops and the First Vatican Council* (Publ.
Louvain, 1971), pages 298 – 301. The author says in a footnote on page
301 that the original is in the *Clifford File of Letters* (Part I) in the
Clifton Diocesan Archives. Sadly what is there now is the final text (in
Clifford's hand) as sent to Bonomi. [J.A.H.]

On reading this exchange of letters between Bonomi and Clifford,
Cuthbert Butler wrote to Bishop Burton:

Ealing Priory,

London W.5

2 Apr. '28

My Dear Lord

I return with grateful thanks the letters of Bonomi &
Clifford. The latter is of especial interest as manifesting the
mentality of the Minority, which has been misrepresented by
the extremists on both sides, notably by Quirinus.

There are some very interesting letters illustrating same
point from Moriarty of Kerry to Newman – & of Clifford to
Newman . . .

E. C. Butler

Note: When Butler sent this letter he was still writing his *Vatican Council*. Yet he chose to ignore Clifford's central point about the pressure brought to bear on the Bishops. [J.A.H.]

On the Life and Discipline of the Clergy (3.2.1870) (Bishop Clifford's Address at the Vatican Council)

Most eminent cardinals, most reverend fathers:

In this council, we must deal with the subject of the life and morals of the clergy both on account of the grave reasons put forward by other fathers and also because it is expressly stated by the Supreme Pontiff in the bull convoking this council that we must deal with questions relating to the discipline of the clergy, secular and regular. But in my view what we must bear in mind above all else is that we are meeting in a general council – not a provincial council, still less in a diocesan synod. Therefore the laws which we pass must be such as to pertain to the universal church or else principles from which particular [local] churches may derive their laws. Therefore it seems to me that things which have been said by many of the fathers, though excellent in themselves, are not in any way appropriate to what should be said in this council.

For example: it is fine to praise in general terms [the importance of] spiritual exercises; but to pass laws about 'when' or 'how much' or 'in what manner' is not for us to do: and if we try to do so, we may well do more harm than good. Thus, for example, some have said that we must prohibit priests from practising medicine. In general this is true, but there are seminaries, founded with the authority of the Pope for the work of the foreign missions, in which priests are very definitely taught the principles of medicine because this is necessary for them in their missions. And do we wish to pass a law which would go against this arrangement?

Again, what has been said about cohabitation with women: we know well what is the mind of the church on this subject; we know that bishops must be most vigilant in passing laws about this matter in their dioceses. But if the most reverend fathers think that, once a law has been passed prohibiting a priest from having anyone except men in his house, this of itself guarantees the good name of the priest, I know for certain that this is not the case. For it often happens that much greater scandals and more serious difficulties arise from the fact of young people (either married or unmarried) living in the houses of priests than if there were living in the house a woman who was respectable and well known among those people where the priest, too, was living. And I am sure that in England, where parents often send their daughters to schools run by Catholics, they would not do so if they were aware that in the priest's house there were also living ordinary young people who looked after the priest.

What has been said by others about passing a law regarding bigger and richer benefices: I for one was full of admiration when I heard these things. For I ask myself where nowadays are such richer benefices to be found? If there is any such abuse still in the church, then our enemies will do us a service; for they have put their finger on all these 'desirable' things and, *pace* the Bishop of the Canary Islands, in our times it would be difficult to find a golden apple even in the Hesperides. were we to pass such a law, I think it would appear more of a harsh irony than a paternal correction. Therefore my wish is that the laws we pass should not go into such detail.

But especially I should like to underline what the most reverend the Archbishop of Strigonia has said about the preface with regard to the dignity of the clergy, both on account of the very compelling reasons which he put forward and also because, in these times, it is very necessary both for the clergy and for the people. The fashion grew up of speaking of the *secular* clergy; so much so that often both priests and people think that priests belong to this world and that they are not called to the inheritance of the Lord, not called to perfection. It is wholly necessary, and part of the duty of this Council, that priests and people be educated regarding the dignity, the holiness and the perfection of that office.

Another matter which His Excellency the Primate touched upon and which today is of very great importance for the whole church; the question of incorrigible priests. It is now a very great evil in the Catholic Church, and it is getting worse from day to day, for now we do not have the power of forcing such priests by secular means; and so these, wearing the priestly garb, wander amongst the people as priests to the great detriment of the people. The most excellent primate has said that such men should be expelled from the ranks of the clergy. I am absolutely certain in my own mind that the ancient discipline should be restored. If bad monks are expelled from a monastery, why shouldn't bad priests be expelled from the clergy? Most reverend fathers, what is worse is that if a bad monk, who is a priest, is expelled from his monastery, he does not join the ranks of the laity but the ranks of the secular clergy, and so we are left carrying not only our own ills but also the ills of others.

In places in our own country, England, and I believe it is also the case in Ireland and in America and elsewhere, there is another serious evil which arises from the same cause. You know that among us there are no benefices for clerics; that the clergy are maintained by the diocese, by the bishop, either because the cleric is given charge of a community of people, or a part of such, who maintain him by their offerings, or else by the offerings of the faithful which are handed to the bishop for the good of the diocese: he must maintain his clergy. Now it is not a rare occurrence, for example in England, for a congregation of people in a small town where there are twenty, thirty or fifty Catholics: they cannot by themselves maintain a priest and so they go without the Mass and every help of religion because often they are some thirty, forty, fifty or even more miles distant from the nearest Catholic priest. These people come to the bishop and say: we cannot do everything but we will do what we can: if you will give us half the money to support a priest we will find the other half. And what is the bishop forced to answer? I would agree willingly except for the fact that I have two or three priests who are suspended. The bad

belong to the clergy, and because we are clerics you will not
permit us to do manual work and so provide for ourselves.
The bishop must maintain these bad priests, and because he
has to do so from the offerings of the faithful, must he leave
all those good Catholics without Mass and without all the
helps of religion? Certainly this is an abuse which should be
completely removed.

I say that when a priest, after many attempts at correction
does not reform, then, after due process of law, he should be
expelled from the ranks of the clergy, should be regarded as
completely secularised, should be allowed to earn his living
in any honest manner but that he should no longer belong to
the clerical state: in no way should he again exercise the
office and ministry of priest: he would be freed from office.
If he wishes to lead an honest life amongst the laity, then let
him do so: if not, then so much the worse for him. But we
must not deprive such good Catholics of the means of
religion merely because he wishes to lead an evil life. And
let us also prohibit other bishops from readmitting such a
priest to the clerical state once he has been expelled from it.

There is another matter which affects the universal church
and which seems to me to be of great importance and that is
the question of the *Missa pro Populo*. You are aware that
from a decree of the Council of Trent all parish priests and
those who have the cure of souls must offer a mass for the
people on each Sunday and feast day. At the time of the
Council of Trent there were omissions as there are now, and
so those who were bound to offer mass for the people were
bishops and parish priests: but now the situation is
different. In a great part of the Church people receive the
sacraments from missionaries, from men who administer
'parish sacraments' but do not have the 'cure of souls' in the
sense in which that term is used in canon law. And so it
happened that when recourse was had to the Sacred
Congregation, the reply came back that these missionaries
are not bound '*ex justitia*' to say the mass for the people on
feast days. I am not calling into question the decision of the
Sacred Congregation: it gave a correct decision because

that indeed is the law; but t am asking that it be decided according to the mind of the Council of Trent what the people and clergy hold, namely, that all who have the cure of souls, whether they be parish priests in the proper sense or missionaries who do the work of parish priests and are maintained either by the bishop or by the people, have the duty of saying mass for the people on Sundays and feast days. For this was in fact the mind of the Council of Trent when it decreed that parish priests should do this because in those days no one had the cure of souls except parish priests.

And certainly even amongst ourselves there has been no little scandal from the decree which we published in which it is stated that priests amongst us are not bound to offer Mass for the people: a scandal to both priests and people – to priests because they feel that this is the natural duty of those who have the cure of souls that they should offer Mass for the people, and to people because, when they expect this of their priests, it is difficult to explain that they are not bound in places where the Catholic religion is established and where (if anything) the people give greater support to their clergy than elsewhere. It would therefore be right to have a general law which said that whenever a priest is given the charge of souls by a bishop, in whatever sense this might be, and where he administers the 'parish sacraments', then such a priest should be bound to offer Mass for the people.

Now let me speak briefly about the breviary. It is right that priests should be enjoined to recite the breviary. But, as many fathers have said, we really must call for the setting up of a commission to revise the breviary. The first reason can be gathered from the very words of the bull summoning this council where it is expressly stated: 'In this ecumenical council all those things which are especially concerned with the dignity of divine worship are to be submitted to a most thorough examination with the purpose of making decisions about them'. Now nothing contributes greater dignity to divine worship than the offering of Holy Mass and the

recitation of the canonical hours. And indeed if we do
nothing about it during this council, then I do not see what
we can do to give effect to these words in the bull which
summoned us; I do not see how we can decide anything
effective with regard to divine worship unless we do
something about the divine office.

We have heard a great deal from prelates concerning both
bishops and clergy regarding meditation, prayer, the
frequency of spiritual reading, and the like. All these things
are excellent: but I say, has not the Church from ancient
times given us a breviary precisely to meet this need which
on the one hand we commend to our priests so that they
may do all these things, and yet on the other we give them
the sort of book which prevents them from doing precisely
that? And we hear priests sometimes saying: I must say it
quickly otherwise I shall have no time for prayer. How is
this? Is not that the very prayer which the Church has
given you? Is it not true that from the most ancient times,
even in the Old Law and much more in the New, the psalter
was the treasure-house for all prayer? Do we not read in
the lives of the saints that when someone wished to
advance in the spiritual life, the first requirement was that
he should be able to recite the psalter by heart? And
indeed we have been given the whole psalter printed in our
breviary, but in practice no one ever recites the psalter
during the course of a year.

Certainly this is a matter we should take a stand on, and if
we want our priests to pray, to read the sacred scriptures
and to know how to meditate, to know the lives of the saints,
then we must put into their hands a book which is so
ordered that they can recite the psalter each week, and so
arranged that, without repetitions, they can do it with ease.
If we do this then it is most certain that within a year of
ordination, or at the most two years, all priests will know
the psalter by heart: and this would be of greater assistance
to them in prayer and meditation than any other means that
we might provide. If the scriptures were to be so arranged in
the breviary that priests would read the whole bible within

a year, then they would know the scriptures, and by this means it would become of great assistance to them in prayer, meditation, spiritual reading and in their preaching. I strongly urge, therefore, that we desire the Holy Father to set up a commission for the revision of the breviary so that it may truly fulfil the purpose for which it was put into the hands of priests.

There is another matter which pertains to the whole Church: the title of ordination to the priesthood. I am not referring here to the title of poverty because this refers to the regular clergy; but the secular clergy are ordained with the title either of patrimony or of benefice or of mission. The title of mission was established originally for the Chinese, and then gradually it was given to all missionary areas in the Church; and now a considerable part of the clergy of the whole world is ordained with the title of mission. This title of mission is not understood in the same way in all countries: some bishops can ordain a certain number of priests with the title of mission; others have permission to ordain for a certain period from their consecration. I hear different things from different places. But what I wish to point out is this that those who are ordained *titulo missionis* are not ordained by virtue of the ordinary law but only by apostolic dispensation. It follows, therefore, that in a great part of the Church where hierarchies have been properly constituted the bishop nevertheless has no right with regard to the ordination of his own clergy. This certainly is a considerable anomaly.

For if any duty pertains to the office of bishop it must surely be that of providing his own clergy, and it must appear as a very great anomaly that even where hierarchies have been properly constituted, a bishop still has no right to ordain clergy except with permission. It might be argued that because a man is ordained *titulo missionis* he does not have a benefice with the result that a bishop must take upon himself the responsibility of supporting all such clerics. It could happen that a bishop because of misfortune ['*iniuriam*'] or some other reason might ordain *titulo missionis* more priests than the church could support and so do injury to others who would not be ordained because his diocese would not have sufficient means to support them. But if some such danger were to arise, I would like to see an arrangement which would require provincial synods to decide how many priests a bishop might prudently ordain in one of the dioceses of the province; and when such a decree of the provincial synod had the approval of the Holy See then a bishop would have the power to ordain his clergy '*de iure ordinario*'.

Several bishops, especially the Cardinal of Seville, the Bishop of Savannah, the Bishop of Augustanus [Augsberg?] and others have requested that no mention be made in this council on the subject of clergy living in concubinage. I wholeheartedly agree with their request because, most reverend fathers, it is impossible – as you will appreciate – to imagine what harm would be done in Protestant areas if within a month of the publication of this council – the proceedings of this council will be published not only in Latin but also in the vernacular and will be available in the homes of Catholics and Protestants alike and will be read not only by grown men but also by young girls – it becomes apparent to everyone that the General Council had to consider and deliberate upon this great evil in the Church, namely that of priests living in concubinage. I have no doubt that the scandal will be immense; that many Protestant fathers and husbands would henceforth prevent their wives and daughters from going to Confession as soon as they saw this being given publicity in the Council.

Besides, I do not know what good it would achieve. I cannot deny that in some parts of the Church it is a great evil. But bishops from those areas tell us that this is not due to any defect in the law [i.e. the laws of the Church], but because the civil authorities favour such priests and prevent the bishops from applying the ecclesiastical laws against them. To what purpose do you pass many laws? If these authorities prevent the enforcement of laws that already exist, then they will do the same with any new legislation.

Now if a law does seem necessary – which certainly I am not sure about, now that I have heard what many of the bishops from those places have said – but if it is necessary to have some formula, though not strictly legal, so that bishops can deal with the cases of these men: I most earnestly request that we do not publish a law dealing with priests living in concubinage, but that the title should be *Concerning Serious Offences Committed by Priests*. For if in treating of priests living in concubinage can also be the occasion for dealing with priests who are drunk or guilty of similar offences, it would be much better to speak in general terms about the more serious offences committed by priests than if one should read in our proceedings something specifically on the subject of priests living in concubinage.

Till now, most reverend fathers, I have spoken about some specific matters: now I wish to turn my attention to the schema in general; but I confess that this seems to me – as to you – altogether impossible. There are three sections of this schema *On the Life and Good Name of the Clergy*: if I were to examine everything that is here it would be impossible to judge whether what has to be added comes under these headings or not. I most earnestly beg that, if possible, we be given, if not an index of everything we are examining, then at least a schema of one subject ['*materia*'] with an index of all the matters relating to that subject.

I admit that it is impossible for anyone judging this to say whether he approves of the schema or whether in his opinion it has been well put together; because it is impossible for him to say whether the part of the schema which he knows fits in with those things which he does not know. And now, most reverend fathers, I am afraid lest you will say to me that I have kept the best wine till now. For, without doubt, what I am now about to say is of greater importance than what I have said already. It is something which concerns us all and I desire to say those things which I must say in the sight of God, and with the greatest respect first of all to the most reverend presidents and secondly to the rest of you.

A general Council (this is of Catholic faith) can be convened only by the Supreme Pontiff; to the Pope also it belongs to decide the way in which we deal with matters in the Council. This the Holy Father has done first through the Bull which convened the Council and secondly through the Constitution *Multiplices inter*. If we are able to speak in this Council, if our decrees have any force at all, it is only in so far as they are in accord with what is contained in this constitution. None of us has any right to propose, to discuss or to decide anything in any other way from that which is set forth in this constitution. And this is entirely necessary for the authority of the Pope himself; because if we act in any other way we shall be doing so contrary to that obedience which is due to our head: but it is also entirely necessary on account of the rights of bishops, because if we act in any way different from what is said here we offend the rights of our brothers in the episcopate. It is for this reason that I say that if in our deliberations we act in any other way from that which has been laid down in this constitution, not only do we offend against the rules ['*contra formas*'] but, precisely because these rules were laid down to protect the rights both of the Supreme Pontiff and of ourselves, we would be wrong in essentials: and sooner or later people would be calling into question the validity and authority of our proceedings unless we act strictly in accordance with that constitution.

Having said this, I must now say that I have been studying this constitution very closely; and it appears certain to me that we are acting contrary to what we have been instructed. I wish to put my difficulty clearly before you and then you, most eminent presidents, will decide whether what I say is right or not. Chapter VII of this constitution deals with general congregations of the bishops, and in particular on page 12 it is laid down how we should act. The Supreme Pontiff puts forward three cases or hypotheses and instructs us as to how we should conduct ourselves in each case.

The first is this: "Moreover, if in a congregation a schema is brought forward which presents either no difficulty or only such as could easily be dealt with at the meeting, then, without further delay, once the differences have been settled and the votes of the fathers taken, let the formula of the decree or conciliar canon in question be decided." Here the Holy Father puts forward a case where the proposed schema can give rise to slight difficulties to the fathers. Therefore the first thing to be done, before proceeding further, is to ascertain whether the fathers regard the difficulties as serious or slight.

Over many days now we have heard more than twenty addresses, we have heard of the difficulties of this or that bishop; but whether the fathers believe these difficulties to be grave or light, I certainly do not know nor do any of you. Now this first arose when the Holy Father asked of us that we should ascertain whether the difficulties were serious or not. If they are not serious, then we are not allowed, nor do we have the right, to send them to a deputation, but it is very much enjoined upon us that, when our discussions have been resolved – therefore there must be *some* discussion – concerning these minor difficulties, we take the votes of the fathers in that very congregation. When such a situation obtains, there is no provision made for us to send these difficulties to a deputation.

But there is a second case: "But if difficulties arise about the schema which are such that, when opposing points of view have been debated, there is still no way in which the difficulties can be resolved at that meeting, then the following procedure is to be adopted". Here it is assumed that the difficulties are of a more serious nature. Therefore, before we proceed any further, it is necessary to know whether the difficulties which are put forward are seen by the fathers to be serious or only slight. This must be determined before we can proceed any further. Then, once we know this, we are instructed that "where difficulties are such that when opposing points of view have been debated, etc.". There must therefore be a conflict of views. We must know what the fathers think on one side and what others think on the other because it states quite clearly that we must not act unless the contrary views have been discussed. Furthermore, under the same heading it is repeated that in such a case a third mode of proceeding is to be followed. In other words when it happens that the question about the proposed schema cannot be resolved. In such a case, what are we directed to do? Before we have recourse to outside means, we must try all means within the congregation itself to resolve the difficulty. Now, as I have said, we know nothing about what the fathers think: whether the difficulties are great or whether they are slight – we have no means of knowing the nature of these difficulties. And not only do we have no means of knowing this before the schema is handed over to the deputation, we do not even have the means whereby we can make an attempt to see whether the difficulties can be resolved in this congregation.

All these things are required of us in this congregation in the decree of our most Holy Father and Lord. And yet we are not doing a single one. We have long dissertations, some relevant, some not: but concerning the views of the fathers on these matters we know nothing.

Finally, in the third place, the Holy Father says: "If it should happen – when someone speaks thus he is certainly referring to an extreme, not an ordinary, case – as we indicated above, that in a general congregation there arises a question about a proposed schema which cannot be resolved, then the cardinal presidents of that same congregation – what are they to do? – they are to ensure that the schema etc."[is followed] as [provided for] in the constitution *Multiplices inter*. It is understood therefore that after we have found it impossible to resolve our differences, then we must not send to the deputation all the speeches that have been read in this aula, but that we do send to the deputation the schema and those difficulties that we could not resolve. Now if this is the case then I say that we have done none of these things and that we are in very grave danger of people saying, and of everyone saying, that what we are doing is not in accordance with what the Supreme Pontiff has laid down and that as a result our decrees will be null.

I have spoken only for conscience's sake. I beg you, most eminent presidents and most reverend fathers that, if there is anything which I may have unwittingly said which could injure the dignity and very great reverence which I have towards you and all my brothers, you sincerely forgive me.

(*Mansi*, Tomus 50, Col. 602 *sqq*. My translation).

APPENDIX 7

On the Universal Small Catechism (15.2.1870)
(Bishop Clifford's Address at the Vatican Council)

Most eminent presidents and most reverend fathers:

From what is proposed in the schema and from what has been said by the other fathers, two things are clear –

First, that there is something amiss, a definite harm in the Church which it is our desire to remove; secondly, a method or way has been put before us whereby we can rid ourselves of this evil. In order therefore to enable us to evaluate these statements correctly, it is essential that we know precisely what this evil is which we wish to correct, and then we must consider whether the remedies which are being suggested are in fact suited to ensure the removal of that evil.

To be sure, the evil under consideration is not a false or dangerous or uncertain doctrine which might be being taught in the Church. This is neither implied in the schema nor have the fathers said as much, except perhaps the Bishop of Carcassonne who has just put before you something about Jansenism in the Church which I, for my part, do not think you will find taught nowadays in any catechism approved by Church authorities. Therefore our duty is not one of dealing with some false or doubtful or dangerous teaching which might be taught in the Church – this is not the evil for which we are being asked to find a remedy. Nor is it a question of negligence either on the part of parish priests or of bishops in the way in which Christian doctrine is being taught. But the evil to which many fathers have drawn attention and which really exists – as we have learned both from their speeches and from private conversations with them – is that often in the same country, amongst people speaking the same language, often indeed in the same diocese, the small catechisms are being altered, quite easily, between the death of one bishop and the appointment of his successor.

The result is that Christians passing from one part of the same kingdom or province to another find that their sons and daughters are being asked to learn new forms of the catechism. Indeed this problem, which undoubtedly exists in the Church, will, from the nature of things, increase with each passing day as communications become more easy, with the result that we shall become all the more conscious of its existence. And so if we can find a remedy whereby we may be able to forestall this problem then it will certainly be a worthwhile task for this council.

But now I come to the remedy which has been proposed, and I must confess that I do not find it at all appropriate. There are two proposals. The first is 'to remove for the future all types of small catechisms'. In other words, it is being suggested that in the first instance catechisms now in use in the Church – catechisms, mark you, not of false but of solid doctrine by which Christian people have till now been instructed – that, at a stroke, all these catechisms be abandoned. Secondly, it is proposed that another catechism be put in their place. It is not being suggested that we adopt the catechism of Bellarmine; only that we have something along the lines of Bellarmine.

I would doubt whether there has ever been in the Church a proposal which so affected the lives of individuals as the removal of the catechisms now in use in the Church. Some catechisms are of but recent origin, but there are others which are held in the greatest esteem among various nations and peoples. For simple folk the catechism is their very religion. They know nothing of their religion except that which they have learned from the catechism, and so, if we all too lightly destroy all the catechisms of proven worth throughout the Church, we shall not avoid causing scandal and harm to many people.

But what is the other proposal? It is being suggested that another catechism be put together for use in the whole Church. The authors of the schema do not say that we should take one of the better catechisms that have so far

appeared and put that to universal use. But by the very
fact of their having made up their minds that a new
catechism was necessary, they are admitting that three
centuries of labour by men so learned, so holy and so
practical – that all their efforts have not been sufficient so
as to enable us now to put a catechism before the
Universal Church for the use of young children. For if one
of the catechisms by Bellarmine, or Canisius, or by some
other learned individual, had appeared to them to be ideal
for use as a small catechism throughout the Universal
Church, then surely they would have put forward such a
catechism. With the same breath we are told that what
those learned men, for three centuries up to the present
day, were unable to do is now to be achieved within a
matter of months by some commission.

I admit that I am familiar with the writings of Canisius, of
Bellarmine and of others in this field, but I am not going to
say whether it might be possible to adapt one of these
catechisms for use throughout the world. But this I certainly
know that if these men who were so learned and so practical
– and after so much effort – were unable to produce a
catechism as would win the approval of all the bishops here,
then certainly I believe I am doing no one an injustice if I say
(although I do not believe) that if there is anyone who can,
in the absence of all others, produce a catechism then let
him prove himself to all of us present here. At least there is
no such catechism available to us at the moment. But we are
being asked to vote on a proposal which calls for the
abolition of all catechisms so far produced, and yet in fact
we do not know, we do not see, nor can we judge what sort
of catechism would suffice to take their place.

Many reasons have been given by the fathers showing how
difficult it is to compose a catechism that would suit people
everywhere. I do not wish to repeat what has already been
said, but I will add two points which seem to me to be very
necessary at this particular time. The first is this: the wise
legislator is one who always keeps that which is good, that
which is perfect in a state of perfection, but who eliminates,

effectively and to the very root, only those things which in themselves are bad. In our own day Reformers have always followed a rule whereby, when they wish to introduce changes among the people, they invariably first destroy what is already there, and then, having achieved a '*tabula rasa*', they then proceed to put new laws and new institutions before the people. I do not believe that it behoves us to imitate them: better rather that we improve on what we already have than to destroy it only to embark on what is uncertain.

I take my second point from the circumstances of the present time. You will have noticed how everyone speaks of our Council – you know how we read about it every day. The objection has been made to us by Protestants and by others, namely that the purpose of the Council is to establish a new religion in place of the old. Daily this is what we hear, and not only ourselves but the people even more so, and I do not believe we could give greater credence to this idea than if we were to change all the catechisms throughout the world. However, I do not want you to think, fathers, that I am averse to achieving some sort of unity, as far as that is possible, in the way we teach the Christian faith. My great desire is that this unity be introduced, not forced or pushed, but that things proceed naturally as of themselves, and that they grow in the same way. You cannot present a doctrine in such a way that it suits everyone. But we can first of all, now and to a large extent, provide a remedy (as I said at the beginning) for those evils which are gaining ground in the same province: we can certainly urge provincial councils to strive prudently to ensure that unity be achieved by a gradual process whereby the same doctrine is taught through the use of identical terms. But it is my wish that we not only exhort the fathers to do this, but that we also provide them with a sort of guide as to how to proceed – a model only, which it would not be our intention to impose.

The model to be proposed could be taken from the heritage of the Church which we undoubtedly possess. The Catechism of the Venerable Cardinal Bellarmine is not one that I would wish to suggest as such a model. Of course the name Bellarmine, both as theologian and as the author of books of controversy, is held in the highest esteem not only in Europe but throughout the world. However, there can be no doubt either that the teaching of Bellarmine was not widely held [*non in multis regionibus evasit communis*] for the simple reason that it is more suited to local conditions than to the Universal Church.

On the other hand, since the time of the Council of Trent Blessed Canisius has written for this express purpose and in fact gave his whole life to this one aim: to produce an exposition of Christian doctrine – first, a simple outline for young children, then something more advanced for use in schools, and finally a major work for those who are more widely read. He first published this catechism in 1554 [1] and, through the Roman Emperor King Ferdinand I, it was made obligatory throughout the whole of Germany. And I would draw your attention to the fact that the [catechisms of] Christian doctrine which were later to be drawn up, not only in Germany but also in England and in many other parts, always used as a foundation this exposition of Christian doctrine by Father Canisius.

But this is not all. Before scarcely fifty years had elapsed since he had drawn up his catechism, translations had been made of the advanced, large, and small catechisms into all the languages throughout the world, so much so that in 1615 (to quote Matthew Rader [2]) Canisius himself could be said to speak in nearly every tongue – German, Slovac, Italian, French, Spanish, Polish, Greek, British [*Brittanica*], Scottish, Ethiopian and – as I have learned from members of my household – Indian and Japanese.

---

1   Brodrick puts it at the Spring of 1555 (*op. cit.*, p. 234).

2   The name is omitted in *Mansi* because at this point Clifford was inaudible to the scribe. It is clear, however, that he was citing Rader whom Brodrick later quoted when making the same point.

It was translated into English by Father Garnet who shed his blood for Christ; this doctrine was in use in his time for teaching the catechism. During his life Canisius wrote a very brief summary for young children, and this whole exposition of the Faith appeared in four different forms: first of all, an extremely brief account for the very young; secondly, one for everyone but in which the creeds and signs and symbols which are used in teaching are introduced; thirdly, for the use of those young people who have some familiarity with scholastic thought; and finally, a complete work which the more erudite would have at their disposal.

Most reverend fathers, let me repeat what I have said already: I mean no disrespect to the way things are taught at the present time, but I do believe it to be impossible for anyone to put together an exposition of Christian doctrine which would win such universal approval, and be embraced by everyone – even before it had received the approbation of the Church – in the same way as this teaching of Father Canisius was welcomed.

In order therefore to serve the interests of unity of teaching, as far as I am able, my proposal is not that we should ban all catechisms now in use, but rather that provincial councils be especially urged to take a close look at the question of how to achieve unity in the teaching of doctrine in their provinces. Then I would suggest that this book of Christian doctrine by Father Canisius be presented to everyone as a norm, a model which has the approval of this Council, a book which in fact expresses in an ideal way the teaching of Holy Church. I am certain that in many areas the bishops will adopt it because it is written with such simplicity and brevity; and even in those places where it is not adopted, they will nevertheless take those brief definitions of the sacraments which are to be found in Canisius with the result that from now on we shall have them described in the same way. Furthermore, we would always have them ready to hand when Protestants and Catholics start asking us questions about the precise teaching of the Church.

This seems to me something practical which can be done. If, on the other hand, we set about composing something which is new and which we then try to impose on everybody, we shall indeed be destroying that which we have which is old but without producing something that will truly stand the test of time.

[My translation].

(*Mansi*, Tomus 50, Col. 769 *sqq.*)

The Constitution on the Catholic Faith (24.3.1870)
(Bishop Clifford's Address at the Vatican Council)

Most Eminent Presidents, Most Eminent and Most Reverend Fathers: The greater part of what I wished to say has been so clearly stated by the Bishop of Birmingham that there is nothing that I wish to add apart from an observation about the same phrase which I submit to your wise consideration.

It should be noted that in our second session, we made our profession of faith in the following words: "I affirm that the power of indulgences was granted by Christ to His Church and that their use is of the greatest benefit to Christians". This statement refers to the Church spread throughout the world. Then immediately we added: "I acknowledge the Holy Catholic and Apostolic Roman Church to be the mother and teacher of all churches". This statement refers to the particular church of the City of Rome.

However, one should notice that in the [printed] Acts of this Council these words which I have just quoted will be found as almost the last words spoken in the Second Session, to be followed immediately by headings relating to those matters discussed in the Third Session where we shall have these words: *The Holy and Apostolic Roman Church thus decrees* . . . It seems to me that readers will come to one of two conclusions: on the one hand that those words are to be taken in the first sense as explained in the final part of the Second Session, namely for a particular church – the Roman Church – in which case the sense of this first chapter would be that we are describing the faith of the Roman Church which is the mother and teacher of all the churches and that we are not speaking of the Church spread all over the world.

If, on the other hand, we say that the words "the Church, Catholic and Roman" are to be taken to refer to the Church spread throughout the world, then they will say that within the space of two pages, and without any explanation or note, we have used the expression in two senses.

I am therefore of the opinion that if we are to speak not only correctly but also in an ordered fashion, it would be better if in this first chapter we were to speak after the manner of the Council of Trent: the Holy Catholic Church teaches ... If later in the schema on the Church – when it is expressly dealing with the Church – those things be described which we hold concerning the Holy Roman Church, let us state clearly that not only is it the teacher and mother of churches, but that this term *ROMANA* should rightly be seen as a sort of *TESSERA* by which particular churches throughout the world can prove their catholicity, so much so that by this one fact of a particular church being in communion with the Church of Rome it is proved to be also in communion with the Catholic Church. Conversely, whatever society is shown not to be in union with the Roman Church, it is *ipso facto* proved not to be in communion with the Catholic Church.

(*Mansi*. Tomus 51. Col. 106 *sq*. My translation)

The following should be noted:

Clifford's suggestion was accepted by the Deputation de Fide. [See col. 397, No. 23, and Bishop Gasser's reply, col. 416].

Minor emendations to conciliar documents, proposed by Clifford, are referred to in *Mansi*, Tomus 51:

• Col. 764 (No. 144)

• Col. 770 (No. 185)

• Col. 832 (No. 479)

• Col. 854 (No. 557)

APPENDIX 9

On the Universal Small Catechism (30.4.1870)
(Bishop Clifford's Address at the Vatican Council)

Most eminent Cardinals, most reverend Fathers,

A few of the things which I wished to say have been partly
dealt with by several speakers, but there are some things I
wish to state because in certain respects I wish to differ. I
should like, therefore, to propose a change in page 5 which
first of all I shall read and then give reasons for the change.
In place of what is proposed in the schema I would like to
see the following:

> "with the approval of the Council and taking
> into account first and foremost the
> aforementioned catechism of the Venerable
> Cardinal Bellarmine as well as catechisms
> now widely used among Christian people, not
> to mention selected works of some Bishops in
> various parts of the world, the new small
> catechism etc."

I think that those words *"after the model of the
aforementioned Venerable Cardinal Bellarmine"* should
not be put as if we wished to limit those who have to produce
a new catechism to such an extent that they follow slavishly
all that is contained in Bellarmine's small catechism. My
view is that we wish to leave it open to the authors to take
from any catechism whatever seems to be of better quality
or more useful.

Since therefore that seems to be the sense – as I see it – of
that paragraph, and since those words *"after the model of
Bellarmine's catechism"* have seemed to some Fathers,
and indeed have led many to conclude, that we wish to
demand the retention of the longer responses and examples
given by Bellarmine, even though they are less suited to our
times, I think that it would meet the wishes both of the

Commission and of the Fathers if the words were to be changed to: *"taking into account first and foremost the catechism of the Venerable Cardinal Bellarmine as well as catechisms now widely used among Christian people"*.

As regards the second part, namely that we add: *"not to mention selected works of some Bishops in various parts of the world"*. It is true that, if put at the end of the directive it may appear to be (a) alien to the scope of the schema and (b) that that which should be left to the prudent solicitude of the Holy See would seem to be handed over to the Commission.

But I do not think that the sense of the words argue against their being included. The words *"as well as catechisms now widely used among Christian people"* show that we are giving a sense of direction to those entrusted with the task of composing the catechism. Therefore the question is not whether we should propose anything to them, but rather in what directions we suggest they could profitably look.

Whenever there is talk of putting together a small universal catechism, there are two serious difficulties in the way. The first arises from the fact that it is said to be new. This difficulty can be met, as far as that is possible, by our observation that we are proposing that a catechism be put together which takes into account those better catechisms which are already in use throughout the world. It is not so much something new that is being proposed; rather it is a work which already exists in the Universal Church but is being reduced to a unified text.

The second difficulty is a very practical one and arises from the fact that it is extremely difficult to compose a catechism which can meet the needs of so many different people. There is no other way of dealing with this problem other than by consulting Bishops from the different countries. We had an example of this during the present Council when there was a discussion about that famous comma! The Bishops had no problem in regard to the main argument, the difficulty was entirely about what was necessary for any particular country.

As soon as the difficulty was recognised there was no problem about overcoming it. The same thing is bound to happen – not once but a hundred times – when it comes to composing the small catechisms.

Let us therefore make these two comments; that we take into account first and foremost Cardinal Bellarmine's catechism and also those which are more widely used by Catholics, and also that we use what appears appropriate from the works of various Bishops from different parts of the world; and that the Council bear in mind the two chief difficulties which occur when a small catechism is being proposed and that it suggest the best way in which these difficulties can be met.

(*Mansi*. Tomus 51, Col. 481 *sq*. My translation)

On the Definition of Papal Infallibility (25.5.1870)
(Bishop Clifford's Address at the Vatican Council)

Most eminent presidents, most eminent and most reverend fathers.

I am afraid that you will regard it as most inopportune that I should speak to you at this hour on *opportuness* after so much has been said to you on this subject. However, I could not keep completely silent since from the very beginning I have always expressed myself as being opposed to the opportuness of dealing with this question; and now it seems to me to be no less inopportune, namely the way in which we are treating of it, on its own and separate from the Church (as a whole).

What we have heard from the most reverend and wise Archbishop of Westminster has not caused me to alter my position. Indeed, some of the things which he said have confirmed my words in that very opinion, especially in regard to the necessity of not separating the question of the authority and infallibility of the Roman Pontiff from the question of the authority and infallibility of the Church.

For he has said that this opinion is not something which has arisen suddenly, as some have asserted, but is a view which was already being discussed in the 17th and 18th centuries; and it was because of this fact – that the question was being debated at that time – that the doctrine of the infallibility of the church has become obscured. It seems to me that there is no clearer conclusion to be deduced than this; namely, that the two questions are inextricably bound together, and therefore, that if we wish to proceed properly in this matter, that we must not treat the authority of the Roman Pontiff separately but we must also deal at the same time with the authority of the Church.

The example of our own country confirms this. He has said that English people, who must come to the truth, will be best attracted in this way, that the infallibility of the Church be proved to them and then it will be demonstrated that the infallibility of the Roman Pontiff is necessary to that infallibility of the Church. If it is therefore necessary that the question be presented in this way to the people so that they can grasp it, it is necessary that we put it forward in that way so that we can make them clearly understand what this connection is between the infallibility of the Church and the infallibility of the Roman Pontiff.

And besides he has confirmed this with quotations from four leading journals which are published in England. You have heard what is said there about the necessity of this definition. It is obvious, most reverend fathers, and needs no proof from me that these Protestant publications were not written to promote the Catholic cause. The very fact that they write in this way should make us suspicious that here lies a snake in the grass.

And if it really is true, as the most distinguished archbishop has said, that things have to be demonstrated logically to the English people, certainly in order to be able to convert an Englishman to religion then it must in the first place be necessary to demonstrate to him that the Catholic Church is not despotic [*signs of disapproval*].

The whole problem which Protestants have against the Catholic Church, which they call papistical, is this that they are always seeking to prove that the Catholic Church is in fact tyrannical, and these men who will write in these articles, in these publications, will make every effort with their arguments so that they will make English people believe that by this proposed definition what will clearly appear, what will logically follow, will be that the Catholic Church is indeed tyrannical and that the Roman Pontiff truly is the tyrant. For this, it seems to me, one must come to the unavoidable conclusion that if we by this definition – whatever form it may take in the end – wish not to hinder but to help people, it is necessary that we do not give them a separate definition which relates to the infallibility and authority of the Roman Pontiff, but it is necessary that we clearly and logically demonstrate to them what is the nature and essence of the Catholic Church, what is the true authority in the Catholic Church, how the authority of the Church and the authority of the Pope come together [*sibi invicem conveniant*: are in accord, are in harmony with each other], and how in all these matters it is neither tyranny nor despotism. But if, after so many months of labour, we have done nothing except to put before the people some decree about the infallibility of the Roman Pontiff, no matter in what way the decree may be worded, this will be the overriding impression of the people that we had done nothing other than to constitute the Pope as a despot. [*Murmurs and sounds of disapproval*].

Besides, most reverend fathers, it is true that this question was the cause of troubles in the Church during the 17th and 18th centuries, and in this sense it is not new; but as far as our people are concerned it is certain that it will be a matter which has arisen all of a sudden. There was no question among English people on this point; we have always taught our people in England about the infallibility of the Church in controversies with Protestants both in writing and in addresses. We used to teach that the question of whether the final source of infallibility resided in the Pope alone or in the Pope with the Church was a matter of theology ['*ad scholas*'], not of faith; and in our popular catechisms mention was made only of the infallibility of the Church. Preachers whom I have often had in my churches speaking on controversial matters in the presence of both Protestants and Catholics, always explained the matter in this way as presented in the books which we are accustomed to give to people when we instruct them in the faith, either Catholics, or Protestants whom we wish to convert.

I pass over Milner, Challoner, Gother and others like them so that (I can quote) the exposition given by the most eminent Cardinal Wiseman on the supremacy of the Pope in his

Lectures to People on the doctrine and practice of the Catholic Church which are much used by English Catholics. In Lecture Eight he writes as follows: "The idea of the supremacy of the Pope includes two distinct but closely connected ideas: the first is that the Holy See is the centre of unity: the second is that it is the supreme authority. Through the first is signified that all the faithful must be in communion with the Roman Pontiff through his pastors, and in this way a chain is formed, unbroken from the least member of the flock right up to him who has been constituted the pastor of all. But he is also the source of authority because all lower rulers in the Church are subject to him, and from him or through him, either directly or indirectly, receive their jurisdiction." Then he adds: "If perchance serious and widespread troubles should arise, either in matters of Faith or practice, he will call a general council of the pastors of the Church, and with him as president – either personally or through his legates – he will approve the canons and decrees".

But in the 3rd Lecture, on the subject of the way in which matters are transacted in a council, he gives this explanation to the people: "Suppose there were to arise some question about a particular doctrine about which no one could agree and no one knows what is to be thought, what is the mind of the church, and what is prudent and necessary in regard to an enquiry and what is to be done. The method of proceeding is this: a close examination would be instituted of the writings of the ancient fathers of the Church, and so would be known what was held in various regions in different centuries: and thus, having collected the votes of the whole world of all ages, it would not be a new doctrine that would be handed down, but a definition would be made of what had always been held in the Catholic Church. In each case the matter would be dealt with as an historical enquiry, and, so that a right definition would be arrived at, nothing would be omitted; then at last, the decree passed by the Church would be infallible".

We are all agreed in this, and we have instructed our people about the infallibility of the Church along these lines; but it cannot be that this new definition, especially if it is done in such a hurry, without any explanation, can be reconciled with the doctrine of the infallibility of the Church as we have handed it down to them up till now. For many, not only Protestants but also Catholics, it cannot but seem to be a new doctrine. Indeed, both before I left England and since my arrival in Rome, several priests and lay people have either written or spoken to me to say how much contention there had been among the people and in their families, and how great was their fear that if a definition, as if *de fide*, were passed in a hurry, the faithful would defect from the Faith, and names have been given to me not only from recent converts but also born Catholics. To all I have given this one reply: Do not, I said, be worried about what is being commonly put about – things which say that the council was only summoned for this purpose, these voices, I said, only belong to the writers of journals but have absolutely no authority. I know that Rome does not deal with matters in that way: many wicked things are put about by the enemies of the Roman Church: no one has accused her of being precipitate: Rome must not be judged by the fervent desires of some.

I must confess that things have turned out in a way different from what I was expecting: and indeed the judgment I had made was based on my experience which I thought was in accord with the prudence and dignity of this great City. How very differently does Saint Augustine teach us to act when he says: "How can this matter, shrouded as it is in so many disagreements, be brought to a clear exposition and ratification by a full council (*ad plenarii concilii luculentam illustrationem confirmationemque perduci*) unless it has first been debated for a very long time in various parts of the world and is clear from many discussions and meetings of the bishops?" Now we are dealing with a question which is so grave that it radically concerns not only the authority of the Pope but all episcopal authority in the Church. And not only have we not discussed it in any manner "for a very long time", not only

have we been summoned here without any prior warning
that this matter would be raised in the council, but
furthermore the question was introduced in haste and
outside the prescribed order of business and, what is worst
of all, on its own, that is without at the same time raising the
issue of the relationship which exists between the primacy
and infallibility of the Roman Pontiff and also between the
authority and teaching power of the bishops.

No one can be ignorant of the exaggerated opinions, beyond
all reason, which in these days are being put about amongst
the people. If the Vatican Council does nothing other than to
publish some sort of decree on the infallibility of the Roman
Pontiff, saying nothing about the Church, nothing about the
Bishops, offering nothing to contain the false views which
are going about; then not only can that peace not be hoped
for from our labours, but beyond doubt anger and
dissension will increase. I cannot help thinking, most
reverend fathers, that we are underestimating the
difficulties which can arise in many dioceses – as already
mentioned by their bishops.

The most reverend Archbishop of Caesaraugusta wants the
Church to be ruled by Truth, not by public opinion.
Undoubtedly this is most true if it is understood to mean
that the Church must not be silent about truth because of
the fear of men, that in other words it should appear to
please God rather than man. But if it is understood to mean
this that, although it is the whole truth, prudence in acting
is not the most important thing in the running of the Church
but everything is to be committed to the care of Heaven;
then this pertains rather to Fatalism than to Faith. The
Church has its unconquered firmness, but it also has its
political wisdom; it does not separate the simplicity of the
dove from the astuteness of the serpent since it is amongst
wolves that it must feed its lambs. It is necessary that the
servant whom the Master places in charge of his household
should be not only faithful but prudent so that he may give
food to all in due time. The Church should not be ruled by
public opinion, but nor should she dismiss it out of hand.

Most reverend fathers, consider, I beg of you, the Catholic Church; gaze on this Sion and embrace her. There was a time when the kingdoms of Europe comprised one republic, Christian and Catholic. By a long series of evils it eventually happened that a great part of Northern Europe was torn from the Church: in other regions mobs and rebellions rose up against the Church. The Catholic Church, built on rock, does indeed remain unconquered; but who is there that would not weep over such terrible calamities? Who would say that it is not a matter for the greatest prudence in the Church to ensure that something similar does not happen again? Now new enemies are pressing upon us; the gates of hell are rising against the Church, not only in those regions which are more remote from the centre of light but also in those lands which are nearer and have not hitherto been separated from the Catholic Faith. There can be no doubt that our enemies are striving to tear even other regions away from the Church.

Of course I know that the gates of hell will not prevail; but what will prevent what has happened before from happening again – I mean their inflicting great damage upon the Church – unless we use the utmost prudence? If now great men, from wheresoever they come, where the enemies of the Church are mixing with her children and where men are more easily torn away from the Church – whether from Germany, Hungary, France, Lusitania, Switzerland, even Italy itself – if these vigilant pastors raise their voices and warn us of the grave danger, who will dare to say that one should not take them too seriously? Who is it that will persuade himself that the business of the Church is only to preach the truth and to disregard the signs of the times and public opinion? If only one tenth of those evils which these pastors fear were to befall the Church, is it not true that the Eternal Shepherd will exact the most severe reckoning from those who have neglected the signs of the times? But there is also another point which I feel I must make.

After that most tragic defection of the XVI century, the Church, ever faithful to the mission which it had received from its Founder, with the Holy See giving the lead – as is right and proper for the successors of Peter – with notable success set about recovering the lands which had been lost and of gaining new ones for Christ. Many conversions took place in England and Germany, and in America where the land is new, new and extensive churches [dioceses] have sprung up. Can there be anyone who is not aware of the toil, matched with wonderful success, that has enabled these things to take place in our own day? If we were to ask: where in the Church is to be found the principal cause of our sorrow, would not the answer be particularly in the older churches, Italy, Spain and South America?

If, on the other hand, we were to seek out the source of our joy, would it not be found in those churches which have but recently been won? New conversions are taking place in America, also in England and in the British Empire in which daily new conversions are happening. Can there be any doubt, therefore, that the greatest harm would be done to the Church, if, while (still) suffering in those areas where Christianity first took root we were to give rise to religious difficulties precisely in those places where the hope of the Church now lies? Not only would difficulties be placed in the way of conversions – we would even be giving cause for offence. How therefore can we term 'small' the difficulties and fears of the bishops who come from those places?

The most reverend speaker who replied to the Bishop of Saint-Gall said, speaking on this subject, that it was a question either of good Catholics who doubtless would receive anything which the Church decided, or of bad Catholics and Protestants who, as they are not to be offended by a proposal, equally are not to be listened to in the matter. First of all, this distinction is both defective and childish. There are good Catholics and bad Catholics – but bad Catholics are not to be ignored because they are bad. Besides, amongst Catholics, especially those who are educated, there are degrees of fervour which are both many and varied. Yes indeed, they are good Catholics who lead a good life, who quite often receive the sacraments, who bring up their families in the fear of God, who use their talents for the good of the Church either in civil affairs or in education, or in the law or armed services, or in other ways.

All these men, especially those who live among Protestants, are more or less involved in controversy, and this of necessity because they must defend their position *vis-a-vis* their colleagues. There is a very grave danger, and it is a great temptation against the Faith, to place on these men a new yoke, and to impose it in such a way that it looks like – whatever it may be in fact – a further curb on their freedom. But if the decree on the infallibility of the Roman Pontiff is decided in the form in which it has been proposed, without any further explanation about the authority of the Church, then it is impossible – especially if we think about the extreme theories which are going around, fostered by their promoters and now in the hands of everyone with no answer by way of remedy – that many such men will not be troubled and be thrown either into Indifferentism or into a complete loss of Faith.

I know that in these times it has been very much the custom to lump all these people together indiscriminately as of little importance and firmly to number them among the heretics. But, most reverend fathers, if the Catholics in Britain and America now enjoy their liberty, if the Church there and in North America is free, if the bishops exercise their power there with a degree of freedom, then this is due after God to the persistent efforts of such men devoted as they are to the interests of the Church. No one will convince me that that man will not inflict great harm upon the Church who forces such people either to leave the Church or to become lukewarm in her defence.

But neither is it true to say in this regard that Protestants are in no way to be taken into consideration. People who speak like that are ignorant of how in England and America Catholics live amongst Protestants, of how they exist in the relationships of everyday life, and of how they depend upon the goodwill between themselves and Protestants. In

England and America Catholics – who are in a minority – for
the most part are ruled by Protestants, nor are they able to
achieve anything for the Church unless they are supported
by Protestants. Our laws are made by Members (of
Parliament) who in great part are Protestants; the whole
freedom of the Church, the titles of ecclesiastical property,
freedom of instruction, the status and liberty of regulars
and monks, even the rights of Catholics to hold office as
magistrates, in the army or in the law – all these things
depend upon the way in which Protestants regard their
fellow Catholic citizens. No one can possibly declare,
therefore, that it is not a matter of great prudence to the
church to consider whether it is opportune to provoke
Protestants in these regions against the Church. Bad times
are pressing in upon us; in our assemblies laws are being
considered for the elementary schools, also on ecclesiastical
goods. This is the beginning of evils: we shall have no way of
defending the cause of the Church unless we have the help
of Protestants and of those ministers of the realm who are
well disposed towards us. Our present way of doing
business has already alienated many people from us, has
weakened our cause, and will alienate many more as the
days go by. Experience has taught this and also the writings
of men holding high office in the kingdom, this I know and
others can testify with me.

I cannot but be offended when I hear some dismiss these
fears so lightly, fears which several bishops have described
of defections or of schism in their dioceses. I have heard
many say: so be it, it is their loss not the Church's; the
Church will triumph and in the end will be even more
vigorous. This is not the voice of the Catholic Church, the
voice of that Church which we confess to be mother as well
as teacher. That wisest of kings when judging between two
women gave orders that the child was to be cut in two. He
pronounced that woman to be the true mother who was
moved to pity over the child. She who was able to say "let the
child be divided" was declared no mother at all [1 Kings iii,
16 – 28].

His Eminence the Cardinal of Dublin quoted as an example the people of Ireland so as to show how vain is the attempt when Governments try to establish national churches amongst Catholic races. Would that I could corroborate the Cardinal's argument about my own country with that of the Scots, the Belorussians, the Prussians, the Danes, the Swiss and the Norwegians! The governments in all these regions have been all too successful in being able to form national churches. Furthermore, what the Cardinal has said about the Irish nation he said not only with truth but with modesty; Englishman though I am, I can bear witness quite boldly, which I am happy to do in this gathering, to the loyalty and faith of that [Irish] people: now indeed the English are striving to put right – as far as they can – the wrongs which they inflicted in Ireland. But if we cast our minds back to those times of which the Cardinal was speaking, there is no doubt but that never at any time was there a people which daily bore such harsh and ruthless persecution for the Catholic Faith with such a noble and loyal heart. But it was not only harshness – there was also a certain providence [*sapientia*] in the oppression by the English of nearly all the Catholics in Ireland. For that noble people, not only could it never be seduced so as to change or repudiate that faith which through saint Patrick it had received from the Holy See, but far more than that, they were able to provide not only for themselves but also for England, America, Australia, India and for all our colonies. Wherever the English tongue is heard there the Catholic Faith has been planted by the Catholics of Ireland.

Yet despite the truth of all this, most reverend fathers, which of us would not pay the highest price – even to the shedding of blood – in order to avoid all these evils, or that our indomitable sons should not have to fight against them? Indeed, as I read through the pages of English history I am not convinced that those are wrong who are of the view that, if Queen Elizabeth had been treated with more caution and prudence before she ascended the throne and during the early years of her reign, then that tragic tearing away of England from the Apostolic See with all its horrible consequences could have been averted. This is even more true of the time of James II. We had a Catholic king; more than half the population still held the religion of their ancestors, and for the rest the Protestant religion was more a question of recent practice than of conviction. The more influential people were mere time servers and were easily drawn to the party which appeared more likely to win. At that time there was great hope of re-establishing the Catholic religion in England. And yet one can scarcely credit the blind stupidity of the King's advisors, both clerical and lay, who constantly urged on him policies that were extreme in matters both political and ecclesiastical. King James followed the example of King Roboam, and met a fate which though similar was worse. In the baptistery of this church there stands a monument, the work of Canova, on which are inscribed the following words; 'The Last of the Stuarts'. What one does *not* read there is that hope of restoring the Catholic Faith to England disappeared, that the persecution in Ireland and of the Catholics in England was renewed. If only James II had lent a timely ear to those who warned of the evils which would surely come if, without due consideration, burdens were to be placed on the people which would be more than they could sustain or even understand.

How much different, and happier, have things been in the past century when the first relief was granted to the Catholics of England and the foundations were laid of that most complete religious freedom which in recent times has come to fruition. The result is that nowhere in the whole world is there to be found a place where the practice of religion is more free or where the spiritual authority of the Roman Pontiff is more fully acknowledged or more freely exercised.

At that time there was a question of swearing an oath of allegiance because the English Government did not wish to grant any easing to the Catholics until they had first of all taken the oath which asserted that the Pope had no power or temporal jurisdiction (either direct or indirect) in the

domains of the King of England, and swearing at the same
time that they were bound in such a way that neither the
Pope nor anyone else could release them from the oath once
it had been taken.

There were not lacking those who insisted that it was not
right for Catholics to swear such an oath, among whom were
the most reverend Ghilini, papal nuncio at Brussels.
However, the bishops of both England and Ireland, having
given the matter serious consideration and bearing in mind
the serious harm which would be done to the Church – harm
which they were quite right to fear – were of the opinion that
the oath should be taken. In fact both they and the superiors
of the religious orders took the oath and recommended both
clergy and people to do likewise in the year 1778.

The most reverend Monsignor Butler, Archbishop of
Cashel, writing in the year 1786 to Viscount Kenmare
states that he had given a complete explanation to His
Eminence Cardinal Marefoschi who at that time was the
Protector of Ireland. Butler adds that in his reply the
Cardinal 'gave complete approval to what I had written to
him'; and this approval of the Cardinal was later confirmed
by the Pope and by the Congregation of Propaganda Fide
who also approved the form of the oath. The letters of
approval written by the Sacred Congregation are
absolutely authentic and are in my possession.

An English author who has written on the history of that
period, after describing the prudent way of proceeding
adopted by those church leaders, concludes as follows: It is
to these venerable men that we are debtors in that we enjoy
the free exercise of our religion and the secure possession
of our property." If at some future date it should happen that
we can gain further rights, it will be to these, before all
others, that our success will be due. But when such
prudence is lacking, alas! how often greater evils have
befallen us, because the worst enemies of religion are its
reckless propagators, [*quod maximi hostes religionis
sunt immoderati religionis assertores*].

Just as I have always been sorry that this question had ever
arisen – nor have I changed my mind in this regard – so now
I am certain that not only can no good be hoped for from an
isolated definition of this question (howsoever it be
phrased) unless at the same time, with the decree on the
authority of the Roman Pontiff, the whole question of the
authority of the Church and of the bishops is clearly,
logically and coherently (*splendide*) explained to the
people. Unless this is done, strife and disturbances
everywhere will not decrease but increase. But I have said
enough on this subject.

I had prepared a great deal to say on the arguments put
forward by the Fathers on the schema in general, but since
you have heard so many learned men speaking on this
subject I do not wish to tire you any more with my words
[*signs of approval*]: but there is one thing I must note.
Many have spoken saying that we were dealing with
something that was clearer than the mid-day sun. To me,
however, it seems that not only are we lacking the mid-day
sun but, the more we proceed, the greater the darkness.
There is absent the first requisite of clarity, namely that
the state of the question [*status questionis*] between the
contending parties be clearly understood. The more
fathers speak the more obvious it is that the same words,
the same phrases are being used in different senses by
different people.

The most reverend Archbishop of Westminster had said
that, although there is disagreement among us regarding
the opportuness, we are nevertheless dealing with a fact
about which we are all agreed. Many argue as if all those
who are opposed to a decree about the personal and
separate infallibility of the Pope, were also opposed to the
primacy and supreme authority of the Holy See. There are
others who wish us to use terms which speak of a *personal
and separate* infallibility. But the proposers of the schema
themselves explain the gift and privilege of infallibility in
different ways. Not only do books recently published on this
subject speak expressly about a personal infallibility, but

yesterday you heard the most reverend Bishop of Urgello arguing at great length that the core of the whole question is that the infallibility be applied to a person. Anyone can see that there is a whole world of difference between, for example, what the Archbishop of Mechlin has said about the issue and the Bishop of Urgello. And still the matter is treated as if we were talking about one and the same thing. But if the nature of the question is not clearly stated – and I do not mean orally or by one or other member of the Deputation, but in writing and authoritatively – then very long speeches will profit us nothing.

The Cardinal Archbishop of Dublin [Paul Cullen] has rebuked the Cardinal of Prague [von Schwarzenberg] as if he had wished to deny that the charge of the whole of the Lord's flock had been committed to Peter alone, or as if he had said that it was within the competence of one bishop to interfere in the affairs of another diocese. The Cardinal of Prague said no such thing. What he wished to show was how strong was the link between the question of the primacy of the Pope and the question of the rights of bishops, and so he concluded that it would not be right for a consideration of one to be treated separately from a consideration of the other. He said that some of the rights of bishops pertained to their own dioceses, while others pertained to the Universal Church, by which words he was making a clear allusion to the rights of bishops in General Council. Were we acting beyond our rights when we were discussing a Small Catechism for the whole Church, when we were dealing with bishops, *vicarii* and other matters pertaining to the discipline of the whole Church? And because these rights of bishops are intimately connected with the question of the infallibility of the Pope, one can be left in no doubt about those who assert that, in defending the infallibility of the Roman Pontiff, bishops in a General Council are not true judges but that they make an assertive judgement [*iudicium assertionis*] only. In other words, they accept that which, even before a hearing of the case, has already been judged.

But in recent days we have heard and react even more serious statements. From the beginning of this Council nothing has been more solemnly or more clearly stated than that the bishops would be properly seen in the Council as true judges, judging with the Pope matters of Faith, and that a strict interpretation was to be placed on the words of the first Dogmatic constitution: *'with the bishops of the whole world sitting and judging with us'*. But not only have several whittled down this judgement, but others, including the most reverend Archbishop of Edessa, whose recently published book is of no small authority in explaining what he wishes to see established through the decree on Infallibility, expressly reduces the office of the bishops – even in a General Council – to this, that they provide the Pope with advice; and he further puts them in the same category as other theologians. Here are his words (art. 3, p. 151): *"Although in publishing decrees, Roman Pontiffs are in the habit of using the advice of bishops, gathered either in ecumenical or local synods, or of cardinals or of other learned men; however, although these external helps are required so that they may act lawfully and prudently, they are not to be thought of as necessary in order to demand adherence from the faithful"*. It is expressly stated here that bishops, even when gathered in General Council, only offer advice to the Pope. Surely you can see that this question touches the very roots of the rights of bishops.

In saying this I do not wish for one moment to imply that the Cardinal of Dublin had any wrong intention in interpreting the Cardinal of Prague's words in a different sense: for my part the greatest injury and injustice was done to the Cardinal Archbishop. But I have pointed this out so that I can give you an example of how wrong we are to proceed in this way. Each bishop puts forward his view from the ambo: but first of all, since the point at issue has not been clearly defined, although as regards words they are talking about the same thing, namely Infallibility, nevertheless in reality they are talking about different things. Then again, either because of the nature of the subject or by reason of the place or of the speakers, it is bound to happen that some things are not properly understood, or even wrongly understood, as in the example I have given. The result is that not only are old obstacles and causes of disagreement not removed, but daily even new ones are accumulating without there being any way of explaining or of interpreting or of correcting those things which have been either badly expressed or wrongly understood.

Most reverend Fathers, whenever a question arises among brothers or friends, whenever there is a disagreement among those in government, then brothers and friends – wishing to put things right – are torn in two directions; in order to restore unity, before all else one must seek to establish what precisely is the point at issue between the contending parties so that the points of agreement become clear, together with the points of difference. In this way, with the question precisely stated, the arguments and evidence on both sides by which each party will strive to support his case are brought forward and examined, and then one finally proceeds to a decision on the point of disagreement. But this cannot be achieved by a long series of speeches which have no connection one with another, but only by a genuine, bona fide meeting for discussions between select Fathers – advocates from both sides – who, talking among themselves, responding to each other and equipped with all that is necessary to examine the question, are able to determine on which points we are indeed agreed and on which we disagree, and to what extent and why. Several Fathers for a long time earnestly requested that this be done, but unless it is done, we shall never arrive at a resolution of this question.

Had we assembled here – which in fact we have not – in order that a question already determined and decided could be imposed on all, there would have been no reason why we should have delayed here a moment longer. We would have been asked to give our votes and, with each one deciding according to conscience, the rest would be left to God. But we have in fact reached this point – where I believe we certainly have come in the same way as the apostles and elders came – whereby we see this matter and realise that it cannot be determined in any way other than by having a full investigation with a true, sincere and honest meeting between selected Fathers from both sides.

The most reverend Bishop of Santa Concepcion yesterday eloquently urged those who have asked for the definition to pray, to do apostolic work and to support the authority of the bishops. I totally agree. But is it true that those bishops who think otherwise, and who now ask that the matter be fully examined by representatives from both sides, that they are not your brothers and that they are enemies of the Holy See? Look at France, Germany, America, Portugal, Switzerland – look at all these countries from which your brothers have come. And now consider the history of the church for a quarter of a century, in Europe stricken by the evils of persecution, yet in other respects elsewhere most glorious on account of the spread of the Faith.

If when in these times the faith is to be preached or the freedom of the Church guaranteed or colleges for the education of Catholic youth have had to be protected against unbelievers, or the See of Peter with its rights, either divine or temporal be defended, or help brought to alleviate the necessities and afflictions of our most beloved father, then they have never been second to anyone either in writing or in toil or in help to fight the battles of God, and to expose themselves and their possessions to the enemy for the sake of the House of David. There are amongst those, not less than among you, who, like Paul and Barnabas, can speak of what God has done through them for his people; nor should it be thought that if *you* close your ears against their pleas, whatever the outcome, that history will pass a harsh judgement against *them*.

This is the only way in which there can be hope for a return of peace and tranquillity, that brothers agree among themselves so that in the end true doctrine about the Church and about its Supreme Head is stated in a clear and worthy manner and in this way they will be able to hear the message of the Gospel through the mouth of Peter, and believe.

(Mansi. Tomus 52, Col. 274-284. My translation)

On the Definition of Papal Infallibility
(Written Submission at the Vatican Council)

- What I have often said I now repeat; the definition of this opinion as *de fide* will be a great hindrance to conversions in Protestant lands. Indeed, it will also be a stone of scandal to not a few Catholics. On the other hand what benefit it will bring I just do not see.

- But in England there will be another harm and it is this. Before Catholics were freed from the penal laws and admitted to full civil liberties and equality with their fellow citizens, bishops and theologians were asked publicly by Parliament whether English Catholics believed that the Pope could impose on the people definitions relating to faith and morals without the express or tacit consent of the Church. All the bishops (among whom were two predecessors of the Cardinal of Dublin) and the theologians replied that Catholics held no such belief. It says as much in the printed acts of Parliament. Relying on these replies the English Parliament admitted Catholics to a share in their civil rights. Who is now going to persuade the Protestants that the Catholics were not acting dishonestly or in bad faith? For when it was a question of obtaining their rights they claimed in public that the doctrine of the Infallibility of the Roman Pontiff formed no part of their Catholic Faith. However, immediately they get what they want, they renege on what they publicly professed and declare the very opposite!

- The difficulties which occur against the doctrine of the Infallibility of the Roman Pontiff acting alone are such that, even before they can be addressed, one cannot see how the proposition is in fact amongst those truths which for certain have been revealed by God.

- In the proposed schema the definition is deduced from two premises: for it states *"Hence this sacred Council approving etc.".* But the consequence does not follow from the premises. For the first is deduced from the fact that in the Profession of Faith which

Gregory X [1271 – 1276] sent to the Greeks and which they professed in the Second Council of Lyons, it states that questions of faith must be defined by the judgment of the Roman Pontiff. But Gregory X himself at the very time that he was seeking such a declaration from the Greeks, when he wished to define that the Holy Spirit proceeded from the Father and the Son, did this in a General Council. Such being the case he showed that, when he said that questions of Faith should be settled by the Roman Pontiff, he did not exclude the necessity of the Pontiff doing this with the consent of the churches. All he was excluding was what the Greeks wanted, namely, that in order to settle questions of faith, it was not necessary to have the judgment of the Roman Pontiff. One cannot therefore conclude *from those words* that the Roman Pontiff, acting either alone or with the Church, is infallible.

Secondly, the Infallibility of the Roman Pontiff is deduced from the words of the formula which was signed by the Fathers of the Eighth Ecumenical Council in which it is stated that *"In the Apostolic See the Catholic religion has always been preserved untainted"*.

But because until that time the Apostolic See had defined nothing for the Universal Church without the approval of the churches, one cannot conclude that the Catholic Religion would have been preserved in the same way as if it had acted in a different manner. What is there to stop one believing that it was precisely the care the Roman Pontiffs took in summoning General Councils and in requiring the consent of the churches that was the means whereby the Faith was kept pure and the words of Christ were to be disregarded? The conclusion in the schema exceeds the premises.

• Why is it that, in the note, the words *"and because it cannot etc."* are said to come from the formula of Pope Saint Hormista, signed by the Fathers of the Eighth Ecumenical Council? In the Acts of the Council I have found (in the Collection of Isadore) between the letters of Saint Hormista [elected 514, died 523] a statement of faith of John, Bishop of Constantinople, *addressed to* Pope Saint Hormista. What I did not find was that it was *written by* Saint Hormista. In that statement the words quoted are not to be found in their entirety but only in part. However, they *are* to be found in their entirety in the formula sent to the Greeks through Pope

Hadrian II [867 – 872 and were signed by them in the Second
Council of Lyons. But Anastasias the Librarian who was at the
Council wrote about this formula: "*it should be noted and not
forgotten that this libellus conveys the mind of Pope Nicholas
[858 - 867] of happy memory, but because prevaricators at that
time would not accept it, it was again sent by Pope Saint
Hadrian but under another name, namely that of a Bishop of
Constantinople.*

(Mansi. Tomus 51. Col. 1032 seqq. My translation)

Text of the Definition of Papal Infallibility (1870)

Therefore, faithfully adhering to the tradition received from the beginning of the Christian faith, for the glory of God our Saviour, the exaltation of the Catholic religion, and the Salvation of Christian people, with the approval of the Sacred Council, we teach and define that it is a dogma divinely revealed:

That the Roman Pontiff, when he speaks *ex cathedra*, that is, when in discharge of the office of Pastor and Teacher of all Christians, by virtue of his supreme Apostolic authority, he defines a doctrine regarding faith or morals to be held by the Universal Church, is, by the Divine assistance promised to him in Blessed Peter, possessed of that infallibility with which the Divine Redeemer willed that His Church should be endowed in defining doctrine regarding faith or morals; and that therefore such definitions of the Roman Pontiff are of themselves, and not from the consent of the Church, irreformable.

Clifford's Pastoral on the Syllabus of Errors (Lent. 1865)

Dearly Beloved,

Each year in the discharge of our duty, we address some words of exhortation to you at the approach of the holy season of Lent, but we are in a more special manner called upon to do so on the present occasion. Our Holy Father Pope Pius IX., ever mindful of the interests of the Catholic Church, and ever watchful to repel the insidious approaches and open assaults of error, has lately addressed a letter to all the Catholic Archbishops and Bishops throughout the world, directing their attention to the increased activity with which wicked men labour to subvert the truth, and to propagate errors and false principles regarding revelation, the authority of the Church, and the nature and duties of civil society; endeavouring, above all things, to persuade men to regard as an evil that union and community of purpose between the Church and Civil Governments which has ever been of such salutary advantage both to Church and state. The Holy Father expresses his earnest expectation that the Pastors of the Church will exert their zeal *by taking the sword of the spirit which is the word of God, and that, strengthened by the grace of our Lord Jesus Christ, they will daily redouble their efforts to induce the flocks committed to their charge to abstain (as the great Bishop and Martyr St. Ignatius expresses it) from those poisonous herbs which Jesus Christ does not cultivate because they are not of his Father's planting; and that they will unceasingly press on the faithful that whatever true happiness man can enjoy, flows from our august religion, its doctrine, and its practice and that that people is happy whose God is the Lord.*

How can we more effectually discharge this duty than by calling your attention to this very Letter of the Holy Father, wherein he sums up these noxious doctrines, and repeats the condemnation which he and his more immediate predecessors have, on former occasions, pronounced against them?

The Encyclical of the Holy Father has been brought before the public in so many ways that it is unknown to none. You have heard the clamour and opposition raised against it, even in this country, but more especially abroad. You have heard with what fidelity, and how fearlessly the Pastors of the Church elsewhere have fulfilled their duty of warning the faithful against the errors it condemns, and how they have interposed the shield of their eloquence and of their learning, between the Holy Father and the malicious attacks of those who have sought either to vitiate the meaning or to weaken the authority of his teaching. It is not to be wondered, if in the midst of the clamour which has been raised, even some good men have taken alarm, have hesitated as to the meaning and purport of some of the doctrines condemned, and have looked for some explanation of expressions to which so many different meanings have been attached. We shall therefore endeavour to call to your minds some of those Catholic principles and doctrines which will enable you more readily to understand the nature of the errors condemned, and thus furnish you with the means both of giving an account of that faith which is in you, and of silencing the ignorance of foolish men.

To the Encyclical, the Pope has appended a list of the errors condemned, classifying them under various heads. We shall therefore best consult both brevity and clearness by following the order thus pointed out to us. The limits of a Pastoral would not allow us to comment on each individual error condemned, neither does the nature of the case require we should do so. Except in instances where particular propositions require more detailed explanation, it will be sufficient for us to refer to various classes of errors, and to point out to you the principles they are opposed to, as well as the grounds for their condemnation.

The first class of errors falling under the ban of the Supreme Pontiff are those which strike at the root of Christianity. Errors denying that God exists as a distinct spiritual and eternal Being, that He watches over and governs the affairs of men, or that He has given revelation to man. Errors asserting that revelation and reason are opposed to one another, or that reason is independent of, or superior to, revelation, – that the sacred volumes are not really inspired by God; and the like. It is not necessary that we should detain you with remarks on these blasphemous doctrines. Their falsity and impiety is manifest to all true children of the Church, and they have been repeatedly and convincingly refuted by many learned apologists of the Christian faith.

Next to these infidel and rationalistic errors, are condemned the doctrines, so called, of indifferentism and latitudinarianism. That is to say, of those who vainly seek to promote unity amongst men, and to destroy religious differences, not by drawing men to truth, but by sacrificing truth for unity; and who would avoid all dissensions about dogma, by relieving men of all dogma concerning which they may disagree. This is simply to deny all objective value to revealed truth. They who hold such opinions necessarily deny the existence of anyone true divinely-guided Church. They look upon all religious sects as bodies of men striving more or less earnestly to discover truth, and each attaining some degree of success; but they do not look on the whole of revealed truth as the absolute inheritance of any; all religions are to them but various roads, leading more or less circuitously to one end. How widely opinions of this kind are spread amongst men, we know from daily experience. But nothing is more directly opposed to the teaching of the Catholic Church.

We believe that there is but one holy Catholic and Apostolic Church. That this Church is "*the pillar and groundwork of the truth.*" – (1 Tim. iii. 15). That "*Christ will be with her all days. even to the consummation of the world.*" – (Matt. xviii. 20). Out of this Church there can be no salvation, "*For whosoever revolteth and continueth not in the doctrine of Christ hath not God.*" – (2 John, 9). And "*he that believeth not shall be condemned.*" – (Mark xvi. 16). All other sects being cut off from this one true Church are not with Christ but against Him, as He Himself has said, "*He that is not with me, is against me; and he that gathereth not with me scattereth.*" – (Matt, xii 30). With St. Paul we believe that there is but "*one Lord. one faith, one baptism.*" – (Eph. iv. 5); "*and if any man will not hear the Church, he is to us as the heathen and the publican.*" – (Matt xviii. 17). Justly, then, does the Pope condemn those who teach that man is free to choose any form of religion that appears good to him by the light of reason, and that man may find out the way of eternal life and make sure his eternal salvation in the observance of any religion.

But it is necessary we should here make some remarks on one proposition, the condemnation of which has been singled out in a special manner for attack. It is the seventeenth amongst the condemned propositions, and runs thus:-" *The eternal salvation of all those who are not in any way in the true Church of Christ, may at least well be hoped for.*" The condemnation of this proposition appears, to the minds of some, to exclude from all hope of salvation not those only who contumaciously resist the teaching of the Catholic Church, but also all those who do so in error and in good faith. Such, however, is not the teaching of the Catholic Church; nor is it in any way implied by the condemnation of the proposition before us.

For the right understanding of this proposition, it is necessary in the first place to remark that its condemnation does not imply that it is vain to hope for the salvation even of the most wilful and obdurate heretics by means of their conversion to the Catholic faith. On the contrary, in this sense the Church teaches us constantly to pray, and consequently to hope, for the salvation of all men: *"For this is good and acceptable in the sight of God our Saviour; who will have all men to be saved and to come to the knowledge of the truth."* – (1 Tim. ii. 3, 4). But when it is said of persons who are not in the true Church, that we cannot well hope for their salvation, it is meant that such hope cannot be entertained, so long as they remain, as they are, out of the true Church.

Secondly, we must bear in mind that by eternal salvation is here meant, not any manner of reward naturally due to man, but that wonderful and supernatural happiness which consists in the vision of God, which He has prepared for those who are faithful to Him – a reward to which man has naturally no claim, which has been purchased for us by the Blood of Christ, which is promised indeed as a crown to those who are faithful, but to obtain which, our actions, however good, are of no value in themselves, unless they be first prevented by God's grace, – unless we be incorporated in Jesus Christ, made members of His body, and thus through Him acquire for our actions a supernatural value.

Bearing these observations in mind, let us enquire, who then are those who are altogether separated from the true Church of Christ, and for whose salvation, consequently, we may not hope? They belong to one of two classes. For either they have never been members of the true Church, or else, having been members, they have, of their own free will, abandoned it.

And first, as regards those who have never been members of the true Church. To this class belong all those infants or adults who have never been cleansed from the original stain in the waters of baptism. It is by means of this sacrament that we become members of Christ, partakers of His merits, and heirs to His kingdom, and *"unless a man be born again*

of water and the Holy Ghost, he cannot enter into the kingdom of
God." – (John iii. 5).

As regards, therefore, all those who die before baptism, there can be no
hope of their ever enjoying that supernatural beatitude which can be
acquired only through the merits of Jesus Christ. The Church does not
teach thereby that those who die before baptism, but without actual sin,
are condemned to eternal torments. She tells us indeed that they are
excluded from that supernatural glory which the saints enjoy, and of
which St. Paul says, "*That eye hath not seen, nor ear heard, neither
hath it entered into the heart of man what things God hath prepared
for them that love him.*" – (1 Cor. ii. 9). But she neither teaches that they
are condemned to suffer pain, nor that they are excluded from such
natural happiness as becomes their state. Those unbaptised persons who
have known the truth and have refused to embrace it, shall indeed be
condemned with the wicked, "*For he that doth not believe, is already
judged.* – (John ii. 18). They also who have not known Christ, but have
been guilty of actual sins against that law which is written in our
hearts, shall also be punished for them, "*For God will render to every
man according to his works . . . For whosoever hath sinned
without the law, shall perish without the law; and whosoever
have sinned in the law, shall be judged by the law.* – (Rom. ii. 6, 12).
But no man shall be accountable for not having embraced the faith
when he knew it not. Hence the Catholic Church condemns as
erroneous the sixty eighth proposition of BAJUS, wherein he asserts
that *the purely negative unbelief of those to whom Christ has not
been preached, is a sin.*

There remains the second class, of those who are separated from the true
Church. These are they, who, having been admitted into the true Church
by baptism, and having thereby become members of Christ and heirs to
the kingdom of heaven, have afterwards, of their own free will, separated
themselves from that Church, either by denying some article of faith
which they knew, or by refusing to enquire after truth when doubts arose
in their minds concerning it. such baptised persons, and such only, are
altogether out of the true Church. For heresy, like all other sins, requires
full knowledge and free consent. Hence, not only are all baptised infants
members of the true Church, but those persons also who, after attaining
the use of reason, are brought up in error and imbued with prejudices
against the truth, who are outwardly separated from the Catholic Church

and addicted to false sects, but who never have had doubts concerning the errors they have imbibed, or who, having doubts, seek faithfully from God, light and grace to know the truth: these, we say, though outwardly not in communion with the Catholic Church, are nevertheless true members of the same.

As ST. AUGUSTINE says, – *"Those who defend their opinion, not through obstinate animosity, even if that opinion be false and perverse, more especially if it be not the result of daring presumption on their part. but an inheritance coming to them from parents who had been led astray and fallen into error: who seek cautiously and anxiously after truth, ready to embrace it when they discover it, are not to be ranked amongst heretics."* – (Aug. Ep. 43). Of such as these, the condemnation does not speak, for they are not altogether out of the true Church, their separation being only external. That such cases exist, experience testifies. To enquire as to their number is idle speculation. It can be known to God alone, who searches the hearts and proves the reins of men. But they who after having known the way of justice, have turned back from the holy commandment which was delivered to them; they who resist the truth; men corrupt in mind, reprobate concerning the faith: they also who have doubted, but have refused to examine; or who see the truth, but from worldly motives refuse to embrace it, – who, consequently, are, through their own fault and of their own will, separated from the Church and resist the call of God, they are not in any way in the true Church, and against these, Christ Himself has pronounced sentence, when He says, *"He that shall deny me before men, I will also deny him before my Father who is in heaven."* – (Matt. x. 33).

We must now pass on to the consideration of other errors concerning more especially the authority of the Church, – that of the State, – and the relation of these to each other. And first let us call to mind the teaching of the Church on these points. The Church claims to be not a mere free association, a brotherhood, or a school of philosophy, but a complete and organised society, ordained and constituted by God, deriving her authority not from man but from God, and therefore claiming, as a right, the obedience of men in all those matters over which that authority extends. She is the city built on the mountain; – she is the kingdom of God. The supreme authority in this city, the keys of this kingdom, were given by Christ Himself to Peter, and to his successors; and under him the

Holy Ghost has placed Bishops to rule the Church of God. As this authority, which regards all spiritual things, comes direct from God, not through the State, so neither is the Church dependent on the will of the State for the exercise of the same. Most justly, therefore, does the Holy Father charge with error those who teach that the Church is nothing more than an association dependent on the state, deriving its powers from the state, and exercising its authority only so far as the state sanctions and permits, or who seek to make the State and not the Church the supreme arbiter in matters relating to faith, morals, and instruction. The propositions condemned by the Pope as containing or implying this doctrine are very numerous.

But if the Church claims for herself in spiritual matters an authority which is derived from God, she not only recognises the authority of the civil power in temporal matters, but she teaches that such authority is likewise in its own sphere derived from God. It is necessary to bear this truth in mind while considering the present question. It is a truth to which our reason bears witness. Reason tells us that man is by nature made for society. For of all animals man alone is unable to bring his natural qualities, whether physical or mental, to perfection except through society; and as society cannot exist without laws and without a co-ordination of its members one to the other, some of whom must command whilst others obey, it follows that the existence of temporal rulers holding authority in the State, is part of the design of nature, or rather of that God who is the author of nature. Temporal rulers are, then, an ordinance of God, and consequently the duty of subjects to obey them is a portion of that law of nature which God has written in the hearts of men. This moral duty, which reason points out to us, is most distinctly confirmed in the revealed word of God. "*Let every soul be subiect to higher powers* (says St. Paul), *for there is no power but from God; and those that are, are ordained of God. Therefore he that resisteth the power. resisteth the ordinance of God. And they that resist. purchase to themselves damnation . . . Wherefore be subject of necessity, not only for wrath, but also for conscience' sake.*" – (Rom. xiii. 1, 2, 5).

To these principles of reason and revelation is directly opposed the teaching of those who recognize no other source of power than material strength, or the will of majorities, who see in right, nothing more than a material fact, or who assert that rebellion against lawfully constituted authority is no sin; and therefore most justly are these and such like doctrines condemned by the Pope.

What if temporal rulers be not unfrequently raised to power through violence, cunning, or other unjust means? Does this overthrow the truth that the temporal power comes from God? Most assuredly not. Such evil acts are undoubtedly sinful, nor can they give any rightful title to those who have recourse to them. But it happens not unfrequently that power thus unjustly acquired becomes afterwards necessary for the welfare of society; either because they who have wrongfully possessed themselves of it use it wisely and for the good of the community, or because unsuccessful resistance to their usurpation would cause much greater evils to society than the usurpation itself. Thus Governments, which owe their origin to violence or injustice, may at times become legitimate, and rightly claim conscientious obedience from their subjects; but such right is founded not on the violence which has placed such rulers in power, but on the fact that their rule has become, under the circumstances, necessary for the good of society, for which object the temporal power was ordained by God. Hence they are truly the ministers of God. It was when the Emperor Nero ruled over the world that the Apostle wrote that *"princes are the ministers of God serving unto this purpose."* – (Rom. xiii. 6). It follows that the Pope in his Encyclical Letter rightly condemns the doctrine "that in the political order accomplished facts have the force of law from the mere circumstances that they are accomplished." There are indeed cases when an unjust fact having been accomplished, prudence and the interests of society forbid its being undone. But if such fact acquires the force of law it is by reason of the relation it bears to the interests of society, not from the mere circumstance of having been successful.

As to the various forms of government by which nations are ruled they are the work of human wisdom, they vary at different times and in different countries, nor has the Church ever condemned or disapproved any of them; content with pressing on her children the duty of obedience to all duly constituted authority.

We have already remarked that in treating of the relationship between Church and State it is necessary to bear in mind that power in the State is derived from God. For if the State owes its existence and its authority to God, then has it duties to fulfil towards God; it owes service to God; it is bound to look on the service of God as the groundwork of society, and therefore foremost amongst those interests for the guardianship of which authority is given to the State. Even heathens, by the light of reason, understood that religion was the true groundwork of all wise government. A godless State is as unnatural and impious as a godless man, or a godless family. If, then, religion is a duty of the State, and if the Church is, by God's ordinance, the sole depositary of all true religion, there necessarily arises a relationship between these two powers.

It becomes a duty of the State to recognize the Church – to acknowledge her authority – to respect her rights – to protect and to uphold her. To say, as some do, that the best state of society is that in which the Church is not recognized by the civil power, is to affirm either that the Church is not the divinely appointed guardian of religion, or that the State has no duties towards God. Such doctrine cannot but meet with the most emphatic condemnation of the Church and of its supreme Pastor. But whilst the Holy Father recalls to the minds of men that the harmonious action of Church and State is a blessing to society, and condemns those who seek to destroy it where it exists; whilst he denounces the ravings of those who say that in all well regulated societies the law ought to proclaim that each man is free, not only privately but publicly, to teach, write, and act as he pleases in all religious matters, without interference of any kind from any authority, ecclesiastical or civil; whilst he recalls the words of his predecessor, ST. CELESTIN, that *the Catholic faith is the foundation which gives stability to kingdoms*, and in the words of another Pope, ST. INNOCENT I, reminds men that the *kingly power was instituted not only for worldly government, but chiefly for the protection of the Church*; he does not thereby teach, as detractors have sought to make believe, that the Gospel is to be propagated by the sword, that all toleration is bad, or that those governments which exercise toleration are acting contrary to the principles of the Church.

It is the duty of the State to uphold and protect the Church; but the mode of fulfilling this duty must, like all such duties, depend, in great measure, upon the nature of the society that has to be governed. When our Saxon forefathers were converted from heathenism to the faith, conversion began, in most instances, with the kings, and descended to their subjects. They were Christian princes presiding over heathen populations. Never was there, perhaps, a race of kings under whose rule the principle of union of Church and State was more fully, more successfully carried out.

They were the first founders of that wonderful constitution under which we live, and which, after so many ages and so many vicissitudes, still bears uneffaced the marks of its Catholic origin. Our Saxon kings not only aided and protected the Church, but the triumph of religion under that protection was complete. The Anglo-Saxons became a most Catholic nation. Yet it was not by violence that this change was effected. Venerable BEDE thus relates the conversion of the men of Kent:- *"When King Ethelbert believed and was baptised. great numbers began daily to flock together to hear the word, and forsaking their heathen rites to associate themselves, by believing, to the unity of the Church of Christ. Whose faith and conversion the king so far encouraged, as that he compelled none to embrace Christianity, but only showed more affection to the believers, as to his fellow-citizens in the heavenly kingdom. For he had learnt from his instructors and leaders to salvation that the service of Christ ought to be voluntary, not the effect of compulsion."* – (BEDE, *Hist.* i. 26.) In like manner were the other Saxon kingdoms brought to the faith through the example of their princes, and the encouragement they gave to religion.

But if Anglo-Saxon kings presided at first over pagan populations and by their wise support of the Church led their subjects to embrace the true faith; there are other rulers who preside over populations professing various religions, and whose duty it equally is to support the true faith. As regards these our blessed Lord Himself has pointed out to us the right course to be pursued, in the parable of the good seed and the cockle which had grown up together in the same field. To the enquiry of the servants concerning the cockle, *"Wilt thou that we go and gather it up?"* the master of the field replied, *"No, lest perhaps gathering up the cockle, you root up the wheat also together with it;."* – (Mat. xiii. 28, 29). Whence we learn that toleration under such circumstances is commendable, not because all religions are equally good, any more than wheat and cockle are of the same value, but because a contrary course is far more apt to damage the interests of truth than to promote them.

It is different, again, in countries where governments and people alike belong to the true Church; for it is then the duty of the State to prevent strangers from introducing error where it exists not. It is no longer the question of allowing wheat and cockle to thrive till harvest time after they have once grown up in the same field, it is a question of allowing cockle to be sown where only wheat has grown before. This is the work of an enemy, and it is the duty of the state to guard against it. Hence, though strangers frequenting Catholic countries are laudably allowed themselves to practise their own religion, the Pope justly condemns the doctrine of those who say that in such countries it is laudable to allow to immigrants the *public exercise* every man of his own religion. – (Prop. 78). And the Holy Father further shows the reason why such conduct is not laudable, viz., because the public practice of false worship, and the public manifestation of false opinions, tends to corrupt the minds and morals of men, and leads to indifferentism – (Prop. 79). If we believe ST. PAUL when he says *"Be not seduced, evil communications corrupt good manners,"* – (1 Cor. xv. 33), it is impossible to deny the truth of such a statement. The manner of dealing with the evil must needs, as we have remarked, be different under different circumstances. Still an evil it must be acknowledged to be. ST. PAUL, who warns us against the danger of evil communications, tells us in the same epistle that evil communications must oftentimes exist, and that the remedy against them does not always lie in avoiding them, *"otherwise* (he says) *you must needs go out of this world."* – (1 Cor. v. 10). Thus where religious dissensions unfortunately exist, toleration is laudable. Where unity still exists, it is a real good for society, and one which it is the duty of the State to protect.

Such is the doctrine, such the practice of the Catholic Church and of her Supreme Pontiff. But because the Pope will not allow that there can be more than one true Church, and denies the right of men to reject her teaching and her authority; because he will not recognize in might or in majorities the source of the civil power, but teaches that the power of Kings and Governments comes from God, and therefore imposes on them the duty of making the interests of God and His Church paramount to all others; because he will not admit the Church to be a mere function of the State, and denies the power of the state to regulate her teaching and her discipline; because being himself invested with temporal power for the good of the Church, he refuses to give up that trust into the hands of those who hold doctrines so subversive of her principles, therefore is he denounced *as refusing to be reconciled to. and to enter into competition with progress, liberalism and modern civilisation.* – (Prop. 80). What teachings and principles are concealed under these high sounding words the condemned propositions clearly show. With such progress and civilization the Pope never can, never will be reconciled. With that progress and civilization which recognizes religion as the foundation of society; which respects and upholds alike the authority of the Church, the authority of the state, and the liberty of the subject; which, whilst it seeks to extend learning, forward commerce, develop the material interests of nations, and assuage the miseries that man is heir to, remembers on the other hand, that *"Unless the Lord build the house, they labour in vain that build it: unless the Lord keep the city, he watcheth in vain that keepeth it* (Ps. cxxvi. 1.); with such progress and civilization the Pope needs not to be reconciled, for he has never been at variance with it.

The importance of this subject has obliged us to address you at greater length than usual.

APPENDIX 14

The Vatican Council
and a Duty of Catholics in Regard to it.
A Sermon Preached on Whit-Sunday 1870,
by George Case

THE FOLLOWING SERMON was preached very much as it now stands. In order to prevent any misconception, the Author takes this means to call attention to these two points:- First, that he has abstained from speaking of the Vatican Council as oecumenical, for the obvious reason that no council can justify its claim to that title until its close. Secondly, that he has spoken of the decision of the Holy Ghost as being made known through the Church's utterance, rather than the Council's, because whatever weight the decrees of a council may have must depend upon its oecumenicity and its freedom.

Whether the accounts that have come from Rome of the want of freedom of debate at the present Vatican Council are true or not, God now knows, and time will show to the world.

The Vatican Council
and a Duty of Catholics in Regard to it.

> When He, the spirit of Truth, is come, He will teach you all truth.

> John XVI. 13

SEVERAL MONTHS have now elapsed since our Holy Father, Pope Pius IX., having determined to collect together the Bishops of the Catholic Church for the celebration of that Council which is now assembled in the Vatican, ordered that the collect for Whit Sunday should be added to the proper prayer of the Mass on all days, even the greater festivals of the Church not excepted. And I need not tell you that his reason for so doing was, that the prayers of the whole body of the faithful might thus ascend as a continual incense to the throne of Grace, and draw down a blessing upon this council; even the Holy Ghost, that He might descend upon the Fathers who compose it in the fullness of His sevenfold gift, and endow them with the spirit of wisdom and of understanding, the spirit of counsel and of fortitude, the spirit of knowledge and of true godliness, and the spirit of the fear of the Lord; that so their deliberations might be brought to a happy termination, to the preservation of the faith, and the good of the Church, and the glory of Almighty God.

And now the great festival of Pentecost has come; and while we commemorate the first outpouring of this same Holy Spirit on the Apostles, we are led to rest calmly and with confidence on those loving promises of our Lord which were fulfilled indeed as on this day, more than eighteen centuries ago, but which are our inheritance also to the end of time. – 'I will ask the Father, and He shall give you another Paraclete, that He may abide with you for ever – the Spirit of Truth'.[1] And again: 'The Paraclete, who is the Holy Ghost, whom the Father will send in my name, He will teach you all things, and bring all things to your mind, whatsoever I shall have said to you'. [2] And again: 'When He, the Spirit of Truth, is come, He will teach you all truth'. [3] yes, my brethren, it is this which is our confidence; this our assurance that we shall never be misled; this which is our consolation when the truth is attacked, and we, in our faintheartedness, seem to tremble for the faith – that, so long as we cling to the Church of Christ, we are dwelling under the shadow of the Most High, and are abiding under the protection of the God of Heaven. 'He will overshadow thee with His shoulders; and under His wings thou shalt trust. His truth shall compass thee with a shield'. [4]

---

1   John xiv. 16.

2   *Ibid*, 26.

3   *Ibid.* xvi. 13.

4   Ps. xc. 4, 5.

Observe – there are, so to speak, two sets of promises with regard to the gift of the Holy Ghost. The first such as these, 'He shall abide with you,' 'He shall be in you'.[5] The other, 'He shall teach you all things . . . whatsoever I shall have said to you;' [6] 'He will teach you all truth'. [7] And these correspond to two elements in the life of the soul.

(1) First, there is the inward action of the Holy Ghost upon the soul, inspiring it with holy thoughts and desires, with which it must co-operate, else there can be no real vital religion of the heart. But this is not enough. So far there is no safeguard against spiritual delusions. In fact, there is no absurdity of fanaticism which has not set up its claim to be the work of the Spirit of God. How, then, are we to be certain that our religiousness is not a delusion? Here (2) comes in that other and outward action of the Holy Ghost, manifesting itself in the teaching of the Church, and it is this which gives a man a certainty that his religion is not self – deception. Both these actions of the Holy Ghost are necessary. Without the former, our faith would be but a barren, cold, heartless assent to a set of formulas, a faith without works, a faith without charity, a faith altogether dead and valueless. Without the latter, we should be liable to be the prey of any false religion or superstition, and to be as 'children, tossed to and fro, and carried about with every wind of doctrine, in the wickedness of men, in craftiness by which they lie in wait to deceive'. [8]

This is the reason why a Catholic lays such stress upon the decisions of the Church; this the reason why he feels bound by those decisions which are made by the Church, with the aid of the Holy Spirit; this is that which gives him such confidence, such 'peace in believing'.[9]

He knows that his faith is founded upon a rock. The rain may fall, and the floods come, and the winds blow, and beat upon the house, but it cannot

---

5   John xiv. 16, 17.

6   *Ibid.* 26.

7   *Ibid.* xvi. 13.

8   Eph. iv. 14.

9   Rom. xv. 13.

fall, for it is founded upon a rock, and that Rock is Christ. He knows that he belongs to a Church, against which the gates of hell can never prevail, that in that Church he may rest secure, even as Noe [*sic*] was secure in the Ark from the perils of the flood, that, although dangers may arise to the Church from without, and difficulties and anxieties and fears even from within, yet that he is in that Barque which, while it is tossed about with the waves and contrary winds, has Christ at the helm, who, though He seems to sleep, yet is awake to the distress ('I sleep', saith He, 'but my heart watcheth'[10]), and He is only waiting till we arouse Him with our cry for help. Then He arises, and rebukes the winds and the waves, and there is a great calm.

But although this confidence and 'peace in believing' is the rightful inheritance of Catholics, still from time to time there have arisen, and yet arise, in the Church great and burning questions, which seem to threaten this peace and to shake this confidence – controversies which so divide man from man who have been baptised into the faith, that it would seem as though the powers of evil had already in their hands the seamless garment of Christ, and were ready to rend it in twain.

Such, for example, was the controversy of the fourth century concerning the divine nature of Christ; so that it became necessary to assemble a General Council of the Church, in order that the true faith might be vindicated. Not that there was really any doubt in the Christian Church, in order that the true faith might be vindicated. Not that there was really any doubt in the Christian Church about the divinity of our Lord – the question was, whether the subtleties of the heretics were compatible with the orthodox faith. And the reason of this is, because the doctrine of the Church is old, it is the doctrine of Christ – there never can be a new doctrine. Such, again, was the controversy which arose in the fifth century on original sin. Such, again, the disputes on the Eucharist which began to be agitated as early as the ninth. I cite these merely as examples. Time will not allow us to dilate upon them. Enough to say, that at length the Church settled those questions; and then peace was restored till some new controversy arose. The cries of the faithful aroused Jesus sleeping at the helm, yet watching albeit sleeping – 'Then He arose and rebuked the winds and the waves, and there was a great calm'.

---

10   Cant. v. 2.

But there are also controversies which affect not the substance but the outskirts of faith. On such questions believers take different sides. If they are to be decided there is only one person which can decide them – the Church speaking by her rightful organs. Till she has decided, there is no earthly power that can condemn. Till she has decided, liberty of thought is left to Christians. Who are men that they should judge one another? You may discuss this or that doctrine, you may argue for or against it, you may endeavour to win over your opponent to your own way of thinking, you may privately feel convinced that he is in the wrong, that his opinion on the subject is most pernicious; but you cannot condemn him, you cannot anathematise him, or treat him as though he were not as good a Catholic as yourself, lest you be found to be cursing one 'whom the Lord hath not cursed.'

Now, the present time is one in which one of these controversies has arisen. A great question is now agitating the minds of Catholics. Some take one side, and some the other. The Supreme Assembly of Christendom is now debating it. Men wonder how it will eventually be decided. Hence, till by the aid of the Holy Ghost this question shall be settled, and such a decree be put forth as shall enlist the obedience of the whole Church, both parties have a right to exist, both have a right to argue; but neither has the right to excommunicate the other, nor to impute to the other a want of sincerity or of orthodoxy of faith. And, more, it is the positive duty of both parties to tolerate one another. There, in the Vatican Council, you have Bishops on the one side, and Bishops on the other, alike distinguished for their piety, their learning, and their zeal for the glory of God. Yet, though thus divided, they are in full communion with one another. The clergy here in England and abroad are also divided on this question, yet are they in full communion with one another. The laity also discuss the question freely among themselves; and however widely their opinions differ, still they also are in full communion with one another. How is this? Because the question has not yet been decided; and until it has been decided in such a way that no man can remain a Catholic unless he bow to the decision, they have a right to argue and to speak their mind, and to speak freely.

No man, be he a Catholic or not, can be ignorant of what that question is which is now agitating the Church and being discussed in the Vatican Council. You know, of course, that I refer to the question of Papal Infallibility.

Now, let us examine for a moment the state of the question. The doctrine of the Church is, that in matters of faith and of morals her formal teaching is always right, and can never lead her children into error; that she is 'the pillar and ground of the truth'; [11] that to her was committed the 'deposit' of the faith, which she is bound to keep intact and pure, and to defend from all corruption of doctrine; and that she possesses this great gift of infallibility in virtue of the promise of her Lord, (1) that 'the gates of hell shall not prevail against her;' [12] (2) that He would send the Holy Ghost, the Spirit of Truth, to lead her into all truth; [13] and (3) that He Himself, although withdrawn from the sight of men, would yet remain with her to guide and to direct her. 'Behold, I am with you all days, even to the consummation of the world'.[14]

With regard to this, there is no dispute or question among Catholics. So far we all are of one mind. The only question among us on this point is, What is the rightful organ of the Church's infallible utterance? or, from another point of view, Where does the Church's infallibility reside?

On this point there are varieties of opinion among Catholics, and of these varieties innumerable combinations and modifications. But these three seem to stretch over the whole ground of the controversy.

I. There are some who hold that the infallibility of the Church is, as it were, gathered into a head in the Pope alone, personally, and without the aid of the Bishops.

II. Others maintain that it resides in a Council, with the Pope at its head: provided that the Council be (1) really oecumenical, that is to say, be really a fair representative of the entire Catholic Church; and (2) there be in its deliberations full and perfect freedom of discussion and debate; so that, if either of these two conditions is wanting, its decrees, as such, are not infallible, and therefore are not irrevocable, but may at some future time be abrogated, or altered, or modified.

---

11   1 Tim. iii. 15.

12   Matt. xvi. 18.

13   John xiv. 26; xvi 13.

14   Matt. xxviii, 20.

III. Others insist that the infallibility of the Church is diffused throughout the body; so that the proceedings of a general council do not acquire their full force until they have been accepted by the Universal Church.

I am not going to argue in support of one or other of these opinions. I merely state these as opinions which are held among Catholics.

You may naturally, then, be curious to know to what conclusion the present Vatican Council will ultimately come. My brethren, on this point you know as much as I know, I as much as you. But this we do know, that the Church will never be formally committed to a decision to which she is not guided by the Holy Ghost, who 'breatheth where He will, and thou hearest His voice, but thou knowest not whence He cometh, or whither He goeth'.

Remember, once again – there is no controversy at all about the Church's infallibility. She was infallible centuries ago, as she is infallible now. Therefore, whatever is ultimately decided to be the right method of her utterance will of course be conformable to former decisions of the Church, and compatible with the historical facts of eighteen centuries.

Therefore it will, of course, be conformable to the decisions of the sixth, seventh, and eighth general councils, and compatible with the historical fact that Pope Honorius was by those councils condemned as a heretic.

Therefore it will be compatible with the fact that bulls and codes of law have been put forth by Popes, as, for example, those on usury, persecution of heretics, and the rights of the Tiara over civil governments, which either are now become obsolete, or are rejected as shocking and barbarous by the conscience of Christendom.

What, then, is our part, my brethren, at this time of excitement and agitation? What is our duty with regard to the Vatican Council? 'It is good', says the author of the Lamentations, 'to wait with silence for the salvation of God'.[15]

---

15   Lam. iii. 26.

To wait in quietness of spirit, and to rely calmly and serenely on the strong arm of God; to remain in prayer and supplication, even as the Apostles and the ever blessed Mary, for the outpouring of the Holy Ghost; to be ready with all humility and cheerful submission to hear His voice when it shall please Him to speak, and when we hear it to obey – this it is which is our duty now. 'But before all things have a mutual charity among yourselves.[16] Though all may not agree together in this matter, yet learn to respect one another. Remember that you profess the same faith and partake of the same sacraments, that all ought to have the glory of God and the welfare of the Church at heart, and that your differences here (and how should there not be differences so long as we see through a glass darkly, and know only in part!) – your differences here, I say, will all fade away in the glorious presence of Him whom we all hope one day to know as we are known, and to see face to face.

There is no proof that the general body of Catholics is not so waiting. But, unfortunately, there is every proof that certain self-elected representatives of Catholics sin grievously against this patient and charitable expectation, and act as though they were the infallible exponents of the Catholic mind. What! Because a man has a ready pen and a printing press at his command, is he therefore to set himself up and to act as though he were chosen to express the opinions of a body of men whose thoughts he cannot possibly know, except in so far as this or that man has communicated his own to him? Or is a priest so to degrade his pulpit as – (I do not say to express or to advocate, which he has a perfect right to do) – but so to express and advocate his views as to imply pity, or scorn and contempt, for those who differ from him?

No, my friends: it is not thus that God's truth is maintained. God does not need the violence and unscrupulousness of men for working out His own designs. Remark, I do not quarrel with men for stating their views, for arguing, for endeavouring to persuade others to adopt them: but I do protest against the tone of pharisaic insolence which certain organs of the Catholic press assume. I do protest against the abuse which they heap upon those who differ from them. I do protest against the low wit with which they strive to heap contempt even on some of those who are sitting as Fathers in the Council, and whose office and position they profess, forsooth, to hold in such unbounded veneration!

---

16   I Pet. iv, 8.

These organs (1) would make us believe that all Catholics worthy of the name are unanimous in their opinion of what the Council ought to decide – that the few dissentients who cannot conscientiously adopt their views are to be regarded as virtually heretical, as men who have no business in the Church. Here is a grave fault against veracity. For (a) they ought to be aware that, at any rate, some time ago it was not so. They should call to mind the fact that, 'instead of avowing their belief in the Pope's infallibility, the Catholics of England and Ireland have again and again declared that they did not believe it; and these denials have been deposited in the Government archives; that in the "*Declaration and Protestation*," signed by 1,740 persons, including 241 Catholic clergymen, it is distinctly affirmed, "We acknowledge no infallibility in the Pope;" that in the "*Oath and Declaration*," taken by all Irish Catholics in the thirty-third year of George III, the following words occur: "I also declare that it is not an article of the Catholic faith, neither am I thereby required to believe or profess that the Pope is infallible;" and that the Irish Bishops, assembled in Synod on February 26, 1810, allowed that this Oath and Declaration are "a part of the Roman Catholic religion as taught by the Bishops, are received and maintained by the Roman Catholic Churches in Ireland, and as such are approved of and sanctioned by the other Roman Catholic Churches"'. [17]

Besides which, (b) it is not true that even now Catholics are unanimous on this point. The mere fact that a controversy is going on proves this. And how can they be said to be unanimous, when the very Fathers of the Council are arrayed on opposite sides, some maintaining and some opposing the doctrine, some dreading its promulgation, others looking forward to it as the panacea for all evils?

And even (c) suppose that there were this unanimity, how are these private writers to know it? And how can they possibly know the minds of men who have never made known their minds to them? To affirm that I know to be true that which I do not know to be true, is as distinct a falsehood as to affirm to be true that which I know to be not true.

---

17   Letter of S. T. P. to the *Weekly Register*, headed, '*Faith and Opinion*'.

But (2) when to this is added the almost outrageous condemnation of Catholics suspected of not coinciding in this pretended unanimity, I confess I am inclined to ask, Where is Christian charity fled? And I can but call to mind the terrible warning of the Lord Jesus Christ, that whosoever shall say to his brother, Thou fool! shall be guilty of hell fire.

But (3) there is something yet, if possible, more grave to be added. For these writers lay themselves open to the charge of presuming to dictate to the Holy Ghost, when they hint that if the council, which they declare to be in all things inspired by Him, were to separate without promulgating a decree, it would be 'abdicating its office' , 'not doing its duty,' and would prove itself 'a false teacher.' All I can say on this head comes to this, that a man who presumes to dictate what shall be the ultimate decision of the Holy Ghost before it is made known, commits the same kind of sin as he who refuses to receive that decision when it is made known.

A man, of course, cannot but have hopes and wishes; but they must be expressed (1) as what they are in truth, simply private and personal. They must be expressed, (2) further, with perfect charity, and not only with the tacit admission, but with the inward feeling that those who object may be as good Catholics as those who affirm the point in dispute. And lastly, (3) the expression must be made in humility and perfect patience to await the guidance and decision of the Holy Spirit.

It is good for a man to hope; and that hope we have as an anchor of the soul, sure and steadfast, a more than hope, a confidence, a positive assurance founded on the Word of God, that the Lord Jesus Christ will not forsake His Church, which He has purchased to Himself with His most precious blood; that the Holy Ghost is even now abiding with her, and leading her into all truth: that, as in the beginning He brooded over the face of the waters, and then the light broke forth over the yet unformed universe, and beauty and harmony spread itself like a fair mantle over the whole, so that it became an Eden and the garden of the Lord, so now also is He looking down on the Church, and overshadowing it with His wings, as it were brooding over this confusion of controversy and uncertainty and anxiety; and then presently the light will break forth, and the mists will be dispelled, and His voice will be heard, 'This is the way, walk ye in it'.

The Lord our God shall make our darkness to be light, and the days of strife shall be ended; for He is our Light and our Salvation. 'Expect the Lord, do manfully, and let thy heart take courage, and wait thou for the Lord'. So we will pray and hope, and wait patiently for the salvation of God.

APPENDIX 15

Catholic Allegiance:
Clifford's Reply to Gladstone (Pastoral Letter, Advent. 1874)

"Render therefore to Caesar the things that are Caesar's,
and to God the things that are God's." – Luke xx. 25.

Dearly Beloved,

The precept contained in these words of our Divine Lord has been familiar to you from your childhood. You have been taught how at your birth you became members of a worldly kingdom, entitled as such to all the rights and privileges of free men, but subject to the laws, and owing allegiance to the sovereign, of the land of your birth.

When you were born again in the Sacrament of Baptism, you were enrolled citizens of the heavenly Jerusalem, thereby acquiring rights and privileges far superior to any that earthly kingdoms can bestow: you became subject to the laws of the Church of Christ; and henceforth owed allegiance to the Vicar of Christ upon earth, the Pope.

But, as your Baptism deprived you of none of those rights and privileges which you had acquired by your birth, so neither did it free you from the duty of obeying the laws of your country, nor was the allegiance due to your temporal sovereign in any way relaxed; on the contrary, the sanction of religion was now added to the natural sanction, and you were taught to obey civil laws, and to be loyal to your temporal sovereign, not only from fear, but also from conscience sake. You were henceforth both Englishmen and Catholics: in civil matters you recognize the Queen as your sovereign, in all spiritual matters you obey not any temporal authority, but the Vicar of Jesus Christ; and as the temporal allegiance due to the Queen is perfectly distinct in its nature from the spiritual allegiance which is due to the Pope, so to the one and to the other you owe a full and perfect allegiance.

You know how the Catholics of this country and of Ireland who, steadfastly adhering to this doctrine refused to recognize the authority of the temporal power in things spiritual, were for many long years persecuted and deprived of the rights and privileges due to them by their birth as British subjects.

In the year 1829 this grievance was in great measure redressed by the Act of Catholic Emancipation: subsequent enactments have removed all remaining disabilities, and our Protestant fellow-countrymen have acknowledged that it is possible for Catholics and Protestants to live in harmony as loyal subjects of the same temporal sovereign, and that Catholics may be faithful to the Pope without failing in their allegiance to their Queen. But within the last few weeks this harmony has been rudely threatened, and Mr. Gladstone, in whom Catholics not only recognize a great statesman, but one to whom they owe gratitude for his exertions in removing many past grievances, and who is the head of a great party mainly instrumental in obtaining Catholic Emancipation, has proclaimed that, since the publishing of the decrees of the Vatican Council it is no longer possible for English Catholics to pay to their temporal sovereign a full and undivided allegiance.

This is a matter of such grave importance to you as Englishmen and as Catholics, that we consider it our duty to address you specially upon it, not so much with the view of urging you to the fulfilment of a duty which you already faithfully practice, as of instructing you how to give an account of the faith which is in you, and how to rebut the charge now brought against you.

Mr. Gladstone, in challenging an answer, points out what sort of reply to his accusation would not be deemed satisfactory, as well as what would. "What is not wanted," he says, "is a vague and general assertion of whatever kind and however sincere". Now before we proceed further, we must protest against this assumption, that our Protestant fellow-countrymen have any right not to be satisfied with a general assertion of our loyalty. Protestant controversialists may essay to draw infidel or revolutionary consequences from Catholic doctrine, and may challenge Catholic divines to show that they are wrong. But in our proceedings with our fellow-countrymen we have a right to be judged by our actions.

Nearly half a century has elapsed since the passing of Catholic Emancipation. During that period Catholic peers and Catholic members have sat in Parliament; Catholic judges and Catholic magistrates have administered justice on the bench; Catholic barristers have pleaded at the bar; Catholic soldiers have fought in the army; Catholics have served their country in every office of trust. During the whole of that period the public voice of the country has proclaimed that Catholics have proved themselves to be loyal. Nobody then has a right to put Catholics on their trial, and say that they shall be considered guilty of a want of loyalty unless they can prove themselves innocent of the charge. Our conduct is before the world. we *say* we are loyal, and we claim it as a right to be taken at our word.

Having entered this protest, we shall proceed to examine what it is that Mr. Gladstone says is wanted of Catholics. What is wanted, he says, is either a demonstration, that not even by any powers asserted for the Pope by the Vatican Council, can he claim any right to impair the integrity of their allegiance, or else a declaration, that if any such claim is made it will be rejected, even if resting on definitions of the Council. We ask, what are the decrees of the Vatican Council which he deems fatal to our allegiance, and he points out two:–

1st. The decree which states that obedience is due to the Pope in all things which belong to faith and morals and the discipline of the Church.

2ndly. The decree which states that when the Pope, speaking *ex cathedra*, by right of his supreme Apostolic authority, defines that any doctrine appertaining to faith or morals must be held by the universal Church, such definition is infallibly true. Morals, says Mr. Gladstone, include every human action, whether belonging to the temporal or spiritual jurisdiction, and the Pope claims power over all. "I care not," he exclaims, "if there be dregs or tatters of human life such as can escape from the description and boundary of morals. I submit that Duty is a power which rises with us in the morning and goes to rest with us at night. It is co-extensive with the action of our intelligence. It is the shadow which cleaves to us go where we will, and which only leaves us when we leave the light of life. So then, it is the supreme direction of us, in respect to all Duty, which the Pontiff declares to belong to him, *sacro approbante concilio*: and this declaration he makes, not as an otiose opinion of the schools, but *cunctis fidelibus credendam et tenendam*".

To these words of Mr. Gladstone we give our most cordial assent; but we utterly deny the conclusion which he draws to the detriment of our allegiance. The region of morals is fully as vast as he describes it, but it is not a *terra incognita*, a land without roads, or landmarks, or fixed boundaries of any kind. On the contrary, no department of human research has been more thoroughly explored, mapped out, and circumscribed in every direction; all through it roads have been traced, and boundaries marked, which it is beyond the power of Pontiff or Caesar to remove. The Vatican Council has not abolished the decalogue. The Pope cannot change moral precepts, or reverse articles of faith already defined. Every human action comes within the sphere of morality, but the morality of by far the greater number of our actions has been long since fixed and determined; and the supreme power of direction, which the Pope claims in respect of them, is that preaching to all men the duty of duly performing them.

Again, all human actions are moral actions, but it by no means follows from that that they belong to the sphere of the spiritual power. It is a moral action to pay taxes, to buy and to sell, to plead at the bar, to try criminals, just as much as it is a moral action to administer the sacraments and preach the Gospel. Yet whilst these latter belong to the spiritual power, the former belong to the temporal power, and the supreme direction of the Pope regarding them shows itself in preaching to all men to be honest and just in the performance of such actions; to *"admonish them to be subject to princes and powers, to obey at a word, to be ready to every good work"* (Titus, iii, 1.) but the Pope has no more power to assess our taxes, regulate our trade, or interfere with the administration of our law courts than he has to sit and deliver judgment in the Court of Queen's Bench.

The limits of the temporal and spiritual jurisdiction are *in the main* definite and understood. Men go on from day to day and year to year rendering unto Caesar the things that are of Caesar, and to God the things that are of God, without any hesitation or doubt as to what belongs to each; and of the conflicts which have occurred between Church and state, the greater number have arisen not from any uncertainty as to whether the point contended for was of a spiritual or temporal nature, but from the unjust violation of the well-known territory of one party by the other.

When Catholics were required to conform to the Established form of worship and abjure the spiritual supremacy of the Pope, there could be no doubt that the temporal power was exceeding its own limits, and that

Caesar was coveting the things of God. In all matters which belong to the spiritual domain we obey the Pope, in all matters which belong to the temporal domain we obey the Queen.

When we say that the supreme direction of all that regards morals belongs to the Pope, we no more assert that he has the power to make wrong right and right wrong, or that he may ignore or transgress boundaries already fixed between the temporal and the spiritual powers and so interfere with our allegiance, than we mean to assert that our lives and liberties lie at the mercy of the sovereign, when we say that she reigns supreme over this realm. This is a question which touches the *Authority* of the Pope, not his *Magisterium*. Infallibility regards the latter not the former, and to say that the Pope is Infallible is not to say he is Impeccable. It does not follow that because the Pope has supreme power no Pope has ever abused it. But, as regards the cases in which it is alleged that Popes have done so, the truth or falsehood of the charge must stand or fall with the evidence adduced in each case. If a Pope were so to abuse his power as to seek to interfere in that which undoubtedly belongs to the civil authority, Catholics would resist him.

An illustration of what we have said may be drawn from the oath of allegiance required of Catholics by the Emancipation Act, and taken by them down to the day when all religious tests were abolished. In it they declared their belief that the Pope had no power to depose the sovereign and free them from their allegiance. What Catholics swore then they profess with equal readiness now. The morality of this action is fixed and determined, and may be clearly demonstrated. Allegiance, as the name itself implies, is the tie which binds the subject to his sovereign. It consequently differs in nature and extent under different forms of government. England is a constitutional monarchy, and the allegiance of Englishmen is co-extensive with the terms of the Coronation Oath.

The Queen swears to govern according to the Constitution, and her subjects are bound to her so long as she continues to do so. It is a solemn bilateral contract between the sovereign and her subjects. Now –ç

1st, the Pope cannot deny the general proposition that subjects owe allegiance to their sovereign; that is a moral principle established beyond doubt. Nor,

2ndly, can he deny that Queen Victoria is the lawful sovereign of this realm, and that English Catholics are her subjects. This is a matter which belongs to the temporal domain: the Pope acknowledges it, and every Catholic Bishop in England, in the oath he takes at his consecration, acknowledges not only spiritual obedience to the Pope, but also that his civil allegiance is due to the Queen. And,

3rdly, the Pope cannot release one party from the obligation of complying with the terms of a solemn and lawful contract without the consent of the other. It follows that the Pope has no power to free English Catholics from their allegiance.

When the whole Christian world reverenced in the Pope the supreme judge of the Christian commonwealth, the Pope passed judgment on the question whether the sovereign had complied with the terms of the tenure on which he held his crown, and consequently whether he had forfeited his claim to the allegiance of his subjects. In so doing he no more interfered with the rights of the temporal power of sovereigns than the Geneva arbitrators, by giving their award, interfered with the independence of England and the United States.

To aid in the defence of Queen and country against all comers is part of the temporal allegiance due from Englishmen by their birth. So is it part of the civil duties owed by soldiers to obey the commands of their officers without questioning the nature of the service on which they are employed. The Pope has no power to absolve them from their temporal allegiance, nor to oppose in any way the performance of civil duties which are due to the Queen. In the words of Dr. Doyle, quoted by Mr. Gladstone, "*the allegiance due to the King and the allegiance due to the Pope are as distinct and as divided in their nature as two things can possibly be*".

Nevertheless beyond these and such like cases which are firmly established there still remain some open questions, and occasions may arise when on a demand being made of a subject by the civil authority, that subject (whether Catholic or Protestant) must ask himself this question, "Is this a thing which belongs to Caesar or a thing which belongs to God"? If I obey shall I be transgressing the precept that we must obey God rather than man?

Neither Catholic nor Protestant leaves the decision of this doubt to the State. Catholics say the ultimate decision rests with the Pope. A dogmatical definition need not be issued, though perhaps at times even this may be done, and we shall presently consider whether the fact of such a definition resting with the Pope speaking *ex cathedra* instead of with the Pope in Council, in any way affects the allegiance of Catholics. All that is necessary, for our present argument, to state is, that Catholics maintain, and always have maintained, that the ultimate decision in such doubtful cases rests with the Pope, whereas Protestants claim the right of removing the doubt by private judgment. The difference is fundamental: but the question we have to decide is not whether Catholics are right and Protestants wrong, but rather whether it is possible for Catholics and Protestants, holding such opposite views, to live together as loyal subjects of the British Crown.

Protestants may ask Catholics, "What security have we that that authority which you believe to be from God, but which we do not, may not some day solve the doubt (should it arise) in a sense incompatible with your allegiance?" Catholics, on the other hand, may in their turn inquire of Protestants, "What security have we that that private judgment which you trust in, but which we believe leads you into error on many points, may not lead you into error in this instance also, and so bring you to persecute us for refusing to give to Caesar what belongs to God?"

Protestants, we presume, would reply somewhat in these terms:– "We have given you all the security we can give – we have granted you Emancipation, we have recognised your right to the free exercise of your religion, and we have pledged ourselves to preserve to you these rights so long as you stand by the assurances of loyalty you have given. Our conduct towards you during the period which has elapsed since the passing of the Emancipation Act, the well-known moderation of English statesmen, and the good sense of your English fellow-countrymen are a guarantee that we shall continue to act towards you 1n the same way for the future." Such is the security which Protestants tender to Catholics.

And now, on the other hand, what security can Catholics offer to Protestants? Catholics say:- "We pledged ourselves at the time of the passing of Catholic Emancipation to acknowledge the then King and his successors as our legitimate sovereign, to the exclusion of all other claimants; and we promised to pay him perfect and undivided allegiance.

We declared our belief that neither the Pope nor any other ecclesiastical person has the right to interfere with the civil government of the State, nor to oppose in any manner the performance of civil duties which are due to the King; and we declared that the Pope has no power to depose the King, or free us from our allegiance. What we held then we hold now. We have paid due allegiance ever since Emancipation; and during that time the Pope has never given any decision calculated to impair our allegiance. This is your guarantee that we shall act in the same way for the future."

Further guarantee than this it is not in the power of Catholics to give, for Protestants do not believe, as Catholics do, that the authority of the Pope is from God, and that therefore his decision may be better trusted than that of private judgment. If, therefore, Protestants refuse the security we offer, which is the same as they offer us, and which is the only one we can offer short of turning Protestants, there is but one course open to them – persecution.

It remains to be seen whether the allegiance of Catholics has been imperilled by the decree on Papal Infallibility. Mr. Gladstone lays stress on the fact that, prior to the granting of Emancipation, the Catholic Bishops declared "*on oath their belief that it is not an article of the Catholic faith, neither are they thereby required to believe that the Pope is infallible*." It is true, they did so, and, at that time, lawfully did so; but no such declaration was inserted in the oath required to be taken of Catholics; and that, for the obvious reason that such a declaration was no security at all for their allegiance.

For 1st – Though the bishops could then declare, and did declare, that they *were not required* to believe that the Pope is infallible yet they could not, and did not, deny that even then many Catholics *did* hold, and all Catholics *might* hold, that the Pope is infallible when speaking *ex cathedra*; and *if* such belief be incompatible with due allegiance to the sovereign, it was no security against a divided allegiance for Protestants to be told that Catholics were not *obliged* to hold it, when at the same time it was certain that a large number of them *did* and all *might* do so. Accordingly it was not required of Catholics to swear that they did not believe that the Pope was infallible, but only to swear that the Pope could not release them from their allegiance. Hence, no guarantee given by Catholics at the time of the passing of the Emancipation Act has been removed.

2ndly. – If the allegiance of an English Catholic is a divided allegiance at all, it must be so for the reason that his allegiance is paid to an authority distinct from the English Crown, whatever that authority may be. It matters not whether such authority resides in priest or layman, Christian prelate or Mahometan caliph, General Council, or infallible Pope. The allegiance is either divided in each case, or in none. And, therefore, as Catholics are admitted to have been loyal so long as they acknowledged the authority of the Pope when defining in council, they cannot be charged with a divided allegiance for admitting the infallibility of the Pope defining *ex cathedra*.

3rdly. – It has been argued (though not by Mr. Gladstone) that "as long as infallibility was invested in the teaching body of the Church united to the Pope, it was comparatively harmless, for it could scarcely be exercised at all. But now that it is concentrated in the breast of a single man, it is a thunderbolt which may be launched at any time. Allegiance to a Church dispersed was simply a theoretical inconsistency with English loyalty."

Now this argument, if it proved anything, would prove too much. It would prove, that prior to 1870, Catholics really paid a divided allegiance, only they had not the power of showing their disloyalty, whereas it has been admitted that up to that date Catholics were quite capable of rendering an undivided allegiance, and did so, in fact. But the truth is that the argument has no force whatever, as far as the loyalty of English Catholics is concerned. Whenever a question has arisen concerning which the Catholics of England or Ireland required the decision of the spiritual power, neither General Councils nor Definitions *ex cathedra* have had anything to do with the matter; application has always been made direct to the Pope, who has sent his answer through the Propaganda, and nothing more has been requisite.

Does anybody suppose, for instance, that in order to settle the question about the lawfulness of Catholics attending the Queen's Colleges in Ireland, it was ever thought necessary either to convoke a General Council, or to elicit a dogmatic definition *ex cathedra*? The notion is simply futile. The Bishops applied to the Pope through the Propaganda, and received back the Pope's answer through the same organ. That was the process observed in all similar cases prior to the decree of the Vatican Council about Infallibility, and the same procedure down to the minutest detail is observed to this day. It is easy to refer a matter to Rome now, but it was equally easy then. The decision was obeyed *then* as *now*, neither more nor less; and, as the process was held to be compatible with loyalty *then*, so it must be held to be compatible *now*.

Therefore, the argument founded on the greater facilities supposed to be afforded by the Vatican decree for Catholics to violate their allegiance, is wholly visionary.

Since, therefore, neither the decree about the obedience due to the Pope, nor the decree about the Papal Infallibility, or any other decree of the Vatican Council, empowers the Pope to interfere with the civil allegiance of Catholics more than before those decrees were enacted, and since, before their enactment, the Pope had no right, in any way, to interfere in the civil government of England, nor to oppose in any manner the performance of the civil duties which Catholics owe to the king, or otherwise to impair the integrity of their allegiance; so neither has he any such right now. And as it is acknowledged that English Catholics were then able to pay perfect and undivided allegiance to their temporal sovereign, so must it be acknowledged that they are equally capable of doing so at the present time.

Mr. Gladstone has thought proper, by way of testing the loyalty of Catholics, to inquire what may be their mental attitude towards the question of the Temporal Power of the Pope, in the supposition that the duties of England, as one of the guardians of the peace of Europe, led it to take measures hostile to that temporal power.

We know nothing of the secret conspiracies hinted at by Mr. Gladstone, nor have we any idea what measures might be framed by any English Minister to guard the peace of Europe against them, neither are we in any way authorised by English Catholics to speak in their name and say what would be their mental attitude under these hypothetical circumstances. But this much we say (and it is all that need be said, as far as the question of Catholic loyalty is concerned), that the English Catholics, without any imputation to their loyalty, are as free to oppose, by every constitutional means in their power, any measure brought forward by ministers in a sense hostile to the Temporal Power of the Pope, as they are to oppose any other measure of domestic or foreign policy, of which they disapprove; and that as for unconstitutional measures, it would neither be asked of them to have recourse to them, nor would they do so.

We have, dearly beloved, detained you at great length; we therefore briefly conclude by praying that the Prince of Peace, whose advent we are preparing to celebrate, may avert the ill feeling, which accusations of this kind are but too apt to generate amongst those who have hitherto lived peaceably together as fellow countrymen, that He may promote peace and goodwill amongst all, and keep you ever faithful to that doctrine preached alike by St. Peter, and by his successor, Pius IX., – "Honour all men: love the brotherhood: fear God: honour the King". – *Peter*, ii. 17.

The blessing of our Lord Jesus Christ be with you all. – Amen.

A DISCOURSE
Delivered at the Funeral of
George Errington, Archbishop of Trebizond

Fear Not The Judgment of Death (Ecclus, XLI, 5)

There is a judgment that awaits all men after death. It is a strict and terrible judgment: God Himself is the judge and the witness. *If thou, O Lord, wilt mark iniquities, O Lord who shall stand?* But faith, which makes us acquainted with this awful fact, tempers our fear and cherishes our hope by the comforting assurance that He who is to be our judge is also our Redeemer. Our Lord Jesus Christ is Himself our advocate, and *He is the propitiation for our sins: and not for ours only. but also for those of the whole world.* (I John ii. 2.) He it is *who His own self bore our sins in His body upon the tree. that we, being dead to sin, should live to justice; by whose stripes we are healed.* (I Peter ii. 24.) His blood was shed for the remission of sins; and because we believe that the holy and unbloody sacrifice of the altar is one with that which with shedding of blood was consummated on Calvary, and because we profess that in the Mass a true, proper, and propitiatory sacrifice is offered to God for the living and the dead, therefore are we this day assembled round the remains of one we have loved and venerated in life, engaged in solemnly offering up his holy sacrifice for the repose of his soul, before we consign his body to the grave.

But besides this tremendous judgment of man by God, there is also another judgment which follows death, immeasurably inferior in importance, it is true, but still one which Holy Scripture teaches us not to disregard. It is that judgment which men form of the lives and actions of those who have gone before them. Of the wicked it is said that *their memory shall perish* (Wisd. iv. 19); *but the just man shall be in everlasting remembrance, he shall not fear evil repute.* (Ps. cxii. 7.) *Some there are of whom there is no memorial, who have perished as though they had never been ... Others are men whose godly deeds have not failed ... Their glory shall not be forgotten; their bodies are buried in peace, and their name liveth unto generation and generation.* (Ecclus. xliv.)

The venerable Archbishop, over whose mortal remains we mourn, has not been called away from us at the dawn of life, neither was his long career hidden from the eyes of men. His days reach beyond the span of fourscore years, allotted by the psalmist to the strong among the children of men: he died in his eighty-second year. His life was an eventful one, and is inseparably connected with the history of the Catholic Church in this country. What manner of name does he leave behind him? What is the verdict men will pass upon him? Shall he fear the judgment of death? In answer to this question, I – as one who during four-and – thirty years was united to him by bonds of the closest friendship, and who, with few exceptions, knew more of him than most men now living – will endeavour to lay before you a brief sketch of his life.

George Errington was born of an old English Catholic family at Clintz, his father's property, near Richmond, in Yorkshire, on the 14th of September, feast of the Exaltation of the Holy Cross, in the year 1804. At an early age he was sent to Ushaw College, near Durham, where he distinguished himself for his talents and assiduity in his studies. He always retained a sincere attachment to this his Alma Mater, and cultivated through life the friendship of many of the superiors and fellow-students with whom he had there become acquainted. In the autumn of 1818 he went to Rome to study for the Church, in the Venerable English College which, during the days of persecution, furnished so many zealous missionaries and holy martyrs to the Catholic Church in England, and which having been closed during the occupation of Rome by the French, had lately been reopened by Pope Pius VII, Dr. Gradwell being appointed Rector. Here, as at Ushaw, he continued to apply himself with great earnestness to study, and at the end of his course he took the degree of Doctor of Divinity, and was ordained priest in the Patriarchal Basilica of St. John Lateran, about the year 1828. Shortly after this, Dr. Wiseman (afterwards Cardinal), having succeeded Dr. Gradwell as Rector of the English College, Dr. Errington was appointed to be Vice-Rector under him, an office in which he at once began to display signs of that ability for administration and the management of funds for which he was distinguished in after life. He also devoted much of his time to the study of ecclesiastical history, and of Roman archaeology, in which he became well versed.

After a few years his health broke down, he was obliged to retire from his post at the College, and fears were entertained that he would never recover health and strength sufficient to enable him to resume active duty. For the space of about eight years he travelled with his eldest brother through France and Spain and other parts of the Continent, spending the winters chiefly in the south of France, for the benefit of his health. During his travels he gathered for himself much useful information and added the knowledge of French and Spanish languages to that of Italian, with which he was already acquainted. His health being re-established, he returned, about the year 1836 or 1838, to Rome, and resumed work at the English College, under Dr. Wiseman, who highly valued his talents and ability, and who was warmly attached to him. In Rome he cultivated the acquaintance of many of the distinguished prelates and learned professors of the day, with some of whom he formed friendships which lasted through life.

In 1840, Dr. Wiseman was named by Pope Gregory XVI. coadjutor to Bishop Walsh, then Vicar Apostolic of the Midland District. After being consecrated Bishop in the chapel of the English College, Dr. Wiseman took his departure for England, and Dr. Errington either accompanied him to England or went there shortly after. Dr. Wiseman, whilst coadjutor to Dr. Walsh, resided as President at Oscott College, where, in August, 1843, Dr. Errington joined him, and presided over the studies for the space of four years, down to June, 1847. In the summer of this year, Bishop Wiseman went to London as Pro-Vicar Apostolic, and Dr. Errington left Oscott. Henceforth he devoted himself to the life of a missionary priest, first in Liverpool, whither he went in February, 1848, and afterwards in Salford, where, in July, 1849, he took charge of the important Mission of St. John's.

The magnificent Church of St. John's, now the Cathedral of Salford, had only just been built, mainly through the munificence of two well-known Catholic gentlemen of Manchester, Mr. Leigh and Mr. Leeming, with whom and with the members of whose families Dr. Errington formed a most intimate and lasting friendship, equalled only by the esteem and veneration in which they held him ever afterwards. A great friendship also existed between Dr. Errington and Dr. Turner, the late venerable and holy Bishop of Salford, who at that time was Rector of the neighbouring Mission of St. Augustine, in Manchester. There was still a heavy debt on the Church of St. John's when Dr. Errington took charge of the Mission, and the zeal, energy, and self-denial with which he laboured to overcome the financial difficulties of the situation earned for him the admiration and gratitude of the Catholics of Salford and Manchester. But he was no less esteemed for the zeal and energy with which he devoted himself to the duties of his sacred ministry, his assiduity in the confessional, his earnestness in preaching and catechising, his punctuality at the various services, and the care with which he visited and instructed the poor.

In September of the year 1850 Pius IX. re-established the Catholic Hierarchy in England. Salford was one of the newly erected Sees; and Dr. Turner, the great friend of Dr. Errington, was named first Bishop. Dr. Errington himself was appointed to the See of Plymouth. They both received episcopal consecration, at the hands of Cardinal Wiseman, in the now Cathedral Church of St. John's, Salford, on the 25th of July, 1851. Bishop Errington arrived in Plymouth early in August.

On his way he stopped at Prior Park, where I first became acquainted with him, and accepted the offer of becoming his secretary. The esteem I then conceived for him ripened into a friendship which remained unbroken during four-and-thirty years, to the day of his death. I lived with him as his Secretary and Vicar-General at Plymouth, and thus became intimately acquainted with his manner of life. This was but little changed after his elevation to the Episcopacy from what it had been before. Bishop Errington at Plymouth was the same hard-working, self-denying missionary priest that he had been at Salford. The conditions of his labour were harder than they had previously been. At Plymouth Catholics were few, and the poverty of the new diocese was extreme. Nobody who now visits Plymouth can form any idea of what the condition of the Mission was when Bishop Errington, surrounded by a few priests and altar-boys took possession of his See, in the little barn-like Chapel of St. Mary, on the 7th August, 1851.

The beautiful Cathedral of St. Boniface, the Bishop's residence, the Convent and the Schools, that form such an imposing group on the heights of Plymouth, are the fruit of the zeal and labour of Bishop Errington's successor. Nothing of this existed thirty years ago. Bishop Errington's work, like that of St. Paul, was, as a wise architect, to lay the foundation on which others might build; and when, not long ago, he visited Plymouth, he expressed his delight and admiration that the work raised was not indeed either wood or stubble, but so precious and noble.

The house in which Bishop Errington lived at Plymouth, the furniture, the food, and all the surroundings were of the poorest description, and in later days they frequently formed the subject of the good-natured jokes of his friends. There was but one object of value in the house, and that was his library, which he had collected with great care, and which he carefully preserved through all the many vicissitudes and changes of his life. It was, I believe, the only article on earth to which he had any attachment, and his frequent request to me was not to allow it to be scattered after his death.

At Plymouth he had to organise the Diocese, which was of vast extent, yet exceedingly poor, and with very few Catholics widely dispersed. But, besides the work of the Diocese, he did the work of an ordinary missionary priest at Plymouth. The young priests who worked under him felt at times inclined to resent the work required to be done, and the hard living they had to put up with; but all felt it was impossible to complain when they saw that the Bishop was always foremost in the work and took the hardest share of it upon himself.

Numerous examples might be given of his endurance and his indefatigable zeal. To mention one instance. I remember how on one Palm Sunday he said an early Mass and heard confessions in the church at Plymouth. He next performed the pontifical ceremony of blessing the palms; and then, leaving me to sing the mass, he started in a gig for the convict prison of Princetown, some ten miles distant, on the top of Dartmoor, there to perform service for the prisoners. Having gone little more than half way, he was stopped by snow, which had fallen heavily the night before; and at last, having vainly attempted to force his way over a snowdrift, he was compelled to return to Plymouth, where he arrived late in the afternoon, half perished with cold. Yet he preached that same day at the evening service. Many are the examples that might be given of his indomitable perseverance in struggling with difficulties, and his untiring zeal in labouring both for the Diocese and for the Mission of Plymouth. Suffice it here to say that he thoroughly organised the Diocese; and when, after four years, he was called to Westminster, he was able to hand it over, though poor, yet free from debt and in excellent order, to his successor.

He held the first Diocesan Synod of Plymouth with his clergy at Ugbrooke Park, which had been kindly lent to him for the purpose by the late Lord Clifford, who ever entertained for him deep admiration and a sincere friendship. He also attended with the other Bishops of England the first

Provincial Council of Westminster, and greatly helped Cardinal Wiseman, who always set great value on his work and assistance, in the preparation of the decrees. At a later period, the decrees of the second Provincial Council were almost entirely drafted by him.

In the year 1855, Cardinal Wiseman, requiring assistance in the work of governing the Diocese of Westminster, asked and obtained of Pope Pius IX that Dr. Errington should be promoted to the rank of Archbishop, and appointed his coadjutor. Dr. Errington accordingly left Plymouth, and went to Westminster in June that year to reside with the Cardinal, and laboured with him during five years. He was also during this period thrown much in contact with Dr. Grant, the saintly Bishop of Southwark, who held in high estimation his talents and virtues. Whilst he was coadjutor to the Cardinal in Westminster, an event occurred which is in a strange way associated with his abode at Prior Park during the latter years of his life. The financial condition of the Clifton Diocese, and especially of the College of Prior Park, had, owing to several unfortunate circumstances, become gravely embarrassed; and at the death of my predecessor, Bishop Burgess, it seemed unavoidable to close the College.

The Holy Father Pope Pius IX resolved not to appoint a successor to the See of Clifton till the financial question had been settled; and in October, 1855, Archbishop Errington, on account of his well-known financial ability, was appointed by His Holiness Administrator of the Diocese. In this capacity it fell to his lot to acquiesce in and regulate the sale of Prior Park, to wind up the affairs of the College, and apportion the losses to be borne by the various dioceses concerned in the undertaking. Fourteen years later, when I had re-purchased Prior Park and re-opened the College, he came to reside here, and here he spent fourteen of the most peaceful and happy days of his life.

After Dr. Errington had settled the affairs of the Clifton Diocese, it pleased His Holiness Pius IX to appoint me to that See. He was graciously pleased further to confer upon me the great honour and favour of consecrating me with his own hands, and on that occasion he chose Archbishop Errington to assist him as one of the Consecrating Bishops, in the Sixtine Chapel at the Vatican, on the 15th February, 1857.

Not long after this, events took place which gravely affected the fortunes of Dr. Errington during the remainder of his life.

One great feature in the character of Archbishop Errington was that he not only was always led by a strong sense of duty, which was with him paramount to all other considerations, but he always went straight to the point; and having once made up his mind as to what in his view ought to be done, he suffered no obstacle to deter him from the course resolved upon. He acquired the name of the "Iron Archbishop." This quality of mind, most valuable in itself, was not always accompanied with an equal appreciation of the difficulties to be encountered and of allowances to be made. Nobody knew better or more highly valued Archbishop Errington's sturdy character than Cardinal Wiseman. But the Cardinal had a greater feeling for the weaknesses of men, and was more disposed to meet opposition by striving to bend it than to break it. He was also more sensitive of obstacles, and suffered much when compelled to encounter them. The character of these two men – both highly gifted, both highminded, and both holding each other's qualities in high esteem – was essentially different. The difference up to a certain point had the effect of making them feel the advantage of mutual co-operation, and so of drawing them nearer to each other; but there was always danger of a rupture, and that rupture occurred at last.

In matters of Church government, as in matters of business or politics, good and great men are not rarely found to hold different views, and feel urged to take opposite courses. So it happened in the present instance. In the Catholic Church, there is but one supreme authority recognised by all priests and laymen as the arbiter in matters, not only of faith, but of discipline. That authority rests with the successor of St. Peter, the Bishop of Rome. We have nothing here to do with the matters in dispute: it suffices to know that Pius IX, who adjudicated the question, decided that it was not expedient that Dr. Errington should continue to be coadjutor to Cardinal Wiseman. This decision sufficed for Dr. Errington and from that date he ceased to be officially connected with Westminster, and retired into private life.

On two subsequent occasions, the Holy Father offered to appoint him to the government of important Archiepiscopal Sees; but having now reached an advanced period of life, he did not feel equal to enter upon fresh fields of labour and anxiety, and he asked and obtained leave to remain in his retirement.

But though the nature of his differences is not matter to be treated of on an occasion like the present, the humility and the patience with which he always bore trials and anxieties, which might well have broken the courage of other men, deserve our highest praise, as they always excited the admiration of those who knew him. Never, save at times to his most intimate friends, was he known to refer to his past struggles and griefs, and when speaking to them his language was that of a man discussing an abstract question of discipline, rather than of one occupied with matters closely affecting himself and his nearest interests. Never was he heard to utter an unkind word in reference to anybody connected with those disputes.

But, though retired from public life, he could not be without occupation; and in September, 1865, at the invitation of his friend Dr. Goss, Bishop of Liverpool, he accepted the charge of the Missions in the Isle of Man, and there, for three or four years, he again resumed the labours of a simple missionary priest. In December, 1869, Archbishop Errington went to Rome, and there, with the Archbishops and Bishops assembled from all parts of the world, he assisted at the sittings of the General Council of the Vatican till the month of July, 1870, taking throughout the liveliest interest in its deliberations. During these ten months he resided at the Convent of the Irish Dominican Fathers at St. Clemente, with his great friend the learned Father Molooly, well known in connection with the archeological discoveries made by him at that ancient basilica. Father Molooly always had a great veneration for the Archbishop, and the two friends constantly corresponded till Father Molooly's death.

Dr. Errington had now reached his sixty-seventh year. His life had been one of unremitting hard work, and he had had to struggle with severe mental anxieties. It is not surprising, therefore, that he should no longer feel his strength equal to the hard work of a missionary priest, and that he should seek some rest. But rest, as understood by Archbishop Errington, could never be dissociated from work of some kind. I was well acquainted with his views and feelings, and as I journeyed back with him from Rome to England after the Council (visiting on our way his brother-in-law, Count Spada, at his country house near Ancona), I proposed to him that he should come and reside at Prior Park, and undertake the tuition of the young theological students there preparing for the priesthood. He was pleased with the suggestion, and shortly after he came to visit the College, and took up his abode here in October, 1870.

He began forthwith to deliver courses of lectures to the students, and in the performance of this self-imposed duty he persevered with most scrupulous fidelity up to the day of his death. His profound knowledge of Scripture, theology, and canon law was a source of immense advantage to the young men who studied under him: he laboured, not only to instruct them, but to make them interested in their studies, and to inspire them with a love of knowledge for its own sake: whilst his earnestness, regularity, and punctuality was felt to be a constant and powerful incitement to duty and labour, not only by his scholars, but by every superior and professor in the College.

Amongst many instances of this earnestness and punctuality to duty, it will long be remembered how on one occasion having gone to spend the Christmas vacation with his relatives in Italy, and finding on his way home that the route through Mont Cenis had been blocked by an avalanche so as to impede his return to England in time for the opening of the term at the College, he telegraphed me, deploring the inevitable mishap, and asking me to provide that no delay might occur in the commencement of his class in consequence. Meanwhile he at once retraced his steps to Genoa, where he took steamer for Marseilles, and by this circuitous route he managed to reach Bath after midnight of the day preceding the opening of the term at Prior Park. Next morning he proceeded up to the College, and presented himself in the class-room as unconcernedly as if he had come down from his apartment, and had not hurried day and night in the depth of winter, over more than a thousand miles, in order to be ready at the appointed time.

A still more striking instance of his eagerness to be strictly faithful to the punctual discharge of duty is to be found in the circumstance, that on the morning of the day of his death, lying as he was on the bed on which only a few hours later he breathed his last, he assembled his pupils in a room adjoining his own, having appointed them the work they had to prepare, and busied himself about the papers they had written on the subjects he had assigned to them. A few hours after that he had breathed his last. He died as he had ever lived, and as he would have wished to die, busy at work to the end.

The fourteen years which Archbishop Errington spent at Prior Park form that portion of his life with which the majority of those here present this day are best acquainted. It was that of the most humble, unassuming, and gentle of men. He won the esteem and affection of every member of the College. The superiors, the professors, the students, the servants, all venerated him for his virtues and admired his humble and unassuming bearing. He was ever ready to give others the benefit of his learning. He took a sympathetic interest in the conversation and discussions of the masters, and in the labours and games of the boys. To all his conduct was a constant incitement to regularity in the observances of college life. Even in his advanced age he rose punctually at six, and never, except when prevented by illness, omitted to celebrate Mass at seven, and spend some time in prayer. It was also a constant practice of his to read each day a portion of the Holy Scriptures, besides his meditation. He was most methodical in reciting the divine office, and his well-known figure pacing up and down at stated hours in the portico in front of the College, saying the canonical hours, will be long missed as one of the standing features of the place. During the whole of his life he was exact in the daily recital of the holy Rosary. Up to a very late period he took his turn in preaching the Sunday sermon at the High Mass of the College. His attitude in prayer was most devotional. He was a favourite confessor, and he was very exact himself in approaching the sacrament of penance. Every year, during the long vacation, he devoted ten days to a spiritual retreat, which he spent in one of the houses either of the Jesuits or the Redemptionist Fathers.

But I must draw to a close. As the Archbishop lived, so did he die: engaged in work and true to duty to the last. He had been on a visit to friends in Ireland during the Christmas holiday, and had parted from them in excellent health and spirits; but on reaching the College on Friday, January 15th, he felt ill, and suffered from loss of appetite. A chill, caught on the journey during this very severe weather, seems to have settled on his lungs. It was difficult at first to persuade him to take to his bed. When he did so at last, on the Sunday, the disease had made rapid progress. On Tuesday, the 19th, hearing from his medical attendant that his end was probably drawing near, he, at his own request, received the Last Sacrament, whilst in full enjoyment of his faculties, with great devotion joining aloud in the prayers that were recited. This was shortly after two o'clock in the afternoon. After awhile he felt easier, and seemed to fall asleep; but presently his breathing grew fainter, and about half-past five, without pain or struggle of any sort, he quietly breathed his last.

Such, in brief, was the life and death of Archbishop Errington. He was a man of high principle; he had a thorough ecclesiastical spirit; he was indefatigable in action, never knowing what it was to be idle; he had a stern sense of duty, and was scrupulously exact in all that concerned it. He had an iron will, and the vigour with which he applied it weighed heavily at times on those who worked with him or under him. But he was always most just, and no one of his subordinates ever complained of having received from him an unjust or unfair command. When hard or unpleasant work had to be undertaken, he was always foremost in claiming his share. with all this he had a kind heart, and was ever ready to assist both by words and by deeds those that were in distress. He was most true and sincere in his friendship, and no man ever had friends more numerous or more attached than he had. He had a particular gift of interesting and gaining the affection of children. He was a man of high intellect, and was well versed in ecclesiastical learning, and also in various branches of science. But he was most humble and unassuming in his manner; most patient under adversity and trials. He was profoundly religious, exact in prayer and in the performance of his religious duties, and faithful in offering the Holy Sacrifice daily. Every day he read and meditated on the Holy Scriptures, and he loved to talk on and to discuss religious subjects.

As he lived, so did he die: faithful to his God and engaged in work to the very last.

Shall he then fear the judgment of death? What is the verdict that those remaining behind shall pass upon him? Shall he fear evil report? Will not, rather, his memory be long handed down under the appellation you have so often heard bestowed upon him during life, of "the good Archbishop"?

We shall now perform the last sad office of laying his body in the grave, there to await the general resurrection. We shall bury him at the entrance of this church – a most appropriate spot. All who enter the church will pass by his grave, and thus be reminded to pray for him. But this is not all. Passers by that spot, masters, students, and all, who will no longer have before their eyes the encouragement of his presence, will still be reminded by the sight of the tablet marking his tomb of the examples he gave them. As with the prophet of old, *even after death his bones will prophesy*: as day by day we pass by them, they will be to us a constant reminder to be true to duty, to be exact in observance, to be manly and patient in adversity, always to walk humbly before our God, and so, like Archbishop Errington, *not to fear the judgment of death.*

APPENDIX 17

Sermon
Preached at the Funeral of
His Eminence John Henry Newman
Cardinal of the Holy Roman Church
by
William Clifford

Wisdom led the just man through the right ways and showed
him the Kingdom of God, and gave him the knowledge of
holy things, and made him honourable in his labours and
brought his labours to completion. – WISDOM x 10.

My lords, my rev. brethren, my dear brethren: As we stand here to assist
at the last holy rites about to be performed round the mortal remains of
the great and holy man who it has pleased God to call away from the
midst of us, we must all feel that we are witnessing an event of no
ordinary kind. Looking round at the present assembly, and being aware
of the much larger number desirous to be present, but who are precluded
by the narrow limits of available space, still more when we call to mind
and reflect on all that we have heard, and all that has appeared of late in
the public press, we feel that we are assisting at the funeral, not only of
one who has left a mark on his generation, but of one whom a nation
admired and a nation loved. And who is he? He is a Catholic priest, a
Prince Cardinal of the Holy Roman Church, one, moreover, who has come
over to her, and who has devoted his wonderful genius and great learning
to the propagation of that Church in this Protestant land. What a change
is this since he himself was a young man! Could that which we now
witness have taken place then?

Would anybody then have believed it possible that the kind words, the
honourable sentiments, the fair and generous appreciation of character
and actions which we have heard and read of late would ever have been
uttered and published in this country regarding a Catholic priest and a
Roman Cardinal? And yet not only has this wonderful change taken place
in his lifetime, but it is in no small degree his work. Others, indeed, have
had their share; but in the work of disarming prejudice and drawing men
to judge fairly and kindly of others who differ from them in religion, no

man has accomplished what he has done. And more than with his learning he has done it by his gentle and kind manner, by his patience and sympathy, by knowing how to bear with the weaknesses of others, and how to handle, not only the minds, but the hearts of men. "The meek shall inherit the land". God, in His tender mercy towards this land, chose him for a special work, and endowed him with gifts specially fitting him for that work. He gave him not, from the first, a knowledge of the truth, but led him to it through the dreary path of anxiety and doubt, that so he might become a fitter instrument in the hand of God to help those who have to pass through similar trials. How many of those who assemble round his mortal remains this day look back with feelings of deep gratitude at the kind words and helping hand that led them into the Kingdom of God, and brought them to the knowledge of holy things? I wish, indeed, that it had fallen to the lot of some one more gifted than myself to speak to you of his life and virtues; but I was unable to deny the request of those who asked me to address you, and you must bear with me.

John Henry Newman was born in London on the 21st day of February, 1801. His parents were members of the Established Church. He was baptized and religiously brought up at home. At an early age he was sent to a private school at Ealing, where he remained till the year 1816, when he went to Trinity College, Oxford, of which he became a scholar two years later. In 1820 he took his Degree, and three years later he was elected Fellow of Oriel. Having taken Orders in the Anglican Church, he was in 1829 appointed Vicar of St. Mary's with the out-lying chaplaincy of Littlemore. Newman's connection with Oxford, which began in 1816, lasted for thirty years, and terminated in February 1846 by his reception into the Catholic Church. It was a most eventful period, and fraught with the gravest consequences to him and to the Established Church. It was not without its effect on the Catholic Church in England, and in the events which then took place we may well admire the merciful hand of God leading the just man through right paths till it showed him the Kingdom of God. His residence at Oxford may be divided into two periods. During the first, which extended to the year 1832 or thereabouts, Newman was mainly occupied in forming his own opinion on religion. His parents had trained him chiefly in Calvinistic principles, but these he gradually dropped before he had been long at the University. From his earliest days he had given evidence of a bright intellect and great activity of mind. He had also shown a very religious disposition, and an earnest desire for religious truth. At Oxford he came under the influence of men of great abilities, of different schools of religious thought. He also read books advocating widely opposite views of religion. At one time he tells us that he was on the verge of acceding to anti-dogmatic theories; but it was not for long. The men with whom he entered into the closest friendship – friendships which endured for life – were all firm adherents of the principle of dogma, and of a teaching authority, and it was with these that he cast in his lot.

In the year 1832 his mind was made up upon three points:– First: The necessity of upholding the dogmatic principle, as opposed to freedom of thought in religion. Secondly: The necessity of a certain definite teaching by a visible Church and episcopal authority. This he recognised in the Established Church. Lastly: He felt no sympathy with the Church of Rome. That year he travelled abroad. He went to Rome, where he met Cardinal (at that time Dr.) Wiseman, but no change took place in his views. He travelled in Sicily, where he fell ill, and on his recovery he returned to England strongly impressed with the conviction that he had a mission to labour in the reformation of the Church of England. His object, and that of those who laboured with him, was to restore the purity of dogmatic teaching in the Church of England, on the ground of maintaining ecclesiastical authority as opposed to the Erastianism of the State. This was the origin of the Tractarian party of which Newman became the chief exponent, of which he was for some time practically the head, and which derived its name from the *Oxford Tracts* that were started by him, and to which he was one of the chief and most influential contributors. In his *Apologia* he has left us a detailed account of the movement, its origin, its progress, and the labours of himself and friends during upwards of twelve years. It is not my purpose here to enter into the details of the struggle which Newman endeavoured to carry on at first under the covered opposition, and later on with the open condemnation, of that external authority, submission to which formed the basis of the movement. When, after the publication of *Tract 90*, he saw to his own grief the storm of indignation which rose against him on all sides, he felt, as he says, that his occupation was gone, his position was untenable, and he withdrew from the conflict. He retired to Littlemore, where he dwelt for some time with a few intimate friends; and, finally, on the 8th of October, 1845, he sent for Father Dominic, the Passionist Father, and on the following day was by him received into the Catholic Church.

As we read the account which Cardinal Newman wrote in later years of the long struggle he went through during the period that he was connected with the Oxford Movement, we are forcibly struck in the first place by the utter disregard for self which he manifested throughout. He was void of all personal ambition; he sought no personal advantage; he shrank from no personal sacrifice or loss. He coveted not the honour of leadership. It was not I, says he, that sought friends: my friends sought me. Secondly, we cannot fail to remark his earnest desire for truth. I remember how, at the time when these events were passing, Catholics, both in England and abroad, used to grow impatient and wrathful at the long delay which took place before Newman submitted to the Church. They used to say that he was not sincere, that he must be keeping back from selfish and unworthy motives. And yet how different is the truth when we come to know it. Never was a man so earnest and sincere in his search after truth as he, Newman, was at that time. When he was lying dangerously sick at Palermo, and was anxious to return and take part in the work of the movement in England, he would say to his attendants: "I shall not die, for I have not sinned against the truth." Those beautiful lines which he wrote about the same time, *Lead. Kindly Light*, express not only his own yearning, but have been used by hundreds of others in similar circumstances to give vent to their similar feelings. The ordeal that Cardinal Newman went through during those years not only helped to purify his own soul and prepare him for the grace of conversion, but the tender sympathy and compassion which he always felt for souls suffering under doubts and perplexity, as well as the power of aiding and encouraging them under such trials, was, in no small degree, acquired at the price of what he then went through himself. And this may be said further, that his example and a knowledge of the path through which he was led by the Holy Spirit before his doubts were removed and he was shown into the city of God, whilst all the time outsiders were in wonder at his delay, has, in no small degree, tended to make others more charitable and more just in their appreciation of the motives and difficulties of those who are still outside the fold of the one Shepherd.

"From the time that I became a Catholic" (writes Cardinal Newman), "of course I have no further history of my religious opinions to narrate. In saying this, I do not mean to say that my mind has been idle, or that I have given up thinking on theological subjects: but that I have no variations to record, and have had no anxiety of heart whatever. I have been in perfect peace and contentment. I have never had one doubt."

These words effectually silenced the foolish reports at one time circulated that Newman would ere long repent of the step which he had taken in submitting to the Church of Rome. But at the time of the Vatican Council, after the definition of the Infallibility of the Pope when speaking *ex cathedra* had been promulgated, similar rumours were again set afloat. It was said that he refused to accept the Decree, and that at one time Dr. Newman was on the point of uniting with Dr. Döllinger and his party, and that it required the earnest persuasion of several members of the Roman Catholic Episcopate to prevent him from taking that step. In his letter addressed to the Duke of Norfolk on the occasion of Mr. Gladstone's *Expostulation*, Cardinal Newman refers to these rumours, and characterises them as "the most unfounded and erroneous assertions," and says that the report "is an unmitigated and most ridiculous untruth in every word of it." To you, right rev. prelates, and to you, my Catholic brethren, it is needless to recall to mind this disclaimer. The high trust which the Holy See placed in Cardinal Newman by promoting him to the Sacred College of Cardinals is of itself ample refutation of this silly charge; but I have deemed proper to allude to it lest by others my silence might be imputed to wrong motives.

The news of Newman's conversion to the Catholic Church caused a great sensation, as well amongst Catholics as amongst Protestants, not in England only, but abroad also, and especially in Rome, where his name was already well known, and the movement in which he formed such a prominent figure had been watched with much interest. Cardinal Acton wrote to him a letter of congratulation, anticipating that his great talents would henceforth be of valuable assistance to the cause of God in the Catholic Church. Dr. Newman tells us that after his reception he had proposed to retire from the public gaze and to betake himself to some secular calling. But God, who had thus far guided him on his journey, and found him faithful, had other designs regarding him. It became evident that he was further destined to serve his Divine Master in the sacred calling of the priesthood. Long before he entered the Catholic Church, before he had reached the age of 16, he had become convinced that it was the will of God that he should lead a single life. There can be no mistake, he tells us, about the fact; and he was faithful, as usual, to the Divine calling. He never had a taste for worldly pursuits or worldly pleasures. He had no worldly ambition; his one desire in all his actions was to work for God and for His Church. Cardinal (at that time Dr.) Wiseman, who had for years past taken great interest in Newman and the Oxford Movement,

invited him to Oscott, and placed him for some time at Maryvale, or Old
ascott, not far from the New College, where Dr. Wiseman at that time
resided. Shortly after, by Dr. Wiseman's advice, he went to Rome in
company with his dear friend, Father Ambrose St. John, and after due
preparation he was ordained priest by Cardinal Franzoni on Trinity
Sunday, 30th May, 1847, and said his first mass in the private chapel of
Propaganda on the following Thursday, the Feast of Corpus Christi. I was
a student in Rome at the time, and had the pleasure of serving it.

Cardinal Newman was a man utterly detached from the pleasures and
cares of the world, but he felt no call to a monastic life, and, though he
had plenty of internal resources, and never was less lonely than when
alone, he felt the necessity of living with others who would sympathise
with him and with the work he was doing. The Oratory of St. Philip Neri,
which is an institute of secular priests living together under a common
rule, presented to him the kind of life which he wished for. He conceived
a great admiration and love for St. Philip, whose gentle and winning
manners were so congenial to his own taste. He embraced his institute,
and having, together with his companions, gone through his novitiate in
Rome, he returned to England and became the Founder of the
Birmingham Oratory, which was first established in Alcester street, and,
after some years, removed to its present site in Edgbaston. The Oratory
in London was also started under his auspices, but the union of the two
oratories was only temporary, as it is a rule of the institute that, though
all Oratorians follow the same rule, each house shall govern itself and be
independent of the others. The whole of Cardinal Newman's life, from the
time of his return from Rome in 1848, till the day of his death, has, with
one short exception, been spent with his spiritual children in the
Birmingham Oratory. He was there perfectly happy; he found there the
peace and retirement and leisure for thought and writing which he loved
so much, and in the society of his spiritual children, the Fathers of the
Oratory, who loved him dearly and reverenced him deeply, he found that
union of hearts which his sympathetic nature required. He was never at
ease when absent from the Oratory, and was always anxious to return
and be amongst his own. He received from Pius IX the title of Doctor of
Divinity, and he became commonly known by the title of "Dr. Newman".
Since his promotion to the dignity of Cardinal by the present Pontiff, he
has been addressed as "his Eminence" but the title which he loved most
was that which he claimed in his own community of "Father Newman"
or "The Father". The one break in the continuity of his residence at

Birmingham, to which I have alluded, occurred in 1852. In that year the Catholic University was established in Dublin, and Cardinal Cullen, Archbishop of Dublin, and the Irish Bishops invited Dr. Newman to assume the office of first Rector of the University. He obeyed their summons, and went to reside in Dublin, still retaining his office of Superior of the Oratory in Birmingham. He continued to fill the office of Rector of the University for six years, during which time he made the acquaintance and acquired the esteem, and in many instances the friendship, not only of the Irish Bishops and many of the clergy, but also of many eminent Irish laymen. It was during his stay in Ireland that he published his *Nine Discourses on the Idea of a University*, and other occasional lectures on cognate subjects.

The life of Dr. Newman in Birmingham before he went to Dublin and after his return was always an active one. He preached and took part in all the works of the Oratory and of the mission. He was always ready to answer to the call of his Bishop to come forward in the defence of Holy Church, and to promote her cause. Here he preached his *Discourses to Mixed Congregations*, and here at the institute he delivered his lectures on *Difficulties of Anglicans*, a passage in one of which gave occasion for the Achilli trial, to which I need not do more than allude. During the discussions which arose after the publication of the Decrees of the Vatican Council he was engaged in controversy with his old friend Dr. Pusey, and wrote an answer to his *Eirenicon*. Likewise, when Mr. Gladstone rashly accused Catholics of want of loyalty to their sovereign, Dr. Newman took up the challenge, and nobly refuted the charge in a letter which he published, addressed to his Grace the Duke of Norfolk. But the preaching and writings of Dr. Newman, a portion only of which I have here enumerated, are far from constituting the whole or even the greater part of what, at this time, he was doing for the Church of God. His kind and gentle nature, the sympathy he always felt for those who were in anxiety and doubt, and the art he had of gaining their confidence and ministering to them comfort and advice, no less than the high esteem in which his learning was held, caused men of all classes and callings to have recourse to him in their difficulties, and he was most indefatigable in giving them his assistance both in person and by letter. There is scarcely an individual of any note who had been received into the Church during the last thirty years who has not in the course of his search after truth received assistance from Cardinal Newman. Many owe their conversion, under God, entirely to him.

I shall not attempt an enumeration of all Cardinal Newman's writings, but I cannot avoid noticing that interesting work his *Apologia pro Vita Sua*. It owes its origin, as everybody knows, apparently to a mere accident – the necessity which he felt of repelling a wanton attack made upon his veracity. But it proved a most providential work. It has placed the workings of God in the soul of his holy man in a most wonderful light before the whole world. It brought great comfort to Cardinal Newman himself, for it was the means of breaking down the barrier which, since his conversion, had up to that time existed between him and old friends, and it has had the effect of destroying many prejudices, and of removing to a great extent that wall of separation which centuries of mutual distrust had erected between Catholics and Protestants in our country.

As a writer, it is impossible to speak too highly of him. He was a perfect master of the English language and of English style. As a preacher, he had wonderful powers of his own: he relied not on the outward forms and graces of delivery; but he had a sweet voice, a distinct utterance, and an earnestness of diction which captivated his hearers, and impressed them with the conviction that he meant what he said, and that what he said was true. He attended the first Provincial Synod of Westminster, held at Oscott in July 1852, and the sermon which he there preached, *The Second Spring*, greatly delighted the assembled fathers, most of whom then heard him for the first time, but not less, perhaps, was the impression made by his sweet voice, his simple enunciation, and his saintly appearance, as he read the points of mental prayer at the public sessions of the Synod.

Time compels me to pass over much that Cardinal Newman has done for the Church, but any account of his work in Birmingham would be incomplete which omitted to record the foundation by him of the Oratory School. The large number of scholars, children of old Catholic families no less than of recent converts, testify to its efficiency and success. It was a work of Cardinal Newman's own creation; he always took the greatest interest in it, and even a few weeks before his death, though borne down by age and infirmity, he assisted at the Latin Play performed by the scholars – an annual institution which owes its origin to his special care and supervision. All who have been educated at this school, from the Duke of Norfolk downwards, have preserved a sincere love and deep veneration for the good Cardinal, and the old boys of the Oratory are foremost this day amongst those who mourn his loss.

Dr. Newman had reached the advanced age of four score, and, though he was still sound in constitution and vigorous in mind, it was clear that in the ordinary course of nature the end of his career could not be very far distant. That Divine Providence, which had watched over him and led him through wondrous ways to the Kingdom of God and had enriched his mind with the knowledge of holy things, had also made him honourable in his labours for the Church of God. One thing still seemed to be wanting to crown that work. Newman's idea of God's Church had always been that of a visible active authority. His conception of work done for God was work done under the sanction of authority. When he found that he could not do this in the Established Church, he felt, as he says, that his occupation was gone. Since his reception into the Catholic Church, his veneration for the authority of the successor of Peter had been unlimited. Between him and his Bishop, the late Dr. Ullathorne, there had existed the greatest intimacy and a cordial friendship founded on the high appreciation which each had of the other's character, and that venerated and holy man used often, in speaking of Dr. Newman, to tell of his great humility and of his tenderness of conscience in all that regarded obedience to his Bishop.

When the reigning Pontiff, Leo XIII, was raised to the see of Peter, one of his first acts after his accession was to offer the Cardinal's hat to Dr. Newman. Dr. Newman had no ambition: the proffered dignity had not been sought for by him; his natural love of retirement would have prompted him to draw back and decline the dignity so graciously proffered. But this offer was the seal of approval placed by the highest authority on all that he had endeavoured to do for the Church: it was an answer to all detractors, it was the crown of the edifice, the accomplishment of his labours. God had vouchsafed him the accomplishment of his greatest and only ambition, the approval of his work by the authority of his vicar. *Complevit labores illius*. In this light Dr. Newman viewed the kind offer of Leo XIII; in this spirit he accepted it. For this he was always most grateful to the Holy Father, and was most anxious to show his gratitude. Of the high nature of the dignity offered to him he had the greatest estimation, and, though he was naturally averse to any display of pomp, though on his return to his Oratory at Birmingham he was anxious to make as little change as possible in his former habits of life, he was scrupulously observant that nothing should be done, and nothing omitted by himself or by his attendants, the doing or omission of which might in the slightest degree detract from the respect and observance due to the Cardinalatial dignity. The news of the elevation of Cardinal Newman to the Sacred College was received with universal applause, and addresses of congratulation poured in from the continent, from America, and all parts of the world. On his return to England he received numerous deputations and addresses, not only from the Catholic Bishops, the clergy and laity of England, Ireland, and Scotland, and from his old friends, but Protestants throughout the country expressed their satisfaction at this recognition of his talents and virtue, and regarded his elevation as an honour done to the country in the person of one of the most illustrious of her sons. That this kindly feeling was not due to a mere transitory excitement of the moment is evinced by the grief and sympathy which at the present day has been shown throughout the country when the news of his death became known, and by the numerous kindly notices concerning him which have appeared in the public press of all shades of opinion.

Cardinal Newman survived his elevation to the Cardinalate for eleven years, having been created Cardinal Deacon of the title of St. George in Velabro in the year 1878. He had now reached the advanced age of 89. For the last three years his strength had been gradually failing, and his sight had become dim, which was a great trial to him, as it deprived him of the pleasure of corresponding and reading. But his mental faculties remained unimpaired to the last. When the Catholic Truth Society met in Birmingham in July of this year 1890, he received a deputation of its members, and said a few words in answer to their address. Shortly after, on Saturday, August 9th, he expressed himself as feeling better than he had been for a long while, but in the evening he complained of shivering, and it was evident he had caught a cold. He was promptly attended by Dr. Jenner Hogg, but the illness made rapid progress. Dr. Blunt, his medical adviser, who had for years attended him with the most kind and unremitting care and assiduity, was summoned by telegraph from Blackpool, whither he had gone a few days previously, and arrived that same evening. By Sunday morning it became clear that he was suffering from pneumonia, and henceforth all hope of recovery ceased. He still remained conscious, and about mid-day on Sunday asked Father Neville, his secretary and attendant, to recite with him a portion of the Breviary. On Monday morning he fell into a comatose state. Extreme Unction was administered to him by Father Mills, but he was not able to receive Holy Viaticum. He had received Holy Communion on the Saturday two days previous. Dr. Ilsley, Bishop of the Diocese, had been absent from

Birmingham for some days, and the news of the Cardinal's illness had not reached him. He unexpectedly returned to St. Chad's, and, on hearing the sad news, went at once to the Oratory, where he found the Cardinal still alive, but apparently unconscious. He remained with him some time in prayer, and recited with the Fathers the "Commendation of the Departing Soul". At twelve minutes to nine Cardinal Newman quietly, and without any struggle or pain, surrounded by the Fathers of the Oratory, breathed his last.

I wish I could delineate to you his virtues and holy life as he deserves, but I feel myself quite unequal for such a task. I must, however, say a few words about his private life. Cardinal Newman had from his childhood a great idea of the majesty and greatness of God. He was truly a man of God. He always felt himself to be in the presence of God, and the duty of serving God and doing His will was prominent to all other thoughts. His descriptions of the Divine attributes and the great works of God are some of the most beautiful and most powerful portions of his writings. Great was his devotion to the Blessed Sacrament of the Altar. He never omitted saying daily Mass except when incapacitated by bodily infirmity, and in his latter days he felt the impossibility of being able to say Mass as the greatest of his trials, and often spoke of it as such. His fervour and devotion when saying Mass was most edifying to those who assisted. He had also a tender devotion to the Mother of God, which shows itself in many of his writings; and he was specially fond of saying the Rosary. He spoke of it as a most beautiful devotion, and often said that when deprived of the power of saying Mass he found his greatest compensation in saying the Rosary and meditating on its beautiful mysteries.

When in health he attended all the devotional exercises of the Oratory. His mode of life was simple, and in conformity with his profession of a son of St. Philip. Of his devotion to St. Philip, whom he tenderly loved as a son loves his father, I need not speak. He has left abundant evidence of this in his writings. When in Rome, he loved to visit the holy places, and it is recorded that when first he went to Rome after his conversion, though he arrived late in the day and much fatigued by his journey, he would neither rest nor take food till he had been to visit the tomb of the Prince of the Apostles, there to renew his profession of faith. His love of truth and a warm sympathising heart were chief amongst the traits of his character. He was void of personal ambition, most unselfish, and always ready to sacrifice himself for others. He was naturally of a retiring disposition, and very sensitive. He was a sincere friend, and, as he was always most considerate to others, he felt keenly any slight or injustice exercised towards his friends or himself. These leading features of his character were plainly noticeable to all, and have many times been commented upon during his life, and now more especially in the many notices which have appeared concerning him in the public press. But, perhaps, the best and fullest description of his character has been unwittingly given to us by himself. Cardinal Newman was essentially an Englishman; such he professed himself to be, and Englishmen, without distinction of party or creed, have been proud to claim him as one of themselves. In a sermon, *Christ on the Waters*, preached in this city on the occasion of Dr. Ullathorne being installed as first Bishop of Birmingham, Cardinal Newman traces the history of our Saxon forefathers as they wandered from the defiles of the mountains in the frontiers of Asia across Central Europe, till they settled themselves in this our island. "It was", he says, "a proud race, which feared neither God nor man – a race ambitious, self-willed, obstinate, and hard of belief, which would dare anything, even the eternal pit, if it was challenged to do so." Such, he says, was the character of our pagan ancestors; but then he proceeds to describe what that character was to become under the influence of Divine grace. "The Almighty Lover of Souls looked again, and He saw in that poor forlorn and ruined nature . . . what would illustrate and preach abroad His grace if He took pity on it. He saw in it a natural nobleness, a simplicity, a frankness of character, a love of truth, a zeal for justice, an indignation at wrong, an admiration of purity, a reverence for law, a keen appreciation of the beautifulness and majesty of order – nay, further a tenderness and an affectionateness of heart which He knew would become the glorious instruments of His high will, illuminated and vivified by His supernatural gifts." In these words Cardinal Newman has painted for us his ideal of the English character under the influence of grace. It is the best and truest description of his own.

And now the end has come. A great and holy man has been taken from the midst of us, a faithful servant and mighty champion of God's Church has gone to his reward, one of the most prominent and most gentle characters of this age and country has departed from our gaze. His years have reached beyond the span of life usually accorded to men. Those who knew him best, his dearest and numerous friends, those who were the companions of his sorrows and his joys, have gone before him; a new generation of men has arisen in their place, yet had he died in the vigour of his manhood, in the midst of his work, the sorrow felt at his departure would not have been more universal, it could not have been more sincere. His memory will always remain in benediction in this land. His writings will be read wherever the English tongue is known, and will continue to do some of the work which he has done. With sorrowing hearts, we commend his dear soul to God, and his ashes to the earth. He is now beyond the reach of our praise, but we may help him by our prayers. Numerous Masses have everywhere been offered up for the repose of his soul; many more will be offered still. When we think of this and remember the pure and holy life he led upon earth, we may not be without hope that even now his happiness is complete. But these are secrets known to God alone. We must never relax in prayer. Remember his own touching appeal:

> Weep not for me when I am gone,
> Nor spend thy faithful breath
> In grieving o'er the spot or hour
> Of all enshrouding death.
>
> Nor waste in idle praise thy love
> on deeds of head or hand,
> Which live within the living Book,
> Or else are writ in sand.
>
> But let it be thy best of prayers,
> That I may find the grace
> To reach the holy house of toll,
> The frontier resting place.
>
> To reach that golden palace gate
> Where souls elect abide,
> Waiting their certain call to heaven
> With angels at their side.

Towards the holy angels he always had a special devotion. It was a sentiment that had grown up with him from his infancy, and, as he advanced in years, he loved to think of them and address them as the ministers of God constantly employed by Him about the works of Creation. For his guardian angel he had a tender devotion, he called him his friend and his brother:

Mine oldest friend, mine from the hour
When first I drew my breath:
My faithful friend that shall be mine
Unfailing till my death.

Mine when I stand before the Judge;
And mine if spared to stay
Within the golden furnace till
My sin is burn'd away.

And mine, O Brother of my soul,
When my release shall come:
Thy gentle arms shall lift me then,
Thy wings shall waft me home.

May they even now perform this loving office as we offer up the prayers of Holy Church before consigning his mortal remains to the tomb: *Subvenite, Sancti Dei, occurrite, Angeli Domini, suscipientes animam ejus, offerentes eam in conspectu Altissimi.* Come to his assistance, O ye saints of God; Make haste to meet him, O angels of the Lord. Receive his soul and offer it up in the presence of the Most High. Amen. Amen. [1]

---

1   For the warm reception accorded to Cliffod's eulogy see above
      pp 323 – 325.

Bishop Hedley's Funeral Oration
on Bishop Clifford

Bishop Hedley based his panegyric upon the words, "O Lord, Thou hast tried me and hast known me" (Psalm cxxxviii., 1). Addressing those present as "My Lords and my brethren in Jesus Christ," he said it was too often true that mourning for the dead was conventional, and even genuine regret for a public loss might frequently leave the heart untouched; but that day there was sorrow of another sort. God tried him, God knew him; not as God knew him could they say that they knew him, but yet they seemed to have known him, they seemed to have tried him. They were there that day, his relatives, his flock, his clergy, the Regular Orders, his fellow Bishops, his friends – all those with whom he lived, with whom he worked in England, in Rome, in the Church, in society, in literature – they thought they knew him. They knew him as an honest man, as a good man, as a God-fearing man, as a kind man, an able man, as one who deserved to be called, like the prophet of old, a lover of his brethren. And be believed that their grief was not only genuine, but that it came out of those deep springs of human nature which were only stirred by personal loss. With so many present who could recall his words and his acts, it seemed idle for one to stand up and to try to put into expression what must be at the best only a very incomplete portrait. And yet reverence for his person and for his office and the custom of the Church, demanded that some last funeral words should then be spoken in the presence of all that remained upon earth of the Right Rev. William Joseph Hugh Clifford, third Bishop of the Church at Clifton.

He was the son of Hugh Charles, 7th Baron Clifford, of Chudleigh and was born at Irnham. He would have been 70 years of age had he lived till Christmas Eve. After his early training he went to Rome, where, when he was 17 years old, in 1840 the Festival of the Assumption, he delivered before Gregory XVI a panegyric on our Lady. He was ordained priest at Clifton by [Bishop Hendren, V.A.] on August 25, 1850, so that had he lived he would in a week have been a priest for 43 years. Afterwards he sought Rome again, and having taken the degree of Doctor of Divinity, he went, as many would remember, to Plymouth with Archbishop Errington, his life-long friend, next to whose remains they should place his body in a few minutes. He took an active part in various departments of Catholic life and again visited Rome for study, to familiarize himself above all with Canon Law. One who wrote a memoir of him at that time said, alluding to the weakness of his health, that if it should please God to re-establish his health, they could justly look forward to his doing much for the Church; and that prophecy had been fulfilled. He was consecrated, Bishop of Clifton by Pius IX on February 15, 1857, and took possession of his see on March 17 – St. Patrick's Day – of the same year. Since then he had been what they had known him at Clifton for 36 years. He was speaking to those who knew Dr. Clifford in many respects much better than he did.

There were some who could have spoken better who had either passed away or were absent that day. He recalled Cardinal Manning whose loss they had so lately lamented; he recalled his own predecessor in South Wales who was five and twenty years his senior, and between whom there was a friendship of a genial, almost playful character, such as between father and son. These had passed away, and there was one whose absence they especially regretted, namely, the Chief of the English hierarchy, who had sat beside Dr. Clifford for many years at the Bishops' meetings and who was bound up with him in many ways. He should have spoken that day. A public man, his character, his attainments, and his learning were solid, and of a sterling English type. He was not easily swayed by sentiment or fashion; his mind and disposition clung to ancient ways and to the practices of the grand old English stock from which he sprung. What his fathers loved he loved; what his fathers practised that he willingly practised.

And yet that spirit which in some men might have been narrow and insular was lifted up and broadened by the education he received, by the life which he lived. For many years he studied among the learned men of Rome; he had heard the greatest of her theologians, had mingled with great prelates. He had been brought into contact with the great stream of universal Catholic thought, and any narrowness of mind and any possibility of prejudice were swept away by that education which he had received and by that constant association which he kept up with the holy city of Rome and with her spirit and long traditions; for the Catholic Church, though an immortal church, was not dead like some stony sphinx of Egyptian deserts silted up by the sand of ages; her immutability is the perpetuity of continual life. Dr. Clifford recognised that, unalterable as she was, nevertheless there was in her the development of leaf and the bursting of flower from year to year from century to century.

In all public questions those who came across the late Bishop Clifford recognized in him an anxiety to know, an anxiety to be serious, an anxiety to discuss. He seemed to think and feel that anything unreasonable and irrational was unworthy of his mind, and hence he was ever sincere; he never would give an opinion which he had not thought out and which he did sincerely hold. They could turn to him therefore, and though he could be eager in dispute, and though he held the ideas which he did hold with tenacity, he never in the heat of argument for a moment lost his temper and in a moment when all was over there was serenity in that beautiful mind, and that charity, which was a mark of Christ's children, was never overshadowed. A more loyal friend, probably never existed, as they well knew. He supposed that there were few men who put self-interest on one side more effectively. To his fellow bishops, clergy, and friends, he was a true and loyal friend; they could depend upon his help and guidance whenever and wherever they met him. There were one or two serious occasions in his life to which he could not do more than allude, because it was impossible that they could be properly discussed without fitting and suitable material.

The provincial Synods of this country, upon which the Catholic Church so much depended in her discipline, owed a great deal to his learning, and to his sincerity and earnestness; and at the Bishops' meetings, the presence of Bishop Clifford was always a gain and always an advantage. He said little, but what he had to say was exactly to the point, and was so full of information that it was always of very great profit. This had been going on for many years quietly and silently. It was impossible that the general public could understand what a bishop with qualities like these could do for the advancement of the Church to which he belonged, but those present, especially the clergy, could enter into it. There were at the time of the Vatican Council certain rumours in the public press; he was not going to enter into them. It was in some respects a time of trial; Bishop Clifford's action was steady, cautious, moderate, unaffected by sentiment, full of loyalty to the Holy Father, and he was, to the last, joyous and happy in the full acceptance of the great Catholic dogma. There was another memorable occasion upon which, whatever else might be said, he sacrificed himself – sacrificed what most would call his own prospects – for loyalty to a friend. And there was the great work which few outsiders had even heard of – the part which he took in the negotiations at Rome – which led to the Constitution *Romanos Pontifices*, which had doubled the efficiency of the regular clergy in this country by that thorough order, that thorough organization, that thorough peace, without which there could not be progress in the Church of God.

His brethren knew how interested he was in the building of churches, and of schools, in the education question, in the question of religious education for every child, in the institutions which were more or less established by his means and by his interest, and how he placed himself at the head of every good movement. They remembered how he had what they might call a special devotion to ecclesiastical functions, and how wherever the clergy were gathered together around the altar of God, there was the Bishop at their head. They knew how, without much facility in preaching he was always ready and anxious to preach, and no one ever heard him speak without carrying away something solid and valuable. They remembered, too, his Pastoral Letters and his papers on religious, scientific, literary, and archaeological subjects.

He could not help recalling in connection with his work his dealings with the religious women of the diocese. There were two convents that might be said to have been founded by him. One was the Convent of the Dominican Sisters at Stroud, and the other that of the Adoration Nuns at Taunton, an order which he specially brought over from France to pray for his diocese. In his days, like the High Priest of old, he "strengthened the Temple of God." What he did was not seen to the outside world, but it was unceasing, unassuming, dutiful and wise. Some of them knew that much, God knew much more than that, and he wished that they could follow him into that inner sanctuary of his life where really and truly a man must be judged, and there only; he wished they could follow him in his prayer, his Mass, his reading, his moderate and abstemious life, his readiness to help and to minister.

There was never a man less ostentatious in his piety and his goodness; and there were few men more pious and God-fearing. No one could tell how kind he was, how large-hearted he was. That establishment in which they were now assembled, how much did it owe to him? Perhaps they would never know. He gave what was more than all the rest, he gave his affection – his interest and affection. Perhaps there never was a Bishop who was more anxious to do his best to give employment to priests and to help them in every possible way. He could only allude to that genial spirit which they remembered so well. It reminded one of the first verse of the 49th chapter of Ecclesiasticus where the memory of Josias was spoken of as "a sweet perfume" as "music in pleasant times." Downside, Woodchester, Prior Park, and many another home – how well they knew him! And in every place where the clergy congregated there was he in the midst of them with that beautiful and genial spirit which drew men to him.

But God was to visit and try him by that suffering without which there was no perfect man. When God loved a man he did two things. He purified the heart from other affections except Himself and He drew the heart nearer to Himself. This was going on during the life of the one who lay there. He suffered: he suffered all his life from much anxiety; he felt extremely many things that another person would have felt little. In his life one knew how every day, more than every day, there were stings to touch the heart, and there were wounds of the spirit which a sensitive disposition would feel more severely than any physical suffering. This sensitiveness was more or less covered by a certain shyness. And then there was real physical pain; he suffered some years from a terrible malady. The loss of his friends, one after another, affected his spirits and the disease was working upon him; and at last the end came. It was a solemn preparation for death! He almost looked death in the face before that operation which he consented to; he almost knew, perhaps better than his friends knew, that he would never recover. Calmly and with the spirit of a servant of God he made his arrangements, he put his affairs in order, he held his meetings and he did not neglect his friends.

The very last time he appeared in public was on July 30, on the occasion of a presentation to Father Hill, at Stroud. Then he submitted to the surgeon, and in less than three weeks from that day – in nineteen days – came death. What a preparation! How near he must have grown to God in those final days of suffering which he endured with such truly Christian resignation. During the last prayers one could see him struggle to lift his feeble hand to form the sign of the cross – the sign he had learned to love in his youth, to follow in his manhood, and which was impressed upon him in his suffering and old age. Holy Sacraments comforted him, and sacred inspirations sustained him. The Holy Father's blessing arrived at midnight on Saturday in these words: "The Pope is deeply grieved at the illness of the Bishop of Clifton; he prays for his recovery; and he sends him his blessing." The tears sprang to his eyes as he heard the words read, and he immediately hid his face and seemed to turn altogether to the next world.

Then just as the bells of the Sta. Maria Maggiore were beginning to sound for the first Vespers of the Assumption – that church in which in his Childhood he had praised the Mother of God, his spirit went to his Saviour.

Catholics and non-Catholics had shown their appreciations of his worth. As the days went on let the clergy of the Catholic Church never forget him in their Masses, let the people remember him before the holy altar at all times, in order that soon through God's mercy and the blood of Jesus he might stand before the ever-lasting throne.

(*The Tablet*, 26.8.1893)

The Bishop of Clifton

In another column we quote the salient facts of that distinguished and saintly life which closed at Prior Park on Monday last, after a lingering and painful malady. It was a life which well and fitly deserved both these epithets; distinguished, by its learning, its indefatigable zeal, its secular and ecclesiastical success, saintly, by its steadfast attachment to whatsoever things are pure, holy and righteous. Few messages, as emphasizing and illustrating these facts, could be more pathetic than that which, on Wednesday last, sped out of Rome from the Holy Father to England, through his Secretary of State. "The Holy Father," he wrote, "is deeply affected by the announcement of the death of the excellent BISHOP OF CLIFTON; and will pray for the repose of his blessed soul." And the Pope, too, in a previous message, upon hearing that the BISHOP was near to death, sent him his last and comforting words of affection and encouragement. For the BISHOP OF CLIFTON, to follow thence a natural train of thought, was, in a peculiar sense, the child of the Holy See. By a particular privilege he knelt at the feet of Pius IX to receive his episcopal consecration; and his personal attachment to the see of Rome was ever afterwards evinced in a prominent and deeply affectionate fashion. Upon every celebration at Rome with which the English people were concerned, the BISHOP OF CLIFTON was to be found standing specially and representatively by the throne of the HOLY FATHER. It was he who introduced pilgrims, composed addresses, delivered speeches – for he spoke Italian fluently – and uttered all the words of devotion and love which the English people as a body desired to deliver into the keeping of the VICAR OF CHRIST. It was in Rome that he sat at the feet of the most learned Professors of the time to study from them those sacred sciences of Canon Law and Theology, of which he later proved himself to be so distinguished a master; it was to Rome that he ever turned his mind as confidently and as securely as one should – and, above all, as a prelate distinguished by Rome's favour and Rome's affection should – who acknowledges that there is the centre of the Christian faith, the pivot upon which all the machinery of CHRIST'S Church turns through its measureless path.

With this central and distinguishing feature in his character, it was not wonderful that he trod, both in public and private life, a straight, consistent, and unhesitating way. In all public affairs he strove to follow out this consistent attitude, no matter the unpopularity with which such a determination might be attended. His moral courage was unbounded; and, since he ever founded his general opinions upon the bases of morality, it would not be easy to find many men so capable of adhering to those opinions, despite every aggression and every provocation, once they had been formed. Throughout his life he was singularly beloved by all with whom he chanced to come in contact, and there is more in the phrase than it might be supposed to contain; for he seldom sought out the applause or even the love of the many. His character was so refined that the temptation of aggressiveness or the allurements of seeking large and facile popularity were alike unknown to him. His, on the contrary, were rather qualities of mercy and generosity – qualities, which in one holding a position of responsibility and authority are doubly desirable and delicate. Withal he had no weakness of character about him whatever; but his strength was the elastic and unobtrusive strength of steel rather than the strength of brute force and brute assertiveness. If he desired to carry out a design that seemed good to him – and otherwise he was scarcely capable of a desire – he pursued it with a pertinacity and a resolution that suffered no obstacles to oppose them. Witness the persistent and triumphant manner in which he restored Prior Park from the state of fallen fortune into the successful educational enterprise which it has since become. Witness also the progress of the diocese of Clifton in every direction which has steadily attended the efforts of his personal organization. For a very personal organization it was, which with unceasing care and quiet vigilance directed those complicated affairs very keenly, very resolutely and, above all, very holily.

He died as he had lived; at the College of his choice, the College at which years before he had received part of his education, and which he lived to restore, as its Bishop and diocesan Governor, at Prior Park; and he died unobtrusively, in the full possession of all his faculties, as he had abundantly proved till within a little while before his death. Readers of these columns will remember the eagerness with which, but a few weeks ago, his pen was busy with the loss of the *Victoria* [HMS Victoria sunk at sea with great loss of life, June 1893]; and although his argument was pronounced by the subsequent verdict of the Court Martial to be not in accordance with the conclusions of the expert officers of the Fleet, it was impossible not to recognize the keen vital interests and logical instincts with which he approached that difficult and complex problem. His learning, too, in abundant provinces was ample and unmistakable; his knowledge of archaeology was varied and also practical. He possessed many valuable and most interesting relics which his combined learning and devotion had persuaded him first to discover and then to secure. He never relaxed in his Biblical studies, in the pursuit of which he had collected a fine library, which was to him a source of great consolation and use. Lastly, and this point has been dwelt upon before, he was a master of Canon Law, a subject in which he often had the opportunity of distinction. At a difficult and delicate juncture of public affairs, armed with this knowledge, it was to this journal that he contributed a series of persuasive and independent papers which aroused an attention which they well deserved, and a hostility which might have been expected from their frank and uncompromising independence. But, above all, he was a good and brave and beloved pastor of his flock and of his clergy; his example stimulated them, his refinement educated them, his unobtrusiveness was not lost on them. And he goes to his grave with the love of these and the suffrages of all who understand how great a loss his death means to the English Catholic Hierarchy.

(*The Tablet*, 19.8.1893)

APPENDIX 20

A Personal Recollection of Bishop Clifford

Although Clifton was his habitual place of residence he spent much time at Prior Park, and his intimate connection with it would alone justify a tribute to his memory here. But he was also well known in Bath, much interested in its various scientific societies and especially useful in throwing light on doubtful questions relating to its Roman antiquities and other matters of local history.

The *Athenaeum* justly says that Bishop Clifford was in many ways an uncommon man; by descent indeed almost a curiosity. He was the second son of the seventh Baron Clifford, of Chudleigh who married the daughter of Thomas Weld who, being left a widower, took orders in the Church of Rome and eventually received a Cardinal's hat. Hugh Clifford was thus the extraordinary instance of a Cardinal's grandson, and there is reason to believe that had he lived a little longer he would have enjoyed the dignity conferred on Dr. Weld. So long ago as the early fifties Dr. Oliver in his *Collection illustrating the history of the Catholic Religion in the West of England*, predicted that Dr. Clifford would become a prominent character in the community.

He received part of his early education at Prior Park, at the time when Bishop Baines lived at the mansion, and he was in constant intercourse with him until his death. The next resident prelate was Archbishop Errington, with whom he had the warmest friendship, as is shewn by the desire to be interred by his side in the corridor adjoining the college chapel. Bishop Clifford's love for Prior Park, begun in early life, continued to the end. He was accustomed to say that wherever he was, through the long period of sixty years, no place had greater charms for him. In addition to the surpassing beauty of the landscape and the historic associations, which no one could appreciate better than himself, there would be his attachment to successive heads of college, men of no ordinary intellectual and religious worth.

Great therefore must have been his sorrow when in 1856, the vicissitudes came which broke up the college and deprived the Catholics of the beautiful estate. But great also were his courage and energy, when, after the changes of nine years, he obtained funds for buying back the property and re-establishing a high class seminary. Mention was made of his efforts by Dr. Hedley, Bishop of Newport, in his sermon at the Mass prior to the interment. "No one," he said, "could tell how generous and large hearted the deceased prelate was; no one would ever know how much the place where they were assembled owed to him". As one of the audience I felt indeed it was only necessary to look around on the rows of noble pillars, the ceiling, the windows and other accessories, all in the exquisite style and proportions of an Italian cathedral, to feel the force of the preacher's remark. And while this was evidence of the care, skill and cost with which additions had been made through successive decades, thoughts would crowd upon the mind of the constant care for the educational objects of the establishment and of the love which every member of it cherished for the benefactor.

The contiguity of Clifton made Dr. Clifford's frequent visits to Bath easy. And here a large circle of friends were always glad to welcome so genial and accomplished a visitor. Apart from his episcopal duties many objects of interest in the city had a share of his regard, especially the antiquities, on which he occasionally gave lectures at the Institution. It would be easily imagined by all who knew the tendency of his mind and his intimate knowledge of Rome that the uncovering and development of the magnificent baths within his diocese would be watched by him with peculiar pleasure. On this and other kindred subjects he was always regarded as an authority by the various archaeological societies with which he was connected at Bath and Bristol and in the counties of the district, while his charming simplicity of style and manner attracted all sects and parties and led to the formation of many friendships. But everyone knew that it was to the church of his fathers his most ardent affection and constant service were given. Year by year it was seen how buildings arose, institutions multiplied, congregations increased, under the fostering care of the indefatigable bishop. Yet preaching was not amongst his accomplishments, in consequence of a slight physical hesitancy.

His eminence in the church, however, caused him to be selected for the sermon at the funeral of his intimate friend Cardinal Newman. Few dignitaries were better known in Rome; he had the rare privilege of being consecrated to his bishopric at the Vatican; with Pius IX he appears to have been for a long time a special favourite, and that Leo XIII had sincere regard for him is said to have been shewn by a willingness to give him the post of English adviser when Cardinal Howard left Rome. This would have been unwelcome to him in consequence of the strong ties of Clifton and Prior Park. One reason for the Pope's desire to have such an adviser would probably be his thorough knowledge and excellent pronunciation of the Italian language. It has been even said that Bishop Clifford could preach well in Italian though not in English.

It should be gratefully remembered that the strong religious affections which had been mentioned were combined with much independence of character. Dr. Hedley mentioned this in his eloquent sermon with reference to Dr. Clifford's objection to the celebrated dogma of the Immaculate Conception* for which the Pope required the acceptance of the Church. The preacher attributed the objection to a broadmindedness acquired by Roman experiences, to mingling with the most learned theologians and men of the widest intellects, and to constant contact with the great stream of Catholic thought. "The Catholic Church", said Dr. Hedley, "though an immutable Church was not silent and dead, like some stony sphinx of the Egyptian desert silted up by the sand of ages; no her immutability was the accompaniment of perpetual life." "Dr. Clifford", he continued, "recognised this, and saw that, unalterable as the Church was, there was nevertheless in her the development of leaf and the bursting of flower from year to year and century to century." Another writer remarks that "he aimed at leading his flock by gentle suasion and high example rather than by enforcing blind obedience to the voice of authority".

Prior Park had seen many remarkable gatherings. Statesmen, Philosophers and Philanthropists had often met there in genial conclave. But never probably within that beautiful pile of buildings had there been such a grand and solemn spectacle as on Friday, the eighteenth of August. The preceding circumstances had touched many a chord of loving sympathy. It was known how the good Bishop had gone on with his work until he had found it necessary to submit to an operation. It was known how he wished for it to be performed in the quiet of Prior Park with the aid of his personal medical attendant, Mr. King. It was known how a London specialist had been so successful that strong hopes of recovery were entertained, but how in a few sad days other symptoms appeared, and, after the last solemn ceremonies, the patient sank to rest. And thus were brought together from Bath and Clifton and Bristol and all the country round that large sympathising congregation. Those who were present will long remember the solemn dirges, the array of dignitaries, the eloquent sermon, the universal sorrow; and many must have returned home thankful for having known so good a man.

(Jerom Murch, *Biographical Sketches of Bath Celebrities* Publ. London & Bath, 1893, pages 223 – 227).

Note: The dogma to which the writer should have referred was that of Papal Infallibility, not of the Immaculate Conception.

SOURCES AND BIBLIOGRAPHY

1. ARCHIVAL SOURCES

FAMILY

The Clifford family archives at Ugbrooke Park, Chudleigh, Devon.

ECCLESIASTICAL

A.   **Abroad**

    The Vatican

    The Generalate of the Society of Jesus, Rome

    Propaganda Fide, Rome

    The Venerable English College, Rome

    The English College, Valladolid, Spain

B.   **England and Wales**

    Westminster Diocesan Archives

    Birmingham Diocesan Archives

    Cardiff Diocesan Archives

    Liverpool Diocesan Archives

    Southwark Diocesan Archives

    Clifton Diocesan Archives

    Leeds Diocesan Archives

Northampton Diocesan Archives

Nottingham Diocesan Archives

Plymouth Diocesan Archives

Salford Diocesan Archives

Franciscan Provincial Archives

Archives of the English Province of the Society of Jesus

Public Record Office

2. PERIODICALS, JOURNALS AND NEWSPAPERS

Clergy Review

Downside Review

Dublin Review

Journal of Ecclesiastical History

Pall Mall Gazette

Punch

Recusant History

Somerset and Wilts Journal

The Daily Telegraph

The Month

The Tablet

The Times

The Universe

The Venerabile

Western Daily Press

Whitehall Review

3. PRIMARY PRINTED SOURCES

Abbott, Walter M., ed
The Documents of Vatican II (London, 1966).

Blakiston, N., ed
The Roman question: extracts from the dispatches of Odo Russell
from Rome 1858 – 1870 (London, 1962).

Case, George
The Vatican Council and a duty of Catholics in regard to it. A sermon
preached on Whit Sunday, 1870 (London, 1870).

Challoner, Richard
A Collection of controversial tracts (London, 1747).

Clifford, William
A Discourse delivered at the funeral of George Errington, Archbishop of
Trebizond and First Bishop of Plymouth, in the church of Prior Park
College (Bristol, 1886).

Clifford, William
A History of the Bull *'Romanos Pontifices'* with letters from Cardinal
Manning and others, and extracts from the private diary of Bishop
Clifford (bound typescript, no date, Clifton Diocesan Archives).

Clifford, William
Sermon preached at the funeral of His Eminence John Henry Newman,
Cardinal of the Holy Roman Church (London, 1890).

Code of Canon Law, in English translation (London, 1983).

Codex Iuris Canonici (1918).

The Declaration and Protestation signed by the English Catholic
Dissenters in 1789: with the names of those who signed it (1791).

[Errington and Wiseman].
Special Commission set up by Pope Pius IX to investigate dispute.
In Italian (Roma, 1860).

Gladstone, W. E.
The Vatican Decrees in their bearing on civil allegiance: a political
expostulation (London, 1874).

Gladstone, W. E.
Vaticanism: an answer to replies and reproofs (London, 1875).

Gother, J. L.
A Papist misrepresented and represented or a two-fold character of
Popery (1685).

Guy, Robert E., ed
The Synods in English: being the text of the four Synods of Westminster,
translated into English. (Stratford-on-Avon, 1886).

Hudd, Alfred E., ed
Proceedings of the Clifton Antiquarian Club for 1884 – 1888,
Vol. I (Bristol, 1888).

Mansi, Joannes Dominicus
Sacrorum Conciliorum nova et amplissima collectio; repr. & continued
by L. Petit and J.B. Martin. 53v [in 60]. Paris, 1889 – 1927; tom. 50 & 51.

Maskell, William.
What is the meaning of the late definition of the Infallibility of the Pope?
An enquiry. (London, 1871).

Milner, J,
The End of religious controversy in a friendly correspondence between
a religious society of Protestants and a Roman Catholic divine,
addressed to the Right Rev. Dr. Burgess (Dublin, 1827).

Newman, J. H.
Apologia pro Vita Sua (London, 1864).

Newman, J. H.
Letters and diaries ed, Ian Ker and Thomas Gornall [and others], 32v.,
Oxford, 1978 – 2008.

Ordo Recitandi
1848 – [Forerunner of The Catholic Directory].

Quirinus [pseud. J.J.I. von Döllinger and others]
Letters from Rome on the Council (London, 1870).

Rudderham, Joseph E.,
The Second Vatican General Council [unpublished manuscript held in
Clifton Diocesan Archives].

S.B.
A modest enquiry how far Catholicks are guilty of the horrid tenets
laid to their charge: how far their principles are misrepresented, or
misunderstood: and what may be alleged in defence of those they really
profess (London, 1749).

4. SECONDARY PRINTED SOURCES

Note: this list was compiled in 1991

Altholz, J. L.
The Liberal Catholic movement in England (London 1962).

Anstruther, Godfrey
The Seminary Priests (4 vols.) (Great Wakering 1968 – 1977).

Arnstein, W. L.
Protestant versus Catholic in Mid-Victorian England: Mr. Newdegate
and the nuns (Columbia, 1982).

Beck, G. A., ed.,
The English Catholics 1850 – 1950 (London, 1950).

Bossy, John
The English Catholic community 1570 – 1950 (London 1950).

Brandreth, Henry R. T.
Dr. Lee of Lambeth (London 1951).

Brodrick, James
Robert Bellarmine (London, 1961).

Brodrick, James
Saint Peter Canisius, S. J. 1521 – 1597 (London, 1935).

Butler, Christopher
The Theology of Vatican II (London, 1967).

Butler, Cuthbert
The Vatican Council 1869 – 1870 (1930, London 1962).

Butler, Cuthbert
The Life and times of Bishop Ullathorne 1806 – 1889
(2 vols.) (London, 1926).

Casartelli, L. C.
Sketches in history (London, 1906).

Cashman, John
Bishop Baines and the tensions in the Western District (Unpublished
thesis for M.Litt., 1989, University of Bristol).

Cashman, John
The Clifton Mission, 1830 – 1901 (Bound typescript, 1990, Clifton
Diocesan Archives).

Catholic Encyclopedia
(London and New York, 1907).

Chadwick, Owen
The Victorian Church (London, Part 1, 3rd ed. 1971;
Part 2, 2nd ed. 1972).

Clifford, Hugh
The House of Clifford (Chichester, 1987).

Clifton, Michael
The quiet negotiator: Bishop Grant, Bishop of Southwark (Liverpool, 1990).

Cobb, Peter G.
The Oxford Movement in nineteenth century Bristol (Bristol Branch of
the Historical Association, Local History Pamphlet (Bristol, 1988).

Coulton, G. G. and Lunn, Arnold
Is the Catholic Church Anti-social? (London, 1947).

Crichton, J. D.
Worship in a hidden Church (Dublin, 1988).

Cwiekowski, Frederick J.
The English bishops and the First Vatican Council (Louvain, 1971).

Darby, J. H.
Diocese of Clifton 1850 – 1950, A centenary souvenir (Bristol, 1950).

Dictionary of National Biography
22 vols repr London, (1937 – 1938).

Drane, Mother Francis Raphael
Life of Mother Margaret Mary Hallahan (London, 1929).

Femiano, Samuel D.
Infallibility of the laity: the legacy of Newman (New York, 1967).

Fitzsimons, John, ed.
Manning: Anglican and Catholic (London, 1951).

Fothergill, Brian
Nicholas Wiseman (London, 1963).

Gasquet, Aidan ed.
Lord Acton and his circle (London, 1906).

Gilley, Sheridan
Newman and his age: a biography of Cardinal Newman (London, 1990).

Gillow, Joseph
Bibliographical Dictionary of the English Catholics. 5 vols.
(London, 1885 and later).

Hales, E. E. Y.
Pio Nono (London, 1954).

Harding, J. A.
The Re-birth of the Roman Catholic Community in Frome (Unpublished
thesis for M.Litt., 1986, University of Bristol).

Hemphill, Basil.
The Early Vicars Apostolic of England, 1685 – 1750 (London, 1954).

Hergenrother, Dr.
Anti-Janus: a Historico-theological criticism of the work entitled
'The Pope and the Council' by Janus. English translation by
J. B. Robertson. (Dublin, 1870).

Holmes, J. Derek
More Roman than Rome (London, 1978).

Holmes, J. Derek and Bickers, Bernard W.
A Short history of the Catholic Church (Tunbridge Wells, 1983).

Howell, Brian S.
The Formative years of Catholic boys' secondary education in Bristol,
1890 – 1918, with reference to the Christian Brothers' College, Berkeley
Square. (Unpublished, Main study for degree of B.Ed., 1975, University
of Bristol).

Hughes, Peter, E.
Cleanliness and godliness: A sociological study of the Good Shepherd
Convent refuges. (Unpublished thesis for Ph.D., 1985, Brunel
University).

Janus [Döllinger, J.J.G. von, and others]
The Pope and the Council (London, 1869).

Knox, Ronald A.
In soft garments (London, 1942).

Knox, Ronald A.
Occasional sermons (London, 1960).

Langston, James Newton
The Catholic mission in Gloucester and its resident priests (1788 –
1894) (4 vols. bound typescript, c.1957. Gloucester Library,
Gloucestershire Collection, 31841).

Leslie, Shane
Henry Edward Manning: his life and labours (London, 1921).

Manning, H. E.
The Vatican Decrees in their bearing on civil allegiance (London, 1875).

McClelland, V. A.
English Roman Catholics and higher education, 1830 – 1903
(Oxford, 1973).

McClelland, V. A.
Cardinal Manning: his public life and influence (London, 1962).

McElrath, Damian
The Syllabus of Pius IX: some reactions in England (Louvain, 1964).

McNabb, Vincent
Infallibility (London, 1927).

Mill Hill Father
Remembered in blessing: the Courtfield Story (London, 1955).

Morley, John
The Life of William Ewart Gladstone. 2 vols. (London 1908).

Murch, Jerom
Biographical sketches of Bath celebrities ancient and modern with
some fragments of local history (London and Bath, 1893).

Norman, Edward
The English Catholic Church in the nineteenth century (Oxford, 1984).

Oliver, George
Collections illustrating the history of the Catholic religion in the Counties of
Cornwall, Devon, Dorset, Somerset, Wilts and Gloucester (London, 1857)

O'Meara, K. [Grace Ramsay]
Thomas Grant: first Bishop of Southwark (London, 1874).

Pawley, Bernard and Margaret Pawley
Rome and Canterbury through Four Centuries (Revised ed. 1981).

Pius a Spiritu Sancto
The Life of Father Ignatius [Spencer] (Dublin, 1866).

Plumb, Brian
Arundel to Zabi: a biographical dictionary of the Catholic bishops of
England and Wales (Warrington, 1987).

Purcell, Edmund Sheridan
Life and Letters of Ambrose Phillipps de Lisle (edited and finished by
Edwin de Lisle). 2 vols. (London, 1900).

Purcell, Edmund Sheridan
Life of Cardinal Manning. 2 vols. (London, 1896).

Reynolds, E. E.
Three Cardinals (Newman, Wiseman, Manning) (London, 1958).

Roche, J. S.
A History of Prior Park College and its founder, Bishop Baines
(London, 1931).

Roskell, Dame Mary Francis
Memoirs of Francis Kerril Amherst, D.D., Lord Bishop of Northampton
(London, 1903).

Schiefen, Richard J.
Nicholas Wiseman and the transformation of English Catholicism
(Shepherdstown, 1984).

Shepherd, James
Reminiscences of Prior Park (London, 1894).

Snead-Cox, J. G.
The Life of Cardinal Vaughan. 2 vols. (London, 1910).

Strachey, Lytton
Eminent Victorians (Repr, London, 1948).

Sweeney, J. N.
Lectures on the nature, the grounds and the home of faith, delivered in
the Pro-Cathedral Church of the Holy Apostles, Clifton (London and
Bristol, 1867).

Tristram, Henry, ed.
ed., John Henry Newman: centenary essays (London, 1945).

Walsh, Michael
The Tablet 1840 – 1990: a commemorative history (London, 1990).

Ward, W. G.
A Letter to Rev. Father Ryder on his recent pamphlet (London, 1867).

Ward, W. G.
A Second letter to Rev. Father Ryder (London, 1868).

Watkin, E. I.
Roman Catholicism in England from the Reformation to 1950
(London, 1957).

Williams, Michael E.
The Venerable English College, Rome (London, 1979).

Wilson, J. Anselm
The Life of Bishop Hedley (London, 1930).

Wiseman, Nicholas
Lectures on the principal doctrines and practices of the Catholic
Church (London, 1888).

INDEX

PIO NONO

Pope Blessed Pius IX was the longest reigning pope in history
(1846 – 1878).
He re-established the English and Welsh hierarchy in 1850, and in 1857
personally consecrated William Clifford as third Bishop of Clifton.